TWINS: Black and White

FOUNDATION FOR HUMAN UNDERSTANDING SYMPOSIA

TWINS:
Black and White

R. TRAVIS OSBORNE

FOUNDATION FOR HUMAN UNDERSTANDING
ATHENS, GEORGIA   ALEXANDRIA, VIRGINIA

International Standard Book Number: 0–936396–00–8
Library of Congress Catalog Number: 79–92757

Printed in the United States of America

To the memory of Henry E. Garrett

Contents

List of Tables

List of Figures

Acknowledgments

This book includes information that was gathered over a period of eight years and has been in preparation for more than four years. Publication would not have been possible without the cooperation of scores of professional assistants, personal friends, skilled secretaries, and most of all the twins who gave up two days of Saturday vacation to take part in the study.

Many specialists have contributed to the book. Steven Vandenberg designed the original Cooperative Twin Study and supervised the testing of twins in Kentucky. Robert Nichols' invited address to the American Psychological Association Meeting, September, 1976, constitutes the major portion of Chapter III. Arthur Jensen suggested the cross-racial factor analytic study of the twin data. James Fortson was the statistical consultant and wrote the original computer programs used in the analysis of the twin data.

While work on the book was in progress, I relied on the help of many other people, without whose careful and loyal assistance in checking references, verifying computer printouts and quotations, testing, scoring, typing and retyping, proofing, etc., the book would have been less well written. I am indebted to Melinda Lay, Melanie Hammond, Dorothea Reid, Judy Allison, Edna Lee, and many others whose dedication to the work was an encouragement to me.

I am especially indebted to Wilma Sanders and Frank Miele, personal friends and professional associates, for their expert advice at every step in planning the research and preparing the manuscript. Their consistent encouragement and enthusiasm during periods of no perceptible progress are acknowledged with appreciation.

While acknowledging the assistance of these specialists, any errors of fact or interpretation, however, are my own responsibility.

Preface

The study brings together for the first time in one volume an analysis of psychological test results and biometric measurements of large samples of black and white twins—in all, 496 pairs of twins, ranging in age from 12 to 20. In addition to the heritability estimates reported previously (Osborne, 1978), important new analyses of personality, socio-economic status, culture fair and primary mental ability tests, and neurological findings are presented.

In the body of the survey, the reader will find independent chapters dealing with heritability of mental ability, school achievement, and personality by race and by sex. In the appendixes will be found all raw data, including psychological test results and the biometric measurements used in zygosity determination. From the printouts in the appendixes, studies in the body of the text may be verified or unreported relationships among the variables may be investigated. Tapes of the appendixes are available from the author.

I

Introduction

A decade before he published the first scientific twin study in 1875 Sir Francis Galton (1865) stated, "the general resemblances in mental qualities between parents of offspring, in man and brute, are every whit as near as the resemblance of their physical features" (p. 158).

Galton (1869) predicted that native ability, like stature, is distributed approximately normally in any given population. He was, however, not satisfied with his statistical evidence:

"The persons whom you compare may have lived under similar social conditions and have had similar advantages of education, but such prominent conditions are only a small part of those that determine the future of each man's life. It is to trifling accidental circumstances that the bent of his disposition and his success are mainly due, and these you leave wholly out of account—in fact, they do not admit of being tabulated, and therefore your statistics, however plausible at first sight, are really of very little use." No method of enquiry which I have been able to carry out—and I have tried many methods—is wholly free from this objection. I have therefore attacked the problem from the opposite side, seeking for some new method by which it would be possible to weigh in just scales the respective effects of nature and nurture, and to ascertain their several shares in framing the disposition and intellectual ability of men. The life history of twins supplies what I wanted. (Galton, 1875, p. 566)

Since 1875 over 100 scientific studies of the cognitive ability of twins have been published. With few exceptions all support Galton's original thesis that mental ability is inherited, the ratio of variance attibutable to environmental and hereditary factors being approximately one to four.

1

The work of Sir Cyril Burt, one of the foremost proponents of the inheritance of intelligence, became suspect two years after his death in 1971. In reviewing kinship correlations reported by Burt, Arthur Jensen (1974) noted misprints and inconsistencies, involving invariant correlations from unknown or ambiguous sample sizes. After an unsuccessful attempt to resolve the discrepancies in Burt's work, Jensen proposed a strategy for future researchers to make their data more useful and more easily verifiable. Totally ignoring these constructive suggestions, the popular press used Jensen's criticism of Burt as an excuse to headline: CRUCIAL DATA WAS FAKED BY EMINENT PSYCHOLOGIST . . . THEORIES OF IQ PIONEER COMPLETELY DISCREDITED . . . THE FRAUD REOPENED THE DEBATE ABOUT RACE AND INTELLIGENCE.[1]

The Burt controversy is best summarized by Bernard Rimland and Harry Munsinger (1977) who point out that the data demonstrating the heavy dependence of IQ on genetic factors are far too solid to be shaken by the work of any single investigator, even Sir Cyril Burt.

Nicholas Wade (1976), in reviewing Burt's experiments, says:

> The only sure evidence of error, the invariant correlations, is a curious mistake for a cunning forger to make. Perhaps, when old and ill, Burt was too proud to ask for help in doing the calculations and, as Eysenck suggests, carried over the results from earlier papers. (p. 919)

Not all biologists agree with Rimland and Munsinger. Harvard Professor Richard Lewontin believes:

> There is not one jot or tittle of evidence of any genetic basis for any behavioral trait, except schizophrenia—whether it be intelligence or nastiness or aggressiveness. And given the finite resources which support scientists in their playgrounds, it is a waste of taxpayers' money to study IQ heredity or other genetic components of human personality. ("We're all the same under the skin," 1976)

The present study is the first to include test scores, biometric data, and personality profiles of a sizable group (123 pairs) of black twins. It also provides a comprehensive analysis of over 125 different intellectual, biometric, and personality characteristics for 496 pairs of twins and makes available the raw test data and anthropometric measures which can be used by other investigators to verify reported findings or to explore addi-

---

[1] *Sunday Times,* London, Oct. 24, 1976; *The Observer,* London, Oct. 31, 1976; *Times,* London, Oct. 26, 1976.

tional hypotheses. In addition to the above, this study has a strictly practical aspect, the importance of which should not be overlooked. Increasing restrictions on the use of human subjects in research involving psychological tests, blood typing, and anthropometric measurements virtually preclude in the foreseeable future the possibility of locating and testing sizable numbers of twins.[2] The problem is compounded by the scarcity of twins, which occur only once in 88 live births.

In summary, this study has added significance not only because it is the first of its kind; if present trends prevail, it may also be the last of its kind.

[2] For a sample of such restrictions, see: *Institutional Guide to DHEW Policy on Protection of Human Subjects (Revised); The Declaration of Helsinki, 1964,* World Medical Association; *Ethical Principles in the Conduct of Research with Human Participants, 1973,* American Psychological Association; *Professional Ethics—Statements of Procedures of the American Anthropological Association, 1973.*

II

History of Twin Studies

Perhaps no other natural phenomenon stimulates so much interest among so many different types and classes of individuals (physicians, geneticists, dramatists, poets, artists, and parents) as human twinning. Although multiple births occur among all ethnic groups, the birth of twins elicits reactions that range from riotous celebrations by Western African tribes to the ostracism or death of both mother and offspring elsewhere in Africa and in parts of India and Japan. "The fear of producing twins," write Strong and Corney (1967), "was so great that Hottentots about to marry were said to amputate one testicle in the belief that this would prevent such a misfortune!" (p. 1).

Some twins, even those of the same sex, are so dissimilar that even a blind father can easily distinguish between them; others so nearly alike that parents, teachers, and close friends often have difficulty telling them apart.

That there are actually two types of twins was not established until late in the 19th century. About the same time Sir Francis Galton was undertaking his first investigation of twins, "physicians and biologists in several different countries independently developed the concept that 'identical' twins resulted from a single fertilised ovum, whereas 'fraternal twins' occurred when two separate ova were fertilised" (Strong & Corney, 1967, p. 14).

In his long search for statistical evidence to prove the inheritance of mental ability, Galton found that the life history of twins was a veritable treasure house of information. The results of his initial research were published in *Fraser's Magazine* in 1875 under the title "The History of Twins, as a Criterion of the Relative Powers of Nature and Nurture." Galton's scientific insight and writing skill can be appreciated from a few excerpts:

My materials were obtained by sending circulars of enquiry to persons who were either twins themselves or the near relations of twins. The printed questions were in thirteen groups; the last of them asked for the addresses of other twins known to the recipient who might be likely to respond if I wrote to them. This happily led to a continually widening circle of correspondence, which I pursued until enough material was accumulated for a general reconnaissance of the subject. . . .

I have received about eighty returns of cases of close similarity, thirty-five of which entered into many instructive details. In a few of these not a single point of difference could be specified. In the remainder, the colour of the hair and eyes were almost always identical; the height, weight, and strength were generally very nearly so, but I have a few cases of a notable difference in these, notwithstanding the resemblance was otherwise very near. . . .

I have only one case in which nobody, not even the twins themselves, could distinguish their own notes of lectures, &c.; barely two or three in which the handwriting was undistinguishable by others and only a few in which it was described as closely alike. On the other hand, I have many in which it is stated to be unlike, and some in which it is alluded to as the only point of difference. . . .

Enough has been said to prove that an extremely close personal resemblance frequently exists between twins of the same sex; and that, although the resemblance usually diminishes as they grow into manhood and womanhood, some cases occur in which the resemblance is lessened in a hardly perceptible degree. . . .

Hitherto we have investigated cases where the similarity at first was close, but afterwards became less; now we will examine those in which there was great dissimilarity at first, and will see how far an identity of nurture in childhood and youth tended to assimilate them. As has been already mentioned, there is a large proportion of cases of sharply contrasted characteristics, both of body and mind, among twins. I have twenty such cases, given with much detail. It is a fact, that extreme dissimilarity, such as existed between Esau and Jacob, is a no less marked peculiarity in twins of the same sex, than extreme similarity. On this curious point, and on much else in the history of twins, I have many remarks to make, but this is not the place to make them. . . .

The impression that all this evidence leaves on the mind is one of some wonder whether nurture can do anything at all beyond giving instruction and professional training. It emphatically corroborates and goes far beyond the conclusions to which we had already been driven by the cases of similarity. . . . There is no escape from the conclusion that nature prevails enormously over nurture when the differences of nurture do not exceed what is commonly to be found among persons of the same rank of society and in the same country. My only fear is that my evidence seems to prove too much and may be discredited on that account, as it seems contrary to all experience that nurture should go for so little. But experience is often fallacious in ascribing great effects to trifling circumstances. (pp. 566–576)

Galton's pioneering study is remarkable because it was made without knowledge of the now standardized division of twins into two principal types, and without the help of modern statistical procedures. The nineteenth century genius' model could hardly be improved today.

Despite such a promising beginning, progress in twin research was slow. No new study of importance was published until E. L. Thorndike's celebrated monograph appeared in 1905. It was as carefully planned and as well written as Galton's landmark paper. Although the concept of two twin types had been developed a quarter of a century earlier, Thorndike defended with some strong statistical support his belief in the classical theory that twins only come in one variety. R. A. Fisher (1919), after reviewing Thorndike's data, also rejected the idea that there were two types of twins, thereby making it clear that the idea was still not universally accepted.

Thorndike did, however, introduce two new techniques for the study of twins in his 1905 paper: structured psychological tests and the correlation coefficient, the latter corrected for attenuation. In regard to this procedure Thorndike (1905) acknowledges, "I take Mr. Spearman's method of correction for attenuation on trust, as I do not possess the mathematical knowledge necessary to derive his formulae" (p. 4).

Although conducted a quarter of a century apart and on two different continents, the results of the first two methodical twin studies are remarkably similar—even to the extent that both Galton and Thorndike were somewhat apologetic about their findings. Compare Galton's words to these from Thorndike's (1905) study:

> Doubtless we all feel a repugnance to assigning so little efficacy to environmental forces as the facts of this study seem to demand; but common opinion also feels a repugnance to believing that the mental resemblances of twins, however caused, are as great as the physical resemblances. Yet they are. (p. 10)

The next milestone in twin studies was reached in 1924. In a study reported in *Psychological Monographs,* Curtis Merriman (1924) was the first to employ standardized individual and group IQ tests to test the intellectual similarities of twins. The results of his investigation finally convinced psychologists that there are two types of twins, fraternal (two eggs) and identical (one egg). Merriman's other findings were not too different from those of Galton and Thorndike. Environment, he stated, appears to have no important influence on the degree of twin resemblance. He also asserted that twins do not suffer from any particular deficiency in mental capability.

The next significant development in this field was the work of Karl Holzinger. Relying on data assembled at the University of Chicago in collaboration with H. H. Newman and F. N. Freeman, Holzinger (1929) developed two formulas for determining the relative effect of nature and nurture on twin differences. The first measures the relative effectiveness of nature and nurture in determining *mean* twin differences. The second (Holzinger's well-known H index or H ratio), which measures the *variability* of twin differences, was written by Holzinger as $h^2 = \dfrac{i^r - f^r}{1 - f^r}$.

Although the H index is being replaced by more dependable statistical methods, it was used uncritically for over 30 years. To appreciate Holzinger's contribution, the reader is referred to his original paper published in 1929.

With the advent of high-speed computers and large data banks, provided for the most part by National Merit Study and Project Talent Study, twin research was accelerated in the early 60s. Robert C. Nichols was among the first to recognize the weakness of Holzinger's Index and to suggest an improved method of estimating heritability from twin data. Since Nichols' heritability estimate is one of several used in this study, a summary is quoted from his 1965 paper.

> The particular power of the twin method lies in the fact that the difference between the intraclass correlations for identical and fraternal twins is equal to the proportion of the total variance due to hereditary differences between fraternal twins. Since fraternal twins have on the average half their genes in common, this is half the heredity variance in the trait. This fact can be used to construct heritability coefficients from twin correlations which give estimates of the proportion of the variance in a trait attributable to heredity. The coefficient h^2 proposed by Holzinger (1929) is the ratio of half the hereditary variance to the variance within sets of fraternal twins.
>
> $$h^2 = \frac{\sigma^2_{DZ} - \sigma^2_{MZ}}{\sigma^2_{DZ}} = \frac{r_{MZ} - r_{DZ}}{1 - r_{DZ}} = \frac{DH}{DH + DE + E}$$

Since error of measurement enters into the within-set variance the correlations are usually corrected for attenuation. Another coefficient which we have developed for use in our twin study is called *HR*.

$$HR = \frac{2(r_{MZ} - r_{DZ})}{r_{MZ}} = \frac{2DH}{CH_{MZ} + CE}$$

This is the ratio of the hereditary variance to variance due to heredity and environment common to both twins of a set. If one is willing to assume that the major environmental influences on a trait, at least those which might be measured or manipulated, are common to both twins of a set, this ratio is the proportion due to heredity of the variance attributable to heredity and major environmental variables. This ratio also offers the advantage of not including error variance and thus not requiring correction for unreliability of the measuring instruments.

Figure 1 shows a schematic representation of the sources of variance in twin data. The left-hand vertical line represents the total variance of a trait in identical twins and the right-hand line the total variance in fraternal twins. The possible sources of variation are listed between the two lines. Both hereditary and environmental variance is divided into that common to twins of a set and that which is different for the two twins of a set.

The schematic representation in Figure 1 and the logic behind the heritability coefficients make certain assumptions which may or

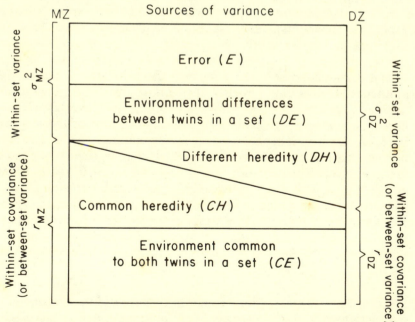

Figure II–1. Schematic representation of sources of variance in twin data.

may not hold in a given study or with respect to a given trait being investigated. The four major assumptions are the following: (a) that the similarity of environmental influence is the same for fraternal and identical twins; (b) that for the trait in question there is no correlation between parents due to assortive mating (although if the correlation between parents is known it can be corrected for); (c) that hereditary variance in a continuous trait being studied shows no dominance or interaction effects; (d) that hereditary and environmental influences are not correlated (although small correlations make little difference). (pp. 232–234)

In his chapter in *Methods and Goals in Human Behavior Genetics,* Steven Vandenberg (1965) proposed a third heritability formula, the *F* ratio, which compares within-pair variance of DZ twins with that of MZ's, and then tests the significance of this ratio by the *F* test:

$$F = \frac{\sigma^2 wDZ}{\sigma^2 wMZ}$$

The limitations of the three heritability formulas of Holzinger, Nichols, and Vandenberg were summarized by Jensen in a paper presented to the National Academy of Sciences in 1967.

The prevailing method of estimating heritability from MZ and DZ twins has been by means of the *H* index devised by Holzinger. That Holzinger's *H* index is not a satisfactory estimate of h^2 is now generally recognized in behavior genetics, but the precise nature of the inadequacy of the *H* index and the problem of estimating h^2 from MZ and DZ twin data have remained conceptually obscure. Nichols proposed an improvement on the *H* index, called the *HR* index, but it, too, is unsatisfactory as an index of h^2. One serious criticism of *H* and *HR* is that one is not a monotonic function of the other, and neither is a monotonic function of h^2. Vandenberg has proposed using *F* (the variance ratio) as a test of the significance of $\sigma w_{DZ}^2/$ σw_{MZ}^2 (DZ within-pair variance/MZ within-pair variance), but this is as faulty as an index of heritability as the *H* index itself, since *F* is a linear function of *H*. Determining the variance ratio *F*, however, is an essential step prior to computing h^2; if *F* is not statistically significant, h^2 cannot be presumed to differ significantly from zero. (p. 149)

Since 1929 the intraclass correlation coefficient rather than analysis of variance has been the method of choice for most investigators studying the resemblance between pairs of twins and other relatives. It has recently been pointed out by Krystyna Last (1977) that the correlational approach is useful only when performing straightforward analysis and when the causes of variation are simple. Since behavior traits are complex in origin, Last warns us it is often misleading to use the correlational approach.

> Using correlations rather than variance components assumes equality of the total variances between groups. Therefore, we must assume that all effects leading to inequality of the total variances are absent. If this is not the case then estimates obtained from the data will be biased, and we will lose information about effects leading to unequal variances. Jinks and Fulker (1970) have enumerated several factors producing inequality of the total variances:
> 1.   The genetical components differ between groups.
> 2.   Between and within pairs environmental components differ between groups.
> 3.   Genotype-environment covariance is present. (Last, 1977, pp. 1–2)

The present paper uses the correlational methods of Holzinger, Nichols, and Vandenberg, despite their recognized weaknesses. However, while the analyses reported in this volume were being prepared, Basic Battery test data were made available to Last for analysis by methods originally proposed by Jinks, Fulker, and Eaves and recommended by her. This analysis will comprise portions of her dissertation written under the direction of Lindon Eaves at the University of Birmingham.

Last uses both the intraclass correlation approach and the method of analysis of variance components, a dual approach which makes it possible to compare results of the two different methods applied to the same data. All the findings of her 730-page dissertation cannot be reviewed here, but conclusions applicable to the present study will be summarized briefly (Last, 1977).

(a)   Last found the usual pattern of sex differences and race differences in mean performance. Mean scores for blacks were lower than those for whites. Males performed better than females on spatial tests (p. 298).

(b)   There was no evidence of a difference in heritability between the races (p. 161).

(c)   Although Last did not have the best data set for detection of sex linkage, there was no evidence whatsoever to suggest its presence in these data (p. 169).

(d)   There was a marked difference between MZ and DZ correlations. This confirmed previous work suggesting heritable variation for measures of ability (p. 170).

(e)   For the seven tests whose total variances were homogeneous and for which an adequate model was found, the results were broadly consistent with those obtained by analyzing the correlations (p. 192).

(f) In the analysis of intraclass correlation coefficients, a heritable component of variation was demonstrated for most tests. No heritable component was found for the more unreliable tests (p. 298).

(g) A general mental factor was extracted and analyzed. Environmental models could not explain the observed pattern of variation. Assuming the between-families component to be produced entirely by assortative mating, Last decided as much as 90% of the variation could be attributed to genetical differences (p. 299).

From this review of the development of the twin method in the study of heritability, it is clear that there is no one perfectly reliable procedure for determining the exact proportion of mental test variation attributable to genetical or enviornmental differences. Even for the same method, heritability estimates of intelligence vary according to the nature of the task.

In subsequent chapters, tests of general intelligence, culture fair intelligence, primary mental abilities and personality, as well as electroencephalographic records, will be analyzed by the classical methods of Holzinger, Nichols, and Vandenberg.

III

Twin Studies of Ability, Personality, and Interests[1]

Nancy Breland (1972) reviewed twin literature from the time of Galton up to 1971, extracting 756 pairs of intraclass correlations. Robert C. Nichols and Breland assigned the traits to the broad domains of ability, personality, and interests, then narrowed the classification within each domain according to the specific trait. In those instances in which an unfamiliar test was used or in which the trait could not be unambiguously grouped with other studies of the same trait, the correlations were temporarily discarded. This provided a means of organizing a large body of data, although tests with similar names, which were grouped together, were no doubt in many instances measuring quite different traits.

Although our research design did not include the measurement of interests, Nichols and Breland's review of twin studies on the topic will be included in this chapter since it adds important information to the study of human behavior genetics.

The results for the ability domain are shown in Figure III–1, which demonstrates considerable variation among studies, as well as a striking overall consistency. The correlations were predominantly high and positive, demonstrating that twins tend to be quite alike in a variety of abilities. Identical twins tended to be more similar than fraternal twins on all 12 traits of ability. If the weighted averages represented by arrows are considered to be one large composite study based on several thousand sets of twins, the difference between identical and fraternal intraclass

[1] This chapter constitutes the major portion of an invited address presented at the American Psychological Association meeting, Washington, D.C., Sept. 4, 1976, by Robert C. Nichols, professor of educational psychology, State University of New York, Buffalo, N.Y. Some of the introductory and explicatory matter has been omitted. The author, needless to say, is most indebted to Dr. Nichols for his generosity in allowing such important information to be incorporated in a book that is not his own.

12

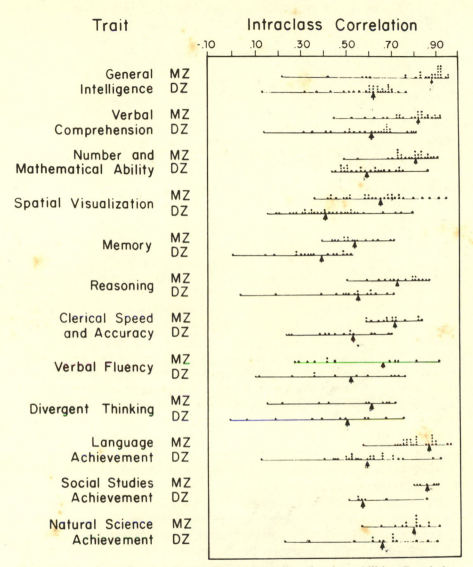

Figure III–1. Intraclass correlations from twin studies of various abilities. Correlations obtained in each study for MZ (identical) and DZ (fraternal) twins are indicated by dots; the mean correlation, weighted by the number of cases, is indicated by an arrow below the horizontal line representing the range of correlations for each trait.

correlations range from .25 for general intelligence to .11 for divergent thinking.

Figure III–2 shows the analogous results for the interest domain. The picture is quite similar to that for abilities, except that the correlations

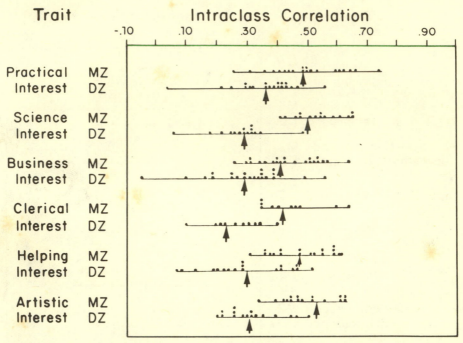

Figure III–2. Intraclass correlations from twin studies of various interests. Correlations obtained in each study for MZ (identical) and DZ (fraternal) twins are indicated by dots; the mean correlation, weighted by the number of cases, is indicated by an arrow below the horizontal line representing the range of correlations for each trait.

are somewhat lower. The difference between weighted averages for identical and fraternal twins ranges from .22 for artistic interests to .11 for business or enterprising interests.

Figure III–3 shows analogous results in the personality domain, which are similar to those for interests except the horizontal lines tend to be somewhat longer, indicating greater variation among studies. The difference between weighted averages for identical and fraternal twins ranged from .27 for extroversion to .19 for masculinity-femininity.

Confronted with the remarkable similarity of results for ability, interests, and personality as well as for the more specific traits within the three domains, the reader might well ask whether this survey of the twin literature reveals any significant difference between traits or between domains.

The weighted composite results of all twin studies are not appropriate for answering this question because different traits were investigated by different studies using different samples of twins. Thus, the large differences noted between different studies of the same trait could produce

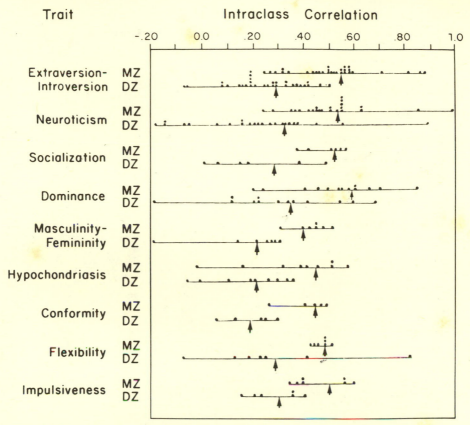

Figure III–3. Intraclass correlations from twin studies of various personality dimensions. Correlations obtained in each study for MZ (identical) and DZ (fraternal) twins are indicated by dots; the mean correlation, weighted by the number of cases, is indicated by an arrow below the horizontal line representing the range of correlations for each trait.

spurious differences between composite results for different traits. The best evidence on this issue, then, comes from considering each study as an independent attempt to estimate population values for a given trait. We can then ask whether studies of different traits produce results that cannot reasonably be attributed to the variation among studies observed when investigating the same trait. For this analysis each study was an equal unit and was not weighted by its sample size.

Table III–A shows the unweighted mean correlations for the various traits dealt with in the previous three figures. The basic data are the same as in the figures, but the results are slightly different because the studies were given equal weight regardless of sample size. It can now be

TABLE III–A
Mean Intraclass Correlations from Twin Studies of Various Traits

Trait	Number of studies	Mean Intraclass Cor.		Difference $r_{MZ} - r_{DZ}$	
		r_{MZ}	r_{DZ}	Mean	SD
Ability					
General Intelligence	30	.82	.59	.22	.10
Verbal Comprehension	27	.78	.59	.19	.14
Number and Mathematics	27	.78	.59	.19	.12
Spatial Visualization	31	.65	.41	.23	.16
Memory	16	.52	.36	.16	.16
Reasoning	16	.74	.50	.24	.17
Clerical Speed and Acc.	15	.70	.47	.22	.15
Verbal Fluency	12	.67	.52	.15	.14
Divergent Thinking	10	.61	.50	.11	.15
Language Achievement	28	.81	.58	.23	.11
Social Studies Achievement	7	.85	.61	.24	.10
Natural Science Ach.	14	.79	.64	.15	.13
All abilities	211	.74	.54	.21	.14
Interests					
Practical Interest	20	.50	.37	.13	.15
Science Interest	15	.54	.29	.25	.11
Business Interest	22	.45	.30	.15	.14
Clerical Interest	10	.44	.26	.18	.09
Helping Interest	18	.48	.30	.18	.14
Artistic Interest	16	.50	.32	.18	.13
All interests	116	.48	.30	.18	.13
Personality					
Extraversion-Introversion	30	.52	.25	.27	.14
Neuroticism	23	.51	.22	.29	.21
Socialization	6	.49	.23	.27	.17
Dominance	13	.53	.31	.23	.18
Masculinity-Femininity	7	.43	.17	.27	.21
Hypochondriasis	9	.37	.19	.18	.28
Conformity	5	.41	.20	.22	.15
Flexibility	7	.46	.27	.19	.27
Impulsiveness	6	.48	.29	.19	.12
All personality	106	.48	.29	.19	.12

Note: Mean correlations are unweighted averages of the studies involved. Because most twin studies employ multiple measures, the same twin sample may be represented in several traits.

asked whether the observed variation among traits in the average difference between identical and fraternal correlations can be attributed to chance. A one-way analysis of variance showed the differences among the traits in the ability domain to be not significant at the five percent level. Similar analyses in the interest and personality domains showed even greater likelihood that the observed differences among traits are due to chance. Thus, the difference in similarity between the two kinds of twins does not differ significantly among traits within the three domains. The mean difference between identical and fraternal correlations for the three domains—ability, personality, and interests—

were .21, .19, and .18 respectively. These three numbers are clearly not significantly different from one another. It follows that a twin study is likely to find a difference between identical and fraternal correlations of about .20 regardless of the domain or the trait that is being investigated!

The tendency for both the identical and fraternal correlations to be higher in the ability domain than in the personality and interest domains was highly significant statistically. The average correlation involving ability measures was higher by about .25 than that involving interest or personality measures.

Without attempting to interpret these correlations precisely at this point, their most obvious implications are that individual differences in all traits of behavior, from general intelligence to fingernail biting, are due in roughly equal parts to genetic differences and to environmental differences. The environmental factors that influence abilities tend to affect members of the same family in the same way, while the environmental factors that influence personality and interests tend to affect members of the same family differently.

The National Merit Twin Study

During the 1960s the National Merit Scholarship Corporation conducted an annual, nationwide testing program in which a three-hour test of educational development was given to selected eleventh grade students in most high schools in the United States. The test form asked whether or not each of the roughly 600,000 students who took the test in 1962 was a twin.

By pairing twins who attended the same school and who had the same last name and home address about 1500 sets of same-sexed twins were identified. These twins were each sent a questionnaire asking for detailed reports on a number of hereditary physical characteristics, which were used for diagnosis of zygosity. Subsequently, blood samples were obtained from 124 sets of these twins, and the questionnaire diagnosis agreed with the diagnosis based on extensive blood typing in 93 percent of the cases (Nichols and Bilbro, 1966). Usable questionnaires were received from about 1200 sets.

These twins were then sent an additional packet of questionnaires concerning their behavior, attitudes, goals, interests, and personality and a separate questionnaire to be completed by a parent. The packet contained the California Psychological Inventory and a long questionnaire developed specifically for the study. Complete data were obtained from 850 sets of twins, of which 60 percent were diagnosed identical and 42 percent were male.

This procedure yielded data on a large number of sets of same-sexed twins, all about the same age with each set raised in the same family.

Though these twins are not representative of any specific group to which statistical generalizations can be made, comparison with available norms suggests that they are not particularly unusual except that they qualified for the National Merit Test. Like other National Merit Test participants, they averaged about one standard deviation above high school students on measures of scholastic aptitude. They showed about the same variability as most students on tests of ability, personality, and interests. Except for the ability tests all data were obtained via mailed questionnaires. Checking internal consistency of the responses and comparing the information supplied by the twins and their parents indicate that the questionnaires were carefully completed. The data appear to be about the same quality as data usually obtained in group testing of college students.

Three years later, in 1965, a second twin sample was obtained. The twins among the almost 800,000 participants in the 1965 National Merit testing program were identified as part of a broader question about birth order. The same-sexed twins from this testing were sent a revised form of the physical similarity questionnaire from which 1300 identical sets and 864 fraternal sets of twins were diagnosed. About two years later David P. Campbell, then at the University of Minnesota, mailed these twins the form of the Strong Vocational Interest Blank appropriate for their sex. Usable Strong tests were obtained from 669 male and 949 female sets of twins of which 61 percent were identical. As in the 1962 sample, females and identical twins were somewhat more cooperative in providing data than males and fraternal twins.

The diverse data on these two large twin samples lead themselves to a number of different analyses, but here our attention is limited to the relative similarity of identical and fraternal twins on the various measures. All told, data were available on the 1962 sample for over 1600 test scores and questionnaire items, and the computer obediently spewed out intraclass correlations for all of them.

Differences Among Traits

When the correlations for the major scores representing ability, personality, and interests are plotted on the figures showing the results of past studies they blend in so well that Nichol's investigation could well serve as the modal twin study. Attention was then directed to a more detailed investigation of the striking implication of the literature that the difference between identical and fraternal correlations, and thus the heritability, is about the same for all psychological traits.

To study this question, John Loehlin performed a series of analyses that took advantage of the relatively large sample of twins and the diversity of variables in this study. Loehlin's innovative method was to compute correlations for a variety of variables separately in random halves of the twins of each sex and to look for agreement between random halves and between sexes in the rank order of differences between the correlations for the two kinds of twins. In this way, any tendency for some traits to show consistently larger differences between identical and fraternal correlations than do other traits could be detected. Traits with high heritabilities should show large differences and those with low heritabilities should show small differences in both random half-samples.

This method cannot be applied to the entire list of 1600 variables, because of the large differences among them in reliability. Unreliable variables would tend to have consistently low correlations with correspondingly small differences between them simply because of their low reliability.

The random-half method was first applied to the 18 standard scales of the California Psychological Inventory, which do not differ greatly in reliability. The scales were ranked according to the difference between identical and fraternal correlations in random half-samples of each sex. There was no agreement in these ranks between sexes or between random half-samples. The average Spearman rank correlation was −.05. There was also no agreement between the rank order of the CPI scales in this study with that reported in a previous twin study of the CPI conducted by Irving Gottesman (Gottesman, 1966; Nichols, 1969).

Using the 1965 sample, a similar random-half analysis was performed with 88 Strong Vocational Interest Blank scales for males and 69 scales for females. Again there was little agreement between random halves in the rank order of the scales in terms of the difference between identical and fraternal correlations.

There was also no agreement between the rank order of identical-fraternal differences for the five subtests of the National Merit Scholarship Qualifying Test either for the two sexes or for the 1962 and 1965 samples. However, this may not be especially surprising, since these subtests are highly intercorrelated.

To give any differences among traits the maximum chance to show themselves, one should use as diverse a set of variables as possible. For this purpose John Loehlin performed a series of cluster analyses on all of the 1500 or so questionnaire items available on the 1962 sample to develop a set of diverse clusters, each with reasonable internal consistency. This process yielded 70 clusters in which no variable was in more than one cluster and every variable in a cluster correlated at least .30 with every other. The number of variables in the clusters ranged from 3 to 13 with a median of 4. Although the clusters were formed on an entirely statistical basis, in almost all cases the content was fairly homogeneous and readily interpretable. There was great diversity of content among the 70 clusters, which included abilities, interests, life goals, selfconcept ratings, ideal-self ratings, activities, descriptive adjectives, physical complaints, attitudes, and CPI items.

Differences between identical and fraternal intraclass correlations were computed for the 70 clusters for random halfsamples of males and females. There was no agreement between sexes or random half-samples in the rank order of these differences. The average Spearman rank order correlation was .02.

Thus, it seems that it is quite difficult to find evidence of greater genetic involvement with some psychological traits than with others, even with the relatively large sample of twins available for this study.

In a final attempt to find such evidence, differences were checked between identical and fraternal twin correlations of individual CPI items in random half-samples. To avoid the difficulties presented by low item reliability, only those CPI items that could stand alone psychometrically were selected. Goldberg and Rorer (1964) obtained 3- to 4-week test-retest data for the CPI item pool for three samples of college students ranging in size from 95 to 179. Only those items that had test-retest reliability coefficients of at least .50 in each of the three samples were retained. There were 179 such highly dependable items.

Next, there were sorted out from among these reliable items those in which the intraclass correlation between identical twins was at least .20 higher than that between fraternal twins ("high-difference" items) and those in which either the correlation between identicals was no more than .02 above that between fraternals or the fraternal correlation was higher ("low difference" items). This procedure was carried out separately in the two random halves of the total sample. The question was simply: "Are high and low identical-fraternal differences consistent properties of particular items, or are we screening chance sampling fluctuation?"

Fifty-five and 54 items met the criterion of high difference in the two half-samples; 38 and 31 items met the criterion of low difference. There was a significant tendency for the low-difference items to be the same in the two half-samples, however, there was no such tendency for the high-difference items. Eleven items had low differences in both half samples. Only 6.6 would be expected by chance.

Among the 11 items showing a low difference in both half samples were several expressing social attitudes, a content which did not occur among the high-difference items. These items were: "A person who doesn't vote is not a good citizen," "I do not like to see people carelessly dressed," "I believe women should have as much sexual freedom as men," and "People have a real duty to take care of their aged parents, even if it means making some pretty big sacrifices."

With this hint it was noticed that elsewhere in the questionnaire individual items concerned with attitudes toward racial integration and federal welfare programs and with belief in God also showed low differences.

Thus, there is some evidence that specific social attitudes are less dependent on the genes than are most other psychological traits. It is somewhat reassuring to find that identical twins were not consistently more similar than were fraternal twins. Otherwise it might have been necessary to entertain a hypothesis about ESP at work or, even worse, collusion on answering the questionnaires. In this vein it might be noted with some feeling of relief that the identical twins were not noticeably more alike than the fraternals on such items as reports of the size of their high school class, the size and urbanization of their home towns, or the presence of various items in their home.

Although there were practically no dependable differences among psychological traits in the difference between identical and fraternal correlations, the size of the correlations did differ reliably among trait domains. As in previous studies, correlations tended to be higher for abilities than for personality and interests.

Interpretation of Twin Correlations

Table III–B shows the median correlations obtained for several major groups of variables. A random half-sample analysis showed that the difference between identical and fraternal correlations for the various classes of variables was not dependably different, although the varying size of the correlations (e.g., the mean correlation for the two kinds of

Table III–B

Median Intraclass Correlations for Various Trait Domains

Trait	Intraclass Correlation		
	Identical	Fraternal	Difference (I-F)
General Ability (NMSQT total score)[1]	.86	.62	.24
Special Abilities (5 NMSQT subtests)	.74	.52	.22
Activities (17 activities clusters)	.64	.49	.15
Interests (88 Strong scales, male) (69 Strong scales, female)	.53	.27	.26
Personality (27 CPI scales)	.50	.28	.22
Goals and Ideals (31 clusters of life goal, ideal-self and interest items)	.37	.20	.17
Self Concept (15 clusters of self concept ratings)	.34	.10	.22

[1] NMSQT is National Merit Scholarship Qualifying Test.

twins) was dependable. An attempt may now be made to interpret these correlations in more detail.

First an adjustment should be made for the correlations for two known sources of error in the study—the variables were not measured with complete reliability and the zygosity of the twins was not diagnosed with complete accuracy. Table III–C shows the correlations corrected for these attenuating influences. The reliability estimates used for these corrections are shown in the first column of the table. The best estimate from the blood studies mentioned above is that about 7 percent of the twins of each kind were misdiagnosed, and the correlations were adjusted for the effect of these errors in diagnosis of zygosity. The effect of both of these corrections was to increase the observed correlations. The difference between the corrected identical and fraternal correlations is now about .30, which implies a heritability of about .60. Because the heritability estimate is subject to sampling fluctuation and is fairly sensitive to the estimate of the reliability of the test, one should probably not state this more precisely than to say that about half the variance in these traits seems to be attributable to genetic differences.

Additional correction for assortative mating would not change very much the heritability estimate for personality and interest measures, where quite low positive correlations between spouses are typically found. However, husband-wife correlations on the order of .40 to .50 are generally reported for general intelligence (Vandenberg, 1972), and allowance

Table III–C

Median Intraclass Correlations for Various Trait Domains Corrected for Unreliability of Measurement and Errors of Diagnosis

Trait	Reliability of Measurement	Intraclass Correlation		
		Identical	Fraternal	Difference (I-F)
General Ability (NMSQT total score)	.95	.92	.63	.29
Special Abilities (5 NMSQT subtests)	.88	.86	.57	.29
Activities (17 activities clusters)	.70	.93	.68	.25
Interests (88 Strong scales, male) (69 Strong scales, female)	.85	.64	.29	.35
Personality (27 CPI scales)	.80	.65	.33	.32
Goals and Ideals (31 clusters of life goal, ideal-self and interest items)	.65	.59	.29	.30
Self Concept (15 clusters of self concept ratings)	.65	.55	.13	.42

for this would increase the heritability estimate for abilities to about .70.

There are additional qualifications that should be placed on heritability calculated from twin correlations. Non-additive genetic effects (dominance and epistasis) are included in the heritability figure. Thus, it is often described as "heritability in the broad sense," the total genetic effect, in contrast to "heritability in the narrow sense," which is the heritability that would be realized in selective breeding. Variance attributable to the correlation of genetic and environmental influences is also included in the heritability figure. This correlation might be either positive (those with the more favorable genes are exposed to the more favorable environment), negative or curvilinear (those genetically extreme on a trait are influenced by the environment to be less extreme). Other complications, such as differences in the intrauterine environment for the two kinds of twins, have also been suggested.

Some observers have cautioned that the greater behavioral similarity of identical twins may be due in part to a greater similarity of their environment rather than of their genes. Reports by the twins and their parents indicate that identical twins do in fact spend more time together, have more similar early experiences, and are treated more alike by parents than are fraternal twins. However, this does not seem to be a reasonable explanation for their greater psychological similarity. Within twins of the same type, greater similarity of experience was not associated with greater similarity on the psychological traits with which this study is concerned. In other words, the difference in similarity of environment that has been noted for the two kinds of twins does not appear to result in corresponding differences in psychological similarity. Thus, the best explanation for the twin data in this study and in the literature is that about half of the variation among people in a broad spectrum of psychological traits is due to differences among the people in genetic characteristics.

There is at least one theory which suggests that under long-term evolutionary conditions one might expect traits to tend toward roughly equal (and moderate) heritabilities. The theory derives from arguments outlined by Allen (1970). It holds that, if the heritability of a trait is low, gene mutations affecting the trait will tend to accumulate, increasing its genetic variance. Once the genetic variance becomes large enough relative to environmental variation so that the heritability of the trait is appreciable, stabilizing natural selection will begin to operate on the trait to slow and eventually to stop further increase in its genetic variability and hence to hold heritability at a stable level. If relevant environmental variation were to decrease, the trait heritability would temporarily rise, permitting selection to act more effectively on the genetic variation of the trait, bringing the genetic variation (and thus the heritability) back down again.

Generally speaking, under this hypothesis all traits tend toward moderate levels of heritability because the genetic component of variation of any trait tends to increase until the process of natural selection can "see it" against the background of environmental variation present and hold it stable. This suggests that differences in the importance of different traits for reproductive fitness will be reflected principally in the total amount of variation present, not in the relative proportions of this variation that are genetic and environmental. A trait that is critically important for reproduction will show little variation among individuals and a trivial trait a lot, but their heritabilities will be about the same.

For this mechanism to work, the general level of environmental influence on any given trait must remain fairly constant on the scale of tens of thousands or hundreds of thousands of years on which human biological evolution takes place. The specific environmental influences need not always be the same, but their general level of impact must remain fairly constant. On the face of it, this does not seem very reasonable. The tremendous changes in the human environment that industrialization has produced over the past several hundred years must certainly have changed the environmental impact on human behavior, if only by reducing the privations and noxious circumstances that seem to characterize life in the wild. But we must remember that we are unable to identify the major environmental events that produce differences in human personality. If the critical events are prenatal biological factors or basic parent-child emotional relationships, and if they occur in some relatively short critical period, it may be reasonable to assume that their impact has remained fairly constant over millennia.

It has been customary when discussing the heritability of human behavior to point out that the heritability coefficient is a population statistic specific to a given group at a given time, and it has been suggested that heritability may vary widely even among sub-cultures in the United States. The current line of argument, on the other hand, implies that the genetic and environmental factors responsible for individual differences are rather basic properties of the human condition, and that one would expect to find roughly similar heritabilities over a fairly wide range of circumstances.

Environmental Influences

Another perspective on the character of relevant environmental factors may be obtained by considering the different levels of twin correlation prevailing in different trait domains. Assuming that the degree of genetic influence causing twins to be alike is roughly the same for all trait domains, the differences in the level of correlation (the average of the correlations for both kinds of twins) in the various domains can be attributed to differences in the similarity of environmental influences on the twins of a set. Thus, although it is not known specifically what the environmental factors are, something can be said about the degree to which they affect twins raised together in the same family in the same way. More precisely, if the heritability is known, we can calculate the correlation between twins of the salient environmental influences implied by the intraclass correlations. These environmental correlations for the various domains are shown in Table III–D. Separate estimates of the same environmental correlation were obtained from the intraclass correlations for identical and fraternal twins. The third column in the table shows the average of these two estimates. These environmental correlations indicate the degree to which the environmental influences that produce individual differences in the trait have the same effect on both twins of a set.

These environmental correlations are subject to sampling fluctuation, as shown by the different estimates obtained from the two kinds of twins. They are also somewhat sensitive to the estimate of reliability used in correcting the correlations for attenuation. Thus, small differences between traits should not be taken too seriously. There was a very clear tendency, however, for abilities and activities to have high environmental

Table III–D

Correlation of Twin Environments Implied by the Corrected Intraclass Correlations Shown in Table III–C

Trait	Environmental Correlation		
	Identical	Fraternal	Average (I + F)/2
General Ability (NMSQT total score)[1]	.73	.77	.75
Special Abilities (5 NMSQT subtests)	.65	.68	.66
Activities (17 activities clusters)	.83	.95	.89
Interests (88 Strong scales, male) (69 Strong scales, female)	.10	−.02	.06
Personality (27 CPI scales)	.13	.08	.10
Goals and Ideals (31 clusters of life goal, ideal-self and interest items)	−.02	−.02	−.02
Self Concept (15 clusters of self concept ratings)	−.12	−.42	−.27

Note. Environmental correlations were calculated from the corrected intraclass correlations in Table III–C. The calculation for general ability assumed a heritability of .70 and a genetic correlation for fraternal twins of .57. The calculation for all other traits assumed a heritability of .60 and a genetic correlation for fraternal twins of .50.

[1] NMSQT is National Merit Scholarship Qualifying Test.

correlations and for personality and interests to have low environmental correlations, a finding consistent with previous twin studies.

It is not difficult to accept the high environmental correlation for abilities and activities, since one might reasonably expect that the relevant environmental inputs would be associated with the characteristics of the parents, the home, the school, and the community, all of which are the same for both twins of a set.

But what about the very low or even negative correlation between twins in the environmental influences on personality and interests? Can this possibly be true? Surely such factors as the parents' child-rearing philosophies and the psychological ambience of the community and the home have some influence on the development of personality—factors that are the same for twins reared together. In fact, almost all of the environmental antecedents of individual differences in personality that have been suggested by psychologists and others are similar for twins reared together.

One possible explanation of this paradox lies in the special environmental situation of twins and in our reliance on self-report measures of personality. Each twin has the other twin as a major part of his environment, and this may lead to competition or to contrast effects between them. If a twin's reference point for self-definition is the other twin, and if others around him are continually contrasting the pair members, it seems plausible that they might end up seeing themselves as much less similar in personality and interests than they actually are. Since our personality and interest measures were all based on some form of self report, such a contrast effect could mask the similarity produced by the common environment. This hypothesis obtains some support from the fact that the somewhat indirect self-report measures, such as the CPI and Strong scales, show low positive environmental correlations, while the more direct ratings of self concept show negative environmental correlations.

There are, however, at least three arguments against this explanation. 1) Twelve twin studies in the literature have used non-self-report measures of personality such as hypnotic susceptibility, musical preferences, flicker fusion, autokinetic movement, speed of decision, free association, social intelligence, and color-form movement. The unweighted average intraclass correlations for the more objective personality measures from these studies were .47 for identical and .30 for fraternal twins. These correlations show the usual difference between correlations for identical and fraternal twins near .20, but yield near zero estimates of environmental correlation. 2) The contrast effect would be expected to vary in some systematic way across personality traits and for the two sexes, but no such pattern was observed. 3) The degree to which twins of the same kind tended to associate with each other was unrelated to personality differences between the twins, although one might expect a strong contrast effect to be sensitive to the amount of contact between the twins.

Another possible explanation for the paradoxically low twin correlations observed for personality and interest measures is that the direction of environmental influence may vary depending on the strength or level of the particular trait. It seems likely that a major purpose of social influences on many traits is to make people more alike. The shy person, for example, is helped and encouraged to be more sociable, while attempts are made to calm down the overpowering extravert. Cattell, Stice, and Kristy (1957), in interpreting a similar finding, referred to this effect as "coercion to the biocultural norm." An individual who deviates from the community norm, as set by the biological and cultural central tendencies of his group, will experience a cultural or educational constraint toward the mean. Thus, the major systematic effect of the environment on traits of personality and interest may be to restrict variation, to make the measures less variable than they would otherwise be. Such an environmental effect could produce the observed pattern of twin correlations. The phenotypic manifestation of genetic differences between fraternal twins would be reduced somewhat by coercion to the biocultural norm, but its major effect would be to reduce differences between families, i.e. between twin sets. If the variance-reducing effects of coercion to the biocultural norm were equivalent to the variance-producing effects of systematic between-family environmental influences, only within family environmental effects would show up in the twin correlations.

A third, although unlikely, explanation is that the major environmental influences on personality are actually highly specific situational factors. If the ways in which environment affects personality are sufficiently complex, contingent and subtle, they could appear random in their effects on individuals, and the similar environmental ambiance of twins raised together might have different effects on the individual twins.

Conclusion

Twin studies are remarkably consistent in two major findings: 1) identical twins are more similar than are fraternal twins to about the same degree for a very broad range of traits of ability, personality, and interest, and 2) both identical and fraternal twins are considerably less similar in personality and interests than they are in ability. Both of these findings are startling in that neither was anticipated and both pose problems of interpretation within current theories of individual differences.

Summary

A review of the twin literature and analyses of two large twin samples found identical twin correlations higher than fraternal twin correlations by about .20 for a variety of traits of ability, personality, and interests. This was interpreted as indicating that about half of the variation among people in a broad spectrum of psychological traits is due to differences among the people in genetic characteristics. The data also suggest that the environmental influences on ability affect twins raised together in the same way, while the environmental influences on personality and interests affect twins in the same family differently.

IV

Purposes, Goals, and Definitions

It is manifest that man is . . . subject to much variability.
—*Darwin: The Descent of Man*

This study has four primary goals: 1) To determine the differences in average performance of U.S. blacks and whites on mental ability tests purporting to measure IQ. Such tests cover a broad spectrum of intellectual factors ranging from nonverbal culture-fair performance tasks to sophisticated tests of verbal reasoning. Black-white comparisons on over 25 separate measurements will be reported. 2) To examine the hereditarian proposition that there is a positive correlation for intelligence among members of the same family, the closer the relationship the higher the correlation. Differences between individuals and groups in general intelligence (IQ) are the results of inherited differences, 60 to 80 percent of the variance in IQ test scores being attributable to genetic factors. 3) To ascertain if there is any difference in heritability for general intelligence (IQ) for U.S. blacks and whites. 4) Finally, and perhaps most importantly, to make available to other investigators all test data, biometric measures, and blood test results on the 496 pairs of twins in the study.

In addition to these four primary goals, we will undertake numerous secondary or auxiliary research programs to answer fundamental questions raised by environmentalists. For example, efforts will be made to test the assertion that Binet IQ-type tests are culture biased against members of lower socio-economic groups and minorities. The claim is that standardized intelligence tests do not meet the criteria for valid and reliable tests and that test items are slanted in favor of the white middle class. Cattell's Culture Fair Intelligence Test and other nonverbal instruments will be used to test this assumption.

A second auxiliary research program will test the hereditarian prediction of filial regression. According to the hereditarian view, the correlation for intelligence between parent and offspring will be about .50. Since the variability of IQ remains constant from generation to generation, it follows that children on the average have IQ's halfway between the mid-parent IQ and the average IQ of the general population. The hereditarian thesis also predicts that children, black and white, will have sibs whose average intelligence has regressed toward the population mean of their respective race in accordance with Galton's Law of Filial Regression.

A third auxiliary topic will deal with the claim that the confounding of age and IQ seriously contaminates the correlation between twins. If length of time spent in the same environment has a significant effect on intelligence test performance (IQ), then younger individuals who are genetically identical (MZ twins) should resemble their twins less closely than older identical twins; that is, as age increases, mean difference in IQ between twin pairs should decrease. The same trend would be expected for fraternal (DZ) twins except that initial and final differences would be greater than for MZ twins. We would also expect the correlation between age and IQ difference for both MZ and DZ twins to be negative if environmental influences are cumulative. IQ stability will be examined with 427 pairs of like-sexed twins ranging in age from 12 to 20.

The results of numerous small studies are reported as sections of various chapters. For example, the environmentalist claim that MZ and DZ twins cannot be representative of the population because DZ families come from significantly lower socio-economic levels than MZ families will be discussed in the chapter reporting the analysis of Cattell's Culture Fair Intelligence Test.

The environmentalist hypothesis that within-pair IQ variance of male DZ's is significantly larger than that for female DZ's is examined in Chapter VII.

The claims and questions raised above represent serious challenges to the hereditarian research position. With the new twin data contained in this book, an attempt will be made to respond to these and numerous other arguments of the culture determinists.

Since some terms referred to in earlier sections and used later in the book have special meanings in psychology, they will be defined here.

Intelligence: A hypothetical construct used to describe individual differences in ability to learn, to perceive and understand relationships, to perform tasks requiring logical, spatial, verbal, and numerical reasoning and to recall associated meanings. Intelligence is also called academic aptitude, scholastic aptitude, mental capacity, mental ability, and mental maturity.

IQ: An operational, observable, and measurable representation of intelligence. It is a measure of potential rate of mental growth up to 16, or in some cases, 18 years of age. The formula is IQ = mental age ÷ chronological age × 100. Mental age is the chronological age for which a given score on an intelligence test is average or normal. Chronological age, of course, is the actual age of the subject taking the test. When referring to IQ's, derived from tests, the psychologist usually modifies the term by the name of the test yielding the IQ or by the mental factor measured; for example, Binet IQ; verbal IQ. Figure IV–1 compares the IQ tests used in this book with Wechsler and Stanford-Binet IQ's in relation to the normal curve.

Deviation IQ: A measure of intelligence based on the extent to which an individual's score deviates from the score that is normal for the individual's age. Wechsler IQ's are deviation IQ's. In this study deviation IQ's were obtained for Basic Battery mental tests by standardizing scores for each age to a mean of 100 and a standard deviation of 15 (Figure IV–1).

Heritability: A population statistic describing a property of a given trait in a given population at a given time. It is usually designated as *H, HR,* or *h²,* and it may be determined by a variety of statistical methods (see Chapter II). Technically, heritability is the genetic variance divided by the total phenotypic variance. It is generally expressed as a percentage and decreases with an increasing environmental component of variance for the characteristic under study. For example, an intelligence heritabil-

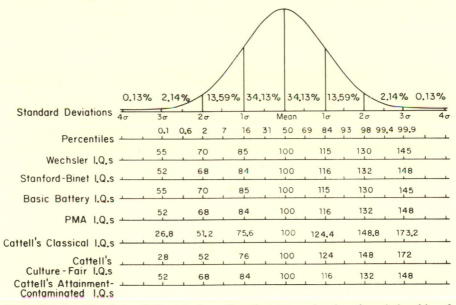

Figure IV–1. The theoretical normal or Gaussian curve showing the relationship of various IQ tests.

ity of .70 does not mean that the intelligence of any individual is determined 70 percent by heredity. What it does mean is that 70 percent of the variation of intelligence in the population is produced by genetic differences between its members.

Monozygotic Twins: Twins derived from one egg fertilized by one spermatozoan. Monozygotic (MZ) twins are sometimes called identical twins.

Dizygotic Twins: Fraternal twins derived by fertilization of two different ova by different spermatozoa. The term is usually abbreviated DZ.

Race: A biological grouping within the human species distinguished or classified according to genetically transmitted differences such as blood gene frequency, skin color, hair type, lung capacity, etc. Only members of two races, Negroid (Negro or black) and Caucasoid (white), will be studied in this book. How membership in a race is determined for this study is described in the following defintion of subpopulation.

Subpopulation: Although this term is widely used and generally understood and accepted in studies of individual differences, Jensen's clearcut definition, which follows, will be used in this study.

> *Subpopulation* has the advantage of being a theoretically neutral term. Unlike such terms as *social class* and *race,* a subpopulation does not connote more than its bare operational defintion. Thus, the term *subpopulation* does not beg any questions with the answers. And it can help to forestall fallacious thinking about social classes and races as Platonic categories. A subpopulation is simply any particular subdivision of the population which an investigator chooses to select for whatever purpose he may have. The only requirement is operational defintion, that is to say, clearly specified objective criteria for the inclusion (and exclusion) of individuals. The reliability of the classification procedure is strictly an empirical question and not a matter for semantic debate. It can be answered in terms of a reliability coefficient, which can take any value from 0 (no reliability whatsoever) to 1 (perfect reliability). A subpopulation can consist of redheads, or females, or owners of a Rolls Royce, or persons with incomes under $4000 per annum, or whatever criterion or combination of multiple criteria one may choose. All other questions follow, their relevance depending on the purposes of the investigator. (Jensen, 1973a, pp. 28–29)

The subpopulations examined in this study are Negroes and whites, boys and girls, MZ and DZ twins, and certain socio-economic groups. Negroes are defined as those individuals who identify themselves or are identified by their parents as Negro and are so identified by others. Whites are those who call themselves white, or Caucasian, and are usually of European ancestry. The white subpopulation does not include Orientals,

Mexican-Americans, and American Indians. Boys are those individuals who identify themselves as boys and are so identified by others. The same classification process is applied to girls. MZ and DZ twins have been defined earlier in this chapter. Socio-economic status is determined by a modified version of Warner's scale (Warner, Meeker, & Eells, 1949).

In the following chapters, subpopulation differences will be examined in a wide range of psychological tests covering the primary mental abilities, school achievement, personality, and Culture Fair IQ. Each chapter represents an independent study involving different tests or different groups of twins in the data pool.

V

Sample and Zygosity Diagnosis

The Sample

Subjects for the Twin Study were drawn from public and private schools in Louisville, Kentucky, and Jefferson County, Kentucky; from public schools in Atlanta, Georgia, and the Georgia counties of Cobb, Fulton, Chatham, Walton, Madison, and Clarke; and from a small number of public schools in Indiana. All together 496 pairs of twins were studied. Most of the analyses will be concerned with the 427 pairs of like-sexed twins. Test scores of 50 pairs of unlike-sexed twins are reported but referred to only occasionally. Nineteen sets of twins, ranging in age from 11 to 20, participated in the EEG study but were not involved in any other aspect of the Twin Study. They are not included in Tables V–A, V–B, or V–C, although their test scores are given in Appendix G.

Table V–A shows the distribution of same-sexed twins by sex, race, and zygosity. In Table V–B the group is broken down by age, race, and sex. In Table V–C the 50 pairs of unlike-sexed twins are shown by age and race.

Table V–A
Distribution of Like-sexed Twins By Race, Sex, and Zygosity

Race	MZ			DZ		
	Male	Female	Total	Male	Female	Total
Black	26	50	76	14	33	47
White	84	87	171	51	82	133
Total	110	137	247	65	115	180

Table V–B
Distribution of Like-sexed Twins by Age, Race, and Sex

Age	White Male	White Female	White Total	Black Male	Black Female	Black Total	Total Male	Total Female	Total Total	Twin Pairs No.	Twin Pairs %
12		2	2		2	2		4	4	2	.5
13	30	46	76	14	30	44	44	76	120	60	14.1
14	46	52	98	24	36	60	70	88	158	79	18.5
15	54	76	130	18	34	52	72	110	182	91	21.3
16	54	74	128	16	32	48	70	106	176	88	20.6
17	56	52	108	6	24	30	62	76	138	69	16.2
18	22	34	56	2	8	10	24	42	66	33	7.7
19	6	2	8				6	2	8	4	.9
20	2		2				2		2	1	.2
Means	15.59	15.41	15.49	14.78	15.01	14.93	15.41	15.28	15.33		
SD	1.60	1.56	1.58	1.29	1.50	1.44	1.58	1.55	1.56		
No. Twin Pairs	135	169	304	40	83	123	175	252	427	427	

Table V–C
Distribution of Unlike-sexed Twins by Age and Race

Age	Number of Pairs White	Number of Pairs Black	Number of Pairs Total
13	1	6	7
14	5	7	12
15	5	6	11
16	8	4	12
17	4	2	6
18	1	1	2
Total	24	26	50
Mean	15.50	14.69	15.08
SD	1.22	1.38	1.37

Zygosity Diagnosis

Since it was not practical to take blood samples from all participants in the Georgia Twin Study, a combination of blood-typing and other methods of twin diagnosis was used. For a detailed explanation of the zygosity determination, see Osborne (1978).

Twins of the cooperative twin studies of Vandenberg (1967a) and Osborne and Gregor (1967) were blood-typed by the following factors: A, B, O, M, N, S, s, P_1, Rho, rh″, rh′, Miltenberger, Vermeyst, Lewis, Lutheran, Duffy, Kidd, Sutter, Martin, Kell, Cellano and occasionally some others. All pairs concordant for all blood types must be MZ while all pairs discordant for any one of the blood types must be classified dizygotic. Some DZ's may be concordant for all blood types and therefore classified as MZ's. When this misclassification occurs, it produces a bias which reduces the proportion of variance ascribable to genetic factors. Thus any obtained estimate of the heritability of a factor will be lower than it would be if it were possible to correctly determine the zygosity of every twin pair.

Smith and Penrose (1955) give tables for determining the probability of misdiagnosis for frequently tested blood groups. Ninety-seven percent accuracy is claimed for MZ diagnosis. Both the Vandenberg and Osborne samples from the cooperative twin studies reported a considerably higher proportion of MZ's than expected.

Two hundred thirty-nine pairs of twins tested by Vandenberg were classified as MZ or DZ using the results of serological tests alone. There were 20 more pairs classified MZ in the Vandenberg sample than would have been expected by chance. The proportion of all twins of questionable classification is relatively small; nevertheless, misclassification of even a small number will lead to the underestimation of the proportion of variance due to genetical causes.

For the twins tested by Osborne, both anthropometric and serological test results were available. The anthropometric measures were: face length, head length, head breadth, head circumference, height and weight. Three other measures were computed: Cephalic index, Kaup's Index (body weight in grams/(height in cm)^2) and Rohrer's Index of body structure (body weight in grams $\times$ 100/(height in cm)^3). Data on color blindness and handedness were also available. Twins concordant for all blood types were then classified as similar (MZ) or dissimilar (DZ) using the nine physical measures described above. Six of 45 pairs of twins concordant for blood type were classified as dissimilar on the basis of physical measures and called DZ's. It was hoped that this procedure would pick out DZ twins who would otherwise be classified as MZ because they were concordant for all blood types by chance. Reclassification of the six pairs on the basis of physical measures would indicate higher misclassification by blood-typing than reported in other studies. Nevertheless, the absolute number of twins involved was relatively small and unlikely to have produced a large bias. This procedure would cause misdiagnosis of the type where true MZ's are mistakenly called DZ's because their physical characteristics differ more than would be expected in MZ twins. But they will not necessarily differ more than expected for abilities being studied here, and therefore the within-pair variance of DZ twins will be reduced. This means that the within-family genetical effect and the proportion of variance due to genetical influences will be underestimated. Thus, the possible sources of misclassification of Vandenberg's sample and Osborne's sample of the cooperative twin studies both lead to underestimation of the genetical components of variance.

Twins tested by Osborne in 1972 were not blood-typed. Physical measures and characteristics were used in conjunction with two questionnaires to determine zygosity. One questionnaire was developed by Nichols for use in the National Merit Twin Study (Nichols, 1965; Nichols & Bilbro, 1966); the other was a modification of the questionnaire used by Schoenfeldt in the Project Talent Twin Study (Schoenfeldt, 1968). On the basis of these data, two computer programs were used to classify the pairs as monozygotic or dizygotic. The Automatic Interaction Detector (AID) Program is explained in detail by Schoenfeldt (1968). The other program was the Discriminant Analysis Program (BMDO7M) from the Package of Biomedical Computer Programs (Dixon, 1973). The latter program utilized the nine physical measurements described in Osborne's cooperative twin studies (Osborne *et al.,* 1978). This group, for which both serological results and anthropometric measures were available, was used as the criterion group for determining the accuracy of diagnosis using the discriminant scores of the 1972 group. The results of the two programs were compared; where these agreed, the twin pair was classified accordingly. Of the 143 pairs in the 1972 group, 61 pairs were classified as monozygotic and 35 as dizygotic. This total of 96 pairs had been classified the same by both programs.

For the 47 pairs of twins remaining, a second discriminant analysis was undertaken using the 96 pairs of twins already diagnosed as the criterion group. Seventeen variables were employed in this analysis: the nine measures from the first analysis plus nose length, eye color, hair color, other hair differences, color blindness (two variables), handedness, and mistaken identity variables from the Project Talent Questionnaire.

Three judges classified the 47 pairs of twins as monozygotic or dizygotic, using front and profile photographs and statements of likenesses and differences reported by the twins in their own assessment of their zygosity. The zygosity of 36 of the 47 pairs were diagnosed the same by the second discriminant analysis and by the judges and were classified as 20 MZ pairs and 16 DZ pairs.

At this point only 11 pairs remained in the doubtful classification. To reach a decision on these, the complete files, except psychological test results, were examined by the principal investigator with the following results:

Twin Pair No. 233: These 16-year-old white girls were called MZ by the discriminant analysis program and DZ by AID. The girls were exactly the same height but differed in weight by 14.5%. Differences in head length and breadth were also significant. One sister was right-handed, the other ambidextrous. The twins reported they were rarely misidentified and believed they were DZ. Twin A said, "There is no resemblance. Everything is unlike." Final classification, DZ.

Twin Pair No. 277: In terms of biometric measurements, these 14-year-old black girls appeared to be identical. They were the same height and had the same head length and head breadth. There were only slight differences in the other physical measurements. However, Twin A was right-handed; Twin B was not. The test for color blindness probably convinced the investigator. Final classification, DZ.

Twin Pair No. 282: These 14-year-old black boys were classified MZ by AID and DZ by the discriminant analysis program. Weight difference was 6%; face length difference 8%. Twin A was color blind; Twin B was not. A was left-handed; B right-handed. Final classification, DZ.

Twin Pair No. 284: These 15-year-old black girls were not classified the same way by the computer programs. Examination of their files convinced the investigator they were DZ. The twins said they were fraternal. A was left-handed; B right-handed. Both said they do not look alike and that Twin A was darker skinned and heavier. Both agreed that their noses, mouths, and eyes looked alike. Teachers, parents, and friends sometimes mistook one for the other. Differences in head length and breadth were significant at the .01 level from Verschuer tables. Final classification, DZ.

Twin Pair No. 309: This pair of 17-year-old white girls was classified DZ by AID and MZ by discriminant analysis. The girls differed by 8% in height and 27% in weight. Twin A was right-handed, B left-handed. The attending physician said they were DZ. The girls believed they were fraternal. Final classification, DZ.

Twin Pair No. 317: These were 14-year-old white girls. A said she knew she was an MZ twin; B was just as confident she was DZ because the attending physician had said so. In the questionnaire, B said their noses were not alike, which was true since their noses differed in length by 9%. Height difference was 5%; weight 13%. A was right-handed; B left-handed. Final classification, DZ.

Twin Pair No. 347: This pair of 14-year-old white girls said their attending physician had told them they were identical. However, Twin B said, "We look nothing alike." A's hair was brown; B's auburn. They never, or only rarely, were mistaken by teachers and parents. Differences in nose length, face length, head length, and height all supported the final diagnosis of DZ.

Twin Pair No. 362: These 13-year-old black boys "know we are identical" but Twin A said that B's hair grew faster than his. They were only occasionally mistaken by teachers, friends, and parents. Differences in five biometric measurements, height, weight, head breadth, nose length, and face length, convinced the investigator they were DZ.

Twin Pair No. 373: These 13-year-old black girls knew they were fraternal. A was right-handed; B left-handed. They were rarely mistaken by friends, teachers, or parents. A's hair was lighter and thinner than B's. Both twins reported their faces, legs, and heads were different. The AID Program called them DZ; the discriminant analysis, MZ. Final classification, DZ.

Twin Pair No. 375: These 17-year-old white girls said they were identical but were rarely misidentified. They indicated their noses, fingers, hands, stomachs, and busts were similar. The discriminant analysis program classified the girls as DZ; the AID Program as MZ. Rohrer's Index of Body Structure and Kaup's Index both supported the diagnosis of DZ. Differences in nose length and face length confirmed the final DZ classification.

Twin Pair No. 379: These 16-year-old black boys said they looked alike and knew they were identical because their attending physician had told them they were. They were seldom misidentified. Face-length difference was the only biometric measure that supported a DZ diagnosis. Other measurements were within MZ limits. Final classification, MZ.

To classify the 19 pairs of twins who participated in the EEG study, the two questionnaires were used in conjunction with physical measurements and photographs. In this group there were 13 MZ and 6 DZ pairs of twins.

The results of the AID Program agreed with the final results in 81.2% of the cases. For the 9- and 17-variable discriminant analysis programs, the diagnoses agreed with the final classification in 85.3 and 76.6% of the cases, respectively. Assuming the final classification to be correct, the reliability of all these methods is not high. However, in the 47 cases where judges were used, the consensus always agreed with the final classification. Of the 11 cases where no decision could be made and the principal investigator decided the issue, 10 pairs were classified as dizygotic. These comments on the zygosity determination are especially interesting if we consider several studies of zygosity diagnosis. Cederlof *et al.* (1961) recorded an accuracy of 98.6% for 145 pairs of twins, using data which had been obtained from two mailed questionnaires asking for the subjects' own opinions about their similarities or dissimilarities.

More recent work by Kasriel and Eaves (1976) showed an accuracy of 96.1% using only responses to two questions on physical similarity and mistaken identity in childhood. The "true" zygosity of the twins was determined by blood-typing 178 pairs of twins for 15 different systems. Of 94 pairs of twins diagnosed as monozygotic by blood-typing, 92 pairs agreed that they were alike and had been mistaken for each other in childhood. Kasriel and Eaves accordingly classified them as monozygotic. If they said they were not alike and not mistaken for each other or if they failed to agree on these two questions, they were classified as dizygotic. Using these criteria only 7 of the 178 pairs were misdiagnosed.

In the Georgia Twin Study (Osborne, 1978), the judges and the principal investigator used responses to questions on similarity and mistaken identity in childhood to help reach their decision. Kasriel and Eaves point out that disagreement between the twins as to their zygosity is usually a good indication that the pair in question is dizygotic. In this study we note that of the final 11 doubtful pairs, 10 pairs were classified as dizygotic.

Zygosity was determined differently in the three subsample studies, leading to misclassification of dizygotic pairs as monozygotic in Vandenberg's cooperative twin study, misclassification of monozygotic pairs as dizygotic in Osborne's cooperative twin study subsample, and to errors in both directions in Osborne's 1972 subsample. However, in each case the bias introduced by the misdiagnosis is predictable and results in the underestimation of the proportion of the variance due to genetical causes.

By way of summary, there are 496 pairs of twins in the Twin Survey— 427 pairs of like-sexed twins ranging in age from 12 to 20; 175 boys, 252 girls; 247 MZ's, 180 DZ's; 29% black, 71% white. Of the 50 pairs of unlike-sexed twins, ranging in age from 13 to 18, 48% are white, 52% black. In the small EEG sample of 19 pairs (13 MZ's, 6 DZ's) only 1 set is black.

VI

Psychological Tests

Psychological tests used in this study represent a broad spectrum, including global IQ, spatial ability, culture fair mental ability, primary mental abilities, spelling, numerical ability, and personality. Complete references for all tests are listed in Appendix B. Since several tests are not well known or readily available, they are here presented in some detail. For each test in the Basic Battery for which a reliability coefficient is not reported in the literature, an estimate of the reliability was made by using the split-half method corrected by the Spearman-Brown formula.

All tests were not administered to all 496 pairs of twins. The tests given to the 427 sets of same-sexed and the 50 sets of unlike-sexed twins are described fully in this chapter. Psychological tests given to the EEG group are described in Chapter XV.

In the *Calendar Test,* developed by Remondino (1962), the examinee is given 50 statements about the days of the week. In a factor analysis, Remondino found that this test loaded on the number factor. The split-half reliability coefficient, corrected by the Spearman-Brown formula, is .78. The Calendar Test, scored number right minus number wrong, yields a single test score. Two sample questions follow:

If today is Sunday, then tomorrow will be Monday.   T   F
If yesterday was Wednesday, then today is Saturday.   T   F

The *Cube Comparisons Test* was developed from Thurstone's Cubes. Each question presents two drawings of a cube. Assuming no cube can have two faces alike, the subject has to decide whether the two drawings *can* represent the same cube or *must* represent different cubes. The right answer can be found: (1) by mentally turning one of the cubes so that its face is oriented in the same way as the similar face of the second cube and then comparing the sides one by one; (2) by noting whether two faces that are side by side have the same letters or numbers in the same relative position. Obtaining the answers by the second method is largely accomplished by verbal reasoning, although it does require a "static" awareness of three-dimensional relations as opposed to a more "dynamic" moving around of the blocks in space. The Cube Comparisons Test, scored number right minus number wrong, yields two part scores and a total score. The reliability coefficient is .58. Two sample items are shown below.

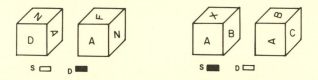

The *Simple Arithmetic Test,* taken from an unpublished study by Mukherjee (1963), contains seven parts, each consisting of a number of simple arithmetical problems. Part I has 15 problems; Part 2, 20 problems; and Parts 3–7, 25 problems each. Speed is an important factor since the examinee is allowed only 2 minutes per part. Problem complexity *decreases* from Part 1 to Part 7. There are five choices for each item on the Simple Arithmetic Test, scored number right minus one-fourth number wrong. The seven subtest scores are summed to obtain the total score. Correlating Part 4 with Part 5 and correcting with the Spearman-Brown formula yields an estimated reliability coefficient of .85. Examples from each subtest are given below:

Part 1: $4(77 + 39 - 4)/7 = 60$ 68   74   64   84
Part 2: $5(69 + 18 - 3) = 420$ 400   410   415   425
Part 3: $69 + 25 - 9 = 85$ 95   90   89   80
Part 4: $640 \div 5 = 120$ 128   88   136   126
Part 5: $8 \times 91 = 738$ 728   732   739   737
Part 6: $19 - 7 = 12$ 13   14   15   16
Part 7: $83 + 17 = 90$ 110   100   109   101

The *Wide Range Vocabulary Test,* adapted from the Cooperative Vocabulary Test, is a five-choice synonym test ranging from very easy to very difficult. It is scored number right minus one-fourth number wrong. There are no part scores. The reported test-retest reliability coefficient for the Wide Range Vocabulary Test is .88. Samples:

JOVIAL: 1. refreshing   2. scare   3. thickset   4. wise   5. jolly
DULLARD: 1. peon   2. duck   3. braggart   4. thief   5. dunce

The *Surface Development Test* is a modified version of Thurstone's Primary Mental Abilities Test. Here the examinee has to imagine or visualize how a piece of paper can be folded to form some kind of object. Each item consists of a drawing of a piece of paper that can be folded on the dotted lines to form the object drawn at the right. The subject is to imagine the folding, to figure out which of the lettered edges on the object are the same as the numbered edges on the piece of paper at the left, and to identify the letters of the answers in the numbered spaces at the far right. He is told that the side of the flat piece marked with the X will always be the same as the X side of the object. This task apparently requires mental movement of the parts of the pattern and probably cannot be performed by verbal reasoning only. The test, scored number right, yields two part scores and a total score. Reliability coefficient is .80. Sample problem:

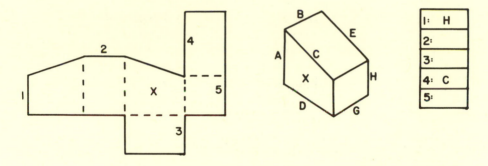

Each item of the *Form Board Test* presents five shaded drawings of pieces, some or all of which can be put together to form a figure depicted in outline form. The task is to indicate which of the pieces, when fitted together, will form the drawing. The test is scored number right, with the two parts added to yield the total score. The reliability coefficient is .73. A sample item is shown below:

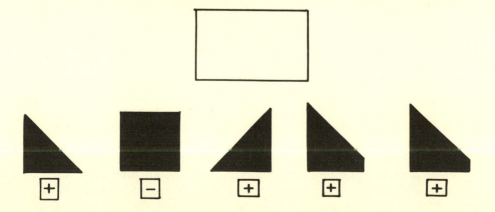

The *Self-judging Vocabulary Test,* developed by Heim (1965), contains two parts. The first contains 128 words, each of which is to be marked A, B, or C. (A = I know this word and could explain it to someone unfamiliar with it, B = I am doubtful as to what this word means, C = I have never seen this word before and have no idea what it means.) The second part of the test consists of the first 80 words of the 128-word list presented as a six-choice test. This part of the test combines the advantages of multiple-choice and creative-answer techniques. It allows the examinee, who thinks he knows the word but is dubious about all the choices, to write his answer in his own words. The test is scored number right minus one-fifth number wrong. In this study, only the second part of the test is used. The Kuder-Richardson reliability coefficient for age 15 is .801, with a median coefficient of .83 for ages 12, 13, 14, and 15. Two examples:

AUTHENTIC: 1. writer   2. to allow   3. respectful   4. a bargain   5. antique   6. genuine

VERSATILE: 1. of varied activities   2. pouring out   3. form of poetry   4. having masculine vigor   5. intense 6. kind of turnstile

The *Paper Folding Test* was suggested by Thurstone's Punched Holes. For each item, successive drawings illustrate two or three folds made in a square sheet of paper. A drawing of the folded paper shows where a hole is punched in it. The subject selects one of five drawings to show how the sheet would appear completely unfolded. While the problems can probably be solved more quickly by imagining the folding and unfolding, verbal reasoning can also provide a solution. The latter method, however, is more likely to lead to incorrect answers. The items are scored number right minus one-fourth number wrong. The two subtests are summed to obtain the total score. Reliability coefficient is .73. Sample question follows:

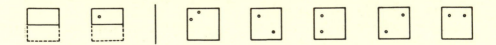

In the *Object Aperture Test,* a spatial visualization test developed by Philip H. DuBois and Goldine C. Gleser (1948), a three-dimensional object is shown, followed by outlines of five apertures or openings. The subject is to imagine how the object looks from all directions, then to

select from the five apertures the opening through which the solid object would pass directly if the proper side were inserted first. This usually requires mentally turning the object into other positions. The test is scored number right minus one-fourth number wrong. It yields two part scores that are added for the total score. Reliability coefficient is .58. A typical item follows:

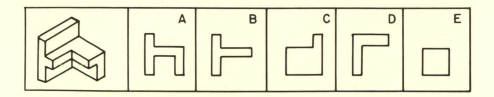

The *Identical Pictures Test* was another adaptation from Thurstone. For each item, the examinee is asked to check which of five geometrical figures or pictures is identical to a given figure at the left end of the row. The test is scored number right minus one-fourth number wrong. Two subtests are summed for the total score. Reliability coefficient is .87. A sample item follows:

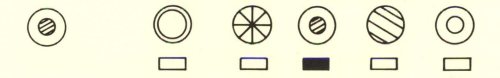

The *Newcastle Spatial Test*, developed by I. McFarlane Smith and J. S. Lawes (1959) for the National Foundation for Educational Research in England and Wales, consists of six different subtests ranging in difficulty from simple recognition of regular solids to the more complex problems of surface development.

Subtest 1 consists of 10 sets of drawings in which the end views and middle section of a solid object are shown. The task is to determine which one of 12 solid objects on the opposite page fits each set of drawings. This test requires some idea of perspective drawing but no strongly developed spatial ability.

Subtest 2 asks which of four choices is a view from above of the solid model shown at the left of the row. This test also calls for only a modest amount of spatial visualization.

In each item for Subtest 3, the examinee is given three sides of a cube in a flat pattern and a drawing of a solid cube, part of which is shaded. The subject is to draw lines on the pattern to indicate where he would cut to remove the shaded parts on the solid model. Spatial visualization helps to solve this problem, although it seems possible to perform the task by verbal reasoning.

In Subtest 4, each item shows a block of wood. The examinee must imagine a cut made along the dotted lines and indicate which of the three drawings on the right shows the shape of the cut face. Here it is obvious no highly developed ability to visualize three-dimensional objects is needed.

In each item on Subtest 5, there is a drawing of a solid object, called Shape, and a place to copy it, called Framework. The examinee is to put circles around the crosses in the Framework that could be joined to make the Shape. It is not necessary to visualize the Shape in three dimensions to copy it. In fact, the task may be easier if one regards the Shape as a flat pattern and merely counts units of distance.

Each item in Subtest 6 shows a model built from the shapes shown beside it. The subject is required to indicate the number of times each shape was used to make the model. Although the examinee could rely largely on verbal reasoning to solve these problems, visualization probably contributes to the speed of solution.

For each subtest, the score is the number of correct answers. Total score is the sum of the six subtest scores. The test-retest reliability coefficient reported in the test manual is .94. Samples of each of the six subtests follow:

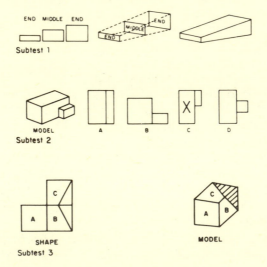

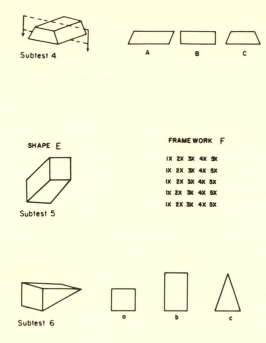

The *Spelling Achievement Test* is taken from the Metropolitan Achievement Test (Allen, Bixler, Connor, and Graham, 1946). Each word is pronounced by the examiner, who then uses it in a sentence, then pronounces it again. The student is then told to write the word. The test, consisting of 60 words, is administered to small groups of subjects by trained examiners. There are no parts scores. Total score is the number of words spelled correctly. Test-retest reliability reported in the test manual is .93. Examples are given below:

garage	I keep my car in a garage.	garage
instructor	One who teaches is an instructor.	instructor
tuberculosis	Tuberculosis is a serious lung disease.	tuberculosis

The *Mazes Test* is taken from a laboratory manual by McKinnon and Henle. The task, typical of earlier maze problems, is to draw a line from the entrance to the exist of the maze without crossing any line or entering blind alleys. Although this test does not require visualizing a three-dimensional or even a two-dimensional figure, the proper solution is probably facilitated by the ability to remember briefly sections of the correct path before drawing a line. A sample maze follows:

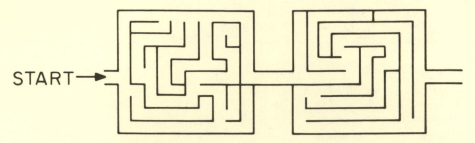

The *Logical Reasoning Test* was originally developed by Hertzka and Guilford in 1955 and later adapted by French, Ekstrom, and Price (1963) for use in the ETS Kit of Reference Tests. It consists of 40 items. As shown in the sample below, the examinee must indicate which of the four conclusions can be drawn from the two statements.

12.   All loans are profitable.
       Some loans are investments.
         Therefore:
             A.   All profitable things are investments.
             B.   Some profitable things are loans.
             C.   Some investments are profitable.
             D.   Some investments are not profitable.

The *Cancellation Test* is considered to be a test of perceptual speed. The examinee is asked to draw a vertical line through each group of five dots and a horizontal line through each group of four dots, while ignoring the group of three dots. The task involves eye-hand coordination. Differences in motor speed probably play an appreciable role in the score. Samples are shown below:

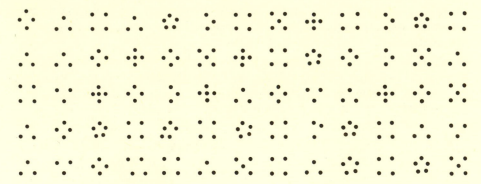

The *Social Perception Test* was developed by Martin Whiteman (1954) to investigate the hypothesis that the social perceptual performance of schizophrenics falls below that of normal subjects. The test consists of 20 sets of 4 or 6 drawings. The examinee must indicate the drawing which does not belong with the others in the set. A sample set of drawings follows:

A

B

C

D

The *Card Rotation Test* is taken from the ETS Kit of Reference Tests. Here the examinee has to decide which of the eight figures on the right show the same side as the model on the left and which ones are mirror images. While this task is usually performed by mentally sliding the figures around, it can be done by verbal reasoning or by naming, such as saying "Is it a 'b' or a 'd'?" or "If the little knob is on top, is the larger bulge toward the right or the left?" Occasionally one notices a subject tilting his head or turning the test paper. It would appear that this is a weak test of spatial ability. It is divided into two parts, 14 items per part. Sample figure:

The *Ship Destination Test,* thought to be a measure of logical reasoning, was developed by Christensen and Guilford in 1955. It consists of 48 items. Questions are asked about a diagram such as the one shown below. Part of the instructions follows:

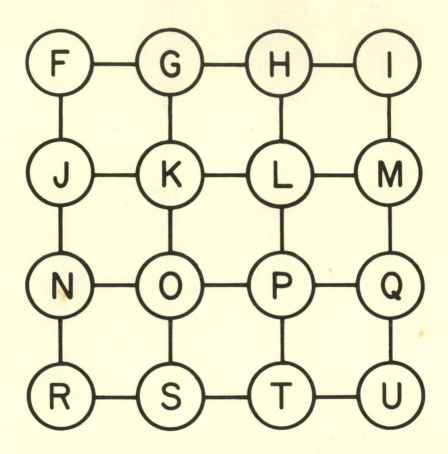

Each circle in the diagram above represents a point on the ocean. Consider the distance along a line from one point to the next to be two miles. That is, point L is two miles from point H. Point M is four miles from point H. The *only* pathways are along the lines.

Consider that you are the captain of a ship that is located at one of the points on the diagram. Other points represent possible ports to which the ship can go. In each of the items below, you will be given the location of your ship and the location of a port. Your task is to figure the distance from your ship to the port. For item 1 below, how many miles is the journey from ship N to port O? For item 1 on your answer sheet blacken the "2" space to indicate that port O is 2 miles from ship N. Next indicate on your answer sheet the number of miles from the ship to the port for item 2 and for item 3.

1. Ship N—Port O
2. Ship J—Port G
3. Ship U—Port M

For the situations below, the wind direction must be considered in figuring the number of miles from ship to port. If your ship must travel against the wind for any part of the journey, this will have the effect of increasing the distance to the port. For every two miles traveled against the wind, add one mile. For every two miles your ship travels with the wind, subtract one mile. For example, if your ship travels with the wind for six of the eight miles to a port, the total distance to the port becomes eight minus three, or five miles. That part of the journey in which the wind strikes your ship from the side is not affected by the wind.

The arrow shows the wind direction for each set of three items. Mark on your answer sheet the number of miles from ship to port for items 4, 5, and 6; then for items 7, 8, and 9.

Wind: ↑	4. Ship F—Port J	Wind: →	7. Ship R—Port U
	5. Ship J—Port O		8. Ship L—Port G
	6. Ship P—Port L		9. Ship Q—Port M

There are 12 items of this kind in which the wind velocity has to be considered. In the next 12 items the subject has to consider wind velocity and current, in the next 12 the effect of the wind velocity or current is doubled, while in the last 12 items added time may be required for the journey if turns have to be made, depending on the direction in which the ship is heading when the choice of port is given.

To make the test battery more interesting to the subjects, we used the *Mooney's Faces Test,* a closure or perceptual ability test that features human faces. Using item difficulty as reported by Mooney (1957), the 10 easiest and 10 most difficult items were selected. To make group administration possible, examinees were asked to indicate the sex of the person shown and the direction in which the person is looking. Examples:

TOP

TOP

E.   MAN   WOMAN

Right   Left   Front

F.   MAN   WOMAN

Right   Left   Front

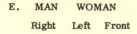

For picture E, you should have circled MAN and RIGHT.

For picture F, you should have circled MAN and FRONT.

The test of *Primary Mental Abilities* was developed by L. L. and Thelma Gwinn Thurstone. The rationale of the research technique underlying "primary mental abilities" is explained in *Multiple-Factor Analysis* (L. L. Thurstone & T. G. Thurstone, 1947).

Thurstone once maintained that each primary factor was largely independent of the others. Later research convinced him that in addition to the primary abilities a "second-order general factor" was at work. Scores on the Primary Mental Abilities Test were, consequently, combined into a single quotient score, which provides a reliable estimate of intelligence comparable to estimates obtained by the Stanford-Binet and the Wechsler Intelligence Scale for Children. The five primary mental abilities measured by the PMA Test are, briefly:

> *V-Verbal Meaning:* Ability to understand ideas expressed in words.
> *N-Number Facility:* Ability to work with numbers.

R-Reasoning: Ability to solve logical problems.

P-Perceptual Speed: Ability to recognize likenesses and differences between objects or symbols quickly and accurately.

S-Spatial Relations: Ability to visualize objects and figures rotated in space and the relations between them.

According to the test manual for Cattell's *Culture Fair Intelligence Test,* most current intelligence tests are looking backward instead of forward. Instead of measuring a child's capacity to learn in the future, they are recording what he has had the opportunity to learn in the past. Cattell and Cattell (1965) say, "The Culture Fair Tests are figural and geometrical in content . . ." (p. 3). They are not, however, limited to measuring mechanical or spatial abilities.

The Culture Fair tests consist of two parallel forms, each totaling 46 items arranged in four subtests and each requiring 12.5 minutes of actual testing time. One relatively easy sample from each subtest is shown below:

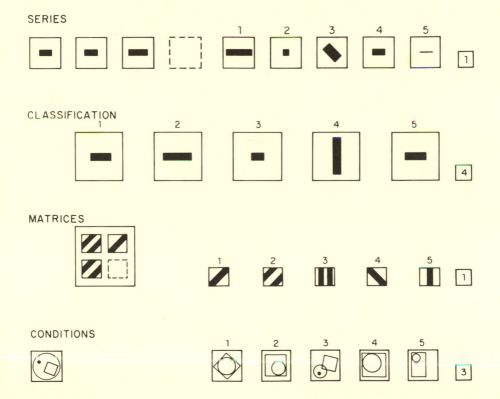

Personality Tests

The Twin Survey test battery includes two personality tests in addition to the Minnesota Multiphasic Personality Inventory which was administered only to the 19 sets of twins in the EEG study. The MMPI will be discussed in Chapter XV.

The other two personality scales are similar in that each attempts to measure factorially independent dimensions of personality. Cattell's *High School Personality Questionnaire* contains 14 dimensions or scores. Jenkins' *How Well Do You Know Yourself?* measures 17 personality factors. Predictably, the two tests overlap on some dimensions. For example, both have scores measuring submissiveness, persistence, and emotional control. Other factorial scales are similar but the authors have different names for them. The Cattell scale has an intelligence factor not found in Jenkins' test. Factors measured by the two personality tests are shown below:

High School Personality Questionnaire Factors

A. Reserved—warm-hearted
B. Less intelligent—more intelligent
C. Emotionally less stable—emotionally stable
D. Inactive—over-active
E. Submissive—dominant
F. Serious—happy-go-lucky
G. Weak superego—strong superego
H. Shy—bold
I. Tough-minded—tender-minded
J. Zestful—restrained
O. Secure—insecure
Q_2. Group-dependent—self-sufficient
Q_3. Uncontrolled—controlled
Q_4. Relaxed—tense

How Well Do You Know Yourself? Factors

1. Irritability
2. Practicality
3. Punctuality
4. Novelty-loving
5. Vocational assurance
6. Cooperativeness
7. Ambitiousness
8. Hypercriticalness
9. Dejection
10. General morale
11. Persistence
12. Nervousness
13. Seriousness
14. Submissiveness
15. Impulsiveness
16. Dynamism
17. Emotional control

The Twin Study test battery is composed of 31 different cognitive tests representing the full range of both verbal and nonverbal measurements of the primary mental abilities. In addition to the mental tests, three personality scales and a test of creativity were administered. Altogether 79 psychological test variables will be analyzed and discussed in subsequent chapters.

VII

Basic Test Battery: Subpopulation Differences

In this chapter we shall examine subpopulation differences in performance and in heritability of mental abilities as measured by the Basic Test Battery, which represents the unique primary mental abilities identified by Thurstone and Thurstone (1938), Cattell (1957), and Guilford (1967). These are called Level II abilities by Jensen (1973a) and "gc" by Cattell (1971).

Jensen says Level II abilities include mental manipulation and transformation of information in order to arrive at a satisfactory output. Level II is much the same as the ability which Spearman termed g (Jensen, 1973a).

Cattell's crystallized general mental ability "gc" emerges strongly in such primary mental abilities as verbal factor, numerical ability, reasoning, mechanical information, and experimental judgment (Cattell, 1971).

The 12 tests in the Basic Battery are the Calendar Test, Cube Comparisons, Surface Development, Wide Range Vocabulary, Form Board, Arithmetic, Heim Vocabulary, Paper Folding, Object Aperture, Identical Pictures, Spelling, and Newcastle Spatial Relations (all of which have been described fully in Chapter VI).

The first step in the analysis was to examine mean raw scores by age and test for all 427 sets of like-sexed twins. Since, on the average, older children are expected to outperform younger children on mental ability tests (see definition of IQ, Chapter IV), it would not be unreasonable to find a monotonic increase in the means of the Basic Battery test scores with age. In Table VII–A, in which test scores are broken down by age, it is seen that the mean scores for all tests increase with age. The increases from age 12 through 18 are steady and in most cases fairly uniform from year to year. The Form Board Test is one exception.

Table VII-A

Means and *SD*'s for *Basic Battery* by Age Groups (Raw Scores)

Name of Test	Ages 12 & 13 (N = 124)			Age 14 (N = 158)			Age 15 (N = 182)			Age 16 (N = 176)			Age 17 (N = 138)			Age 18 (N = 66)			Ages 19 & 20 (N = 10)		
	No.	Mn	SD	No.	Mn	SD	No.	Mn	SD	No.	Mn	SD	No.	Mn	SD	No.	Mn	SD	No.	Mn	SD
Calendar	122	8.3	6.0	158	9.0	6.8	180	9.7	6.3	175	12.1	7.0	138	13.2	7.6	66	14.7	6.9	10	9.8	4.8
Cube Comparisons	122	2.4	6.6	157	3.5	8.5	178	6.1	8.7	175	6.8	9.1	138	7.8	9.8	66	8.8	7.2	10	5.6	7.8
Arithmetic	123	45.6	24.3	157	49.9	28.8	182	56.5	23.9	175	63.8	24.3	138	69.9	31.9	66	75.4	27.5	10	49.2	18.4
Wide Range Vocabulary	124	2.4	2.7	158	3.3	3.2	182	3.7	3.1	176	4.1	3.1	138	5.8	4.1	66	6.9	3.6	10	3.5	2.5
Surface Development	124	16.5	7.6	158	18.7	11.4	182	21.9	11.2	176	21.9	10.4	138	26.0	13.6	66	27.5	13.4	10	22.6	12.3
Form Board	124	7.5	5.7	155	7.8	6.4	181	9.5	6.1	176	10.9	6.6	137	12.1	7.5	66	11.8	6.6	10	13.2	9.1
Heim Vocabulary	124	20.0	14.6	158	27.9	18.0	178	30.6	19.1	176	37.2	17.9	138	43.2	21.1	66	47.7	18.8	10	17.5	9.8
Paper Folding	124	4.3	4.2	158	5.2	4.8	180	6.2	4.4	176	7.0	4.7	138	7.5	5.0	66	8.4	4.7	10	6.1	4.9
Object Aperture	123	1.4	4.9	158	2.2	6.0	181	3.3	5.1	176	3.3	5.1	138	5.6	7.2	65	5.9	6.8	9	6.9	6.9
Identical Pictures	119	47.8	15.9	153	50.9	16.3	181	52.3	16.1	174	55.0	15.6	136	56.6	15.0	64	58.2	16.2	9	50.6	12.9
Spatial Relations	118	38.7	18.3	146	42.8	20.2	172	47.1	19.0	175	51.7	19.7	136	54.3	21.2	64	57.0	18.6	5	50.0	11.7
Spelling	124	23.7	12.3	158	25.6	15.6	182	29.1	14.8	175	34.7	14.0	138	36.1	15.9	65	41.3	12.4	9	30.8	17.6

Note. All twins did not take all tests. Number represents individuals, not twins, in this table.

It follows the usual pattern through age 17 but then shows a slight decline between ages 17 and 18.

The mean scores for age group 19–20 show a decline from age group 18 for all tests except Form Board and Object Aperture, each of which shows a slight increase. Examination of the scores for the ten students in the 19–20 age level reveals that these older students have not progressed normally. Their average Arithmetic and Spelling scores are like those of boys and girls of 14 and 15, children five years younger. All ten students were from the Kentucky sample. All were white—eight boys and two girls; two pairs DZ, three MZ.

With two exceptions, mean scores of twins at any age from 12 through 18 are greater than scores of children a year younger, less than those of children a year older. At ages 15 and 16, mean Surface Development scores are identical. The mean of Form Board scores for age 17 is 12.1; for the 18-year age group, the mean is 11.8.

Although in this study we are primarily interested in twins, Table VII–A reflects scores for all subjects, including a very small number of twins whose co-twins for some reason did not take a particular test. For example, in the 12–13 age group one twin did not take the Arithmetic Test; six students failed to take the Spatial Test; whereas all subjects took the Spelling Test. The purpose of Table VII–A is to give the reader an overview of the range of abilities and ages covered in the Basic Test Battery.

In order to compare the tests in the Basic Battery on score change with age, raw scores for each test were converted to T-scores with means of 50 and standard deviations of 10. Figure VII–1 shows for each test the score change curves, which are strikingly similar and each of which seems to follow the typical growth curve. The obvious exception is the point representing mean scores for the ten overage students.

Since we have demonstrated that, as expected, age is a significant factor in determining average scores on each of the tests in the Basic Test Battery, our next step was to adjust all scores by age so that further analyses of the data could be made without the necessity of age classification. Subjects were divided into five age groups (12–13, 14, 15, 16, 17–20). Within each group scores on all tests were standardized to a mean of 100 and a standard deviation of 15, thereby making these scaled scores comparable to deviation IQ's used in the Wechsler intelligence scales. These age-adjusted scores are used in all of the analyses of the Basic Test Battery reported in the remainder of this chapter.

Since all subjects are classified by race, sex, and zygosity, a three-way analysis of variance was used to determine if score variances of the 12 tests (as well as an average of the 12 tests) are attributable to any or all of these three classifications. Race, sex, and zygosity differences may well be significant sources of variation in the overall score, as well

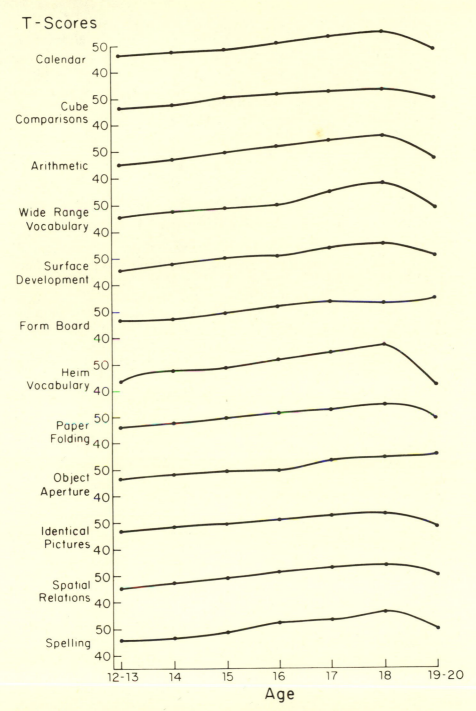

Figure VII-1. Score change with age for tests of the Basic Battery.

as of interesting interactions. For example, an earlier analysis (Last, 1977) found that on the Arithmetic test white MZ boys earned higher scores than white MZ girls. The situation was reversed for blacks. If significant, this interaction would be important in the study of variation in the different racial and sex groupings.

In addition to the three classifications discussed above, 142 pairs of twins or 284 individuals were also classified by socio-economic status. A separate analysis of variance, therefore, was used to determine if such status contributed to score variances.

Since a small number of twins did not take all tests in the battery, there are unequal numbers in some of the classifications. Because of the unbalanced design, an analysis of variance procedure based on least squares fitting of multivariable models was employed. The program, described in *A User's Guide to SAS* (Barr, Goodnight, Sall, & Helwig, 1976, pg. 127), also yields least squares means which are estimates of arithmetic means that would be expected if equal subclass numbers had been obtained. Tables VII–B and VII–C show the results of the two analyses of variance. From these tables it can be determined that race, sex, zygosity, and socio-economic status all significantly contribute to score variances on some or all of the 13 test variables. Consequently, it seems appropriate to divide the total group into subpopulations based on race, sex, and zygosity and, additionally, to divide the smaller group for which socio-economic status is available into three subpopulations.

Table VII–D shows the least squares means for age-adjusted standard

Table VII–B

Effects Contributing to Differences in Means of Various Subpopulations: Race, Sex, and Zygosity

Test (Age-adjusted Standard Scores)	Race	Sex	Zygosity	Z × R	Z × S	R × S	Z × R × S
Calendar	**		*				
Cube Comparisons	**	**					
Surface Development	**						
Wide Range Vocabulary	**		**				
Form Board	**	**					
Arithmetic	**	**					
Heim Vocabulary	**						
Paper Folding	**		*				
Object Aperture	**	**	*				
Identical Pictures	**	*				*	
Spelling	**	**	*				
Spatial Relations	**	**					
Average	**		**				

* $p < .05$.
** $p < .01$.

Table VII–C
Effects Contributing to Differences in Means of Various Subpopulations: Race, Sex, Zygosity, and Socio-economic Status

Test (Age-adjusted Standard Scores)	SES	SEX	RACE	ZYGOSITY	SES × SEX	SES × RACE	SES × ZYGOSITY	SES × SEX × RACE	SES × SEX × ZYG	SES × RACE × ZYG	SES × RACE × ZYG × SEX
Calender	*		**						*		
Cube Comparisons	*	*	**		*				*		
Surface Development	**		**								
Wide Range Vocabulary			**		*				*		
Form Board	*		**								*
Arithmetic	*	*	**								
Heim Vocabulary	**		**								
Paper Folding		*	**		*						
Object Aperture		**	**	**	*	*		*	**		
Identical Pictures	*		**				*				
Spelling		**	**								
Spatial Relations	**	**	**					*			
Average	**		**								

* $p < .05$.
** $p < .01$.

Table VII–D
Least Squares Means for Age-adjusted Standard Scores by Sex, Zygosity, and Race (Deviation IQ's)

	Male				Female			
	MZ		DZ		MZ		DZ	
Test	White	Black	White	Black	White	Black	White	Black
Calendar	104.6	93.1	100.9	88.8	103.2	91.5	101.7	90.4
Cube Comparisons	105.0	94.6	103.8	97.6	100.7	92.0	100.4	89.9
Surface Development	104.5	92.6	102.7	91.7	102.6	93.2	100.0	90.8
Wide Range Vocabulary	103.2	98.4	99.4	91.8	103.2	93.3	100.1	92.7
Form Board	106.8	93.5	103.1	93.6	101.3	90.4	100.5	89.2
Arithmetic	102.0	90.9	100.5	88.8	103.1	94.9	101.8	94.8
Heim Vocabulary	102.3	95.1	101.3	91.0	104.1	93.4	99.4	94.0
Paper Folding	104.7	93.1	102.8	90.8	103.8	90.9	101.5	86.9
Object Aperture	107.5	97.5	105.8	94.6	99.2	92.4	98.0	88.6
Identical Pictures	100.2	94.5	100.1	93.0	101.0	101.9	99.6	96.3
Spelling	99.4	90.6	97.2	86.1	105.2	96.5	103.9	94.6
Spatial Relations	106.7	95.3	106.9	92.4	102.0	89.0	100.2	86.7
Average	103.9	94.1	102.0	91.7	102.5	93.3	100.6	91.3

scores for the 13 test variables for subpopulations by race, sex, and zygosity. Differences in the means are in the same direction and of about the same magnitude as those reported by Eysenck (1975), Jensen (1973b), Shuey (1966), and others.

For every test there is a significant race effect. The difference is about ten IQ points for both MZ and DZ twins and for boys and girls (Table VII–D). The question of whether genetic factors are implicated in the race differences in test performance must be delayed until heritability estimates are discussed later in this chapter. Suffice it to say now that least squares means of the two races differ significantly on all 12 tests and also for the average of the 12 tests. In response to the question, "Are there racial differences in IQ?," Jensen (1973b) has this to say:

> In the United States persons classed as Negro by the common social criteria obtain scores on the average about one standard deviation (i.e., 15 IQ points on most standard intelligence tests) below the average for the white population. One standard deviation is an average difference, and it is known that the magnitude of Negro-white differences varies according to the ages of the groups compared, their socio-economic status, and especially their geographical location in the United States. Various tests differ, on the average, relatively little. In general, Negroes do slightly better on verbal tests than on nonverbal tests. They do most poorly on tests of spatial ability, abstract reasoning and problem solving (Shuey, 1966; Tyler, 1965). Tests of scholastic achievement also show about one standard deviation difference, and this difference appears to be fairly constant from first grade through twelfth grade, judging from the massive data of the Coleman study ("Equality of Educational Opportunity," 1966). The IQ difference of 1 *SD*, also, is fairly stable over the age range from about 5 years to adulthood, although some studies have shown a tendency for a slight increase in the difference between 5 and 18 years of age. (p. 362)

Jensen's position is not shared by all other workers in the field (Kamin, 1974; Ehrlich, 1977; and Layzer, 1975). Probably the most outspoken on the question is Harvard professor David Layzer who asserts, "Published analyses of IQ data provide no support whatever for Jensen's thesis that inequalities in cognitive performance are due largely to genetic differences. . . . Under prevailing social conditions, no valid inferences can be drawn from IQ data concerning systematic genetic differences among races or socio-economic groups. Research along present lines directed toward this end—whatever its ethical status—is scientifically worthless" (p. 216).

In addition to the consistent differences in means for the two races, there are significant sex differences for 7 of the 12 Basic tests. Four of the seven load on the spatial factor. Cube Comparisons, Form Board, Object Aperture, and Spatial Relations all show a significant sex effect; that is, on all four spatial tests in both racial groups boys earned higher scores than girls. This finding is not too surprising since Maccoby (1966) reported higher scores for boys on all visual, spatial ability tests beginning at about six or eight years of age. Keogh (1971) also reported higher spatial test scores for 8- and 9-year-old boys. Droege (1967) and Flannagan, Dailey, Shaycoft, Gorham, Orr, Goldberg, & Neyman (1961) found boys superior on the spatial factor throughout high school, their scores exceeding girls' by at least .4 standard deviation at the end of high school. The question of whether or not genetic factors are implicated in the visual-spatial factor, as suggested by Maccoby and Jacklin, will be discussed later.

The Spelling and Arithmetic tests show consistent and significant mean differences in favor of girls, whose superior verbal achievement on the Spelling Test is not unexpected. Maccoby and Jacklin (1974) found that girls have higher verbal ability than boys. "At about age eleven, the sexes begin to diverge with female superiority increasing through high school and possibly beyond" (p. 351).

The arithmetic superiority of girls is somewhat of a surprise because Maccoby and Jacklin and other workers report significantly higher male performance on tests involving mathematical factors. Examination of the Arithmetic Test might offer some clue for the elevated scores for girls. The test is short and requires no reasoning or problem solving, only the fundamental operations of addition, subtraction, multiplication, and division. Verbal processes would seem to be needed to answer most test questions. In an earlier factor analytic study of these data (Osborne, 1978), arithmetic was found to load with vocabulary on a verbal factor.

The last test of the battery showing significant main effects sex differences is Identical Pictures, significant at the .05 level. The score difference between white boys and girls is small, less than one point for both MZ and DZ twins. Black girls are consistently above the black boys. White DZ boys score about one-half point above white DZ girls. Since the scores obtained by those who took the Identical Pictures Test differ only slightly, barely significant at the .05 level, and there is no significant interaction of any type, no effort will be made to explain the sex differences for this test.

Consistent and significant zygosity differences, however, were found for 5 of the 12 Basic tests. Three load on the verbal factor, Calendar, Wide Range Vocabulary, and Spelling; two load on spatial, Paper Folding and Object Aperture. MZ twins of both races and MZ's of both sexes outperform comparable DZ twins on these tests. The reason is not clear. Using a design similar to that of the present study, Koch (1966) found

Primary Mental Ability scores for MZ twins to be significantly lower than those of DZ's. For all but one PMA subtest, MZ's were below matched singletons.

Husen (1960) anticipated that DZ's would test higher than MZ's because identical partners tend to spend more time together and have more contact with each other. For this reason, we would expect verbal retardation to be greater in MZ's than in DZ's. Husen found just the opposite. Identical twins exhibited throughout his study a tendency toward higher means.

Since findings from other studies are contradictory and the present study is only suggestive of significant MZ-DZ performance differences for selected tests, the question of MZ-DZ differences will be examined with additional biometric, social, and psychological data in later chapters.

In spite of the report by Tyler (1965), Shuey (1966), and Jensen (1973a) that the relationship of measured intelligence to socio-economic status is one of the best documented findings in mental test history, this section of the Twin Study offers a new analysis of SES differences as they relate to mental test performance. Because the subjects are twins and the test battery covers a wide array of mental tests, the present study is unlike others designed to investigate SES parameters primarily because it enables comparisons to be made by race, sex, zygosity, and SES for separate verbal and spatial tests. For example, the environmentalist prediction that subjects from low SES classes do not perform as well on verbally loaded tests as they do on culture fair scales will be examined by race, sex, and zygosity. The environmentalist program also predicts that since general cultural and socio-economic status are important IQ determinants high SES blacks should outperform low and middle SES whites on tests of mental ability.

The first step in our analysis is to determine the main effects contributing to the differences in means between the various subpopulations. Confidence levels are shown in Table VII–C. This analysis of the smaller group of twins for whom SES data were available enables us: (1) to compare the main effects of race, sex, and zygosity shown by the least squares analysis of the sample with a similar analysis made for the total group; (2) to determine if socio-economic status contributes significantly to the differences in means between subpopulations.

Table VII–C shows that for every test there is a significant race effect. The same finding was reported in the analysis of the total group (Table VII–B). Significant sex effects are common to five tests in each analysis. Only three tests in the SES sample show significant zygosity effects.

Although Tables VII–B and VII–C are not perfectly congruent, the pattern of significant main effects in the two tables suggests the smaller group is not very different from the base group in respect to the effects due to race, sex, and zygosity.

Since the levels of confidence of interaction for the three subpopulations were shown in Table VII–B, they will not be repeated in Table VII–C. However, confidence levels for the main effects and for SES interactions are shown in Table VII–C.

Socio-economic status makes a significant difference in means for 8 of the 12 Basic tests. Scores on two verbal and two spatial tests are not influenced significantly by SES. The question raised earlier concerning differential performance for high and low SES groups can now be answered in Table VII–E which reports least squares means by SES level for race, sex, and zygosity. To make the comparison easier, mean scores for the 5 tests which loaded on the verbal factor and the 6 tests which loaded on the spatial factor, along with the one-test perceptual speed factor and the average of all 12 tests, are shown in Table VII–F for each SES level by race.

There is no apparent difference in mean IQ's between the average of the culturally loaded verbal scales and the nonverbal spatial tests. Race and SES differences are obvious, but for any SES level within race there is no consistent pattern of verbal-spatial difference. Low SES whites show verbal greater than spatial by one IQ point but low SES blacks show spatial greater than verbal by two IQ points.

The second environmentalist claim that, since general cultural and socio-economic factors are important IQ determinants, higher SES blacks should outperform middle or low SES whites on tests of mental ability is answered clearly in Table VII–F. The claim is simply not supported by the evidence. Verbal, spatial, and full scale IQ's all show that low SES whites outscore the highest SES blacks.

It is clear from the above discussion that there are significant race differences for all tests of the Basic Battery. Several tests show significant sex differences which follow the usual pattern, boys excel girls in the tests that load the spatial factor; girls are better at verbal tasks. Zygosity differences were found for five tests. The MZ's of both sexes and of both races outscore DZ twins on 5 of the 12 tests. Eight of the 12 Basic tests show significant SES differences.

In summary, the data so far presented strongly support the hypotheses that sex, race, zygosity, and socio-economic status all contribute significantly to score variances on some or all of the components of the Basic Test Battery. It should also be noted that, for the total group, only 1 of the 52 interactions among sex, race, and zygosity is significant (Table VII–B). When SES is added to the analysis of variance, making a four-way classification, we find that there are now 91 chances for interaction. Table VII–C shows that only ten of these interactions are significant and that the significant ones are not clustered under any one interaction variable or any one test. We are able to state, then, that the significant effects on test scores of the four classifications are, in general, consistent

Table VII-E

Least Squares Means for Age-adjusted Standard Scores by Socio-economic Status Group (Deviation IQ's)

Test	White			Black			MZ			DZ			Male			Female		
	1	2	3	1	2	3	1	2	3	1	2	3	1	2	3	1	2	3
Calendar	104	103	102	97	93	85	101	97	95	99	99	92	101	98	91	99	98	95
Cube Comaprisons	102	102	99	102	93	91	103	97	96	101	99	94	107	98	96	96	97	95
Surface Development	106	104	95	95	95	91	102	100	94	99	99	91	102	98	90	99	102	96
Wide Range Vocabulary	104	103	105	95	94	92	102	99	101	97	98	96	99	100	102	100	98	95
Form Board	108	109	101	94	92	90	102	101	99	100	100	92	105	101	95	96	100	96
Arithmetic	104	104	101	102	98	87	103	98	96	102	105	93	104	98	90	102	105	99
Heim Vocabulary	110	112	103	103	94	90	107	103	98	106	103	96	108	103	96	105	103	97
Paper Folding	106	106	102	93	90	89	103	98	99	96	98	92	103	99	97	96	96	94
Object Aperture	103	103	104	90	95	91	101	98	102	92	100	93	100	105	97	93	94	98
Identical Pictures	118	107	103	100	98	101	110	102	105	108	103	99	106	103	102	112	102	103
Spelling	101	102	100	98	93	88	99	97	95	100	97	93	98	92	92	101	102	96
Spatial Relations	107	107	103	96	93	86	105	99	97	98	102	93	106	104	96	98	97	94
Average	106	105	102	97	94	90	103	99	98	100	100	94	103	100	95	100	100	96

Note. 1 = High SES group
2 = Middle SES group
3 = Low SES group

Table VII–F
Mean Factor IQ's by Socio-economic Groups for Whites and Blacks (Least Squares Means)

	White			Black		
	High SES	Medium SES	Low SES	High SES	Medium SES	Low SES
Verbal IQ (Average 5 tests)	105	105	102	99	94	88
Spatial IQ (Average 6 tests)	105	105	101	95	93	90
Perceptual Speed IQ (One test only)	119	107	103	100	98	101
Average IQ (Average 12 tests)	106	105	102	97	94	90

among the subpopulations; e.g., race shows a significant effect on all test scores and this effect does not, for most scores, fluctuate between the sexes or zygosities or among the socio-economic statuses.

The next question to be addressed is this: Are the subpopulation differences in test performance due in part to heredity and, if so, is the effect of heredity on test performance equal for all subpopulations?

To determine the heritability of the tests, methods developed by Holzinger, Nichols, and Vandenberg will be used. The rationales for these heritability ratios were discussed in Chapter II. Heritability, it will be recalled, is a population statistic and, technically, is defined as the proportion of total phenotypic variance shown by a trait that can be attributed to genetic variation in the population.

In the heritability computations, raw scores were first adjusted for age for each race separately. Holzinger, Nichols, and Vandenberg heritability ratios were computed for each test and for the average of the 12 tests. In Table VII–G, intraclass correlation coefficients, heritability ratios, and within-pair variances for black and white twins are shown for all tests and the average of the 12 tests. The F tests shown in the next to the last column in Table VII–G refer to Vandenberg's F ratio. To test the significance of the difference between two F's, they are transformed to a unit normal variate after the method described by Paulson (1942), whose U statistic is entered in a Z table to determine its probability level. The probability levels that the F's of the two races are significantly different are shown in the last column of Table VII–G.

Previously we learned that differences in black and white means were uniform over the whole range of tests. Means differed by about ten devia-

Table VII-G
Heritability Coefficients on 12 Mental Tests for Black and White Twins: Classical Methods of Analysis Using Age-race Standard Scores

Variable	MZ		DZ			Heritability Ratios		Within-pair Variances			
	r	N	r	N	T(Cor)	H	HR	MZ	DZ	F	U[a]
Calendar											
White	.48	170	.40	130	.91	.14	.36	119.09	125.78	1.06	
Black	.54	76	.42	46	.78	.20	.43	112.74	103.40	.92	.65
Cube Comparisons											
White	.43	168	.29	129	1.34	.19	.65	117.54	176.04	1.50*	
Black	.28	76	.10	47	.95	.19	1.26	190.22	137.36	.72	3.68**
Surface Development											
White	.72	171	.36	133	4.65	.57	1.02	62.44	138.94	2.23**	
Black	.48	76	.25	47	1.40	.31	.95	110.72	167.98	1.52	3.29**
Wide Range Vocabulary											
White	.52	171	.23	133	2.95	.38	1.12	106.98	165.88	1.55**	
Black	.43	76	.22	47	1.25	.27	.98	128.17	161.81	1.26	1.80
Form Board											
White	.59	168	.44	133	1.77	.27	.52	98.86	112.01	1.13	
Black	.21	75	.33	47	-.68	-.18	-1.18	183.05	135.02	.74	1.86
Arithmetic											
White	.80	168	.53	133	4.29	.57	.68	44.26	109.97	2.49**	
Black	.84	76	.65	47	2.37	.55	.46	31.91	88.91	2.79**	1.57
Heim Vocabulary											
White	.85	169	.57	132	5.24	.66	.66	33.81	89.13	2.64**	
Black	.76	75	.57	47	1.86	.45	.51	57.41	82.78	1.44	4.49**

Paper Folding											
White	.55	169	.45	133	1.07	.17	.34	101.27	118.08	1.17	
Black	.45	76	−.02	47	2.59	.45	2.07	135.04	173.27	1.28	.00
Object Aperture											
White	.49	168	.39	132	1.05	.16	.41	114.04	134.95	1.18	
Black	.39	76	.17	47	1.24	.26	1.13	141.67	154.88	1.09	.67
Identical Pictures											
White	.76	164	.55	128	3.20	.47	.56	56.73	90.57	1.60**	
Black	.51	72	.32	47	1.20	.28	.75	99.57	162.63	1.63*	.96
Spelling											
White	.85	169	.54	132	5.57	.68	.73	32.67	99.66	3.05**	
Black	.79	76	.58	47	2.14	.50	.53	49.22	82.91	1.69*	4.70**
Spatial Relations											
White	.78	158	.60	125	2.91	.45	.47	46.02	95.45	2.07**	
Black	.85	75	.44	47	4.13	.74	.96	39.97	74.06	1.85*	1.92
Subtest Mean											
White	.85	171	.62	133	4.58	.61	.54	14.09	35.71	2.53**	
Black	.88	76	.51	47	4.18	.75	.85	10.64	31.34	2.95**	1.48

* $p < .05$.
** $p < .01$.
[a] difference in U's. Paulson's statistic for determining the significance of difference in F's.

tion IQ points on both the easy, verbal tasks and the more difficult spatial tests. Heritability differences among the tests are not uniform, suggesting that mental abilities, represented by the Basic Battery, are not uniform in their genetic and environmental characteristics. For example, the tasks required in the Simple Arithmetic Test turned out to be highly heritable for both races. Not only are the F tests significant for blacks and whites, but the intraclass r's are all high, the correlations for blacks slightly exceeding those for whites. For whites, 8 of the 12 F ratios are significant at the .05 level or better; for blacks, 4 are significant. On the other hand, one test, Form Board, yields a negative H value; that is, the intraclass correlation for DZ black twins is greater than for MZ's. In all other cases, H values are positive; that is, MZ $r >$ DZ $r,$ the direction predicted by the hereditarian program.

It will be recalled that the Basic Battery was composed of tests designed to cover the wide range of primary abilities between the ages of 12 and 20. Necessarily some of the tests selected were too easy for many subjects, and several tests may have been too difficult for some. The Calendar Test, for example, was selected to be the first, or buffer, test because it was short and easy. Most subjects over 12 were able to answer questions of the type: Today is Friday. Yesterday was _____ ? _____ . Split-half reliability of the Calendar Test is .80. On the other hand, Object Assembly is probably the most difficult test in the battery. To adjust scores for guessing, it is scored rights minus one-fourth wrongs. The mean score for black children in the two lowest age groups was at chance level. The corrected split-half reliability of the Object Aperture Test is only .58. The longer, more stable tests tend to yield the highest heritability ratios. Spelling, Arithmetic, and Newcastle Spatial tests show significant within-pair F ratios for both races. For these tests the MZ intraclass r's approach the reliability of the tests; that is, MZ twins' scores are as much alike as the scores of the same individual who takes the test twice.

It was established earlier in this chapter that there are significant mean racial differences for all the Basic tests. It was also determined that a significant genetic component is revealed by many of the tests. Some tests yield significant variance ratios for both races, some for neither, and some for one but not the other. We may therefore ask, "Are differences between the heritability variance ratios for the two races significant?" For 8 of the 12 tests, the F's are not significantly different. Arithmetic, Identical Pictures, and Newcastle Spatial tests show significant heritability ratios for both black and white twins, but the differences between the F's are non-significant. On the other hand, the heritability ratios for the two vocabulary and the Spelling tests are not quite as convincing as the three tests mentioned above. Nevertheless, in most cases the F's are significant or approach significance.

The 12 tests, standardized for age and race (mean 100; standard deviation 15), were averaged to get a composite score that would give equal weight to the individual tests. Heritability ratios for the composite or total scores are shown in the last two rows of Table VII–G. When all 12 tests are combined into a general mental test score, F ratios for both blacks and whites are significant at the .01 level, but the U statistic indicates no significant difference in the F's; that is, when the 12 tests are equally weighted and combined into a general mental ability score, there is no difference in variance ratios between the two races. We conclude, then, that within-race variances on mental ability test scores are due to heredity to a significant degree and that the effect of heredity on test performance is not significantly different for the two races.

Since, by design, tests in the battery represented the broad spectrum of specific primary mental abilities (number, space, verbal, and perceptual speed), it would have been remarkable if all tests had reflected the same degree of within-pair variance for both races. On the other hand, grouping tests with similar factor structure or combining several short tests into one composite score or general factor score should produce a more reliable measure of mental ability than a specific test alone, if for no other reason than that the composite test represents a larger sample of mental test performance than the specific test.

Factor analysis of the 12 individual tests produced three distinctly separate factors: (1) verbal factor, made up of Calendar, Wide Range Vocabulary, Heim Vocabulary, Spelling, and Arithmetic tests; (2) spatial factor, made up of Cube Comparisons, Surface Development, Form Board, Paper Folding, Object Aperture, and Newcastle Spatial tests; (3) perceptual speed factor, represented by only one test, Identical Pictures. The 12 individual tests were standardized for age and race with a mean of 100 and a standard deviation of 15. The derived factor scores are equivalent to deviation IQ's. F ratios for each of the factor IQ's and the full scale IQ, which represents the average of the three factors, are shown in Table VII–H. With the exception of the spatial IQ, all variance ratios are significant for both races. For whites, all ratios are significant at the .01 level. Full scale IQ variance ratios are significant at the .01 level for blacks, but verbal and perceptual speed reach only the .05 level.

The variance ratios for verbal and spatial IQ's are significantly larger for whites than for blacks. It should be remembered that the four individual tests with significant black-white F within-pair variance differences are included in these factor IQ's. The perceptual speed factor shows no significant difference in F ratios between races; neither does the full scale IQ in which all three factor IQ's are weighted equally and combined.

Table VII-H

Heritability Coefficients for Factor IQ Tests for Black and White Twins: Classical Methods of Analysis Using Age-race Standard Scores

Variable	MZ		DZ		T(Cor)	Heritability Ratios		Within-pair Variances			
	r	N	r	N		H	HR	MZ	DZ	F	U[a]
Verbal IQ											
White	.82	171	.59	133	4.21	.57	.57	24.29	52.54	2.16**	
Black	.83	76	.64	47	2.19	.52	.45	22.44	43.28	1.93*	2.17*
Spatial IQ											
White	.81	171	.57	133	3.98	.55	.59	24.25	53.98	2.23**	
Black	.77	76	.45	47	2.80	.58	.84	28.01	39.82	1.42	3.55**
Perceptual Speed IQ											
White	.76	164	.55	128	3.20	.47	.56	56.73	90.57	1.60**	
Black	.51	72	.32	47	1.20	.28	.75	99.57	162.63	1.63*	.96
Full Scale IQ											
White	.85	171	.60	133	4.68	.62	.58	15.49	36.57	2.36**	
Black	.80	76	.34	47	3.90	.70	1.15	14.84	47.79	3.22**	.73

* $p < .05$.
** $p < .01$.
[a] difference in U's. Paulson's statistic for determining the significance of difference in F's.

In Table VII–I the races are combined, and heritability comparisons are made by sex. For the most part, there are no big surprises since the same subjects are represented as in Table VII–F. Within-pair variance ratios are significant at the .01 level for both boys and girls on the Arithmetic, Spelling, Surface Development, and Heim Vocabulary tests. There are four tests on which variance ratios were different for boys and girls. On the Cube Comparisons, Identical Pictures, and Object Aperture tests, F ratios were significant for boys only. The Wide Range Vocabulary F ratio was significant only for girls. Heritability ratios for the means of the 12 subtests are significant at the .01 level for both sexes.

Only 3 of the 12 boy-girl F ratios are significantly different. The boys' within-pair variance was significantly greater on two spatial tests. The girls' was greater on one. For all other tests, including Arithmetic, Spelling, and Vocabulary, in which heritability differences might be expected to be different, the U statistic shows no significant difference.

In Table VII–J the races are combined, and heritability comparisons are made by sex for the three factor IQ's and the full scale IQ. All variance ratios for factor IQ's are significant at the .01 level except the single-test factor, perceptual speed. The full scale factor IQ variance ratio is significant at the .01 level for both boys and girls.

The differences in F ratios for the verbal and spatial IQ's are insignificant for male and female comparisons. On the one-test factor, perceptual speed, sex difference in the F ratio is significant. Full scale factor IQ's show highly significant F's for both boys and girls, but the within-pair variance difference between the sexes is insignificant.

The 142 sets of twins with both psychological and socio-economic data provide a unique opportunity to examine P. Nichols' (1970) claim that environmental differences are important in determining heritability values and that environmental factors are largely responsible for the observed differences in performance between whites and blacks. The findings of Binet (1895), Tyler (1965), and Jensen (1973a) were confirmed in an earlier section of this chapter where it was established that there are significant differences in mean IQ between socio-economic classes. The pattern of IQ differences for SES is consistent by race, sex, and zygosity (Table VII–E). Using the SES twin group, the claim that environmental differences are important in determining heritability can now be tested by computing general intelligence (IQ) heritability ratios by social class for blacks and whites.

The hereditarian research program predicts that general intelligence (IQ) is inherited; that is, there is a positive correlation for IQ between members of the same family, the size of the correlation being greater the closer the kinship (Galton, 1869). The program also predicts that the relationship is consistent for different subpopulations: rich, poor,

Table VII-I

Heritability Coefficients on 12 Mental Tests by Sex: Classical Methods of Analysis Using Age-race Standard Scores

Variable	MZ		DZ			Heritability Ratios		Within-pair Variances			
	r	N	r	N	T(Cor)	H	HR	MZ	DZ	F	U[a]
Calendar											
Male	.52	110	.36	63	1.25	.25	.62	125.38	117.01	.93	
Female	.48	136	.42	113	.54	.10	.23	110.45	121.56	1.10	−.84
Cube Comparisons											
Male	.45	108	.28	64	1.18	.23	.73	123.51	185.44	1.50*	
Female	.29	136	.20	112	.70	.11	.60	153.41	154.44	1.01	1.80
Surface Development											
Male	.73	110	.44	65	2.81	.51	.79	76.30	157.23	2.06**	
Female	.56	137	.23	115	3.13	.43	1.19	78.09	140.47	1.80**	.06
Wide Range Vocabulary											
Male	.52	110	.31	65	1.61	.31	.81	96.68	132.40	1.37	
Female	.48	137	.19	115	2.55	.35	1.21	127.01	183.14	1.44*	−.59
Form Board											
Male	.60	108	.54	65	.51	.12	.19	114.22	97.38	.85	
Female	.30	135	.32	115	−.14	−.02	−.11	133.35	129.68	.97	−.54

Arithmetic											
Male	.80	109	.48	65	3.63	.62	.81	40.88	124.80	3.05**	
Female	.82	135	.60	115	3.45	.53	.52	40.04	92.98	2.32**	.48
Heim Vocabulary											
Male	.85	108	.50	64	4.31	.69	.81	41.44	116.55	2.81**	
Female	.80	136	.62	115	2.86	.47	.45	40.77	71.27	1.75**	1.61
Paper Folding											
Male	.49	109	.34	65	1.12	.22	.61	130.65	162.19	1.24	
Female	.54	136	.36	115	1.80	.28	.68	96.59	115.70	1.20	−.03
Object Aperture											
Male	.48	109	.29	64	1.38	.26	.79	128.83	211.16	1.64*	
Female	.37	135	.23	115	1.19	.18	.76	117.64	107.64	.92	2.73*
Identical Pictures											
Male	.70	105	.34	63	3.12	.54	1.02	63.78	149.97	2.35**	
Female	.68	131	.57	112	1.48	.27	.34	74.63	87.40	1.17	3.01**
Spelling											
Male	.86	108	.41	64	5.40	.77	1.05	35.00	119.13	3.40**	
Female	.79	137	.59	115	3.05	.48	.51	40.01	81.98	2.05**	1.59
Spatial Relations											
Male	.79	99	.58	61	2.45	.50	.54	55.17	92.43	1.68*	
Female	.81	134	.53	111	4.15	.60	.69	35.87	88.05	2.46**	−2.64**
Subtest Mean											
Male	.87	110	.63	65	3.73	.65	.55	13.41	38.56	2.88**	
Female	.84	137	.57	115	4.56	.64	.64	12.73	32.32	2.54**	−.29

* p < .05.
** p < .01.
[a] difference in U's. Paulson's statistic for determining the significance of difference in F's.

Table VII–J
Heritability Coefficients for Factor IQ Tests by Sex: Classical Methods of Analysis Using Age-race Standard Scores

Variable	MZ		DZ		T(Cor)	Heritability Ratios		Within-pair Variances			
	r	N	r	N		H	HR	MZ	DZ	F	U[a]
Verbal IQ											
Male	.85	110	.53	65	4.06	.67	.74	22.76	58.21	2.56*	
Female	.80	137	.63	115	2.81	.46	.42	24.49	45.55	1.86*	.88
Spatial IQ											
Male	.83	110	.63	65	2.87	.55	.50	24.99	53.80	2.15*	
Female	.74	137	.45	115	3.59	.52	.79	25.74	48.30	1.88*	.01
Perceptual Speed IQ											
Male	.70	105	.34	63	3.12	.54	1.02	63.78	149.97	2.35*	
Female	.68	131	.57	112	1.48	.27	.34	74.63	87.40	1.17	3.01*
Full Scale IQ											
Male	.85	110	.55	65	3.92	.66	.70	15.18	49.01	3.23*	
Female	.83	137	.54	115	4.41	.62	.69	15.38	34.12	2.22*	.97

* $p < .01$.
[a] difference in U's. Paulson's statistic for determining the significance of difference in F's.

black, white, male, and female. The SES sample of MZ and DZ twins, although small, provides the first opportunity to test this hereditarian hypothesis by social class for black and white twins. (Koch's (1966) twin study is similar in methodology, but the subjects were all white).

In Table VII–K mean IQ's and heritability coefficients are shown for three SES classes for each race and for the combined group. The table supports the hereditarian hypothesis. High IQ's are associated with high SES classes. For the middle and low SES classes of whites, Holzinger's (1929) and Nichols' (1970) heritability ratios are high and positive. The within-pair variance ratio of the middle SES class is also significant.

Analysis of the black twins is even more convincing. Within the black sample, twins in the highest SES class earned the highest IQ's. Intraclass correlations for the three SES classes are in the predicted direction, MZ r > DZ r. The Holzinger (1929) and Nichols (1970) heritability ratios are high. In the high and middle SES classes, within-pair variance ratios are significant at the .01 level.

When the black and white samples are combined and the heritability ratios computed, the results are still more impressive. Twins in the highest SES classes achieved the highest general intelligence (IQ). Intraclass r's are high for both types of twins at all three SES levels, resulting in high heritability ratios and significant within-pair variance F's for the high and middle classes. The findings are consistent with the hereditarian hypothesis.

Correlations were computed between social class and IQ for the two races and for the total group. For the 126 whites the r was −.37; for the 158 blacks, −.40; for the combined group, −.48. These correlations are corroborated by the mental test literature from Binet (1895) to Jensen (1973a). Typical correlations reported by Bouchard (1976) are .42, .45, and .57.

From the above analysis of data on IQ and social class, it is clear that twins of both races from the highest social classes earned highest general mental ability IQ scores. Even when analyzed by race, the high SES classes outperformed the middle and low classes. For neither MZ nor DZ twins did the high SES blacks equal or exceed the low SES whites.

The hereditarian hypothesis says that general intelligence is inherited, 60–80% of the variance being accounted for by genetic factors. If the hypothesis is correct, then all subpopulations should show similar patterns of general intelligence heritability ratios. In this analysis the intraclass correlations, heritability ratios, and within-pair variance ratios all yield congruent heritability patterns by social class for each race and for total group.

It should be noted that in this section twin study data were factor analyzed before heritability coefficients were computed. The first step

Table VII-K

Heritability Coefficients for *Basic Battery* Average IQ for Black and White Twins by Socio-economic Status: Classical Methods of Analysis Using Age-adjusted Standard Scores

Socio-economic Status	MZ		DZ		Heritability Ratios		MZ		DZ		Within-pair Variances		
	r	N	r	N	H	HR	Mn	SD	Mn	SD	MZ	DZ	F
White													
High	.48	11	.57	7	−.21	−.37	116.2	6.7	100.1	8.7	31.8	41.2	1.3
Middle	.90	14	.14	11	.88	1.70	103.4	10.1	105.8	4.8	11.4	35.0	3.1*
Low	.77	9	.54	11	.50	.60	103.3	6.8	99.8	7.0	11.9	29.0	2.4
Black													
High	.90	18	.58	11	.77	.72	97.0	7.9	96.5	7.9	6.5	34.0	5.3**
Middle	.85	22	.31	9	.78	1.27	92.0	6.7	91.5	5.8	7.4	35.2	4.7**
Low	.83	8	.61	11	.57	.53	88.4	4.6	89.1	4.7	3.9	10.8	2.8
Total													
High	.91	32	.71	18	.67	.42	104.7	12.2	100.3	9.5	14.9	30.0	2.0*
Middle	.88	28	.31	20	.83	1.30	97.3	9.4	100.3	7.0	11.4	51.2	4.5**
Low	.91	22	.76	22	.62	.33	93.6	8.0	91.6	6.3	6.0	10.8	1.8

Note: Whites, blacks, and total group were each divided into three SES groups, based on the distribution of SES scores for each respective racial group.

78

was to eliminate from the base group those individuals who did not have scores on all 29 tests or subtests of the Basic Battery. Seventy-seven subjects were dropped, leaving 540 whites and 237 blacks.

For the initial factor analysis, the black and white groups were combined, and the first principal component was obtained for the total group. The groups were then separated by race, and the first principal component was computed for each race.

Once weights had been determined by the factor analyses, three factor scores were assigned to each subject: (a) one based on weights from the total group; (b) one based on weights from the white group; (c) one based on weights from the black group. Own-race determined factor scores were then intercorrelated with opposite-race determined scores and total group scores. The purpose here was to obtain a good general factor score for the entire test battery.

To determine if the first principal component factor scores were measuring the same mental factor in the two races, own-race determined factor scores were intercorrelated with cross-race and total group factor scores. All r's were .99+, suggesting that whatever mental factor is measured in the white group is the same as that measured in the black group and in the total sample.

To estimate the reliability of this method of cross-racial comparisons, the two racial groups were randomly split in half. Twins of a pair were always assigned to the same group to avoid spuriously high correlations. The first principal component was then obtained for each of the four new subgroups.

Three factor scores based on the factor analysis were assigned to each subject in the four subgroups. Factor scores obtained for own-race subgroup, opposite-race subgroup, and total racial group were then intercorrelated to test the method of comparing the same group, opposite group, and total group factor scores without introducing the variable of race. Similar factor weights across groups and high intercorrelations would suggest that the first principal component of this complex battery of mental tests is measuring the same general factor in both subgroups of each race. This is exactly what was found. Correlations for own subgroup, opposite subgroup, and total racial group factor scores were .99+ for blacks *and* for whites.

Table VII–L gives the factor loadings for all 29 subtests for each of the seven groups: total group, black and white groups separately, and the four randomly selected subgroups. Similarity of the seven groups with respect to the factor loadings is remarkable. Arithmetic subtests yield especially high loadings across all groups. Spelling and the two vocabulary tests also load heavily on the first principal component.

As an independent check of the validity of the first principal component factor scores, the three scores obtained from the analyses were correlated

Table VII–L

Loadings of the General Factor on 29 Tests or Subtests of the *Basic Battery* by Various Subgroups

Test or Subtest (Age-race Standard Scores)	Combined Total Group	White Group			Black Group		
		Random Subgroup A	Random Subgroup B	Total	Random Subgroup A	Random Subgroup B	Total
Calendar	.63	.64	.65	.64	.57	.60	.58
Cube Comparisons—1	.48	.45	.53	.49	.58	.34	.46
Cube Comparisons—2	.50	.54	.57	.56	.37	.29	.33
Surface Development—1	.63	.63	.74	.68	.48	.47	.48
Surface Development—2	.67	.69	.71	.71	.60	.54	.57
Wide Range Vocabulary	.47	.46	.55	.51	.23	.50	.37
Form Board—1	.60	.63	.68	.66	.49	.35	.42
Form Board—2	.54	.56	.59	.58	.57	.29	.43
Arithmetic—1	.53	.54	.55	.54	.37	.58	.48
Arithmetic—2	.55	.58	.49	.54	.47	.68	.58
Arithmetic—3	.72	.73	.70	.72	.70	.79	.74
Arithmetic—4	.71	.71	.69	.70	.71	.77	.74
Arithmetic—5	.62	.65	.58	.61	.58	.70	.64
Arithmetic—6	.66	.66	.62	.64	.77	.74	.75
Arithmetic—7	.65	.65	.61	.63	.69	.76	.72
Heim Vocabulary	.70	.67	.71	.69	.73	.72	.72
Paper Folding—1	.62	.66	.67	.66	.65	.39	.52
Paper Folding—2	.57	.55	.61	.58	.58	.49	.53
Object Aperture—1	.36	.40	.42	.41	.23	.24	.24
Object Aperture—2	.42	.46	.55	.50	.32	.11	.21
Identical Pictures—1	.39	.34	.51	.43	.26	.27	.27
Identical Pictures—2	.46	.41	.59	.51	.40	.26	.32
Spelling	.59	.60	.51	.55	.72	.69	.70
Spatial Relations—1	.60	.57	.67	.62	.62	.47	.54
Spatial Relations—2	.53	.52	.55	.53	.50	.52	.51
Spatial Relations—3	.65	.58	.70	.65	.68	.62	.65
Spatial Relations—4	.62	.59	.73	.66	.55	.46	.51
Spatial Relations—5	.68	.69	.71	.70	.68	.57	.62
Spatial Relations—6	.60	.57	.57	.56	.70	.68	.69

with results from a standard IQ test, Primary Mental Abilities (Thurstone, 1963).

For whites, the PMA correlates .85 with both own-race and opposite-race factor scores; for blacks, .82 with own-race and .81 with opposite-race factor scores. These r's are significant and approach the test-retest reliability coefficients for the PMA.

From the above cross-race correlations, it is clear that the same general factor is being measured in each group separately and in the composite group when the two races are combined. When the races are split at random and factor analyzed, the high intercorrelations of the resulting factor scores indicate the significant reliability of the first principal components as a basis for the "cross-racial" correlations. The first principal component yields a general mental ability factor that is indistinguishable between races. Total group principal component factor scores correlate highly with an independent measure of IQ—.85 for whites and .82 for blacks.

Once it was determined that the mental test factors generated by the first principal component analysis were stable and represented the same factor in each race, the groups were reassembled as twins for the final step in the analysis. Classical heritability ratios were applied to the nine factor scores derived from own-race, opposite-race, and total group factor analyses.

Heritability ratios for white, black, and total groups are shown in Table VII–M. In the top third of the table, factor scores of the subjects' own racial group were used to compute the heritability ratios. The results are clear, and the F ratios for all comparisons are significant at the .01 level.

In the center of the table, opposite-race factor scores indicate no apparent change in heritability ratios from same-race factor scores. When the total group factor weights are used (lower third of Table VII–M), the results are indistinguishable from those obtained from own- and opposite-race analyses.

When a general mental factor, not unlike Spearman's g, is used to compute heritability ratios, not only are the F ratios highly significant for own-race, other-race, and total group factor scores, but no significant difference is noted between the heritability ratios of the two races.

There were two main purposes of this chapter: first, to compare performance on a battery of mental ability tests for four subpopulations—race, sex, zygosity, social class; and second, to examine the IQ heritability ratios by race, sex, and social class.

Three-way analysis of variance (race, sex, zygosity) and the classical heritability methods of Holzinger, Nichols, and Vandenberg were applied to 427 sets (304 white, 123 black) of like-sexed twins ranging in age from 12 to 20. Although the small number of twins in some classes,

Table VII–M

Heritability Ratios for Factor Scores Based on First Principal Component Analysis of Own-race, Opposite-race, and Total Group

						Heritability Ratios		Within-pair Variances			
	MZ		DZ								
Score	cor	N	cor	N	T(Cor)	H	HR	MZ	DZ	F	U[a]

Factor Weights from Own Racial Group

Score	cor	N	cor	N	T(Cor)	H	HR	MZ	DZ	F	U[a]
White	.85	141	.63	115	3.89	.58	.50	3517.4	9335.4	2.65*	
Black	.91	70	.58	46	4.45	.79	.73	1619.3	6398.3	3.95*	.31
Total	.91	211	.71	161	5.78	.67	.43	2887.7	8496.3	2.94*	

Factor Weights from Opposite Racial Group

Score	cor	N	cor	N	T(Cor)	H	HR	MZ	DZ	F	U[a]
White	.85	141	.64	115	3.83	.58	.50	2839.1	7696.9	2.71*	
Black	.91	70	.56	46	4.46	.79	.77	1955.7	7340.8	3.75*	.62
Total	.90	211	.71	161	5.48	.65	.42	2546.0	7595.1	2.98*	

Factor Weights from Total Group

Score	cor	N	cor	N	T(Cor)	H	HR	MZ	DZ	F	U[a]
White	.85	141	.63	115	3.88	.58	.50	3302.0	8822.3	2.67*	
Black	.91	70	.56	46	4.48	.79	.76	1838.9	7049.7	3.83*	.47
Total	.87	211	.62	161	5.62	.65	.57	2816.6	8315.9	2.95*	

* $p < .01$.

[a] difference in U's. Paulson's statistic for determining the significance of difference in F's.

especially black DZ, lowers the confidence level of heritability estimates, the consistency of the other results corroborates the hereditarian hypothesis.

For all 12 tests in the Basic Battery and for the total IQ, there is a significant race effect of about 10 IQ points (2/3 SD) for most subtests. Significant sex differences were found for 7 of the 12 subtests. These findings are consistent with Maccoby and Jacklin, except for the higher arithmetic scores for girls than for boys.

The question of zygosity differences in test performance is puzzling. MZ twins of both races and MZ's of both sexes significantly outperformed comparable DZ's on 5 of the 12 Basic tests. The reason for the differential performances of the two types of twins is not clear, and the literature sheds little light on the problem. In a similar study Koch, using the PMA, found higher scores for DZ's than for MZ's. Husen reported the opposite.

The 142 sets of twins with both psychological and social class data provide a special opportunity to reexamine test performance differences by race, zygosity, sex, and social class and to examine for the first time IQ heritability ratios for different social classes within races.

Socio-economic status explains a significant amount of difference in mean IQ's for 8 of the 12 Basic tests. There is no apparent difference in mean IQ's between the culturally loaded verbal tests and the nonverbal spatial tests. On the verbal, spatial, and full scale IQ tests, low SES whites outscore the highest SES blacks.

Classical heritability methods of Holzinger, Nichols, and Vandenberg were applied to the base group of 427 sets of like-sexed twins and 142 twin sets for whom social class data were available. Taken individually, the 12 tests of the Basic Battery show a wide range of heritability suggesting that the mental abilities tested are not uniform in their genetic and environmental characteristics. However, when subtests are combined, as they usually are to obtain an estimate of "g" or general intelligence (IQ), the results are unequivocal. In whatever manner all individual tests or subtests were pooled, by simply averaging the 12 standard scores, by combining the factor IQ's to get full scale IQ, or by using weighted scores determined from the first principal component factor analysis of either race singly or of both races combined, the results were the same. Heritability variance ratios for both blacks and whites were significant at the .01 level. In no case was the difference between variance ratios of the races significant.

Mental characteristics measured by the pooled scores of our comprehensive test battery correlate significantly with a standard IQ score and show congruent heritability patterns for blacks and whites.

A significant contribution of this chapter is a comparison of the IQ heritability ratios by social class and by race. Intraclass correlations, heritability ratios, and within-pair variance ratios yield similar heritability patterns by social class for each race and for the total group. On the basis of the analysis of the SES twin group, P. Nichols' *ad hoc* claim that environmental differences are important in determining heritability values should be rejected.

VIII

Primary Mental Abilities Test: Subpopulation Differences

The Primary Mental Abilities Test has gone through numerous revisions. The first experimental edition was published in 1938 by L. L. and Thelma G. Thurstone. Later editions were titled the Chicago Test of Primary Mental Abilities. Since 1962, when Science Research Associates assumed publication of the test, it has been called the SRA Test of Primary Mental Abilities.

According to the manual, the PMA Test (T. G. Thurstone, 1963) is designed to provide both multifactored and general measures of intelligence. The profile of primary mental abilities is useful in understanding individual differences in performance among children who appear to be comparable in general intelligence. The PMA general or total score—IQ—is an index of general intelligence which is comparable to scores on tests such as the Stanford-Binet and the Wechsler Intelligence Scale for Children.

The abilities measured by the PMA subtests are briefly:

Verbal Meaning: Ability to understand ideas expressed in words. In the later school years this is the most important single index of a child's potential for handling academic tasks.

Number Facility: Ability to work with numbers, to handle simple quantitative problems rapidly and accurately, and to understand and recognize quantitative differences.

Reasoning: Ability to solve logical problems.

Spatial Relations: Ability to visualize objects and figures rotated in space and the relations between them. The test measuring this ability appears in every level of the PMA.

The PMA subtest scores are reported as quotient equivalents which are functions of raw scores and ages. The total raw score is the sum of the four subtest raw scores and is converted to an intelligence quotient, which is also a function of raw score and age. Norms are based on a nationwide standardization program of 32,393 school children. Participating schools were drawn randomly from the Directory of Public Secondary Day Schools 1958–59, U.S. Department of HEW, Office of Education.

At least five other twin studies used some version of Thurstone's original test. The results of the studies, including one by Thurstone, are summarized in Table VIII–A. Blewett, Thurstone, and Vandenberg (two studies) used the Chicago PMA Test, which had four subtests common to the SRA PMA, but no total IQ. Although Koch was the first to give the SRA PMA to twins, she had no intention of getting into a discussion of the "heredity-environment problem," although she conveniently provided the PMA intraclass r's for her MZ and DZ twins from which h^2 can be derived. The within-pair variance ratios were computed by the formula Vandenberg used to obtain F ratios for Blewett's study. When we consider that the five studies were conducted independently over a period of 12 years by different investigators with different sampling techniques, the results are remarkably consistent. Despite the small sample sizes, Verbal and Space tests consistently show significant within-pair variance F ratios. Word Fluency, a Chicago but not a SRA PMA subtest, yielded significant F ratios in the four earlier studies. Although no subtest scores were available for the Koch study, the total IQ within-pair variance F ratio is convincingly significant.

In the present study, 143 sets of twins took the PMA Battery, a relatively small number compared to the 427 sets of twins comprising the Basic Battery sample. As often as possible the same analyses reported for the Basic Battery (Chapter VII) will be used with the PMA Test to compare the two samples and the two test batteries.

It will be recalled that the Basic Battery was not standardized as a test battery. Instead, each subtest was selected to represent one of the primary mental abilities based on the analyses provided in the test manuals or on the information in the ETS Kit of Reference Tests (French, et al., 1963). The PMA, on the other hand, is based on Thurstone's theory that certain mental activities have in common a primary factor that distinguishes them from other groups of mental activities, and that each of these other groups has a different primary factor in common. In addition to the primary abilities, Thurstone found high intercorrelations among the subtests and concluded that a second order general factor existed. This position is now widely held by test theorists.

To compare scores of the relatively unknown tests of the Basic Battery with those of the widely used and standardized Primary Mental Abilities,

Table VIII-A
Primary Mental Abilities Test
F ratios of DZ to MZ Within-pair Variances

Name of Score	Blewett[a] (1954) $N_{DZ}26$ $N_{MZ}26$	Thurstone et al. (1955) $N_{DZ}53$ $N_{MZ}45$	Vandenberg (1962) $N_{DZ}37$ $N_{MZ}45$	Vandenberg (1964) $N_{DZ}36$ $N_{MZ}76$	Koch[a] (1966) $N_{DZ}60$ $N_{MZ}66$
Verbal	3.13**	2.81**	2.65**	1.74**	Not reported
Space	2.04*	4.19**	1.77*	3.51**	" "
Number	1.07	1.52	2.58**	2.26**	" "
Reasoning	2.78**	1.35	1.40	1.10	" "
Word Fluency	2.78**	2.47**	2.57**	2.24**	—
Memory	not used	1.62*	1.26	not used	—
PMA Total IQ	—	—	—	—	2.62**

* $p < .05$.
** $p < .01$.

[a] F ratios calculated from h^2 values by the formula $F = \dfrac{1}{1 - h^2}$. This may result in minor inaccuracies that should not affect the general trend of the conclusions arrived at in the discussion.

Note. Data in this table, except for the Koch study, were taken from a table by Vandenberg (1967c).

Table VIII–B

Correlations of Tests in the *Basic Battery* with SRA *Primary Mental Abilities* (143 Sets of Like-sexed Twins)

Basic Battery (Age-adjusted Standard Scores)	Primary Mental Abilities				
	Verbal	Number Facility	Reasoning	Spatial Relations	Total IQ
Calendar	.52	.53	.67	.52	.64
Cube Comparisons	.37	.44	.49	.49	.55
Surface Development	.49	.54	.64	.51	.64
Wide Range Vocabulary	.54	.44	.46	.42	.53
Form Board	.52	.61	.65	.58	.69
Arithmetic	.56	.57	.70	.48	.66
Heim Vocabulary	.74	.66	.80	.57	.79
Paper Folding	.50	.60	.65	.61	.69
Object Aperture	.35	.49	.46	.39	.49
Identical Pictures	.35	.26	.32	.29	.37
Spelling	.57	.49	.66	.40	.61
Spatial Relations	.58	.68	.74	.68	.80
Average (Full Scale IQ)	.73	.75	.87	.71	.89

tests of the two batteries were correlated (Table VIII–B). The table of correlations looks much like the table of Wechsler subtest intercorrelations. Correlation between the Basic Battery Full Scale IQ and PMA IQ is .89, which approaches the test-retest reliability of most paper and pencil intelligence tests.

The same SAS program used in the analysis of variance for the Basic Battery was applied to the Primary Mental Abilities Test sample. The results of the analysis of variance are shown in Table VIII–C. Race shows the only significant and consistent main effect in the analysis. The Spatial Relations subtest and PMA IQ show significant sex differences. SES effects contributing to mean differences are significant for the Verbal and Reasoning subtests and also for the total PMA IQ. Only 8 of the possible 55 interactions among the four classifications are significant, only one interaction (sex x zygosity) being significant for more than one test variable.

Least squares means are reported in Table VIII–D. Since only 8 of the possible 55 interactions are significant, least squares means are given for major classifications only.

Race differences in test performance revealed by the PMA are much greater than those found for the Basic Battery (Chapter VII). In most instances, the differences approach one full standard deviation. For the PMA total IQ, the white mean is 101.7; the mean for blacks is 85.5. Subtest differences are somewhat less than for total IQ, but still remain in the 15 IQ point range.

The two significant sex differences favor boys, whose slight superiority on the Number subtest and significant superiority on the Spatial subtest

Table VIII–C

Race, Sex, Socio-economic Status, and Zygosity Effects Contributing to Differences in Means of the *Primary Mental Abilities Test*

PMA Scores	SES	SEX	RACE	ZYGOSITY	SES × SEX	SES × RACE	SEX × RACE	SES × SEX × RACE	SES × ZYGOSITY	SEX × ZYGOSITY	SES × SEX × ZYGOSITY	RACE × ZYGOSITY	SES × RACE × ZYG	SEX × RACE × ZYG	SES × SEX × RACE × ZYG
Verbal	**		**												
Number Facility			**							*	*			*	
Reasoning	**		**							**					
Spatial Relations		**	**				*		**						
Total IQ	**	*	**							*		*			

* $p < .05$.
** $p < .01$.

were not unexpected (see Chapter VII). What was unexpected was the non-significant difference favoring boys on the Verbal subtest (see Maccoby & Jacklin, 1974).

Although zygosity differences are not significant for any PMA subtest or the total IQ, least squares means are shown by zygosity for the PMA scores.

The PMA test scores for the three SES classes follow the pattern reported by Tyler, a pattern which also appeared in the analysis of the Basic Battery (Chapter VII). Our reports are compatible with Koch's study, "Twins and Twin Relations" (1966), which analyzed the PMA scores by SES. Koch found differences to be most uniform in the social

Table VIII–D

Least Squares Means for the *Primary Mental Abilities Test* by Race, Sex, Socio-economic Status, and Zygosity

PMA Scores	Race		Sex		Socio-economic Status			Zygosity	
	White	Black	Male	Female	SES 1	SES 2	SES 3	MZ	DZ
PMA Verbal	102.0	90.5	96.5	95.9	100.5	96.1	92.1	95.4	97.1
PMA Number Facility	101.5	86.0	94.5	92.9	96.7	94.3	90.3	95.0	92.5
PMA Reasoning	103.6	89.3	96.3	96.6	102.1	98.0	89.2	96.0	96.9
PMA Spatial Relations	101.7	92.0	99.9	93.9	98.7	98.2	93.7	97.1	96.6
PMA Total IQ	101.7	85.5	95.8	91.5	98.2	94.8	87.9	93.7	93.5

Note. 1 = High SES group
2 = Middle SES group
3 = Low SES group

class variable. Subjects from the lowest class performed least well on all subtests of the PMA except the Spatial Test. In this study, however, all subtests, including the Spatial Test, followed the pattern reported by Tyler, with SES effects being significant for Verbal, Reasoning, and Total IQ (Tables VIII–C and VIII–D).

In Table VIII–E, heritability ratios are shown for black, white, and total group. All *F* ratios are insignificant for whites. On the other hand, Number, Reasoning, and Spatial subtests and total PMA IQ show significant within-pair variance ratios for blacks. The pattern of significant heritability components for blacks is much like that of the five earlier studies reviewed in Table VIII–A. The small numbers of twins in each of the six studies in which the PMA has been used make interpretation of the separate heritability coefficients hazardous. However, the consistency of the findings of significant within-pair variance *F* ratios indicates a likelihood of a high heritability component in most if not all subtests and in the total PMA IQ. Examination of the three heritability ratios (within-pair variance ratios, Holzinger's *H* ratios, and Nichol's *HR* ratios) shown in Table VIII–E suggests higher heritability for blacks than for whites.

Table VIII–E
Heritability Coefficients on SRA *Primary Mental Abilities Test* by Total Group and by Race

Variable	MZ r	MZ N	DZ r	DZ N	T(Cor)	Heritability Ratios H	Heritability Ratios HR	Within-pair Variances MZ	Within-pair Variances DZ	Within-pair Variances F
PMA Verbal										
White	.74	34	.53	29	1.37	.45	.57	53.68	85.97	1.60
Black	.33	48	.24	32	.40	.11	.53	112.33	96.08	.86
Total	.65	82	.51	61	1.25	.29	.44	88.01	91.27	1.04
PMA Number Facility										
White	.58	34	.70	29	−.73	−.38	−.39	127.91	56.07	.44
Black	.64	48	.33	32	1.73	.46	.97	62.08	124.67	2.01*
Total	.72	82	.61	61	1.20	.29	.32	89.38	92.06	1.03
PMA Reasoning										
White	.78	34	.52	29	1.76	.54	.67	50.65	70.14	1.39
Black	.73	48	.62	32	.88	.30	.31	49.15	85.72	1.74*
Total	.84	82	.69	61	2.12	.48	.35	49.77	78.31	1.57*
PMA Spatial Relations										
White	.35	34	.20	29	.61	.19	.86	137.63	145.16	1.06
Black	.60	48	.36	32	1.32	.37	.80	59.60	111.52	1.87*
Total	.59	82	.36	61	1.70	.35	.76	91.96	127.51	1.39
PMA Total IQ										
White	.69	34	.51	29	1.08	.37	.52	86.46	106.50	1.23
Black	.71	48	.49	32	1.43	.42	.61	57.41	117.97	2.06*
Total	.81	82	.62	61	2.36	.51	.48	69.45	112.52	1.62*

* *p* < .05.

IX

Cattell Culture Fair Intelligence Test: Subpopulation Differences

To separate the evaluation of "natural intelligence" from school achievement scores, the Cattell Culture Fair Intelligence Test appears to be an ideal instrument to supplement the Basic Battery and the Primary Mental Abilities Test. The Cattell test is specifically designed to avoid the effects of social, educational, and racial background in estimating the real potential of the individual. According to the CCFIT manual, testing is undergoing steady but profound changes. The new movement began with the demonstration that the general ability factor which runs through intelligence-demanding acts can be measured by perceptual, nonverbal, as well as by verbal tests. Cattell and Cattell (1965) say that most current intelligence tests are looking backward instead of forward.

> *That is to say, instead of measuring the child's capacity to learn in the future, they are recording what he has had opportunity to learn in the past.* Such intelligence tests, depending heavily on learned verbal and numerical skills, correlate well with scholastic achievement in the same year because they themselves consist largely of *learned* scholastic skills, as distinct from intellective *capacity* and *potential.* (p. 3)

It is claimed that the CCFIT gives a more honest evaluation of future potential for school children from diverse homes and cultural backgrounds. The nonverbal aspect of the test has encouraged research with children who do not speak English. The same form of the CCFIT has been given to French, Italian, Chinese, and Japanese children with equal success. One investigator (Fowler, 1955) found that groups of whites and Negroes of comparable social status do not differ significantly in test distributions. The usual sex differences found on group intelligence tests are not reported on the Cattell scale. "The test, therefore, deals with the core of general 'relation education capacity,' which many researchers have shown to be largely inborn, and a relatively constant characteristic (IQ) for the individual" (Cattell, 1960, p. 6).

Scale 2 of the CCFIT was designed for children aged 8 to 14 and for average unselected adults. It consists of two parallel forms, A and B, each composed of 46 items arranged in four subtests and requiring 12½ minutes of total working time. Following the suggestions in the manual, both forms of Scale 2 were administered to 143 sets of like-sexed twins. The method of analysis is the same as that used with the Basic Battery and the PMA.

Tables IX–A and IX–B show correlation coefficients between the CCFIT and the two other intelligence scales used in the Twin Study. The r's between the CCFIT IQ's and both the Basic Battery and PMA are consistently high. Whatever the CCFIT measures is also measured by the PMA and by the tests of the Basic Battery. Intercorrelations of the three Cattell IQ's (Table IX–C) are in most cases higher than the reliabilities reported in the CCFIT manual. For Form A, Classical IQ score correlates with the Culture Fair IQ .95 and with Attainment-Contaminated IQ .98, and Culture Fair IQ vs. Attainment-Contaminated IQ is .97. For Form B, the r's are .96, .98, and .97. It would appear

Table IX–A

Correlation of *Basic Battery* Tests With *Cattell Culture Fair Intelligence Test*

Basic Battery (Age Standard Scores)	Cattell Culture Fair IQ's								
	Form A			Form B			Forms A + B		
	C	SCF	SAC	C	SCF	SAC	C	SCF	SAC
Calendar	.60	.61	.60	.58	.58	.57	.62	.64	.62
Cube Comparisons	.48	.50	.49	.47	.49	.46	.50	.53	.51
Surface Development	.60	.66	.62	.55	.58	.54	.60	.66	.62
Wide Range Vocabulary	.39	.40	.39	.36	.35	.35	.39	.40	.39
Form Board	.63	.66	.63	.59	.61	.59	.65	.68	.65
Arithmetic	.54	.52	.54	.51	.47	.49	.55	.53	.55
Heim Vocabulary	.66	.61	.64	.63	.58	.59	.68	.64	.66
Paper Folding	.66	.65	.64	.61	.61	.59	.67	.67	.66
Object Aperture	.53	.56	.53	.47	.49	.47	.53	.56	.53
Identical Pictures	.32	.29	.32	.26	.24	.28	.31	.28	.32
Spelling	.50	.45	.50	.49	.43	.46	.52	.48	.51
Spatial Relations	.75	.73	.74	.70	.67	.68	.76	.75	.75
Average	.79	.79	.79	.74	.73	.73	.81	.81	.81

Note. C IQ = Clasical IQ
SCF IQ = Standard Score, Culture Fair IQ
SAC IQ = Standard Score, Attainment-Contaminated IQ

Table IX–B

Correlations of *Primary Mental Abilities Test* With *Cattell Culture Fair Intelligence Test*

Primary Mental Abilities	Cattell Culture Fair IQ's								
	Form A			Form B			Forms A + B		
	C	SCF	SAC	C	SCF	SAC	C	SCF	SAC
Verbal	.55	.55	.55	.50	.50	.48	.56	.57	.55
Number Facility	.66	.63	.64	.64	.63	.62	.68	.67	.67
Reasoning	.71	.69	.70	.69	.66	.66	.74	.72	.72
Spatial Relations	.61	.61	.59	.58	.58	.57	.63	.64	.62
Total	.74	.73	.72	.71	.69	.69	.76	.76	.75

Note. C IQ = Classical IQ
SCF IQ = Standard Score, Culture Fair IQ
SAC IQ = Standard Score, Attainment-Contaminated IQ

Table IX–C

Correlation Matrix of Nine Intelligence Quotients Derived From the *Cattell Culture Fair Intelligence Test*

Cattell IQ's	1	2	3	4	5	6	7	8
Form A								
1 Classical								
2 Culture Fair	.95							
3 Attainment-Contaminated	.98	.97						
Form B								
4 Classical	.81	.76	.79					
5 Culture Fair	.76	.75	.75	.96				
6 Attainment-Contaminated	.78	.74	.77	.98	.97			
Forms A + B								
7 Classical	.95	.90	.93	.95	.90	.92		
8 Culture Fair	.91	.94	.92	.92	.93	.91	.96	
9 Attainment-Contaminated	.94	.91	.94	.93	.91	.94	.98	.97

that the CCFIT not only measures the same abilities as conventional intelligence tests, but also that the three CCFIT scores themselves exhibit very small differences.

Another way of comparing tests on the Basic Battery, the PMA test, and the CCFIT IQ's is to factor analyze, using the Varimax method, the 19 subtests representing these three tests of mental ability. Six factors were obtained: (1) Spatial Orientation, (2) Verbal Comprehension, (3) Perceptual Speed, (4) Vocabulary, (5) Visualization 1, and (6) Visualization 2 (Table IX–D).

Factors 5 and 6 are very much alike. The CCFIT IQ's load neither factor significantly. Surface Development, Form Board, and Spatial Relations of the Basic Battery load both visualization factors almost equally. Spatial Relations subtest of the PMA loads Viz-2 but not Viz-1. PMA

Table IX–D

Factor Analysis of *Basic Battery, Primary Mental Abilities Test,* and *Cattell Culture Fair Intelligence Test*

Test	Factor 1 Spatial Orientation	Factor 2 Verbal Comprehension	Factor 3 Perceptual Speed	Factor 4 Vocabulary	Factor 5 Visualization 1	Factor 6 Visualization 2
Basic Battery (Age Standard Scores)						
Calendar	.50	.31	−.07	.33	.06	.43
Cube Comparisons	.19	.17	−.04	.02	.20	.82
Surface Development	.32	.32	.14	.05	.42	.50
Wide Range Vocabulary	.15	.27	.02	.86	.12	.09
Form Board	.44	.20	.17	.18	.44	.44
Arithmetic	.22	.81	.18	−.01	.06	.27
Heim Vocabulary	.33	.71	.10	.41	.19	.19
Paper Folding	.48	.13	.22	.30	.35	.45
Object Aperture	.29	.02	.07	.10	.84	.18
Identical Pictures	.13	.16	.94	.05	.11	.05
Spelling	.25	.86	.01	.22	−.04	.03
Spatial Relations	.50	.30	.22	.24	.41	.44
Primary Mental Abilities Test						
Verbal	.16	.59	.21	.45	.30	.20
Number Facility	.38	.49	.08	.24	.45	.24
Reasoning	.41	.63	.13	.23	.28	.36
Spatial Relations	.44	.21	.24	.36	.04	.54
Cattell Culture Fair Intelligence Test (Forms A + B)						
Classical IQ	.84	.35	.11	.12	.26	.21
Culture Fair IQ	.82	.31	.08	.13	.30	.26
Attainment-Contaminated IQ	.84	.34	.12	.10	.26	.22

Number Facility loads Viz-1 but not Viz-2. The two visualization factors are identified by two tests from the Basic Battery, Viz-1 by Object Aperture and Viz-2 by Cube Comparisons. The Object Aperture Test requires the subject to determine how a three-dimensional object looks from all directions and then to select one of five openings through which the object will pass. Cube Comparisons is adapted from Thurstone's *cubes.* Assuming no cube can have two identical faces, the subject is to decide whether the two cubes can represent the same cube or must represent different cubes. The process of obtaining the correct answer may involve verbal reasoning. Viz-2 may also involve two-dimensional space.

There is little question about factor 4, Vocabulary. The two vocabulary tests from the Basic Battery load this factor as does the PMA Verbal Test. No CCFIT IQ loads factor 4 significantly.

Factor 3, Perceptual Speed, is loaded significantly by only one test, the Identical Pictures Test from the Basic Battery. This factor analysis confirms the analysis of the Basic Battery reported in Chapter VII.

Factor 2 is Verbal Comprehension. Spelling, Heim Vocabulary, and Arithmetic tests of the Basic Battery and PMA Verbal, Reasoning, and

Number subtests all load this factor heavily but not the CCFIT IQ's.

Factor 1, Spatial Orientation, is easily identified by the three CCFIT IQ's all of which load this factor above .80. Calendar, Newcastle Spatial Test, Form Board, and Paper Folding from the Basic Battery and the Spatial and Reasoning tests from the PMA identify factor 1. This analysis of the tests used in the Twin Study indicates that the three CCFIT IQ's are factorially very much like the spatial tests of the PMA and the Basic Battery.

The CCFIT manual claims there is good evidence that a high degree of independence from particular social skills has been reached in the CCFIT. The user is cautioned, however, not to interpret this to mean that the test has no correlation with social status. The manual points out that we must distinguish between a truly existing positive correlation caused by the natural tendency of people with greater mental capacity to enter more complex occupations and the spurious correlations due to persons of higher social status tending to have educational advantages with regard to those cultural skills which contaminate conventional IQ tests.

Our data show that the CCFIT by no means loses all correlation with social status. In fact, the combined scores of the two CCFIT scales correlate with socio-economic status as follows: Classical IQ, $-.36$; Culture Fair IQ, $-.38$; and Attainment-Contaminated IQ, $-.37$. (In the Twin Study low scores represent high SES). These r's differ insignificantly from those reported between the Basic Battery and SES, and between the PMA and SES.

So far, there appears to be little real difference between scores obtained on an omnibus intelligence test, a factor-pure IQ scale, and a culture fair intelligence test. The subjects are ranked pretty much the same by the three different tests.

From the CCFIT literature it would be expected that sex and race would contribute less to score variances of the CCFIT than to the more conventional tests, such as the PMA. A fourway analysis of variance was used to determine if score covariances of the nine CCFIT scores are attributable to any or all of the four classes—race, sex, zygosity, and social class.

Table IX–E shows that race and SES are the only significant main effects variables. SES effect is discounted for three reasons: (1) it occurs only on Form B; (2) it is only significant at the .05 level; (3) it disappears when Forms A and B are combined before the analysis is made. On the other hand, the race effect is highly significant. On all nine CCFIT IQ's race differences are significant at the .01 level.

Of the 99 possible interaction terms in the analysis, race-zygosity for the Culture Fair IQ on Form B is the only significant one, and it is most likely to be the result of a sampling accident.

Table IX–E
Effects Contributing to Differences in Means of Cattell Culture Fair IQ's Between Subpopulations: Race, Sex, Zygosity, and Socio-economic Status

IQ	SES	SEX	RACE	ZYGOSITY	SES × SEX	SES × RACE	SEX × RACE	SES × SEX × RACE	SES × ZYGOSITY	SEX × ZYGOSITY	SES × SEX × ZYG	RACE × ZYGOSITY	SES × RACE × ZYG	SEX × RACE × ZYG	SES × SEX × RACE × ZYG
Form A															
Classical			**												
Culture Fair			**												
Attainment- Contaminated			**												
Form B															
Classical	*		**												
Culture Fair	*		**										*			
Attainment- Contaminated	*		**												
Forms A + B															
Classical			**												
Culture Fair			**												
Attainment- Contaminated			**												

$* \, p < .05.$
$** \, p < .01.$

Least squares means for the Cattell test are shown in Table IX–F. Altogether there are nine IQ's: Classical IQ, Culture Fair IQ, and Attainment-Contaminated IQ for both Forms A and B, and three additional IQ's representing the combined scores of the two CCFIT forms. Although race was the only variable showing significant main effects on the CCFIT, means for sex, SES, and zygosity are listed in the table. The white-black differences on the CCFIT are by far the largest found on any test used in the Twin Survey. Classical IQ's for Form A differ by over 20 points for the two races. Even means on the Culture Fair IQ's differ by 14 or more points. Only 14–16% of the blacks earned scores reaching or exceeding the white means. This is not only true for the separate IQ's of each form but for the IQ's of the combined forms. Also shown in Table IX–F are the least squares means for the CCFIT by sex, zygosity, and social class. Differences are not significant. However, the direction of the difference is consistent with that found for tests of spatial ability on the Basic Battery and the Spatial subtest of the PMA. On the CCFIT boys > girls, high SES > middle SES > low SES, and MZ's > DZ's.

Table IX–F
Least Squares Means for *Cattell Culture Fair Intelligence Tests* By Race, Sex, Socio-economic Status, and Zygosity

IQ	Race		Sex		SES			Zygosity	
	W	B	M	F	1	2	3	MZ	DZ
Form A									
Classical	100.15	79.11	91.57	87.68	91.53	90.60	86.75	91.97	87.28
Culture Fair	98.90	82.37	91.99	89.27	92.64	91.97	87.28	92.94	88.32
Attainment-									
Contaminated	98.89	86.33	93.64	91.58	94.47	93.32	90.04	94.09	91.12
Form B									
Classical	98.84	81.49	91.22	89.11	94.33	91.43	84.74	92.54	87.79
Culture Fair	97.22	83.61	91.42	89.42	94.62	91.54	85.09	92.73	88.10
Attainment-									
Contaminated	97.89	87.58	93.51	91.96	95.98	93.14	89.09	94.53	90.94
Forms A + B									
Classical	99.75	80.52	91.62	88.65	93.14	91.25	86.02	92.50	87.77
Culture Fair	98.28	83.18	91.93	89.54	93.82	91.97	86.40	93.04	88.42
Attainment-									
Contaminated	98.65	87.17	93.78	92.03	95.45	93.47	89.81	94.54	91.27

Note. 1 = High SES group
2 = Middle SES group
3 = Low SES group

Since the race effect is highly significant, least squares means are computed for the nine CCFIT IQ's for SES, zygosity, and sex for each race (Table IX–G). Although the interactions are insignificant, interesting trends are observed in Table IX–G. For all nine CCFIT IQ's, blacks follow the pattern: high SES > middle SES > low SES. The pattern for whites is consistent but different: middle SES > high SES > low SES.

White MZ's consistently outperformed white DZ's on all nine CCFIT IQ's with differences ranging from five to ten points. Blacks, on the other hand, show almost no difference in MZ and DZ mean IQ's. On the nine test variables, differences range from zero to one IQ point.

The next step in the analysis of the CCFIT IQ's is to compute the heritability ratios for the nine separate IQ's (Table IX–H). Because of the large significant IQ differences between the races, heritability ratios will be reported for each race separately but not for the combined group. No within-pair F ratio is significant for any CCFIT IQ for the black group. For whites the F ratios for the Classical IQ on Form A and Classical IQ on the A plus B combination are significant. The finding of insignificant heritability ratios for all nine black IQ's contrasts with the PMA analysis which showed significant F ratios for blacks and the combined group but not for whites. The sample size is not a factor since the same twins were subjects for both the PMA and CCFIT anal-

Table IX-G

Least Squares Means for *Cattell Culture Fair Intelligence Test* for Socio-economic Status and Zygosity for Whites and Blacks

IQ	White			Black			White		Black		White		Black	
	SES 1	SES 2	SES 3	SES 1	SES 2	SES 3	MZ	DZ	MZ	DZ	M	F	M	F
Form A														
Classical	100.5	102.2	97.8	82.6	79.0	75.7	104.4	95.9	79.6	78.6	101.0	99.3	82.2	76.0
Culture Fair	100.0	101.4	95.3	85.2	82.6	79.3	103.1	94.7	82.8	81.9	98.7	99.0	85.2	79.5
Attainment-Contaminated	99.4	100.5	96.7	89.5	86.1	83.4	101.6	96.2	86.6	86.1	98.8	98.9	88.5	84.2
Form B														
Classical	99.8	103.3	93.4	88.9	79.5	76.1	103.8	93.8	81.2	81.7	99.4	98.3	83.1	79.9
Culture Fair	99.8	100.9	91.0	89.4	82.2	79.2	102.2	92.3	83.3	83.9	97.5	97.0	85.4	81.9
Attainment-Contaminated	99.5	100.1	94.1	92.4	86.2	84.1	101.3	94.5	87.7	87.4	98.2	97.6	88.8	86.3
Forms A + B														
Classical	100.4	103.0	95.9	85.9	79.5	76.1	104.4	95.1	80.6	80.4	100.4	99.1	82.8	78.2
Culture Fair	100.1	101.3	93.4	87.5	82.6	79.4	102.9	93.7	83.2	83.2	98.3	98.2	85.5	80.9
Attainment-Contaminated	99.7	100.6	95.7	91.2	86.4	84.0	101.7	95.6	87.4	87.0	98.7	98.6	88.8	85.5

Note. 1 = High SES group
2 = Middle SES group
3 = Low SES group

Table IX–H

Heritability Coefficients for Nine IQ's Derived from *Cattell Culture Fair Intelligence Test* for Black and White Twins: Classical Methods of Analysis

Culture Fair Intelligence Test	MZ		DZ			Heritability Ratios		Within-pair Variances		
	r	N	r	N	T(Cor)	H	HR	MZ	DZ	F
Form A—C IQ										
White	.75	34	.35	29	2.27	.61	1.07	118.2	227.6	1.93*
Black	.53	48	.55	32	−.08	−.08	−.05	225.7	178.8	.79
Form A—SCF IQ										
White	.66	34	.27	29	1.93	.53	1.18	177.7	208.4	1.17
Black	.63	48	.57	32	.36	.13	.17	107.5	69.6	.65
Form A—SAC IQ										
White	.69	34	.31	29	1.99	.55	1.11	84.2	104.4	1.24
Black	.54	48	.48	32	.32	.11	.21	92.8	81.9	.88
Form B—C IQ										
White	.63	34	.29	29	1.64	.48	1.07	142.6	189.6	1.33
Black	.61	48	.52	32	.55	.19	.30	151.8	211.4	1.39
Form B—SCF IQ										
White	.62	34	.36	29	1.29	.40	.82	177.0	117.3	.66
Black	.54	48	.44	32	.57	.19	.38	135.6	118.3	.87
Form B—SAC IQ										
White	.64	34	.30	29	1.66	.48	1.05	78.2	76.1	.97
Black	.52	48	.45	32	.39	.13	.28	82.0	104.8	1.28
Forms A + B—C IQ										
White	.82	34	.38	29	2.84	.71	1.08	67.1	161.7	2.41**
Black	.66	48	.58	32	.55	.19	.24	129.6	154.1	1.19
Forms A + B—SCF IQ										
White	.79	34	.41	29	2.44	.65	.98	86.8	110.8	1.28
Black	.76	48	.60	32	1.20	.38	.40	62.4	63.5	1.02
Forms A + B—SAC IQ										
White	.81	34	.38	29	2.78	.70	1.07	38.8	66.2	1.71
Black	.67	48	.52	32	1.01	.32	.46	52.2	74.5	1.43

* *p* < .05.
** *p* < .01.
Note. C IQ = Classical IQ
      SCF IQ = Standard Score, Culture Fair IQ
      SAC IQ = Standard Score, Attainment-Contaminated IQ

yses. The black group is about 25% larger than the white. No explanation is offered for the attenuated heritability ratios on the CCFIT for blacks. However, for what it is worth, it could be pointed out that black DZ twins are much more alike on the CCFIT than on either of the other test batteries. Intraclass correlations for black fraternal twins exceed the theoretically expected *r* of .50 in two-thirds of the cases; while on all tests the white DZ intraclass *r*'s are smaller than .42. While intraclass *r*'s for black MZ's are somewhat smaller than for whites, they are not significantly different from the MZ *r*'s found on the Basic Battery and the PMA tests. If anything, both kinds of black twins seem to be more alike on the CCFIT than on any of the other tests of mental ability.

It is obvious from the above discussion that CCFIT differs from other IQ tests more in appearance than substance. Although the CCFIT lacks the verbal, numerical, and reasoning subtests usually found on IQ tests, individuals and groups perform about the same as they do on other standardized paper and pencil IQ tests. Sex, SES, and zygosity differences are insignificant while differences in means for the two races are highly significant on all nine CCFIT combinations.

If culture fairness is equated with identity, no significant differences in mean scores would be expected between subpopulations. In three out of four comparisons (sex, SES, and zygosity), the Cattell test could certainly be called culture fair. In the fourth case (race comparison), mean differences on the CCFIT are greater than found on standard IQ tests. As Thorndike (1971) has pointed out, it hardly seems useful to equate fairness with identity. This type of definition prejudges the reality of differences between groups, ruling them out *a priori*. Cleary (1968) has proposed another definition of culture fairness which says that a test is culture fair for two populations if a regression equation based on one group neither systematically over or under predicts the level of performance for members of the second group. Using spelling and arithmetic test performance as school achievement criteria and the CCFIT scores as predictors, regression equations were obtained for each race separately. In the case of arithmetic achievement, the regression lines for the two groups almost coincide. For most test scores, the predicted criterion score for an individual is about the same in both groups. Using the Cattell Classical IQ (A + B), a score of 80 predicts an arithmetic achievement score of 95 for a member of the black group and 94 for a member of the white group. For a Classical IQ of 100, the predicted arithmetic score is 103 for members of both groups. A Cattell Classical IQ of 110 predicts 107.7 for blacks and 107.9 for whites. By Cleary's definition, the A plus B combination of Classical IQ scores on the CCFIT is fair when used to predict arithmetic achievement. The regression equations based on whites neither systematically over nor under predict arithmetic achievement for blacks.

The slopes of the two regression lines differ markedly for spelling achievement. A Cattell Classical IQ of 80 predicts a spelling score of 94 for blacks and 95 for whites. A CCFIT Classical IQ of 88 predicts a spelling score of 97 for both groups. For an IQ of 110, the predicted spelling score for whites is 103, for blacks 107.

Spelling and arithmetic scores for all 286 subjects are predicted from CCFIT IQ regression equations, first using own-race derived equations and then opposite-race equations. The object is to determine if school achievement scores of either race are systematically over or underpre-

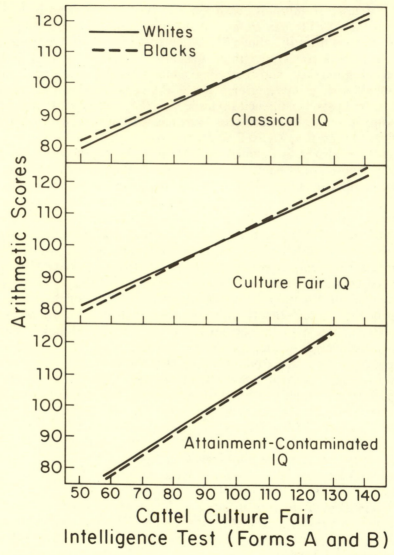

Figure IX–1. Regression lines for predicting arithmetic achievement scores for whites and blacks from Cattell's *Culture Fair Intelligence Test.*

dicted, using the equation for the opposite race. From the regression lines for arithmetic achievement shown in Figure IX–1 it is clear that there is little difference in the own-race/opposite-race equations. Table IX–I shows the difference in percentage of subjects whose arithmetic achievement was overpredicted by the two equations. No difference is significant.

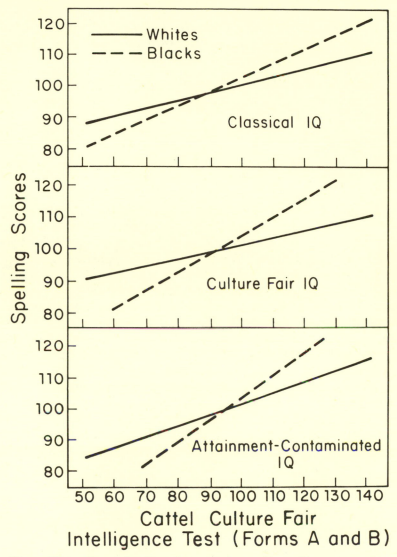

Figure IX-2. Regression lines for predicting spelling achievement scores for whites and blacks from Cattell's *Culture Fair Intelligence Test.*

Inspection of the regression lines for blacks and whites for spelling achievement predicted from the three CCFIT IQ's (Figure IX–2) suggests greater differences than those for arithmetic achievement. For spelling achievement, a higher percentage of whites and blacks was overpredicted by opposite-race regression equations than by own-race equations. However, spelling achievement for neither race is systematically over or under-

Table IX–I

Percentage of Blacks and Whites Whose Arithmetic Test Scores Were Overpredicted by the *Cattell Culture Fair Intelligence Test:* Using Both Own-race and Opposite-race Regression Equations

Culture Fair Intelligence Test (Forms A + B)	Whites			Blacks		
	Own-race	Opposite-race	Difference	Own-race	Opposite-race	Difference
Classical IQ	47	48	1	56	52	4
Culture Fair IQ	50	48	2	54	57	3
Attainment-Contaminated IQ	50	50	0	54	54	0

Note. No percentage difference is significant.

predicted by the opposite-race prediction equation. Low-scoring blacks are overpredicted by the white formula and low-scoring whites are underpredicted by the black equation. For high-scoring pupils, the opposite is true. In no case, however, are the own-race/opposite-race percentage differences significant (see Table IX–J).

Thorndike points out that Cleary's definition of fairness assumes the available criterion score is a perfectly relevant, unbiased, and reliable measure of job competence or school achievement. If the criterion is biased in an unknown direction, no procedure can be set up for fair use of the test. In the present study, spelling and arithmetic were the only school achievement criteria available. The reliability of the Spelling Test is .93; Arithmetic Test, .85. Nothing can be said as to whether the achievement tests are unbiased, although in most school programs spelling and arithmetic scores are relevant criteria of school achievement. In discussing culture fairness, Thorndike makes another point: when two groups differ on both the test and the criterion, the test might not be fair for the group earning the lower mean score. For example, in the case of predicting arithmetic scores from CCFIT Classical IQ's, the two groups differ by .98 standard deviation on the test and by .58 standard deviation on the criterion. If the distributions are normal and the standard

Table IX–J

Percentage of Blacks and Whites Whose Spelling Test Scores Were Overpredicted by the *Cattell Culture Fair Intelligence Test:* Using Both Own-race and Opposite-race Regression Equations

Culture Fair Intelligence Test (Forms A + B)	Whites			Blacks		
	Own-race	Opposite-race	Difference	Own-race	Opposite-race	Difference
Classical IQ	44	56	12	47	51	4
Culture Fair IQ	44	55	11	46	54	8
Attainment-Contaminated IQ	43	54	11	46	54	8

Note. No percentage difference is significant.

deviations equivalent, we would find that about 16% of the black group would reach the mean of the white group on the test, while 22% of the black group would come up to the mean of the white on the criterion. If the white group average was set as a cutoff score, 50% of the whites, compared to only 16% of the blacks, would meet the criterion. Since only 22% of the blacks would reach the critical score on the criterion, a slightly larger percentage of the black group would meet the criterion than would have been predicted by the test.

There is still another way of looking at the culture fairness problem. Jensen (1968) says, though two tests may give the same degree of prediction in college or the Armed Services, if the tests differ in heritability, it is quite possible that a candidate screened out in a selection procedure by one of the tests would be retained by a procedure using a different test as predictor. Jensen sees heritability as a criterion of culture fairness in ability testing because

> the inventors and developers of intelligence tests—men such as Galton, Binet, Spearman, Burt, Thorndike, and Terman—clearly intended that their tests assess as clearly as possible the individual's innate brightness or mental capacity. If this is what a test attempts to do, then clearly the appropriate criterion for judging the test's "fairness" is the *heritability* of the test scores in the population in which the test is used. The quite high values of H for tests such as the Stanford-Binet attests to the success of the test-maker's aim to measure innate ability. The square root of the heritability, ($\sqrt{H}$), represents the correlation between phenotype and genotype, and, is of the order of .9 for our best standard intelligence tests (1968, p. 94).

To Jensen a test may have the same predictability in two populations but still have different heritability ratios. This is exactly what we find for the Cattell test. There is no significant difference between blacks and whites in the predictability of arithmetic achievement from CCFIT IQ's, but there is a difference in heritability between blacks and whites for CCFIT IQ's.

The true meaning of culture fairness testing has to apply to the fair use of test results by psychologists rather than to the culture fairness of a particular test. Thorndike (1971) has pointed out if the criterion measure is itself biased in an unknown direction and degree, no rational procedure can be set up for "fair" use of the test. To determine, for two different groups, what test scores predict a given criterion is fruitless if the criterion does not mean the same thing in the two groups. By the same token, setting up group quotas based on specified criterion ratings previously achieved by others is fruitless if the criterion rating signifies different things in the two groups.

X

Filial Regression of IQ

In *Natural Inheritance,* published in 1889, Galton summarized the ideas on heredity and regression he had developed over the previous two decades. In the book he offers solutions to three questions: (1) How do characteristics of parents relate to the same characteristics in the offspring? (2) What is the relative correlation of each ancestor to the nature of the offspring? (3) How is it possible to measure nearness of kinship?

Unsatisfied with the qualitative assessments in *Hereditary Genius,* 1869, Galton sought advice from Darwin, who suggested his cousin should look at less complex forms of life and try breeding sweet peas. The results of his experiments—conducted with the assistance of nine associates—were reported in an 1877 paper, "Typical Laws of Heredity." In this paper, he used weight of seeds as a parental characteristic, noting that daughter seeds were not as extreme as the parent seeds. He speaks of their "reverting" to the average ancestral type. Reversion, he explained, was the tendency of the mean filial type to depart from the parental type reverting to what may be roughly, and perhaps fairly, described as the average ancestral type. The term reversion has now been replaced by the statistical term regression.

For almost a decade Galton published nothing more on this subject. Recognizing that he needed data from human family records to further test his hypothesis, he said:

> It was anthropological evidence that I desired, caring only for the seeds as means of throwing light on heredity in man. I tried in vain for a long and weary time to obtain it in sufficient abundance, and my failure was a cogent motive, together with others, in inducing me to make an offer of prizes for family records, which was largely

responded to, and furnished me last year with what I wanted. (Galton, 1885a, p. 1207)

Galton provided a graphical representation of his findings that human offspring tend to regress in stature toward the ancestral average. From Figure X–1, it is seen that children of tall parents on the average are not as tall as their parents nor are the children of short parents as short. Galton found the deviation in stature of the offspring from the average to be two-thirds the deviation of its mid-parentage; i.e., the average of the two parents. In his discussion, he was careful to point out that adjustments for sex differences in stature were made and that he had determined that stature was not a factor in choice of a marriage partner. He explains his findings this way:

The child inherits partly from his parents, partly from his ancestry. Speaking generally, the further his genealogy goes back, the more

Rate of Regression in Hereditary Stature.

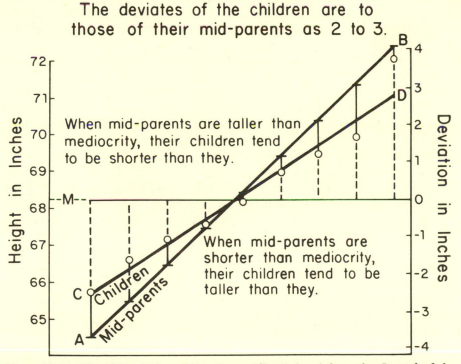

Figure X–1. Regression in hereditary stature. (Reproduced from the *Journal of the Anthropological Institute*, 1885, *15*, 248–249.)

numerous and varied will his ancestry become, until they cease to differ from any equally numerous sample taken at haphazard from the race at large. Their mean stature will then be the same as that of the race; in other words, it will be mediocre. (Galton, 1885b, p. 252)

According to Galton's biographer, D. W. Forrest (1974), *Natural Inheritance* was apparently written in some haste since there were several errors. Forrest believes the work would have been vastly improved if Galton had delayed publication until his paper on correlation was ready since the major fault was Galton's misinterpretation of regression. Offspring are not forced toward mediocrity by the pressure of remote ancestry but because of the less than perfect correlation between parents and offspring.

The Twin Study provides an opportunity to examine the phenomenon of filial regression from a different aspect. Following Galton's reasoning siblings would be expected to depart from the parental type and revert to the average ancestral type.

In one experiment, Galton used stature of mid-parent to demonstrate the heritability and filial regression of stature in children. The relationship between mid-parent and child for stature also holds true for fingerprint ridges and other polygenetically inherited characteristics, including IQ. Since full sibs share the same relationship to each other as mid-parent to child, like-sexed DZ twins should be ideal subjects for a new and different look at the question of filial regression. DZ's not only have the same age, sex, race, and zygosity, but they also have been reared together and have experienced the same or quite similar environmental influences. The twins we will study in this chapter have lived all their lives at home and attended the same schools, though they were not always in the same grade.

To apply the idea of regression to the sample of DZ twins, we must first determine if the system of identifying twins within a set yields random selection; if not, a bias would be introduced into all further computations in this chapter. For purposes of identification, each set of twins was given a three-digit identification number, twins within a pair being assigned in addition a number 1 or 2 (for example, 234–1 and 234–2). The first three digits identified the pair, the last digit the twins within a pair. The mean stature of twins #1 was 64.85 inches; twins #2, 64.73. Mean IQ for twins #1 was 98.68; twins #2, 98.50. The fractional differences are not statistically significant.

The next step was to apply the concept of filial regression of stature to the sample. For each race separately and for the total group, height in inches of twins #1 was correlated with that of twins #2 (Table X–A). Correlations between DZ twins are higher than the correlation

Table X–A
Comparisons of Stature of DZ Twins

	Number	Mean in Inches	Standard Deviation	r_{T1-T2}*	Regression Equation
White					
Twin #1	41	65.71	4.15		
Twin #2	41	65.85	3.50	.7369	$Y = .6215X + 25.01$
Black					
Twin #1	39	63.95	3.46		
Twin #2	39	63.54	2.88	.6671	$Y = .5553X + 28.03$
Total					
Twin #1	80	64.85	3.91		
Twin #2	80	64.73	3.40	.7266	$Y = .6318X + 23.76$

* Pearson r's, not intraclass correlations.

for sibs reported by Burt and Howard (1956), who found an r of .54 for stature but lower than that reported in the classical study of Newman, Freeman, and Holzinger (1937), who found the correlation for standing height for fraternal twins to be .934. The theoretical correlation, assuming assortative mating and partial dominance, is .54.

The purpose of this part of our experiment was not to rediscover what Galton called filial regression but to compare the filial regression of DZ twins on a genetically determined physical measurement, stature, to IQ.

Next we plotted regression lines from the equations in Table X–A. Regressions in stature of twins #2 on twins #1 for whites, blacks, and total group are shown in Figure X–2. The DZ twins in the sample demonstrate the same regression in height that Galton found from mid-parent to child. This was no surprise since DZ twins have the same genetic relationship to each other as mid-parent has to child.

The regression lines in Figure X–2 show the effect clearly. When twin #1 is shorter than the average of his group, twin #2 tends to be taller. The reverse is true if twin #1 is taller than his group average. For subjects near the mean in height, the regression lines are congruent and the effect is less noticeable. By substituting height in inches of twin #1 in the appropriate formula, it is possible to estimate the height of his co-twin.

Although the number of DZ twin pairs with known stature is less than optimum, our results convincingly demonstrate the filial regression of stature for like-sexed DZ twins.

To compare the regression of stature with that of IQ, we repeated the steps of the experiment, this time using all DZ twins—133 white and 47 black pairs. IQ's had been obtained previously as part of the psychological testing reported in Chapter VII. Means, standard deviations, and regression equations are shown in Table X–B. The difference in means between pairs amounts to only a fraction of an IQ point for whites, whereas blacks differ by 1.35 points. Neither difference is statistically significant. The IQ correlations in the sample compare favorably

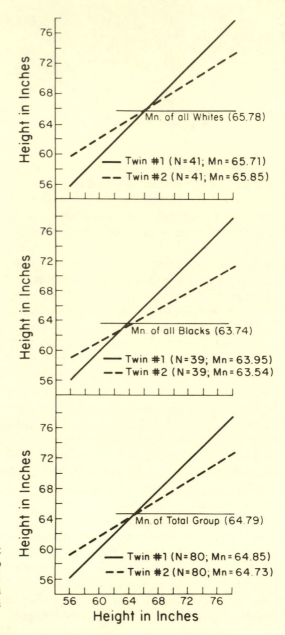

Figure X–2. Regression in height for whites, blacks, and total group of DZ twins. Note: When twin #1 of a pair is taller than average, twin #2 tends to be shorter than twin #1.

Table X–B
Comparisons of Intelligence Quotients of DZ Twins

	Number	Mean	Standard Deviation	r_{T1-T2}*	Regression Equation
White					
Twin #1	133	101.49	9.73		
Twin #2	133	100.77	9.73	.6334	$Y = .6334X + 36.49$
Black					
Twin #1	47	90.74	7.25		
Twin #2	47	92.09	7.46	.5439	$Y = .5597X + 41.31$
Total					
Twin #1	180	98.68	10.29		
Twin #2	180	98.50	9.94	.6839	$Y = .6606X + 33.31$

* Pearson r's, not intraclass correlations.

with those in Jensen's (1969) review of 11 studies of same-sexed DZ twins. Assuming assortative mating and partial dominance, the median r for the 11 studies was .54.

The next task was to plot the regression lines for IQ from the equations shown in Table X–B. The graphs in Figure X–3 are quite similar to those for stature. In the case of IQ, if one twin of a DZ pair has an IQ either above or below his group mean, then the other twin of the pair will, on the average, regress approximately halfway to the mean of his respective population, not to the mean of the combined populations. This regression is in accordance with the genetic prediction.

The regression effect is seen even more clearly in Table X–C where obtained IQ's for all #2 twins are shown opposite those for #1 twins. The same table contains the theoretical IQ values for twins #2, assuming random mating and only additive genes; i.e., the simplest polygenic model. Table X–C should be read this way. For the total group, the #1 twins with IQ's falling in the 80–81 interval (midpoint 80.5) would, theoretically, have co-twins with an average IQ of 89.7, which is about midway between 80.5 and 98.6—the mean for the combined group. The obtained mean for the co-twins was 85.0. Despite the regression not being as great as predicted, it converged toward the group mean exactly as Galton's Law prescribed.

To take another example from Table X–C, the IQ of twin #1 is 110. The theoretical IQ of his co-twin is 104.2; his obtained IQ was 106.1. In this case the IQ of twin #1 was above the group mean. Regression was toward the mean but in the opposite direction of the previous case.

In Table X–D white DZ twins are arranged like the combined group. The regression phenomenon is as obvious as before, except in this instance regression is toward the white IQ mean, 101.1. When twin #1 has an

IQ above his own group mean, his co-twin will tend to have an IQ between that of twin #1 and the group mean. For IQ's around the mean, the differences are only fractions of an IQ point. In Table X–D the regression phenomenon is quite dramatic. Although the obtained

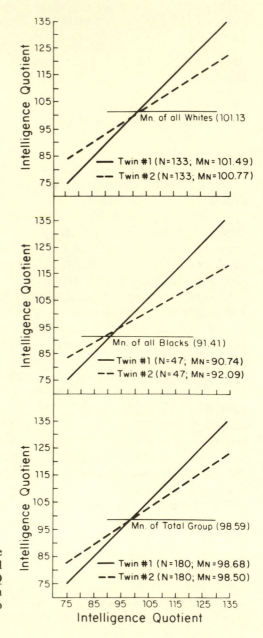

Figure X–3. Regression in intelligence quotient for whites, blacks, and total group of DZ twins. Note: When the IQ of twin #1 of a pair is greater than average, the IQ of twin #2 tends to be lower than that of twin #1.

Table X–C
Distribution of Theoretical and Obtained IQ's for 180 Pairs of Black and White DZ Twins (Mean IQ = 98.6)

	IQ Intervals	Obtained IQ		Theoretical IQ*	
Number of Pairs	Twin #1	Twin #2 Mean	Direction of Regression	Twin #2 Mean	Direction of Regression
3	78–79	83.7	+	88.8	+
2	80–81	85.0	+	89.7	+
3	82–83	84.3	+	90.7	+
11	84–85	88.4	+	91.7	+
5	86–87	89.8	+	92.6	+
15	88–89	90.9	+	93.6	+
11	90–91	94.3	+	94.6	+
10	92–93	95.9	+	95.5	+
9	94–95	95.0	+	96.5	+
15	96–97	99.6	+	97.4	+
15	98–99	98.3	−	98.4	−
16	100–101	99.7	−	99.4	−
10	102–103	102.4	−	100.3	−
9	104–105	101.9	−	101.3	−
10	106–107	103.9	−	102.3	−
7	108–109	104.0	−	103.2	−
7	110–111	106.1	−	104.2	−
7	112–113	108.4	−	105.2	−
5	114–115	110.0	−	106.1	−
3	116–117	110.3	−	107.1	−
4	118–119	106.8	−	108.1	−
3	120 & up	113.0	−	112.2	−

* Assuming random mating and only additive genes; i.e., the simplest possible polygenic model, $r = .50$.

IQ's for twins #2 do not follow the theoretical pattern exactly, the trend is unmistakable.

Black DZ twins are shown in Table X–E. The number of subjects is relatively small, 47 pairs. Nevertheless the regression phenomenon is quite clear. This time regression is toward the black mean, IQ 91.4, not the mean of the combined group. In two different intervals the regression effect does not follow the expected theoretical pattern; that is, the obtained IQ of twin #2 shows a sign opposite from that expected. In the IQ interval 82–83 there was only one #1 black twin. In the 94–95 interval two twin pairs were represented. The #1 twin of pair 034 earned an IQ of 95; his co-twin's was 99. For twin pair 296, however, #1 had an IQ of 94; his co-twin's IQ was 78. This unusually large difference for one set of twins accounts for the apparent shift in the regression effect seen in Table X–E. Otherwise, regression is in the expected direction in accordance with Galton. Blacks regress toward the mean for blacks and not toward the mean of the combined group.

Table X–D
Distribution of Theoretical and Obtained IQ's for 133 Pairs of White DZ Twins
(Mean IQ = 101.1)

	IQ Intervals	Obtained IQ		Theoretical IQ*	
Number of Pairs	Twin #1	Twin #2 Mean	Direction of Regression	Twin #2 Mean	Direction of Regression
6	85 & below	85.3	+	91.6	+
2	86–87	94.5	+	93.3	+
8	88–89	90.3	+	94.3	+
7	90–91	92.6	+	95.3	+
4	92–93	98.8	+	96.3	+
7	94–95	96.9	+	97.3	+
11	96–97	100.5	+	98.3	+
14	98–99	98.5	0	99.3	+
12	100–101	101.3	+	100.3	−
9	102–103	102.8	+	101.3	−
8	104–105	103.1	−	102.3	−
10	106–107	103.9	−	103.3	−
7	108–109	104.0	−	104.3	−
7	110–111	106.1	−	105.3	−
6	112–113	108.3	−	106.3	−
5	114–115	110.0	−	107.3	−
3	116–117	110.3	−	108.3	−
4	118–119	106.8	−	109.3	−
3	120 & up	113.0	−	113.5	−

* Assuming random mating and only additive genes; i.e., the simplest possible polygenic model, $r = .50$.

Table X–E
Distribution of Theoretical and Obtained IQ's for 47 Pairs of Black DZ Twins
(Mean IQ = 91.4)

	IQ Intervals	Obtained IQ		Theoretical IQ*	
Number of Pairs	Twin #1	Twin #2 Mean	Direction of Regression	Twin #2 Mean	Direction of Regression
2	78–79	86.5	+	85.8	+
2	80–81	85.0	+	86.8	+
1	82–83	81.0	−	87.9	+
8	84–85	88.8	+	88.9	+
3	86–87	86.7	+	89.9	+
7	88–89	91.6	+	90.9	+
4	90–91	97.3	+	92.0	+
6	92–93	94.0	+	93.0	+
2	94–95	88.5	−	94.0	−
4	96–97	97.0	+	95.1	−
1	98–99	96.0	−	96.1	−
4	100–101	94.8	−	97.1	−
1	102–103	99.0	−	98.1	−
2	104 & up	100.5	−	101.2	−

* Assuming random mating and only additive genes; i.e., the simplest possible polygenic model, $r = .50$.

Newman, Freeman, Holzinger, and many other investigators have found DZ twin correlations for both physiological and mental characteristics similar to those reported here. Needless to say, the findings of this study are not presented as new evidence but to demonstrate with new and original data Galton's Law of Filial Regression, which is consistent for both physical and mental characteristics and which would be difficult to reconcile with any strictly environmental theory of the causes of differences in height or in IQ.

XI

Stability of IQ

In his reply to Jensen's *Harvard Educational Review* article (1969), Arthur Stinchcombe (1969) claimed that environments accumulate in much the same way as interest does when compounded. A modest initial difference of 2% in environment results after 20 years in a 150% difference. Johnson (1963) found no evidence of early environmental influence on IQ. Based on his analysis of the classical study of Newman *et al.* (1937), Johnson asserted "results do not support the idea that similarity in early environmental enrichment or deprivation is related to later IQ similarity in children" (p. 748).

If length of time spent in the same environment has a significant effect on intelligence test performance, then younger individuals who are genetically identical (MZ twins) should resemble their twins less closely than older identical twins. As age increases, mean difference in IQ between twin pairs should decrease. The same trend would be expected for fraternal (DZ) twins except that initial and final differences would be greater than for MZ twins. We would also expect the correlation between age and IQ difference for both MZ and DZ twins to be negative if environmental influences are cumulative.

Four hundred twenty-seven pairs of twins, living together at home with their parents or guardians, were tested in Kentucky and Georgia with a large battery of mental ability tests described by Vandenberg (1970), Osborne *et al.* (1968), and Osborne (1978). Factor analysis of the 12 Basic Battery tests produced three distinctly separate factors: (1) verbal, (2) spatial, and (3) perceptual speed. The factors were used to generate IQ's. The average of the three factor IQ's is the full scale IQ. Zygosity of the twins was determined by the method described by Osborne (1978).

Among the 427 pairs of twins 123 or 29% are black. According to the U.S. census, the population of Georgia in 1970 was 26% black. The large number of black twins will provide data for the examination of the Stinchcombe hypothesis by race as well as for the total group. In Table XI–A black twins are grouped by age with mean differences in IQ between pairs shown at each age level. With the exception of the 18–20 age level which contains only one pair of MZ twins, the MZ–DZ differences for the full scale IQ were in the expected direction, MZ < DZ. Inspection of the IQ difference means for the various age levels shows no discernible trend for any of the four factor IQ's. The full scale IQ difference of 12.4 points for the one set of MZ twins in the 18–20 age group is almost three times the average difference of the other age levels. There were four pairs of DZ twins in the 18–20 age group. The average difference between these twins was smaller than at any other age level for DZ's.

Table XI–B shows mean IQ differences at six age levels for the white twins. The MZ < DZ full scale difference is found in all age groups from 12 to 20. There is no trend for the IQ difference to be greater at one age level than another.

In Table XI–C the black and white twins are combined. As would be expected the trend of differences is unrelated to age of twins. Although the greatest full scale IQ difference among MZ's is in the oldest age group, the greatest difference for full scale IQ among DZ's is at the youngest age level.

A second test of the cumulative environmental effect on IQ is made by computing intraclass correlations by race at each age level for all four factor IQ's. The intraclass correlation reflects the crucial relationship between the within-family and the between-family variance. The correlation will be 1.0 if co-twins always receive the same score, and 0.0 if co-twins are no more likely to receive the same score than two individuals selected at random (Fuller & Thompson, 1960).

The cumulative environmental hypothesis would predict a monotonic increase in intraclass r's with age. Tables XI–D, XI–E, and XI–F show the intraclass r's for blacks, whites, and the combined group of twins. With the exception of the two extreme age groups for DZ blacks, the findings are remarkably consistent. For the full scale IQ the expected MZ < DZ difference in correlation is found at every age level for each race separately and for total group. Since the intraclass r's in Tables XI–D, XI–E, and XI–F show no systematic change with age, the cumulative environmental hypothesis which would predict a monotonic increase in r's with age must be rejected.

A further test of the cumulative environmental effects is given by the Pearson correlation coefficient computed between individual pair differences in IQ and age. The purpose of this analysis is to examine the claim that twins living in the same environment would become more

Table XI–A
Mean Within-pair Differences of Four Factor IQ's for Black MZ and DZ Twins at Six Age Levels

Age	MZ					DZ				
	No.	Verbal	Spatial	Perceptual Speed	Full Scale	No.	Verbal	Spatial	Perceptual Speed	Full Scale
12–13	14	3.79	8.10	11.35	4.59	9	9.02	9.33	20.79	11.01
14	22	5.26	6.45	8.48	4.03	8	4.78	7.01	15.09	7.65
15	13	7.51	5.44	8.77	2.54	13	7.77	4.09	12.76	6.55
16	17	4.12	5.02	15.04	4.13	7	5.50	8.41	6.41	5.61
17	9	5.92	3.39	9.95	4.23	6	7.08	4.38	12.75	7.25
18–20	1	4.10	15.90	16.90	12.40	4	5.88	5.63	3.73	4.03

Note. All twins did not take all tests. Numbers in this table represent the total number of pairs of twins who participated in the study.

Table XI–B
Mean Within-pair Differences of Four Factor IQ's for White MZ and DZ Twins at Six Age Levels

Age	MZ					DZ				
	No.	Verbal	Spatial	Perceptual Speed	Full Scale	No.	Verbal	Spatial	Perceptual Speed	Full Scale
12–13	21	6.32	5.14	7.88	4.16	18	8.02	10.49	10.44	8.14
14	28	4.88	4.54	6.11	3.40	21	6.57	7.04	11.08	5.83
15	39	6.63	6.52	9.37	4.75	26	8.18	10.33	9.49	6.39
16	33	6.24	5.13	7.89	4.27	31	10.03	7.01	12.31	7.75
17	32	4.74	5.37	8.72	4.01	22	6.73	4.93	9.82	6.13
18–20	18	3.62	4.24	7.98	4.84	15	8.63	8.89	7.39	5.99

Note. All twins did not take all tests. Numbers in this table represent the total number of pairs of twins who participated in the study.

Table XI-C
Mean Within-pair Differences of Four Factor IQ's for all MZ and DZ Twins at Six Age Levels

	MZ					DZ				
Age	No.	Verbal	Spatial	Perceptual Speed	Full Scale	No.	Verbal	Spatial	Perceptual Speed	Full Scale
12–13	35	5.31	6.33	9.29	4.33	27	8.36	10.10	14.02	9.10
14	50	5.05	5.38	7.15	3.68	29	6.07	7.03	12.27	6.33
15	52	6.85	6.25	9.23	4.19	39	8.04	8.25	10.58	6.44
16	50	5.52	5.09	10.37	4.22	38	9.19	7.27	11.20	7.36
17	41	5.00	4.94	8.97	4.06	28	6.80	4.81	10.45	6.37
18–20	19	3.65	4.85	8.50	5.24	19	8.05	8.20	6.58	5.58

Note. All twins did not take all tests. Numbers in this table represent the total number of pairs of twins who participated in the study.

Table XI-D
Intraclass Correlations for Black MZ and DZ Twins for Four Factor IQ's at Six Age Levels

	MZ					DZ				
Age	No.	Verbal	Spatial	Perceptual Speed	Full Scale	No.	Verbal	Spatial	Perceptual Speed	Full Scale
12–13	14	.94	.51	.27	.72	9	-.22	-.20	-.51	-.69
14	22	.77	.60	.64	.79	8	.87	.55	.13	.68
15	13	.75	.88	.49	.91	13	.43	.84	.52	.49
16	17	.85	.79	.50	.78	7	.80	-.33	.66	.47
17	9	.79	.97	.64	.83	6	.11	.56	.54	.05
18–20	1	—	—	—	—	4	—	—	—	—

Note. All twins did not take all tests. Numbers in this table represent the total number of pairs of twins who participated in the study.

Table XI–E

Intraclass Correlations for White MZ and DZ Twins for Four Factor IQ's at Six Age Levels

| | MZ | | | | | DZ | | | | |
Age	No.	Verbal	Spatial	Perceptual Speed	Full Scale	No.	Verbal	Spatial	Perceptual Speed	Full Scale
12–13	21	.79	.72	.76	.87	18	.46	.36	.44	.36
14	28	.87	.87	.86	.88	21	.77	.76	.49	.74
15	39	.72	.67	.65	.77	26	.57	.42	.68	.63
16	33	.78	.84	.80	.85	31	.43	.56	.39	.41
17	32	.89	.82	.73	.88	22	.62	.76	.67	.69
18–20	18	.91	.88	.81	.81	15	.59	.57	.60	.72

Note. All twins did not take all tests. Numbers in this table represent the total number of pairs of twins who participated in the study.

Table XI–F

Intraclass Correlations for all MZ and DZ Twins for Four Factor IQ's at Six Age Levels

| | MZ | | | | | DZ | | | | |
Age	No.	Verbal	Spatial	Perceptual Speed	Full Scale	No.	Verbal	Spatial	Perceptual Speed	Full Scale
12–13	35	.86	.63	.60	.83	27	.33	.23	.02	.05
14	50	.83	.78	.78	.85	29	.80	.73	.45	.73
15	52	.73	.76	.63	.81	39	.54	.53	.62	.60
16	50	.80	.83	.70	.83	38	.51	.49	.45	.44
17	41	.88	.85	.71	.87	28	.55	.74	.66	.61
18–20	19	.91	.82	.78	.76	19	.63	.57	.68	.70

Note. All twins did not take all tests. Numbers in this table represent the total number of pairs of twins who participated in the study.

alike in mental capacity as they grow older; that is, the correlation between age and IQ differences between twins should become increasingly negative as the twins grow older.

In Tables XI–G, XI–H, and XI–I correlation coefficients are shown between IQ differences and age for blacks, whites, and combined group. Of the 24 correlations only 4 are significant; two were on the perceptual speed IQ which is composed of only one test. For MZ black twins the spatial factor showed a significant negative correlation of −.24 which is barely significant at the .05 level. From the tables it is clear that between ages 12 and 20, environmental effects are not cumulative for this sample of 427 pairs of twins. Changes in correlations between age and IQ difference for both MZ and DZ twins from age to age appear to be random rather than systematic or suggestive of a trend.

Table XI–G

Correlations Between Age and Within-pair IQ Differences for Black Twins, Ages 12 to 20

	No.	Verbal	Spatial	Perceptual Speed	Full Scale
MZ Twins	76	.09	−.24*	.07	.02
DZ Twins	47	−.11	−.19	−.36*	−.28

Note. All twins did not take all tests. Numbers in this table represent the total number of pairs of twins who participated in the study.
   * $p < .05$.

Table XI–H

Correlations Between Age and Within-pair IQ Differences for White Twins, Ages 12 to 20

	No.	Verbal	Spatial	Perceptual Speed	Full Scale
MZ Twins	171	−.13	−.02	.05	.04
DZ Twins	133	.04	−.15	−.05	−.07

Note. All twins did not take all tests. Numbers in this table represent the total number of pairs of twins who participated in the study.

Table XI–I

Correlations Between Age and Within-pair IQ Differences for all Twins, Ages 12 to 20

	No.	Verbal	Spatial	Perceptual Speed	Full Scale
MZ Twins	247	−.06	−.10	.03	.04
DZ Twins	180	.01	−.15*	−.17	−.14

Note. All twins did not take all tests. Numbers in this table represent the total number of pairs of twins who participated in the study.
   * $p < .05$.

XII

Subpopulation Differences in Personality

Subpopulation differences in personality will be examined by using *How Well Do You Know Yourself?* (Jenkins, 1959) and *High School Personality Questionnaire* (Cattell, 1969) to measure the various personality parameters. The task will not be simple because test experts do not agree on a satisfactory definition of personality. Even when a tentative definition is reached, the methods of assessing this elusive construct are frequently in dispute. Eysenck's (1976) definition, "semi-permanent behavior patterns characteristic of individuals and of social importance and relevance" (p. 198), seems to be what most psychologists have in mind when they use the term, personality.

Individual differences are obviously central to the personality concept, but there are many accidental and unexpected differences between individuals which would not be part of personality. While Eysenck's definition may be generally acceptable, the surfeit of personality scales attests to the lack of consensus among designers of personality tests. Eysenck finds the most popular personality scales, the *MMPI, Edward's Personality Scale,* and the *California Personality Inventory,* to have face validity but little else to recommend them. Of Cattell's personality test, Eysenck (1972) says, "Cattell's hypothesis of 16 functionally independent factors being measured by his test requires considerable support if it is to continue being accepted by test users" (p. 265).

How Well Do You Know Yourself? was reviewed for the *Sixth Mental Measurements Yearbook* by no less an authority than Lee J. Cronbach (1965), who found the test to be "a reasonably well-edited and well-grouped collection of items" but completely unvalidated with respect to practical decisions. The norm group, he adds, is "damnably inadequate."

Despite its drawbacks, Jenkins' *How Well Do You Know Yourself?*

was administered to 280 sets of twins as part of the battery of the Twin Study. It was replaced by Cattell's *High School Personality Questionnaire* in the battery given to the extended sample of 142 twin pairs. Since there is no overlap between the two samples, the personality test results will be reported separately in this chapter. Had the reviews mentioned above been available at the time the tests were chosen for the twin studies, different personality scales might have been selected.

Part I—How Well Do You Know Yourself?

To follow the pattern of analysis used in previous chapters, a three-way analysis of variance was performed with race, sex, and zygosity as the main effects. However, since Jenkins provides only separate norms for boys and girls, additional two-way analyses of variance were computed for each sex with race and zygosity as the main effects variables. Socio-economic classes were not available for this sample of twins.

On four scales of the Jenkins test there were significant sex differences (Table XII–A). Table XII–B shows that on three of the four scales girls ranked significantly higher than boys. Girls were higher on Scale 15, Impulsiveness; Scale 12, Nervousness; and Scale 6, Cooperativeness. The test manual states that high scores on Cooperativeness indicate a tendency to work with others to achieve common goals. High scores on Scale

Table XII–A

Effects of Race, Sex, and Zygosity on the Subtests of *How Well Do You Know Yourself?*

	Factors	Race	Sex	Zygosity	Race × Sex	Race × Zyg.	Sex × Zyg.	R × S × Z
1.	Irritability	*		*		*		
2.	Practicality	**						
3.	Punctuality	*						*
4.	Novelty-loving	*						
5.	Vocational assurance							
6.	Cooperativeness		*		*			
7.	Ambitiousness		**					
8.	Hypercriticalness		*					
9.	Dejection		*					
10.	General morale							
11.	Persistence							
12.	Nervousness		**				*	
13.	Seriousness							
14.	Submissiveness							
15.	Impulsiveness	*	*					
16.	Dynamism							*
17.	Emotional control							
18.	Consistency	**						
19.	Test objectivity	**						

* $p < .05$.
** $p < .01$.

Table XII–B
Least Squares Means for the Test *How Well Do You Know Yourself?* By Race,
Sex, and Zygosity

	Factors	Race		Sex		Zygosity	
		White	Black	Male	Female	MZ	DZ
1.	Irritability	13.54	12.19	12.78	12.95	13.54	12.19
2.	Practicality	15.07	16.77	15.85	15.98	16.03	15.81
3.	Punctuality	17.49	16.02	16.52	16.99	16.42	17.09
4.	Novelty-loving	20.71	22.25	21.29	21.67	21.63	21.33
5.	Vocational assurance	17.55	18.76	18.43	17.88	18.09	18.23
6.	Cooperativeness	20.28	20.10	19.52	20.87	20.62	19.77
7.	Ambitiousness	14.92	15.09	15.93	14.07	15.16	14.84
8.	Hypercriticalness	11.12	12.18	11.65	11.65	12.18	11.12
9.	Dejection	6.81	7.44	6.85	7.40	6.76	7.48
10.	General morale	16.27	15.81	16.09	16.00	15.78	16.30
11.	Persistence	15.75	16.01	15.79	15.98	16.38	15.38
12.	Nervousness	10.22	9.87	9.23	10.85	10.17	9.92
13.	Seriousness	13.80	14.88	14.11	14.58	14.51	14.18
14.	Submissiveness	14.09	13.72	13.60	14.21	13.58	14.23
15.	Impulsiveness	11.38	10.23	10.23	11.38	10.31	11.30
16.	Dynamism	16.73	16.73	17.19	16.27	16.69	16.77
17.	Emotional control	14.71	14.48	14.96	14.24	14.88	14.32
18.	Consistency	6.43	8.61	8.00	7.04	7.08	7.96
19.	Test objectivity	22.89	17.60	20.31	20.19	20.10	20.39

Table XII–C
Effects of Race and Zygosity on the Subtests of *How Well Do You Know Yourself?*
for Males

	Factors	Race	Zygosity	Race × Zygosity
1.	Irritability		*	
2.	Practicality			
3.	Punctuality			*
4.	Novelty-loving	*		
5.	Vocational assurance			
6.	Cooperativeness			
7.	Ambitiousness			
8.	Hypercriticalness		*	
9.	Dejection			
10.	General morale			
11.	Persistence			
12.	Nervousness			
13.	Seriousness			
14.	Submissiveness			
15.	Impulsiveness	*		
16.	Dynamism			
17.	Emotional control			
18.	Consistency	*		
19.	Test objectivity	**		

* $p < .05$.
** $p < .01$.

Table XII–D

Effects of Race and Zygosity on the Subtests of *How Well Do You Know Yourself?* for Females

	Factors	Race	Zygosity	Race × Zygosity
1.	Irritability	**		
2.	Practicality	**		
3.	Punctuality	*		
4.	Novelty-loving			*
5.	Vocational assurance			
6.	Cooperativeness			*
7.	Ambitiousness			*
8.	Hypercriticalness	**		
9.	Dejection	**		
10.	General morale			
11.	Persistence			
12.	Nervousness			
13.	Seriousness	**		
14.	Submissiveness			
15.	Impulsiveness			
16.	Dynamism			
17.	Emotional control			
18.	Consistency	**		
19.	Test objectivity	**		

* $p < .05$.
** $p < .01$.

12, Nervousness, reveal tension, restlessness, or inability to relax, sometimes manifested by fidgeting and a display of nervous behavior. High scores on Impulsiveness indicate a tendency to act precipitately or to make hasty decisions without careful consideration or deliberation.

On Scale 7, Ambitiousness, boys scored significantly higher than girls. A high score on this scale demonstrates an inclination for personal preferment or advancement in the sense of seeking marks of success or prestige, honor, money, and influence.

Since separate analyses were made for each sex, race and zygosity main effects will be discussed for each race separately but not for the total group.

Table XII–C shows the results of the analysis of variance for males. Of the 17 clinical or factor scales, race or zygosity differences are significant at the .05 level on four different scales for boys. Both control scales also show significant race differences.

For girls (Table XII–D) race differences on six clinical and both control scales are highly significant, whereas no scale shows a significant zygosity difference.

Rather than chart the least squares means for each sex for the Jenkins test, we prepared personality profiles, using percentile norms from the test manual. Figure XII–1 shows profiles for black and white boys; Figure XII–2 for black and white girls. Only two clinical scales show significant

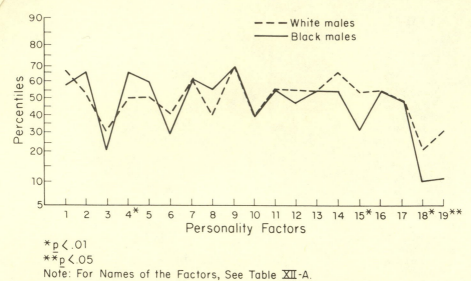

*p < .01
**p < .05
Note: For Names of the Factors, See Table XII-A.

Figure XII–1. Percentile equivalents of least squares means of personality factors measured by Jenkins' *How Well Do You Know Yourself?* for white and black males.

race differences for boys. On Scale 4, Novelty-loving, black boys score significantly higher than whites (Figure XII–1). As the name of the scale suggests, students who earn high scores exhibit a tendency to innovate, to become involved in situations requiring new decisions, plans, and goals. They prefer new ways of doing things in contradistinction to mere variety without novelty.

White boys score significantly higher than blacks on Scale 15, Impulsiveness. Only one race-zygosity interaction effect was signficant. On the Punctuality scale white MZ's were superior to white DZ's. The reverse was true for the blacks.

How Well Do You Know Yourself? profiles for black and white girls are shown in Figure XII–2. Here six clinical scales are significantly different, all but one at the .01 level of confidence. On Scale 1, Irritability, white girls as a group show more of a tendency to feel annoyed and irritable than their black counterparts. Students scoring high on this scale often become annoyed or upset when they feel threatened by people or conditions.

Black girls are more practical than white girls (Scale 2). Pupils who score high on this scale deal with the environment in relation to utilitarian needs.

White girls score significantly higher than blacks on Scale 3, Punctuality.

Black girls, significantly more so than whites, are inclined to note

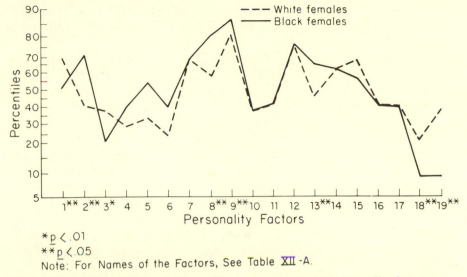

Figure XII–2. Percentile equivalents of least squares means of personality factors measured by Jenkins' *How Well Do You Know Yourself?* for white and black females.

and point out the faults, mistakes, and shortcomings of others as well as to direct attention to and overemphasize these faults (Scale 8). Black girls are also more likely than whites to feel low-spirited, unhappy, depressed, and disheartened (Scale 9).

Scale 13 is Seriousness. Black girls significantly outscore whites on this scale, which is intended to measure attitudes of earnestness or feelings of personal responsibility toward one's work or environment.

Three race-zygosity interaction effects were significant for girls: Novelty-loving, Cooperativeness, and Ambitiousness. For none of these scales were the main effect differences significant. On all three scales white MZ's ranked higher than white DZ's but black MZ's ranked lower than black DZ's.

On *How Well Do You Know Yourself?* there are two control scales—Test consistency, Scale 18, and Test objectivity, Scale 19. Both blacks and whites scored within the normal range on Scale 18, suggesting that each group tended to mark items of similar or identical content in the same manner.

Test objectivity, Scale 19, identifies those subjects who respond to questions in a socially desirable way. Pupils who score high on this scale may have lower than average scores on Scales 1, 9, and 12 and higher than average scores on Scales 4, 5, 6, 11, and 16. Deviant scores on Test objectivity have no meaning in themselves. They merely assist the counselor to interpret the 17 clinical scales.

The reader is cautioned not to attach too much significance to this analysis of Jenkins' test and is reminded that the norms are "damnably inadequate."

Despite the weaknesses of *How Well Do You Know Yourself?*, two observations can be made: (1) black and white boys differ significantly on only 2 of the 17 factor scales; and (2) the real race difference in personality seems to be between black and white girls who differed significantly on 6 of the 17 clinical scales.

The question now arises whether any of the personality factors from the Jenkins scale has significant heritability components. The classical heritability ratios used in previous chapters to determine the genetic component of tests of mental capacity were applied to the 17 factors and to the control scales of *How Well Do You Know Yourself?*.

Because of the relatively small number of blacks in this group, race-sex heritability ratios were not computed. In the present analysis black and white girls comprised one subpopulation, and black and white boys the other.

Heritability ratios for the Jenkins personality factors for boys and girls are shown in Table XII–E. It is immediately apparent that factors measured by *How Well Do You Know Yourself?* show much less of a genetic component than that in the analysis of mental capacity tests. Only 3 of the 17 personality scales yield significant within-pair variance ratios and these only for girls, who demonstrate a significant degree of heritability on Scale 8, Hypercriticalness; Scale 9, Dejection; and Scale 11, Persistence. According to the test manual, high Persistence scores suggest a tendency to resist opposing forces, either outside or within the examinee.

Ten scales indicate a moderate genetic basis for one or both of the subgroups. (Holzinger's heritability ratio (H) is $> .30$.) While a heritability ratio of .30 is not remarkably high, it certainly suggests that some of the personality traits measured by the Jenkins test have a genetic basis. Two scales show high heritability ratios for both boys and girls, Cooperativeness and Persistence. On 5 of the 17 scales only boys show high ($> .30$) heritability ratios: Scale 1, Irritability; Scale 5, Vocational assurance; Scale 7, Ambitiousness; Scale 9, Dejection; Scale 16, Dynamism. Dynamism indicates an active or energetic state of mind, coupled with a sense of vigorous physical well-being. High scores on Scale 5 signify a belief in one's capability to achieve appropriate financial or occupational rewards.

Heritability ratios were $> .30$ for girls, but not boys, on 3 of the 17 factor scales. In addition to Scale 8, Hypercriticalness, which has already been mentioned, Scale 15, Impulsiveness, and Scale 17, Emotional control, show modest heritability components. Emotional control suggests a tendency to inhibit or restrain socially disapproved emotional reactions,

Table XII-E
Heritability Coefficients for Males and Females for Factors Measured by the Test *How Well Do You Know Yourself?*

Factors	MZ Cor	MZ N	DZ Cor	DZ N	T(Cor)	H	HR	Within-pair Variances MZ	Within-pair Variances DZ	F
1. Irritability										
Males	.37	78	−.10	42	2.48	.43	2.57	13.91	19.04	1.37
Females	−.03	86	.20	74	−1.42	−.29	17.44	20.20	15.10	.75
2. Practicality										
Males	.40	78	.14	42	1.38	.29	1.27	15.87	10.80	.68
Females	.23	86	.02	74	1.33	.22	1.81	17.30	18.44	1.07
3. Punctuality										
Males	.07	78	−.02	42	.45	.09	2.51	25.70	24.56	.96
Females	.30	86	.37	74	−.54	−.12	−.52	21.95	14.70	.67
4. Novelty-loving										
Males	.20	78	.14	42	.29	.07	.56	17.78	27.25	1.53
Females	.16	86	.35	74	−1.27	−.30	−2.47	33.96	14.39	.42
5. Vocational assurance										
Males	.32	78	−.02	42	1.82	.34	2.14	21.68	19.55	.90
Females	.28	86	.12	74	1.03	.18	1.13	25.52	18.14	.71
6. Cooperativeness										
Males	.47	78	.18	42	1.61	.35	1.21	13.28	15.07	1.14
Females	.29	86	−.06	74	2.22	.33	2.44	16.45	19.33	1.18
7. Ambitiousness										
Males	.32	78	−.07	42	2.01	.36	2.40	21.08	22.08	1.05
Females	.18	86	.03	74	.95	.16	1.70	25.99	31.70	1.22
8. Hypercriticalness										
Males	.02	78	.01	42	.04	.01	.89	20.04	21.02	1.05
Females	.53	86	−.02	74	3.73	.54	2.06	8.03	17.19	2.14**
9. Dejection										
Males	.27	78	−.03	42	1.59	.30	2.24	14.03	17.29	1.23
Females	.47	86	.37	74	.77	.16	.44	8.41	12.53	1.49*
10. General morale										
Males	.25	78	.20	42	.29	.07	.44	17.03	15.08	.89
Females	.25	86	.15	74	.60	.11	.76	13.12	10.83	.83

Table XII-E (Continued)

Factors	MZ		DZ		T(Cor)	Heritability Ratios		Within-pair Variances		
	Cor	N	Cor	N		H	HR	MZ	DZ	F
11. Persistence										
Males	.47	78	.04	42	2.35	.44	1.83	12.35	12.70	1.03
Females	.40	86	.04	74	2.36	.37	1.81	13.76	22.49	1.64*
12. Nervousness										
Males	-.13	78	-.12	42	-.01	.00	.04	21.58	14.82	.69
Females	.23	86	.25	74	-.17	-.04	-.23	13.93	16.03	1.15
13. Seriousness										
Males	.14	78	-.02	42	.81	.16	2.30	20.37	18.61	.91
Females	.42	86	.28	74	.98	.19	.67	13.77	14.71	1.07
14. Submissiveness										
Males	.19	78	-.06	42	1.27	.23	2.60	15.65	20.83	1.33
Females	.12	86	.17	74	-.30	-.06	-.80	18.69	18.07	.97
15. Impulsiveness										
Males	.38	78	.25	42	.74	.17	.69	14.14	15.88	1.12
Females	.25	86	-.19	74	2.79	.37	3.53	15.50	20.20	1.30
16. Dynamism										
Males	.31	78	-.11	42	2.22	.38	2.73	15.07	15.00	1.00
Females	.17	86	.22	74	-.34	-.07	-.63	18.48	15.59	.84
17. Emotional control										
Males	.16	78	-.16	42	1.65	.28	4.02	11.53	16.43	1.43
Females	.29	86	-.06	74	2.21	.33	2.42	11.52	13.86	1.20
18. Consistency										
Males	.33	78	.16	42	.89	.20	1.01	19.32	22.04	1.14
Females	.49	86	.22	74	1.86	.34	1.08	10.82	10.59	.98
19. Test objectivity										
Males	.33	78	-.10	42	2.20	.39	2.58	19.32	55.63	1.05
Females	.17	86	.17	74	.01	.00	.02	54.10	37.36	.69

* $p < .05$.
** $p < .01$.

such as controlling one's temper in disagreeable situations or remaining calm when others become upset.

No other heritability study using *How Well Do You Know Yourself?* has been located. However, since several of Jenkins' 17 factor scales overlap scales of the other similar test (Cattell's *HSPQ*) in our study, an attempt will be made at the end of this chapter to assess the heritability of personality factors of adolescent twins as measured by the two scales.

Part II—High School Personality Questionnaire

We will now examine subpopulation differences in personality by means of the *High School Personality Questionnaire* (Cattell, 1969). The psychological meanings of Cattell's 14 primary source traits were discussed in Chapter VI. In the *HSPQ* manual, personality traits are described in two ways, first by their technical, psychological names; second by the idiomatic terminology of the man in the street. For example, the technical name for the low end of Scale A is sizothymia; the high end is affectothymia. In the vernacular, low scorers on Scale A are characterized as *reserved, detached, critical,* or *aloof;* high scorers as *warmhearted, outgoing, easygoing,* and *participating.* For our purposes, only the common descriptions will be used. (The common descriptions for all 14 scales are shown as a footnote in Table XII–F.)

Since Cattell believed that there might well be significant personality differences within social classes and geographical, regional subcultures, he employed in the main standardization of the *HSPQ* a proportional, stratified design which was deliberate in regard to (1) socio-economic level of school neighborhood, (2) urban-rural classification, (3) geographical region. Stratification by race was not attempted in the standardization of the 1968–69 edition of the *HSPQ.*

Although the 1972 edition of the *HSPQ* manual reports norms for males and females separately as well as for males and females combined, our analyses use only the combined norms. The scales that are strikingly different in distinguishing masculinity and femininity are A, G, and I, on which girls are higher, and C, E, and Q_2, on which boys are higher. Cattell says these differences are identical with those found on the adult 16 P–F scale.

The first step was to perform a four-way analysis of variance of the *HSPQ* with race, sex, socio-economic status, and zygosity as the main effects variables. Table XII–F shows the level of significance of differences for the four main effects. Since only 4 of the 154 possible interactions were significant, no interpretation of interactions will be attempted.

Significant sex differences for the most part follow the pattern reported by Cattell: girls outscored boys on A, warmheartedness; G, superego strength; and I, tendermindedness. Boys outscored girls on C, ego

Table XII–F

Effects of Race, Sex, Zygosity, and Socio-economic Status on the 14 Factors of Cattell's *High School Personality Questionnaire,* Using Sten Scores

Factors	Sex	Race	Zygosity	SES	Sex × Race	Sex × Zygosity	Race × Zygosity	Sex × Race × Zyg	Sex × SES	Race × SES	Sex × Race × SES	Zygosity × SES	Sex × Zyg × SES	Race × Zyg × SES	Sex × Race × Zyg × SES
A	**														
B		**													
C	**	**	*									*			
D				*											
E	**	**													
F	**	**													
G	**														
H	**		**												
I	**				**										
J															
O						*			**						
Q₂	**	*	*												
Q₃															
Q₄															

Note. Factor A: Reserved—warm-hearted
Factor B: Less intelligent—more intelligent
Factor C: Emotionally less stable—emotionally stable
Factor D: Inactive—overactive
Factor E: Submissive—dominant
Factor F: Serious—happy-go-lucky
Factor G: Weak superego—strong superego
Factor H: Shy—bold
Factor I: Tough-minded—tender-minded
Factor J: Zestful—restrained
Factor O: Secure—insecure
Factor Q₂: Group-dependent—self-sufficient
Factor Q₃: Uncontrolled—controlled
Factor Q₄: Relaxed—tense
* $p < .05$.
** $p < .01$.

strength; E, dominance; Q_2, self-sufficiency (Table XII–G). In addition to the six scales showing outstandingly different sex differences in Cattell's standardization, significant sex differences were revealed by our study on two additional scales—F and H, on which boys ranked higher. A high score on Factor F indicates a happy-go-lucky attitude rather than one of slow caution. Factor H represents the shy-bold continuum. Complete *High School Personality Questionnaire* profiles for boys and girls

Table XII–G

Least Squares Means for Cattell's *High School Personality Questionnaire,* Using Sten Scores by Sex, Race, Zygosity, and Socio-economic Status

Factors	Sex		Race		Zygosity		SES		
	Male	Female	White	Black	MZ	DZ	1	2	3
A	4.79	5.83	5.05	5.58	5.34	5.29	5.10	5.63	5.22
B	4.98	5.25	5.94	4.30	5.18	5.05	5.45	5.25	4.65
C	6.22	5.52	5.49	6.25	6.05	5.70	6.28	5.48	5.86
D	5.25	5.72	5.46	5.51	5.42	5.55	5.45	5.98	5.02
E	6.53	4.90	5.34	6.09	5.60	5.83	6.03	5.75	5.38
F	5.64	4.81	5.64	4.81	5.25	5.20	5.43	5.27	4.98
G	4.89	5.70	5.31	5.28	5.42	5.18	5.44	5.27	5.18
H	5.67	4.95	5.10	5.52	5.68	4.94	5.35	5.55	5.03
I	4.51	6.64	5.54	5.62	5.54	5.62	5.50	5.59	5.65
J	5.73	5.41	5.39	5.75	5.47	5.67	5.34	5.40	5.97
O	4.84	5.30	5.20	4.93	5.08	5.06	4.83	5.17	5.20
Q_2	6.34	5.18	5.41	6.11	5.41	6.10	5.57	5.81	5.89
Q_3	5.47	5.72	5.60	5.58	5.60	5.59	5.87	5.28	5.63
Q_4	5.65	5.95	5.90	5.70	5.56	6.04	5.63	6.08	5.70

Note. For a description of each factor, refer to footnote 1 of Table XII–F.

1 = High SES group
2 = Middle SES group
3 = Low SES group

are given in Figure XII–3. Significant sex differences in least squares means are also indicated.

On five *HSPQ* scales there were significant mean race differences. Blacks were higher on Scale C, emotional stability; Scale E, dominance; and Scale Q_2, self-sufficiency. Whites were significantly higher on Scale B, intelligence, and Scale F, happy-go-lucky. On the other nine scales the differences are nonsignificant. Personality profiles for the two races are shown in Figure XII–4. According to our analysis of the *HSPQ* scores, blacks as a group are more emotionally stable, dominant, and self-sufficient than whites, while whites are more intelligent and less serious-minded.

With respect to zygosity, only 2 of the 14 scales showed significant differences. On Scale H, MZ's earned higher scores than DZ's; on Scale Q_2, DZ's were the high scorers. These results indicate that MZ's are bold and group dependent while DZ's are shy and self-sufficient. Since 12 of the 14 personality scales demonstrated no significant zygosity differences, *HSPQ* profiles were not prepared for the two types of twins.

The proportional, stratified design for standardization appears to have been effective in attenuating personality differences among the three social classes on the 14 *HSPQ* scales. On only two factors, C and D, are there significant differences among the three socio-economic groups, although these differences do not follow a regular pattern. High SES groups were high scorers on Scale C, indicating an emotionally stable personality.

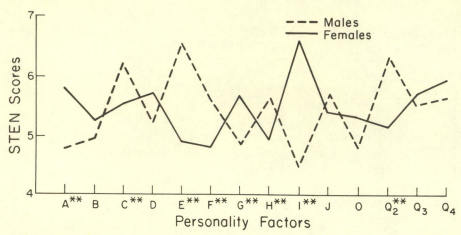

** p < .05

Note: For Descriptions of the Factors, See Footnote of Table XII-F.

Figure XII–3. Least squares means of personality factors measured by Cattell's *High School Personality Questionnaire* for males and females.

The middle SES group earned high scores on Scale D, the inactive-overactive continuum. SES differences on the other 12 scales of the *High School Personality Questionnaire* are nonsignificant.

During the late 50s and the early 60s the Cattell personality scales were undergoing developmental revision and standardization. There have

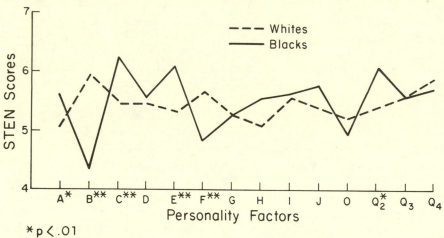

* p < .01
** p < .05

Note: For Descriptions of the Factors, See Footnote of Table XII-F.

Figure XII–4. Least squares means of personality factors measured by Cattell's *High School Personality Questionnaire* for whites and blacks.

been three previous heritability studies based on some form of Cattell's personality test for adolescents—two using the *Junior Personality Quiz,* one the *High School Personality Questionnaire.* Summaries of the three earlier studies and the present study are given in Table XII–H. Cattell, Blewett, and Beloff (1955), relying on the *Junior Personality Quiz* and numbering the factors 1 through 12, found no within-pair variance ratios significant for any of the 11 personality factors. However, for his Factor 12, intelligence, he reports a significant *F* ratio. In Vandenberg's study of 36 DZ and 45 MZ adolescent twin pairs, three test factors of the *Junior Personality Quiz* showed significant within-pair variance ratios: B, nervous tension; C, neuroticism; and D, will control. Finding only 3 of 12 personality scales to yield significant heritability factors, Vandenberg was not enthusiastic about the possibility of continuing research along the same lines. He was fairly sure that our present day measures of personality are inadequate for studies of heritability factors and recommended an open-minded search of all possible test instruments.

The Gottesman study and this study are comparable in two ways. Each used the same form of the *HSPQ,* and the twin samples of the two studies were similar in age and sex distribution. Gottesman's (1963) only reference to socio-economic status was to note "a tendency toward better participation as the economic level of the neighborhood increased" (p. 4). He made no mention of race, but he did indicate that 90% of his twins were of Scandinavian or Western European extraction.

Table XII–H tells us that in Gottesman's study only Scales F, O, and Q_2 show significant within-pair variance ratios. In summarizing his data Gottesman (1963) says:

> . . . the proportion of scale variance accounted for by heredity gave positive results for six of the HSPQ factors. Factors E, Submissiveness versus Dominance; H, Shy, Sensitive versus Adventurous; and J, Liking Group Action versus Fastidiously Individualistic showed appreciable variance accounted for by heredity but with environment predominating. Factors F, Q_2, and O, Confident Adequacy versus Guilt Proneness, showed about equal contributions of heredity and environment. (p. 19)

Comparing the Gottesman findings with ours, two of the three scales with significant genetic components in his study also had significant genetic variance in the Twin Study. Scale F, the sober—happy-go-lucky continuum, and Scale Q_2, group dependency, are the two significant factors common to both.

In the present study the additional parameter of race was introduced. Heritability ratios were computed for 63 pairs of same-sexed white twins and 80 pairs of same-sexed black twins. The two subsamples were com-

Table XII-H

F ratios of Within-pair Variances for Fraternal and Identical Twins on Personality Dimensions Measured by *Junior Personality Quiz* and *High School Personality Questionnaire*

Personality Dimensions	Cattell et al. 1955		Vandenberg 1962		Gottesman 1963		Osborne present study	
	JPQ Factor	F ratios	JPQ Factor	F ratios	HSPQ Factor	F ratios	HSPQ Factor	F ratios
Reserved—warm-hearted	6	1.08	F	1.30	A	1.11	A	1.87*
Less intelligent—more intelligent	12	1.91*	L	1.10	B	1.05	B	1.49
Emotionally less stable—emotionally stable	3	1.60	C	3.20*	C	1.03	C	1.23
Inactive—overactive	5	1.35	E	.93	D	.62	D	1.01
Submissive—dominant	9	.90	I	.97	E	1.44	E	1.19
Serious—happy-go-lucky	11	1.47	K	1.45	F	2.29*	F	1.92*
Weak superego—strong superego	8	1.39	H	1.06	G	.97	G	1.44
Shy—bold	7	1.34	G	.93	H	1.62	H	1.33
Tough-minded—tender-minded	1	1.47	A	1.03	I	1.07	I	1.05
Zestful—restrained	10	1.57	J	1.54	J	1.41	J	1.30
Secure—insecure					O	1.85*	O	.90
Group-dependent—self-sufficient	4	1.08			Q_2	2.28*	Q_2	1.62*
Uncontrolled—controlled			D	1.87*	Q_3	1.13	Q_3	1.36
Relaxed—tense	2	1.56	B	2.08*	Q_4	.53	Q_4	1.35
Number of DZ pairs		32		36		34		61
Number of MZ pairs		52		45		34		82

* $p < .05$.

bined and heritability ratios computed for the total group. Computing heritability ratios by sex for each race might have produced interesting results, but with only nine pairs of black male DZ's, the statistical confidence would have been in short supply.

In Table XII–I heritability ratios are shown for the 14 scales of the *High School Personality Questionnaire* by race and for the total group. Five individual scales, A, E, F, G, and Q_3, produce significant within-pair variance ratios for the smaller white sample, while for blacks two

Table XII–I

Heritability Coefficients on the 14 Scales of Cattell's *High School Personality Questionnaire* by Race and Total Group: Classical Methods of Analysis Using Age-adjusted Raw Scores

Factor	MZ Cor	MZ N	DZ Cor	DZ N	T(Cor)	Heritability Ratios H	Heritability Ratios HR	Within-pair Variances MZ	Within-pair Variances DZ	Within-pair Variances F
A										
White	.44	34	−.11	29	2.18	.49	2.52	7.49	17.12	2.29*
Black	.36	48	.09	32	1.20	.30	1.49	6.44	9.03	1.40
Total	.43	82	−.01	61	2.69	.43	2.03	6.87	12.88	1.87**
B										
White	.35	34	.55	29	−.92	−.43	−1.10	1.87	1.41	.76
Black	.48	48	.18	32	1.44	.37	1.26	1.92	4.09	2.14**
Total	.54	82	.44	61	.73	.17	.36	1.90	2.82	1.49
C										
White	.21	34	.21	29	−.01	.00	−.02	9.47	9.50	1.00
Black	.41	48	.06	32	1.57	.37	1.71	7.32	10.63	1.45
Total	.33	82	.17	61	1.01	.20	.97	8.21	10.09	1.23
D										
White	.21	34	.34	29	−.53	−.20	−1.22	8.71	10.05	1.16
Black	.19	48	.04	32	.65	.16	1.58	9.54	8.50	.89
Total	.20	82	.23	61	−.15	−.03	−.25	9.20	9.24	1.01
E										
White	.39	34	.04	29	1.40	.37	1.78	4.59	9.64	2.10*
Black	.15	48	.18	32	−.14	−.04	−.44	10.18	9.03	.89
Total	.23	82	.12	61	.63	.12	.93	7.86	9.32	1.19
F										
White	.50	34	−.16	29	2.67	.57	2.64	5.21	13.14	2.52**
Black	.41	48	.26	32	.70	.20	.73	5.74	8.25	1.44
Total	.51	82	.12	61	2.54	.44	1.53	5.52	10.57	1.92**
G										
White	.44	34	−.01	29	1.81	.45	2.04	4.99	11.33	2.27*
Black	.13	48	−.11	32	1.00	.21	3.71	8.06	8.36	1.04
Total	.26	82	−.05	61	1.81	.29	2.40	6.79	9.77	1.44
H										
White	.13	34	.04	29	.33	.09	1.35	11.82	13.60	1.15
Black	.21	48	−.26	32	2.00	.37	4.49	8.68	12.91	1.49
Total	.17	82	−.08	61	1.48	.23	2.95	9.98	13.24	1.33
I										
White	.74	34	.67	29	.54	.22	.19	7.27	9.28	1.28
Black	.45	48	.41	32	.21	.07	.18	8.05	7.06	.88
Total	.63	82	.59	61	.35	.09	.12	7.73	8.11	1.05

Table XII–I *(Continued)*

Factor	MZ Cor	N	DZ Cor	N	T(Cor)	Heritability Ratios H	HR	Within-pair Variances MZ	DZ	F
J										
White	.02	34	.08	29	−.23	−.07	−6.22	6.75	9.34	1.38
Black	.21	48	.11	32	.44	.12	.97	6.71	8.14	1.21
Total	.15	82	.11	61	.27	.05	.61	6.73	8.71	1.30
O										
White	−.09	34	.16	29	−.96	−.30	5.59	12.38	10.98	.89
Black	.27	48	.15	32	.53	.14	.89	8.41	7.30	.87
Total	.12	82	.16	61	−.23	−.05	−.62	10.05	9.05	.90
Q₂										
White	.32	34	.24	29	.33	.11	.50	7.88	11.48	1.46
Black	.33	48	.11	32	.99	.25	1.34	5.89	10.33	1.76*
Total	.33	82	.22	61	.69	.14	.67	6.71	10.88	1.62*
Q₃										
White	.29	34	−.11	29	1.54	.36	2.79	7.00	14.17	2.03*
Black	.14	48	.06	32	.35	.09	1.18	8.80	8.03	.91
Total	.20	82	−.04	61	1.41	.23	2.39	8.05	10.95	1.36
Q₄										
White	.27	34	.06	29	.81	.22	1.53	9.25	12.50	1.35
Black	.25	48	.00	32	1.09	.25	2.01	8.11	10.78	1.33
Total	.26	82	.03	61	1.37	.24	1.75	8.59	11.60	1.35

Note. For a description of each factor, refer to footnote 1 of Table XII–F.
* $p < .05$.
** $p < .01$.

scales, B and Q_2, are significant. The five scales showing significant genetic control of personality factors for the white sample would suggest that such traits as warmth, sociability (A), dominance (E), enthusiasm (F), conscientiousness (G), and strong willpower (Q_3) have significant genetic determination. Of the 14 *HSPQ* scales only 2 scales, B, general intelligence, and Q_2, self-sufficiency, indicated significant heritability components for the black group. When the samples of 80 black and 63 white twin pairs were combined and heritability ratios computed, only Scales A, F, and Q_2 showed significant genetic determination. Scales A and F also yielded significant within-pair variance ratios for whites alone.

Since we have reported the results of two separate twin studies of personality—one using Jenkins' *How Well Do You Know Yourself?* the other, Cattell's *High School Personality Questionnaire*—two questions arise: (1) are there common personality patterns on the two scales; (2) do the common personality factors reflect similar genetic components? There are 17 personality factors on Jenkins' test and 14 on the Cattell scale, with no two scales being identified exactly the same. Seven scales on Jenkins' test have no common scale on the Cattell test. Of the ten scales that are somewhat alike on the two tests, no comparable scales yielded heritability ratios greater than .30 for the total samples. In these two studies, two scales on *How Well Do You Know Yourself?*—General morale and Submissiveness—and three on *High School Personality Questionnaire*—restraint, insecurity, and tension—were not significantly influenced by race, sex, or zygosity (or socio-economic status for the three *HSPQ* scales). In addition, all five personality dimensions had non-significant heritability ratios.

Is there a significant genetic component in personality factors measured by the Jenkins and Cattell scales? From our analyses of responses of over 400 sets of same-sexed twins, we find little convincing evidence that these measured personality factors have a significant genetic determination. On most test factors, identical twins are more alike than fraternal. However, our heritability ratios are consistently smaller than those reported by Vandenberg (1967b) and Breland (1972). Summarizing 14 twin studies of personality, Vandenberg reports median *r*'s of .48 for MZ's and .28 for DZ's. Nichols (1976), reviewing over 30 twin studies which reported 106 dimensions of personality, found mean *r*'s of .48 for MZ's and .29 for DZ's. For the 17 scales of *How Well Do You Know Yourself?*, we found median MZ *r*'s of .26; DZ's, .04. For the total group the median MZ *r* of the 14 scales of the *High School Personality Questionnaire* was .26; the median DZ *r*, .12.

Our inability to isolate genetic aspects of personality is not so much a weakness of the twin method of research as it is a weakness of the tests used to measure personality. Such tests are not as reliable as tests of mental capacity. When personality factors are identified and measured with the same dependability as IQ, then and perhaps only then will investigators be able to determine the degree to which personality obeys the laws of genetics.

XIII

The Visual Evoked Response: Heritability Estimates

The fact that the brain wave tracing is a heritable trait can hardly be questioned (Dustman & Beck, 1965; Lennox & Lennox, 1960). At the risk of engaging in twin-study overkill, this chapter, portions of which are taken from a paper by the author (Osborne, 1970), will investigate monozygotic and dizygotic twin correlations for a unique portion of the brain wave tracing, the cortical potential evoked by a light stimulus, otherwise known as the visual evoked response (VER). The MZ and DZ correlations will be compared with those of known biometric resemblances of twins; i.e., face length, head circumference, standing height, weight, and color blindness. Comparisons of VER correlations for co-twins, for age-matched controls, and for bilateral self-correlation will also be made. The periods of the theta, alpha, and beta components of the VER for MZ and DZ twins will be related to scores on a standard test of mental ability. It is recognized that the small number of twins, especially DZ twins, makes intraclass correlations suspect. Nevertheless, the VER self-correlations, co-twin correlations, and twin correlations with matched controls are impressive.

Adolescent and pre-adolescent twins of the same sex from Northeast Georgia served as paid volunteer subjects. The sample was comprised of 13 pairs of MZ twins and 6 pairs of DZ twins (16 girls and 22 boys, age range 11 to 22). One pair of the twins was black. Thirty-eight unrelated control subjects were matched with the twins for sex and age.

Zygosity was established by serological tests performed at the Minneapolis War Memorial Blood Bank. S's were tested for all of the following serological factors: A, B, O, M, N, S, s, P_1, P_2, Rho, rh', rh", Miltenberger,

Vermeyst, Lewis, Lutheran, Duffy, Kidd, Sutter, Martin, Kell, and Cellano. Twins whose serological phenotypes were identical were designated MZ. Those differing on one or more of these serological types were designated DZ (Race & Sanger, 1954). Six pairs of twins were diagnosed as definitely DZ since they differed on at least one independently inherited blood group. Employing only the results of the serological tests it was possible to diagnose the remaining 13 pairs as MZ with a 95% probability of accuracy.

During the experiment the subjects reclined on a hospital bed. Subdermal electrodes were inserted midway between the ear and the vertex on both sides of the scalp. Dominance was determined by handedness. The ipsilateral ear was used as a reference. The ground electrode was inserted in the mid-occipital area.

A Grass Photo Stimulator, ES3B, was placed 30 cm from the face of the subject, who was instructed to relax comfortably with eyes closed. The Grass amplifier was set to the normal 7.5 mm sensitivity, with the high frequency filter set at 70 and low frequency at 1.

The EEG signals were amplified with the Grass Model 6A5 EEG machine. Signals were then fed to a dual-channel, on-line, active band-pass filter system which separated the VER into the three common EEG bands: Theta 3 to 7 cps; Alpha 8 to 13 cps; Beta 14 to 22 cps. The analyzed VER signals were next fed to the four input channels of a computer of average transients, CAT 1000. The output of the filter system was adjusted to unity gain for the raw EEG and for the alpha band, a gain of 2 for the theta band, and a gain of 3 for the beta band. Figure XIII–1 shows in channel 1 the raw EEG signal from electrode 1–A_1. Theta, alpha, and beta activities contained in this raw signal are recorded simultaneously on channels 2, 3, and 4 respectively. The second raw signal from 2-A_2 is recorded on channel 5 with the analyzed portions of this signal recorded on channels 6, 7, and 8.

The CAT was set for 4 milliseconds per address analysis and triggered the photo stimulator after the 64th address of channel 1 or 256 milliseconds after the start of a CAT sweep. Flashes were repeated until the scope tracing was centered in the 10^4 scale, approximately 75 flashes per subject. Each quarter of the memory was plotted separately on a Mosley X-Y plotter allowing one-fourth of the memory for each 14.5 inch graph. Thus for each subject four X-Y plots were obtained from the left hemisphere, one for the VER and one each for the alpha, beta, and theta components of the raw signal. Four plots were also obtained from the right hemisphere.

Visual evoked response tracings of a pair of MZ (ID #902) girls and a pair of DZ (ID #916) girls are shown in Figures XIII–2 and XIII–3. (Each tracing represents an average of 75 responses evoked by the flash stimulus.) These tracings were not selected as being representa-

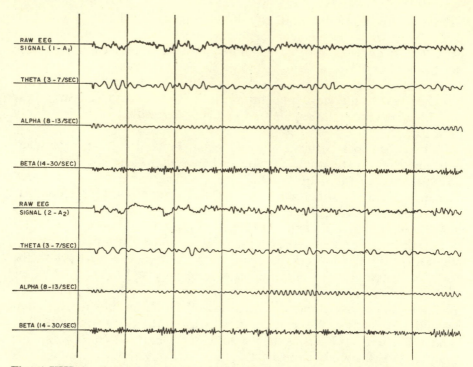

Figure XIII–1. A portion of an analyzed EEG record showing the raw signal from electrode 1-A₁ (right frontal to right ear lobe) on channel 1. Theta, alpha, and beta activities contained in the raw signal are shown simultaneously on channels 2, 3, and 4 respectively. A downward deflection denotes a surface positive wave.

tive of all twins in this study but rather to illustrate the subtle similarities and differences that are observed in the visual evoked response.

The concordance of the VER's of twins 902–1 and 902–2 is immediately apparent in Figure XIII–2. In all four tracings the first significant event after the flash falls within the very narrow range of 10 to 20 ms—remarkable when we consider the VER's in Figure XIII–2 represent four separate experiments: tracing number 1 is the average of 75 flashes from an electrode attached to the mid-parietal area of the left hemisphere of twin 902–1; tracing number 2 is from the right side evoked by 75 different flashes; the other two tracings are for twin 902–2. Tracings of the twins can hardly be distinguished. The VER's from the two hemispheres of the same subject are concordant. The four tracings of these MZ twins are almost congruent.

The visual evoked responses for twin pair 916–1 and 916–2 (W, F, DZ) are clearly different. These four experiments were conducted as were those with pair 902, but with significantly different results that

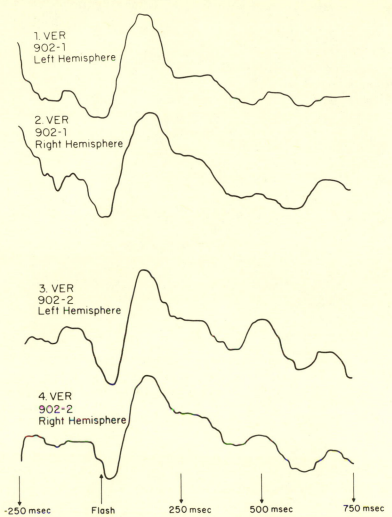

Figure XIII–2. Visual evoked responses for MZ twin pair #902. Left and right hemisphere recordings were not made simultaneously. There was a short rest period between VER 1 and VER 2 and also between VER 3 and VER 4.

will become understandable in the next section. For the first pair of twins the most significant event after the flash for all four tracings fell within a range of 10 to 20 ms, whereas the range for pair 916 was over 200 ms. Note also the spiky waves, especially on the left side of twin 916–1. For this pair of DZ twins the VER tracings are in no way alike. Differences are clearly noticeable between twins and also between hemispheres of the same subject. Neurological reports from the clinical

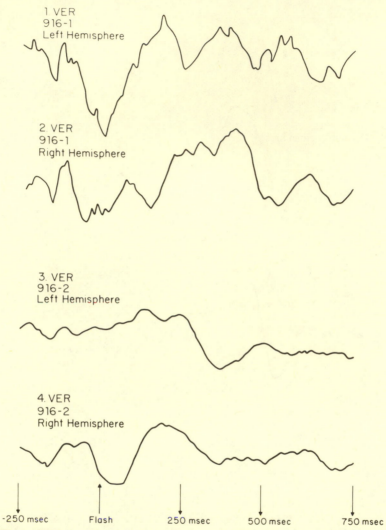

Figure XIII-3. Visual evoked responses for DZ twin pair #916. Left and right hemisphere recordings were not made simultaneously. There was a short rest period between VER 1 and VER 2 and also between VER 3 and VER 4.

EEG's which follow will in part explain the wide differences in the evoked responses.

Twin 902–1, W, F, MZ: There is a well developed alpha rhythm which is slightly spiky at times. Five- to seven-second activity is generalized throughout the record. The tracing is stable on hyperventilation. Flicker adds fast waves. Impression: Quite normal.

Twin 902–2: There is well developed ten cycle per second alpha rhythm. There is a moderate amount of five- to seven-second activity which increases in drowsiness. There is little change in hyperventilation. This is a normal tracing.

Twin 916–1, W, F, DZ: The tracing is characterized by unstable patterns, varying on the two sides with a generally poorly organized pattern of activity. Low voltage fast activity, often spiky, appears throughout the record. There are many sharp waves and a few spikes. With drowsiness, bursts of spiky activity occur. Abnormal slow and sharp patterns build up on hyperventilation. Impression: The tracing is mildly abnormal because of its instability and randomly distributed paroxysmal abnormalities.

Twin 916–2: Tracing begins in the waking state. It is characterized by a great mixture of frequencies in poorly organized patterns and with much difference between the hemispheres. There is a nine per second rhythm. It is often spiky. Four to six per second waves and small sharp waves are common. There are many irregular two to three per second waves present as baseline shifts. Impression: A generally dysrhythmic tracing. One might expect such a record after encephalitis or in a relative of an epileptic.

The wave components of the plot of the raw VER signal are determined by phase change of the evoked response over time. In order to correlate the plots of two subjects, ordinates were erected at one-fourth inch intervals from the base line below the largest positive deflection beginning with the light flash. For each X-Y VER plot, 30 ordinates describing the response were used to compute co-twin, control, and inter-hemispheric correlations for each subject.

For both MZ's and DZ's, Revised Beta Examination (1962) scores and periods of the three major components of the VER were correlated. Intraclass correlations were computed for the Revised Beta Examination and for the periods of the major components of the VER. The periods of alpha, beta, and theta components were determined directly from the X-Y plots (Osborne, 1969).

Table XIII–A shows mean evoked response correlations for MZ's and DZ's with co-twin, with self, and with unrelated age-matched control subjects. The mean r's are in the posited direction, $MZ > DZ >$ controls, but the group differences are not significant. The Duncan multiple range test shows both identical and fraternal twins were significantly more highly correlated with self than with matched controls. The twins were also significantly more highly correlated with their co-twin than with the matched control subjects. VER correlations of twins with controls were at chance level—.13 for MZ's and .11 for DZ's. Both types of twins were more highly correlated with self than with co-twin. After the experiment was begun one MZ twin was found to have an abnormal

Table XIII–A

Coefficients of Correlation of Visual Evoked Responses from Dominant Hemisphere Among Monozygotic and Dizygotic Twins: Correlations Between Twin and Co-Twin, Twin and Self (Left vs. Right), and Twin and Matched Control

	Number of pairs	Mean Age	Age Range		$\overline{X}r$	Range of r's
Monozygotic twins	13	17.4	11–22	With co-twin	.77	.59 to .88
				With self	.84	.08* to .96
				With control	.13	−.52 to .55
Dizygotic twins	6	15.7	11–19	With co-twin	.53	−.22 to .86
				With self	.75	.32 to .88
				With control	.11	−.86 to .55

* See text for explanation of this r.

clinical EEG record with spike and sharp wave focus in the left temporal area.

For this subject the inter-hemispheric correlation was .08. No other MZ subject had self-correlation below .61; several were in the .90s. Four subjects from the monozygotic sample had higher correlations with their twin than with responses from the two sides of their own scalp. When VER records of twins were correlated with those of age and sex-matched controls, no correlation was as great as that of the twin with his co-twin.

Because of the small number of DZ twins, heritability ratios were not computed, but intraclass r's were found for the three primary VER components—alpha, beta, and theta—and for the mental test score. From an earlier twin study (Osborne, Gregor, & Miele, 1968) intraclass r's for face length, head circumference, height, weight, and color blindness were borrowed for comparative purposes.

From Table XIII–B it is seen that the MZ intraclass r's for the alpha and beta VER components are higher than the corresponding DZ correlations. For alpha the MZ r is .60; DZ, .12; for beta MZ r is .30; DZ, .08. For the slow-wave theta component, the DZ r is greater than that for identical twins, MZ, .20 and DZ, .46. In Table XIII–B the DZ intraclass r's for alpha, beta, and theta VER components are smaller than the r's for biometric data (with the exception of color blindness) but greater than r's for the mental test data. The psychometric and biometric control data, it might be added, represent heritability estimates of well-established polygenetic human characteristics (Huntley, 1966).

With the exception of the reversal of the intraclass r's for the theta component of the VER the experimental results support earlier studies indicating that the brain wave tracing is a heritable trait. The lowered intraclass r's for the VER components are a function of the small number

Table XIII–B
Intraclass Correlations for Psychometric, Biometric, and Visual Evoked Response Parameters

	Intraclass r's for MZ's	Intraclass r's for DZ's
Visual Evoked Response Components		
VER alpha, period in ms	.60	.12
VER beta, period in ms	.30	.08
VER theta, period in ms	.20	.46
Revised Beta Examination		
Revised Beta score (IQ)	.89	−.03
Biometric Resemblance		
Face length (mm)	.84	.69
Head circumference (in.)	.81	.54
Standing height (in.)	.88	.68
Weight (lbs.)	.84	.72
Color blindness (Dvorine)	.85	.04

of twins, especially DZ's, and the less than perfect method of determining periods for the alpha, beta, and theta VER components. Although the X-Y plots were read by well-trained judges, it is difficult to determine by visual inspection the periods of VER components when the plots are not sinusoidal.

The mean VER correlation for MZ's was .77, for DZ's, .53. These data compare favorably with Huntley's (1966) MZ of .83 and DZ of .58 for intelligence and MZ r's of .82 and DZ r's of .58 reported by Dustman and Beck (1965) for the visual evoked response. The concordance of correlations for biometric, psychometric, and VER data for the several twin samples is remarkable.

Many investigators, Schwartz and Shagass (1962), Kooi and Bagchi (1964), Dustman and Beck (1963), have reported the visual evoked response to be a reliable and stable physical measurement. Questions have been raised, however, by other investigators, Callaway and Buchsbaum (1965), Pampiglione (1967), Bickford, Jacobson, and Cody (1964), concerning the variability of the scalp evoked response. Is the VER stable over time? Can electrode placement and other laboratory techniques be standardized to yield reliable tracings? Does the number of responses averaged affect the stability of the VER? Are some portions of the tracing more stable than others? Inspection of the X-Y plots would suggest that the portion of the tracing immediately following the light flash is highly reliable while the later portions are unstable. VER records taken for the same subject as long as 17 weeks apart yield reliability coefficients ranging from .82 to .84. For the reliability study the electrodes were removed and replaced as nearly as possible to the original locations. When the electrodes were left in place and the flashes were repeated the same day, the reliability coefficients were all above .90. Inter-hemispheric correlations for the evoked response are no higher on the average than r's for the same subjects taken 4 to 17 weeks apart from the same electrode positions.

After 16 flashes the number of flashes comprising the average VER has little effect on the stability of the tracing. The VER produced from the average of 16 flashes correlates .89 with that produced by 64 flashes and .81 with that produced by 128 flashes. The 64 response average correlates .98 with the average of 128 flashes and .85 with the average of 256 flashes.

By dividing the VER tracing after the flash into three equal 250 ms plots and correlating each part with a corresponding part of another tracing of the same subject, the first third of the plot is shown to be highly stable. For ten tracings involving three different subjects the r's were all above .88. The median r for the first 250 ms was .94; for the middle third of the tracing, .62; for the last third of the plot, $-.07$. From these results it is clear that the visual evoked response is stable over time, although not all parts of the tracing are equally congruent. For all normal subjects the portion of the response evoked the first 250 ms after the flash is almost perfectly reliable. Some subjects' records appeared to be much more stable than others 500 or 750 ms after the stimulus.

Cortical response patterns evoked by a light stimulus were studied for identical and fraternal twins and for age and sex-matched control subjects. The evoked potential (VER) responses were analyzed with a dual-channel, on-line, active band-pass filter system which separated the raw VER into the three common EEG frequency bands. The signals were next fed to the four input channels of a CAT 1000 computer of average transients. For each subject four X-Y plots representing the raw VER and the three major VER components were obtained.

Comment: The visual evoked response determined from subdermal scalp electrodes is a stable and reliable physical measurement. Using only standard laboratory techniques the first 250 ms of the pattern after the stimulus is almost perfectly reliable for periods as long as 17 weeks.

The hereditary nature of the visual evoked response is shown by the high degree of similarity of response patterns for identical twins and by the predictable decrease in similarity for fraternal twins and for unrelated control subjects. The concordance of the visual evoked response intraclass correlations for MZ and DZ twins with those of well established polygenetic, biometric, and psychometric human characteristics is remarkable.

XIV

Electroencephalograms of Twins

In the previous chapter it was shown that the portions of the brain wave tracing known as the visual evoked response yielded intraclass correlations for MZ and DZ twins similar to those of well-established polygenetic, biometric, and psychometric human characteristics. In this chapter the more subjective and clinical aspects of the EEG tracing, including neurological interpretations, will be examined for the twins participating in this phase of the experiment. Heritability ratios will not be computed but records will be compared on the basis of those EEG characteristics known to be reliable indicators of electrical activity of the normal human brain.

The electroencephalogram is made up of electrical rhythms which may be distinguished on the basis of scalp location, amplitude, form, and frequency. Location of the electrical discharge is designated by the scalp placement of the surface electrode which will be fully explained later.

Wave amplitude, measured in microvolts, is determined by comparing peak-to-trough dimensions of a wave form to that of a signal of known voltage. Amplitudes are not always defined exactly. Abnormally high or low voltages are generally indicated in the diagnostic impression, while voltages in the middle ranges are not mentioned or are said to be "within normal limits."

Wave forms are described by technicians to convey important diagnostic information to the neurologist. Except when the wave forms have specific diagnostic significance—for example, positive spikes or spike and wave forms—broad, general, descriptive terms are used. The diagnostic impression may mention such wave characteristics as "small, spiky, sharp waves, low voltage, irregular fast patterns."

Frequency is described in cycles per second (cps) or by the Greek letters, alpha, beta, or theta, which represent relatively broad wave bands. The alpha wave band covers 8 through 16 cps; beta, 14 through 22 cps; and theta, 4 through 8 cps. Occasionally very slow waves, delta waves, are observed in the .5 to 3.0 cps range.

Although the placement of scalp electrodes may vary slightly from one laboratory to another, all systems use standard physiological landmarks as points of reference. Normally a minimum of eight electrodes are placed at symmetrical points in the frontal, temporal parietal and occipital regions. Ear lobes serve as reference electrodes. The system of electrode placement used in this experiment is shown in Figure XIV–

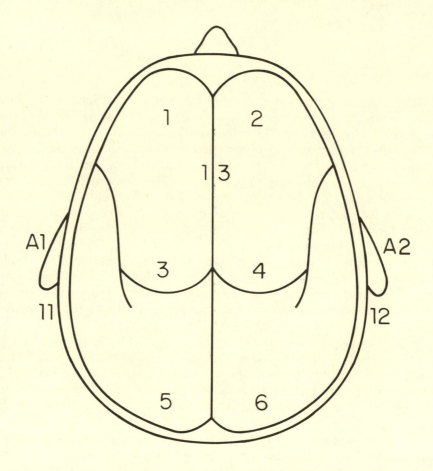

University of Georgia
EEG LABORATORY

Figure XIV–1. System of electrode placement used in the twin study.

1. In addition the technician may vary the entire ensemble of electrodes at the console of the EEG machine.

All areas of the human cortex are able to produce alpha rhythms. However, the amplitude and frequency may differ from one cortical region to the other. For example, occipital areas always show a higher alpha amplitude than the frontal. Furthermore, the alpha rhythm is not the same over the entire scalp. This is demonstrated in Figure 1, Chapter XIII.

Using the system described in Chapter XIII, EEG records of twins were analyzed. Portions of the twin records 910–1 and 910–2 in Figure XIV–2 demonstrate: (1) all areas of the scalp not only produce alpha

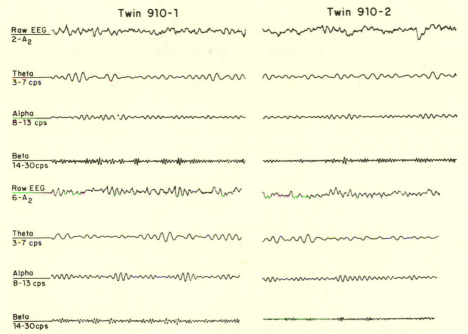

Figure XIV–2. Identical portions of analyzed EEG records of twin pair 910. The raw signal from the right frontal electrode, 2-A_2, is seen in the first channel. Theta, alpha, and beta activities contained in the raw signal are visible simultaneously on channels 2, 3, and 4. Note especially that the alpha activity, not normally prominent in the frontal areas, shows up clearly in the analyzed record.

In the lower half of the figure, the analysis is repeated using the signals from the right occipital areas, 6-A_2. Alpha activity is seen clearly in the raw signal and on the alpha channel. Beta and theta do not show up clearly in the raw signal but are prominent in the analyzed records.

Examination of the left and right halves of the figure demonstrates that electroencephalograms of these twins are remarkably similar in respect to wave form, frequency, and amplitude. (See Chapter XIII for a description of the frequency analyzer used in this experiment.)

rhythms but also beta and theta rhythms; (2) the remarkable similarity of the EEG patterns of MZ twins.

In addition to the frequency analyzer, the EEG technician has other methods of teasing out the information needed by the neurologist to arrive at a valid diagnostic impression. As the subject falls asleep, the electrical activity of the brain goes through a series of changes easily recognized on the EEG tracing. At the beginning of drowsiness in the normal subject, the alpha rhythm is gradually replaced by irregular, mixed frequency activity. As the subject goes from light to moderately deep sleep, bilateral synchronous slow activity is discerned. With the onset of deep sleep the record slows even more, down to .5 cps. MZ twins 906–1 and 906–2 are concordant for most EEG activity except for sleep records, portions of which are shown in Figure XIV–3. Twin 906–1 exhibits a normal sleep record while spike and wave activity in the 906–2 record suggests a convulsive tendency. See Figure XIV–3 and diagnostic impression for twins 906–1 and 906–2 under electroencephalographic findings.

Overbreathing or hyperventilation also alters the normal waking EEG activity. With overbreathing there is a gradual onset of slow waves and a reduction of alpha and beta rhythms. With the cessation of hyperventilation, the record returns to normal within 30 to 60 seconds. The records of DZ twins 917–1 and 917–2 look very much alike except for the hyperventilation runs. In fact, both would be classified normal except that overbreathing by 917–1 elicited paroxysmal abnormalities, especially in the left frontal area. See Figure XIV–4 and the diagnostic impression for this pair of twins.

A third common method used to enhance the EEG activity is a flashing light. Photic stimulation of stroboscopic light produces general cerebral

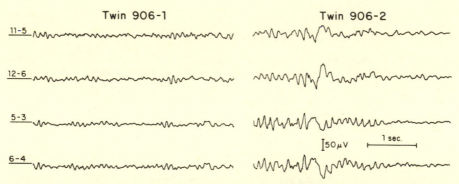

Figure XIV–3. Identical portions of EEG's of MZ twin pair 906 during sleep. The tracing of twin 906–1 reflects a normal sleep pattern. The chart of 906–2 indicates definite and frequent spike activity in sleep, which suggests a minimal convulsive tendency.

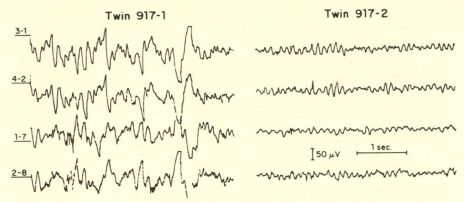

Figure XIV–4. Records of DZ twin pair 917 after 2 min. 40 sec. of hyperventilation. Overbreathing elicits paroxysmal abnormalities especially in the temporal area for 917–1 and increases spiky activity for 917–2, though the overall clinical EEG's of both are within normal limits.

activity over a wide range of frequencies. The stimulation is usually presented with the subject's eyes closed, using a system very similar to that described in the evoked response experiment in Chapter XIII. Records of MZ twins 913–1 and 913–2 manifest the normal response to flicker despite the fact that both records show other abnormalities. (See electroencephalographic findings in the following section.) The alpha rhythm of 913–1 is 9 cps; 913–2, 10 to 11. With the onset of the flashing light, alpha blocking is clearly evident in Figure XIV–5. At higher fre-

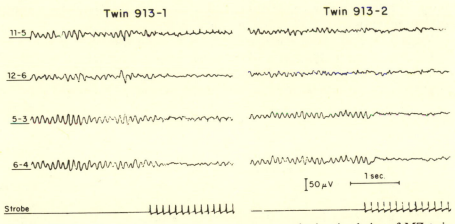

Figure XIV–5. Identical portions of the responses to photic stimulation of MZ twin pair 913. Although records of both twins are abnormal in other ways, their responses to photic stimulation are normal and remarkably similar. At the onset of the flashing light, alpha blocking is clearly visible.

quencies, subharmonics of the flicker frequency are sometimes noted.

Nineteen pairs of twins participated in the EEG experiment. For most subjects, the complete record included frequency analysis, sleep recording, hyperventilation activity, and reaction to variable light flicker. While some tense and anxious subjects were unable to fall asleep, others had to be aroused to get a full waking record. The EEG's were interpreted by a neurologist who was unaware the subjects were twins. Interpretations of the EEG records are given below. Where differences or similarities between the twins are quite apparent, significant portions of the tracings will be shown; otherwise, only the diagnostic impression will be reported.

Electroencephalographic Findings

Twin 901–1 is white, male, MZ, CA18. There is a spiky 11 cps occipital alpha rhythm with a moderate amount of spiky, fast activity in all areas, together with scattered small, sharp waves and some 6 to 7 cps waves. Voltage is higher on the far left portion. Photic stimulation produced a spiky, fast response, higher on the left especially at 15 flashes per second. Diagnostic impression: Despite the spiky, fast activity this tracing is within normal limits.

The tracing of twin 901–2 generally has a very spiky appearance. There is a 12 cps alpha rhythm which is well sustained. Small spikes and occasional sharp waves are mixed in with it. There is a moderate amount of 6 to 7 cps activity. At times this seems more common on the left in the temporal areas. There is little change on photic stimulation. Hyperventilation adds fast activity. Diagnostic impression: The large amount of spiky, fast activity puts this tracing into the borderline category. Could the subject have been on antihistamines or some other medication which might have produced the fast activity?

Twin 902–1 is white, female, MZ, CA20. This tracing was taken in the waking state only, when subject was said to have been very tense and nervous. There is a well-developed 10 cps occipital alpha rhythm, slightly spiky at times because of some superimposed spiky 18 to 24 cps activity. Some 5 to 7 cps activity is noted. At times active scalp and jaw muscles obscure cortical patterns. The record is stable on hyperventilation. Flicker evokes fast waves. Diagnostic impression: Looks quite normal.

For twin 902–2 there is well-developed 10 cps alpha rhythm. Low-voltage fast activity gives the alpha a spiky wave form at times. There is a moderate amount of 5 to 7 cps activity which increases in drowsiness. The tracing shows little change in hyperventilation. Flicker adds fast waves. Diagnostic impression: A normal tracing.

Twin 903–1 is white, female, MZ, CA22. Alpha prevails at 10½ to 11 cps. Muscle artifact is prominent. Hyperventilation produces little or no slowing. Photic driving is present at 8 through 15 cps with added first subharmonic at ten. Very mild depression of activity is seen on the right. Diagnostic impression: Normal.

For twin 903–2 alpha rhythm is 11. Fast and slow frontal and central activity occurs when sleepy. Hyperventilation produces little or no slowing. Photic driving is seen at 8 to 15 cps, mostly with subharmonics. Diagnostic impression: Normal.

Twin 904–1 is white, female, MZ, CA18. A spiky-looking 11 to 12 cps occipital alpha rhythm is better maintained and is bigger on the left. Low-voltage spiky, fast activity is prominent. A moderate amount of 4 to 7 cps activity and a few slower waves are apparent. Spikes occur in both hemispheres. Some display fast activity. Sharp waves appear in #7 and #11, the left anterior and posterior temporal areas. There is little change on hyperventilation. A marked spiky, fast response to photic stimulation is visible. Diagnostic impression: This is a borderline tracing because of the spiky asymmetrical patterns higher on the left, and the spikes and sharp waves.

Twin 904–2 demonstrates an intermittent 12 cps occipital alpha rhythm. Superimposed fast waves give it a spiky appearance. A good deal of 6 to 7 cps activity is present. Small, sharp and spiky patterns often appear in the left parieto-occipital area. Response to flicker creates bigger and spikier waves on the left. Hyperventilation brings out the spiky patterns. Diagnostic impression: Normal except for some very minor spiky patterns in the left parieto-occipital region. These may be a residual of her childhood injury.

Twin 905–1 is white, female, MZ, CA16. Low-voltage irregular, fast patterns and some 6 to 7 cps waves appear at the outset. Bursts of bigger 6 to 7 cps waves and sharp waves are present, along with occasional high-voltage sharp waves, spikes and spike and wave forms. Spikes and sharp waves increase with drowsiness. There are atypical sharp waves with the vertex hump stage. Fourteen cps spindles appear bilaterally. After arousal an 8 to 10 cps alpha rhythm is noted. Hyperventilation increases abnormalities only slightly. Flicker at 15 cps rate triggers spike and wave forms. Diagnostic impression: Mildly abnormal and compatible with a convulsive disorder. There is no focus, with a very marked photic sensitivity at 15 cps flash.

Twin 905–2 has an intermittent spiky 8 to 9 cps alpha rhythm. Spiky, fast waves also occur in runs. A good deal of 5 to 6 cps activity prevails. Spikes and sharp waves are common, especially in frontal and temporal leads. There are bursts of 14 and 6 cps positive spikes and 6 cps waves and 6 cps spike and wave forms which occur in sleep. Abnormal activity diminishes with arousal. Hyperventilation causes slight increase. Flicker at 15 cps evokes spike and wave forms. Diagnostic impression: This is an abnormal tracing and strongly suggests a seizure disorder.

Twin 906–1 is Negro, male, MZ, CA18. There is a well-maintained 11 cps occipital alpha rhythm which waxes and wanes. A few brief episodes of 4 cps waves are noted. Drowsy patterns are normal. Overbreathing elicits bursts of 3 to 4 cps waves with sharp waves, and a few spikes begin on the left and recur. Diagnostic impression: This tracing is borderline because of the bursts of slow, spike and sharp wave patterns on hyperventilation.

For twin 906–2 there is a well-developed and maintained 10 cps waking alpha rhythm. Five to 7 cps activity appears especially in anterior leads. With drowsiness larval spike and wave patterns develop. Four to 5 cps waves are prominent. No significant change on hyperventilation is seen. Diagnostic impression: Although the waking record is within normal limits, definite and frequent spike and wave activity in sleep suggests a minimal convulsive tendency.

Twin 907–1 is white, male, MZ, CA15. Subject displays a well-maintained 10 cps occipital alpha rhythm. Parietally 7 to 10 cps and fast waves are mixed together. Occasional 5 to 6 cps waves are visible. With drowsiness some groups of 5 to 7 cps waves and sharp waves are noted in electrode 7 and in electrode 7–11, dying out on arousal but returning on hyperventilation. Record is stable on flicker. Diagnostic impression: The record of the subject at rest is normal. When the subject is under the stress of hyperventilation or grows drowsy, a sharp wave focus becomes active in the left temporal area. This may be an after effect of trauma, as noted in the subject's history.

For twin 907–2 a 9 to 10 cps waking occipital alpha rhythm is apparent. A great deal of 4 to 7 cps activity takes place, often in brief episodes. The voltage varies and sharp patterns often occur. Sharp waves are displayed in electrode number 11–7 and in 7–8. Drowsiness produces spikes. Bursts of irregular spike and wave and sharp patterns occur at the vertex hump stage of sleep. Sharp waves occur in electrode 5. Sleep patterns are atypical in that the spindle and hump patterns are not well integrated. Hyperventilation evokes sharp waves. Diagnostic impression: This is a mildly abnormal tracing because of the irregular spike and wave bursts in light sleep. Various abnormal patterns are widely distributed in waking and drowsy states as well. They are common in the left temporal area.

Twin 908–1 is white, female, MZ, CA19. Tracing appears to have been taken in waking, drowsy and early sleep stages. There is a 9 cps occipital alpha rhythm but much 6 to 8 cps activity is also present. Low-voltage fast activity often appears spiky. Some runs of spiky 12 cps waves are noted. Four to 5 cps waves and frequent spiky 22 to 24 cps activity appears in early sleep. Some vertex humps are sharp. There are a few questionable spikes. Diagnostic impression: Although fast patterns are very spiky, this tracing can be classed as normal.

Twin 908–2 is characterized by an 8 cps occipital alpha rhythm. Five to 7 cps activity increases as the subject becomes drowsy. Low-voltage fast waves are very prominent in the parietal leads. Spikes and larval 6 cps spike and wave forms appear in this drowsy state. Biparietal activity at 30 to 35 cps appears with some positive spikes. Little change occurs on hyperventilation. Diagnostic impression: There is a great deal of fast activity and a few spikes and larval spike and wave activity occur. Not entirely normal. This subject can be classed as borderline. Further abnormality would probably appear in sleep. Shows atypical fast activity which sometimes correlates with headaches. Significant portions of the EEG's of twin pair 908 are shown in Figure XIV–6.

Twin 909–1 is white, male, MZ, CA11. Alpha exists at 9 cps. Theta is prominent at 6 cps, more rhythmic than alpha. No slowing is noticed during hyperventilation. Photic driving occurs down to 7 cps. High-voltage sleep humps have some sharp components. Diagnostic impression: Normal for age.

Twin 909–2 demonstrates a 9 cps occipital alpha rhythm, higher and spikier on the left. A good deal of 4 to 7 cps activity appears with the alpha, and 5 to 7 cps waves are prominent centrally. There is an average

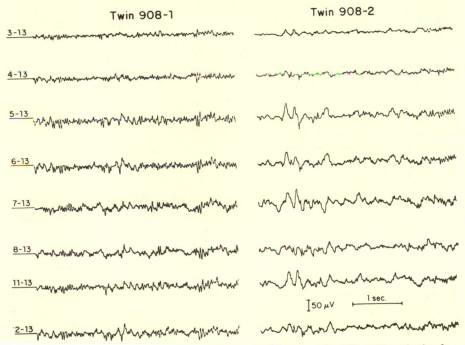

Figure XIV–6. Identical portions of EEG's of MZ twin pair 908. Although the fast patterns of 908–1 are very spiky, the record is classified as normal. Twin 908–2 manifests spike and wave activity and suggests a borderline abnormal record.

amount of 18 to 24 cps activity. The few sharp waves are greater on the left and continue to occur at the onset of sleep. In light sleep positive spike discharges are noted. The vertex sleep humps are spiky. Overbreathing accentuates the asymmetry and brings out sharp waves on the left. There was no significant change on flicker. Diagnostic impression. Borderline. Alpha asymmetry, positive spikes in sleep. Sharp waves on left and atypical sleep humps.

Twin 910–1 is white, male, MZ, CA18. There is a well-developed and well-maintained 10 cps occipital alpha rhythm. A good deal of 5 to 7 cps activity also appears. An average amount of low-voltage fast activity is displayed. No significant change takes place on hyperventilation. Flicker adds fast waves. Diagnostic impression: Entirely normal.

Twin 910–2 shows a 10 cps occipital alpha rhythm. A good deal of 6 to 7 cps activity and an average amount of low-voltage fast activity appear. Six to 7 cps activity is also prominent in the temporal leads. After two minutes of overbreathing, a high-voltage build-up of 2 to 4 cps waves and sharp waves occurs. These waves, which subside slowly, are biggest in the anterior leads, and some are notched. Flicker adds fast activity. Diagnostic impression: While subject is at rest, the record is within normal limits for age 18. The slow and excessive response to hyperventilation does not necessarily correlate with a seizure disorder, but suggests an inefficient homeostatic vasomotor regulation unable to cope with the mild stress of "blowing off" carbon dioxide.

Twin 911–1 is white, female, MZ, CA11. The dominant rhythm is well-established at 9 cps. During drowsiness some 5 to 6 cps waves and some superimposed 12 to 14 cps waves appear. Deeper sleep produces bursts of 3½ to 4½ cps waves. No focal abnormalities were noted. Hyperventilation evokes only a mild build-up, with a fairly quick return to the resting state. Diagnostic impression: EEG is within normal limits.

The basic background activity for twin 911–2 is a fairly well-developed 9 to 9½ cps. During drowsiness and light sleep there are 4 to 6 cps waves and faster 14 to 16 cps super-imposed waves. The record is not technically satisfactory owing to overswitching and excessive eye movement. Hyperventilation is marked by a moderate production of higher-voltage 3 to 4 cps waves, which return to the resting state after 40 seconds. Diagnostic impression: EEG is probably a normal one.

Twin 912–1 is white, male, MZ, CA21. There is a 9½ cps alpha with some beta. In the record there is little or no photic driving. High voltage results in some increase in alpha. Diagnostic impression: Normal.

For twin 912–2 there is a 9 cps alpha activity. Some photic driving is noted. Hyperventilation produces some irregular, diffuse, single delta waves with associated sharp waves. Diagnostic impression: Normal.

Twin 913–1 is white, male, MZ, CA19, who displays a well-maintained 9 cps occipital alpha rhythm. A good deal of 6 to 7 cps activity appears fronto-parietally. There are occasional spikes and sharp waves and a long run of mixed 6 and 10 cps activity. Similar patterns, which continue in drowsiness, occur in short bursts. Hyperventilation elicits mixed 4 to 7 cps waves and sharp waves and some bursts of atypical spike and wave forms. Diagnostic impression: Too much slow activity in the background. The tendency for the 6 to 7 cps waves to be episodic and the abnormal patterns on hyperventilation assign this tracing to the borderline class.

For twin 913–2 there is a well-developed and well-maintained 10 to 11 cps occipital alpha rhythm. At times it increases abruptly in voltage. Low-voltage fast activity appears and with it some 6 to 7 cps activity. A few questionable sharp patterns occur in drowsiness. There is a 5 cps abnormal discharge, which is generalized and consists of 6 to 8 cps sharp waves and some larval spikes. Larval forms of this recur. The tracing is stable on flicker and hyperventilation. Diagnostic impression: Normal when awake; definitely abnormal episode when drowsy. A sleep tracing is indicated.

Twin 914–1 is white, female, DZ, CA11. The first part of the tracing suggests drowsiness. Intermittent 10 cps and much 5 to 7 cps and low-voltage fast waves appear. There are many small, sharp waves and spiky, fast activity. Alpha is often better maintained on the left. Sharp waves are more common in the left anterior and posterior temporal areas than on the right. Hyperventilation evokes big 2 to 4 cps waves, sharp waves and some atypical spike and wave forms. Photic stimulation gives more regular fast activity. Diagnostic impression: This is a borderline fast tracing of a dysrhythmic type. There is a mild asymmetry and more findings in the left anterior and posterior temporal areas than in the right area.

For twin 914–2 waking patterns, composed of 4 to 6 cps waves and 18 cps sharp waves, are poorly organized. Runs of 9 to 10 cps alpha waves appear on the left but are sparse on the right where they are lower and show more slow activity. Sharp waves appear at random. On overbreathing, sharp waves and spiky patterns start on the left and build up generally. Slow waves are greater on the right. Spike and wave forms occur in the left occipito-posterior temporal region. The response to photic stimulation is greater on the left. Diagnostic impression: This is a poorly organized and asymmetrical tracing. Activity is depressed and slower on the right. The left cortex shows more evidence of irritability and suggests some tendency to seizures. With so much asymmetry some organic problem, damage or malformation may be suspected. See Figure XIV–7.

Twin 915–1 is white, female, DZ, CA12. The EEG shows very unstable patterns of 8 to 9 cps alpha with an almost equal amount of 5 to 7 cps activity. There is also much 18 to 24 cps activity in the fronto-

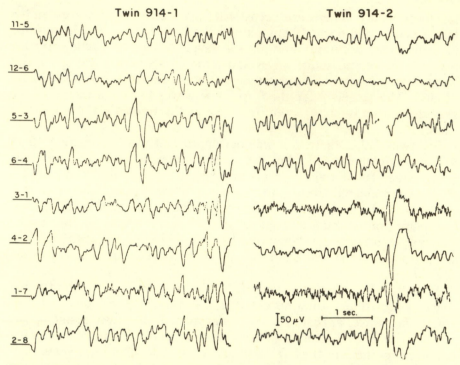

Figure XIV–7. Identical portions of EEG tracings of DZ twin pair 914. Both manifest similar abnormalities with sharp waves and atypical spike and wave forms. The tracing of 914–2 suggests a possible proneness to seizures or to some other organic problem, damage, or malformation.

central regions. Periods of widespread 1½ to 3 cps underlie the other rhythms. The wave forms are frequently ragged with scattered small, sharp patterns especially in the temporal leads. Runs of sharp waves occur more frequently on the left. Runs of 10 to 14 cps plus sharp waves appear in the drowsy state. Local 2 to 3 cps waves are visible in the right occipital. During counting and mental arithmetic there is very little arousal response. Hyperventilation evokes high-voltage fast and sharp waves and bursts of ragged spike and wave patterns. Diagnostic impression: This is a generally dysrhythmic, slow record with much sharp wave activity in both awake and drowsy states. An abnormal response to hyperventilation suggests a convulsive disorder.

Twin 915–2 has an 8 to 9 cps occipital rhythm with a 7 cps rhythm appearing in the parietals. Waves of 4 to 6 cps are very prominent in all areas, together with much 18 to 24 cps fast activity. Underlying 2 to 3 cps waves appear in the occipitals. Spiky, fast and small, sharp waves are widely noted, often in episodes which persist during drowsiness.

Hyperventilation produces an increase in fast and sharp patterns and generalized ragged spike and wave bursts. Diagnostic impression: This is a mildly abnormal, generally dysrhythmic record with a poorly maintained alpha rhythm, much theta activity and some beta activity. There are prominent sharp waves and bursts of abnormal patterns of hyperventilation. See Figure XIV–8.

Twin 916–1 is white, female, DZ, CA12, whose tracing is characterized by unstable patterns varying on the two sides with a generally poorly organized pattern of activity. Ten cps alpha waves appear in groups alternating irregularly with 4 to 7 cps waves. Low-voltage, often spiky fast activity occurs frequently, with many sharp waves and a few spikes. As the tracing continues, sharp waves and spiky patterns increase. With drowsiness, bursts of spiky waves are noted, as well as larval spike and wave forms. At the onset of sleep definite positive and negative spikes are mixed with the vertex sleep humps. These occur in long runs. Sleep spindles appear bilaterally but are not synchronous. Abnormal slow and

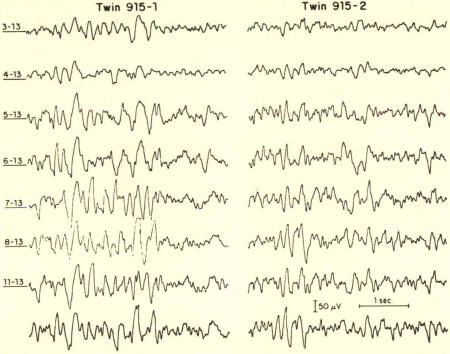

Figure XIV–8. Identical portions of the hyperventilation records of DZ twin pair 915. The response to overbreathing for twin 915–1 is abnormal and implies a convulsive disorder. The EEG of 915–2, mildly abnormal because of the prominent sharp waves and bursts of abnormal patterns of hyperventilation, is little better.

sharp patterns build up on hyperventilation. Lower voltage on the right sides produces a mild asymmetry. Diagnostic impression: This tracing is mildly abnormal because of its unstability and the randomly distributed paroxysmal abnormalities. Sleep patterns are more abnormal than waking activity.

The tracing of twin 916–2 begins in the waking state. It is characterized by a large mixture of frequencies in poorly organized patterns, which exhibit a great deal of difference between the hemispheres. The rhythm is 9 cps, often spiky. Four to 6 cps waves and small, sharp waves are common, with many irregular 2 to 3 cps waves present as baseline shifts. Frequent runs of irregular sharp waves occur in several areas but not as synchronous patterns. Some questionable spike and wave forms appear at times. Overbreathing augments the abnormal patterns. Response to photic stimulation is greater on the left. Diagnostic impression: A generally dysrhythmic tracing. One might expect such a record after an encephalitis or in a relative of an epileptic, though no such information appears on the subject's medical history. See Figure XIV–9.

Twin 917–1 is white, male, DZ, CA18, with a well-maintained 10 cps alpha rhythm which waxes and wanes in voltage. A moderate amount of low-voltage fast activity appears. Voltage occasionally increases and waves look sharp. Five to 7 cps activity appears at random. After 1½ minutes of hyperventilation, sharp waves begin to appear. They are greater on the left. Large 2 to 3 cps waves appear in the left frontal region. A general burst of slow, spike and sharp patterns occurs at the end. The left frontal area is slow to return to normal. Diagnostic impression: The record while the subject is at rest is within normal limits.

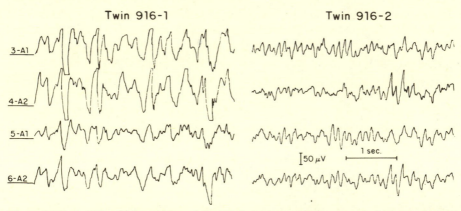

Figure XIV–9. Identical portions of the EEG tracings of DZ twin pair 916. The record of 916–1 is unstable with randomly distributed paroxysmal abnormalities. The tracing of 916–2 is generally dysrhythmic. Such a record might indicate an experience with encephalitis or some form of epilepsy. (See electroencephalographic findings.)

Overbreathing elicits paroxysmal abnormalities especially in the frontal area. All in all, a border-line case.

The tracing of twin 917–2 displays a very high-voltage, almost continuous 10 cps alpha rhythm. At times some associated fast waves give it a spiky wave form. Spiky, fast patterns are also mixed in. A moderate amount of 7 to 8 cps activity is present. Overbreathing increases spiky, fast waves and evokes a few sharp patterns. Diagnostic impression: The record of the subject while awake is within allowable limits although spiky, fast patterns are prominent.

Twin 918–1 is white, male, DZ, CA19. Tracing begins with drowsy patterns of irregular 4 to 6 cps fast waves. There is a mixture of alpha and sleep waves. The vertex hump component is prominent in drowsiness and often looks sharp. Some questionable spikes also appear. An artifact comes and goes and its source is not clearly evident. There are spiky sleep waves and some suspicious sharp waves. Fourteen cps sleep spindles eventually appear bilaterally. A 10 cps alpha follows arousal but slows to 8 cps. Hyperventilation is accompanied by a mild buildup. Flicker produces fast waves and subharmonics. Diagnostic impression: The waking activity seems quite normal. Sleep patterns are not quite typical. They look sharp and spiky with a considerable vertex hump component. The situation is confused by an irregularly appearing artifact.

Twin 918–2 has a well-developed 10 cps occipital alpha rhythm, which waxes and wanes. Low-voltage fast activity is prominent, as is a number of 6 to 7 cps waves. There are occasional sharp waves in the waking state. As subject becomes drowsy, 4 to 5 cps activity appears and the fast patterns become more rhythmic. When sleep begins, some of the bursts of slow waves are ragged-looking, notched slow and spike and wave forms. Runs of sharp waves appear. There was no change on hyperventilation. Flicker adds fast activity especially on the right. Diagnostic impression: The subject is normal awake and while on hyperventilation. Abnormal patterns are mixed with otherwise normal sleep rhythms.

Twin 919–1 is white, female, DZ, CA19. Subject displays an intermittent 11 cps occipital alpha rhythm. Ten cps activity is very prominent and tends to appear as clusters and runs of waves. There is a lot of low-voltage 5 to 7 cps activity. Some small, sharp waves appear at random. After 2½ minutes of overbreathing little buildup of sharp waves is noted. Diagnostic impression: With the subject at rest, the record is within normal limits. The response of the sharp waves to hyperventilation is abnormal, but nonspecific.

Twin 919–2 shows an 11 to 12 cps occipital alpha rhythm, spiky-looking because of the presence of much spiky, fast activity. Much of the time voltage is higher on the left. A moderate amount of 6 to 7 cps activity appears. Sharp waves and spiky patterns are frequent, with less frequent bursts. Overbreathing accentuates the spiky patterns. Diagnostic impression: This is a spiky-looking record with a mild amplitude asymmetry. The left side is higher. The record is just within the limits of normal.

Twin studies discussed in previous chapters emphasized comparisons of MZ and DZ twin groupings on a wide range of psychological tests. In this chapter, intra-twin comparisons were made of EEG characteristics known to be reliable indicators of electrical activity of the normal human brain.

Results from the sample of 19 pairs of twins suggest that, while both types of twin pairs are not perfectly concordant for all EEG characteristics, the similarities are remarkable. When one twin has a normal record, so in most cases does the other. Where abnormalities are observed, chances are that the same type of abnormality will also be noted in the twin partner, though not necessarily to the same degree. Although convincing clinical arguments may be made for the diagnostic impressions, the small number of observations would not support the statistical confidence of a much larger sample of EEG twin records.

XV

Short Reports on Supplemental Tests

In this chapter subpopulation differences in heritability will be examined for several psychological tests not reported previously. Seven tests were eliminated from the extended sample because they were either too time-consuming or too difficult for the majority of the subjects. One test was not included in the Basic Battery because of scoring difficulties and low reliability. It was also decided that results of psychological tests given to subjects participating in the EEG phase of the Twin Survey would be more appropriately included here than with the neurological findings (Chapter XIV).

To make the battery more interesting for the participants, the Mooney Faces Test was included. This examination is a test of closure or perceptual ability in which human faces are pictured (see Chapter VI). For the Twin Study the original test was reduced to the ten easiest and ten most difficult items. Even in its abbreviated version, it was too lengthy and yielded no new information about the subjects. Heritability ratios for the Mooney Faces Test for black, white, and the total group are shown in Table XV–A. Neither heritability ratios *(H)* nor within-pair

Table XV–A

Heritability Coefficients for the *Mooney Faces Test* for Black and White Twins—Raw Scores

Group	MZ r	MZ N	DZ r	DZ N	T(Cor)	Heritability Ratios H	Heritability Ratios HR	Within-pair Variances MZ	Within-pair Variances DZ	Within-pair Variances F
White	.37	137	.34	103	.27	.05	.17	12.73	12.50	.98
Black	.33	28	.19	15	.42	.17	.84	16.32	13.50	.83
Total	.38	165	.34	118	.36	.06	.20	13.34	12.63	.95

variance F ratios show significant MZ-DZ differences. Whatever ability or aptitude the Mooney Faces Test measures (no validity coefficients were reported), there is no difference in the hereditary variance component for the two races.

The Whiteman Test of Social Perception is another buffer test that was eliminated after the first testing. This test was originally designed "to investigate the hypothesis that social and perceptual performance in schizophrenics is impaired relative to that of a normal group" (Whiteman, 1954, p. 266). The justification for using the Whiteman Test was that it provided a change of pace from the tasks requiring mental alertness, attention, and concentration (see discussion of Whiteman Test in Chapter VI). Despite the lack of face validity of the Whiteman Test, for the purpose of this study heritability ratios deserve comment. The within-pair variance F ratio for whites is insignificant (Table XV–B). Heritability ratios are, however, significant for blacks and for the total group, though there could be some sampling error since the number of black twins is small, 28 MZ and 15 DZ pairs.

Card Rotation was the third test dropped from the second test series (see Chapter VI). Since the Basic Battery was overloaded with well-standardized and reliable spatial tests, it was decided to omit from the Basic Battery the Card Rotation Test, at best a weak test of spatial ability, requiring the subject to decide which of eight figures on the right show the same side as the model on the left (see Chapter VI). The task can be accomplished by mentally sliding the figures around or by verbal reasoning. Despite the low reliability and other weaknesses, the abilities required by the test have significant hereditary variance components for whites and the total group and the within-pair variance F ratio approaches significance for blacks (Table XV–C). On hindsight, Card Rotation should probably have been left in the Basic Battery since it requires only four minutes of working time.

Logical Reasoning is a test originally developed by Guilford for use with subjects in grades 11 to 16 and consists of formal syllogisms. The task is to choose a correct conclusion that can be drawn from two state-

Table XV–B

Heritability Coefficients for the *Whiteman Test of Social Perception* for Black and White Twins—Raw Scores

Group	MZ		DZ			Heritability Ratios		Within-pair Variances		
	r	N	r	N	T(Cor)	H	HR	MZ	DZ	F
White	.50	136	.49	103	.09	.02	.04	6.26	7.93	1.27
Black	.70	28	.16	15	1.97	.64	1.53	7.04	17.33	2.46*
Total	.59	164	.46	118	1.43	.23	.43	6.39	9.12	1.43*

* $p < .05$.

ments (see Chapter VI). The Logical Reasoning Test was much too difficult for our twin sample, many of whom were in the eighth grade. Nevertheless, heritability ratios were computed and are shown in Table XV–D. Although whites show no significant heritability component for logical reasoning, blacks, despite a much smaller sample, show a significant within-pair variance F ratio. Considering the small number of blacks, this could well be another sampling accident.

The Inference Test, Rs–3 in the Educational Testing Service Kit of Reference Tests and another in Guilford's Logical Reasoning series, requires the subject to read one or two statements similar to those found in a newspaper or magazine. The statements are followed by various conclusions which might be drawn from them. The subject is to decide which one of the conclusions can be drawn from the statements without assuming additional information. An item from the Inference Test follows:

13.   All human beings fall into four main groups according to the composition of their blood: O, A, B, and AB. Knowledge of these blood types is important for transfusions.
        1—The blood type is determined by genes.
        2—Persons of group AB can receive blood from any other type.

Table XV–C

Heritability Coefficients for the *Card Rotation Test* for Black and White Twins— Raw Scores

	MZ		DZ			Heritability Ratios		Within-pair Variances		
Group	r	N	r	N	T(Cor)	H	HR	MZ	DZ	F
White	.69	131	.53	103	1.93	.34	.47	790.31	1409.09	1.78*
Black	.71	28	.38	15	1.36	.53	.93	727.34	1368.23	1.88
Total	.70	159	.54	118	2.15	.35	.46	779.22	1403.89	1.80*

* $p < .01$.

Table XV–D

Heritability Coefficients for the *Logical Reasoning Test* for Black and White Twins—Raw Scores

	MZ		DZ			Heritability Ratios		Within-pair Variances		
Group	r	N	r	N	T(Cor)	H	HR	MZ	DZ	F
White	.39	135	.44	103	−.46	−.09	−.26	8.27	6.72	.81
Black	.65	28	.17	15	1.70	.57	1.47	4.14	8.90	2.15*
Total	.45	163	.46	118	−.12	−.02	−.05	7.56	7.00	.93

* $p < .05$.

3—Blood transfusions between members of the same group are always safe.

4—Certain percentages of all people belong to each type.

5—Blood from persons of group O can safely be given to persons of any group.

Designed for students in grades 11 to 16, the test was obviously too difficult for average pupils in lower grades. Heritability ratios for the Inference Test are given in Table XV–E. No comparison of twins for either race yields a significant heritability variance component.

The Cancellation Test is another change-of-pace or buffer test which offers the subject a break between more demanding mental tasks. The examinee is asked to draw a vertical line through each group of five dots and a horizontal line through each group of four dots. The test presumably measures differences in eye-hand coordination and motor speed (see Chapter VI). Within-pair variance F ratios are significant at the .01 level for whites and for the total group.

On inspection, the test appears to be the type Jensen would call a Level I test. It involves the neural registration and consolidation of stimulus material and the formation of new associations. Level I abilities are tapped mostly by tests such as the Digit Span, rote learning, trial and error learning, and perhaps certain visually presented material. The Cancella-

Table XV–E

Heritability Coefficients for the *Inference Test* for Black and White Twins— Raw Scores

Group	MZ r	MZ N	DZ r	DZ N	T(Cor)	Heritability Ratios H	Heritability Ratios HR	Within-pair Variances MZ	Within-pair Variances DZ	Within-pair Variances F
White	.56	137	.56	102	−.02	−.004	−.006	3.73	4.64	1.24
Black	.41	28	.07	15	1.05	.37	1.68	2.21	1.90	.86
Total	.57	165	.59	117	−.24	−.05	−.07	3.47	4.29	1.23

Table XV–F

Heritability Coefficients for the *Cancellation Test* for Black and White Twins— Raw Scores

Group	MZ r	MZ N	DZ r	DZ N	T(Cor)	Heritability Ratios H	Heritability Ratios HR	Within-pair Variances MZ	Within-pair Variances DZ	Within-pair Variances F
White	.67	135	.52	100	1.81	.32	.46	1104.15	1826.72	1.65*
Black	.64	27	.69	15	−.29	−.19	−.18	1047.80	1736.13	1.66
Total	.67	162	.55	115	1.53	.26	.35	1094.76	1814.90	1.66*

* $p < .01$.

Table XV–G
Heritability Coefficients for the *Ship Destination Test* for Black and White Twins—Raw Scores

Group	MZ r	N	DZ r	N	T(Cor)	Heritability Ratios H	HR	Within-pair Variances MZ	DZ	F
White	.72	136	.38	103	3.79	.54	.95	25.68	65.98	2.57*
Black	.76	27	−.12	15	3.17	.79	2.31	18.96	31.40	1.66
Total	.74	163	.41	118	4.17	.56	.89	24.56	61.58	2.51*

* $p < .01$.

tion Test deserves more study, starting perhaps with a factor analysis with other tests of the Twin Study.

By far the most difficult test in the battery was developed by Christensen and Guilford and called the Ship Destination Test. The task required is to use knowledge of the position of a ship with respect to a port, wind direction, ocean current, and direction of heading to compute the distance to port following given rules. However difficult the test may be, it still yields for white twins the highest heritability ratio *(H)* of any test discussed in this chapter. The within-pair variance ratio is significant at the .01 level (Table XV–G).

The *F* ratio for the total group is also significant at the .01 level. For blacks it approaches significance. Ship Destination is another test that was eliminated from the second series (see Chapter V).

Although the Mazes Test was given in both sessions, scores were found to be so unreliable that it was not analyzed as part of the Basic Battery. Mazes were among the first nonverbal tests of intelligence and are still basic to individual tests such as the Wechsler or Terman Scales. But difficulties arose when we attempted to adapt an individually administered test for classroom use. After the first testing, scoring problems became apparent. In order to retain the test in the battery, it was decided to use two methods of scoring. The number of half mazes completed was to be one score; the number of errors, the second. The first score measures the speed of response; the second measures accuracy. The younger subjects did not comprehend or did not carefully follow directions of the examiners who were not able to observe all subjects as they marked the mazes. As a result, some children quickly traced a path from start to end, disregarding cul-de-sacs by crossing lines or by retracing their paths. Other children erased their work and started over again. These errors would have been avoided if the test could have been given individually. Even trained psychometrists could not score the mazes consistently. Nevertheless, the Mazes Test results are reported in Table XV–H.

Three psychological tests were given to participants in the EEG phase

Table XV-H
Heritability Coefficients for the *Mazes Test* for Black and White Twins—Raw Scores

Variable	MZ		DZ		T(Cor)	Heritability Ratios		MZ		DZ		T(Mn)	F
	r	N	r	N		H	HR	Mn	SD	Mn	SD		
Mazes ½ blocks													
White	.59	168	.45	127	1.58	.25	.47	29.10	8.61	28.19	7.75	.94	1.18
Black	.48	74	.20	46	1.68	.35	1.17	22.79	7.59	22.26	7.33	.38	1.78*
Total	.60	242	.43	173	2.32	.30	.57	27.17	8.80	26.62	8.08	.66	1.34*
Mazes errors													
White	.43	168	.16	127	2.43	.31	1.23	9.26	6.72	9.72	6.14	-.62	1.49**
Black	.51	74	.22	46	1.76	.37	1.14	14.46	13.84	12.16	9.71	1.06	.97
Total	.50	242	.20	173	3.49	.38	1.21	10.85	9.78	10.37	7.35	.57	1.14

* p < .05.
** p < .01.

Table XV-I
Heritability Coefficients for the *Torrance Test of Creativity*—Raw Scores

Variable	MZ		DZ		T(Cor)	Heritability Ratios		Within-pair Variances		F
	r	N	r	N		H	HR	MZ	DZ	
Fluency-Verbal	.33	11	.51	6	-.33	-.38	-1.13	296.32	276.67	.93
Flexibility-Verbal	.27	11	.17	6	.16	.12	.75	60.00	62.42	1.04
Originality-Verbal	.21	11	-.32	6	.80	.40	5.00	569.41	614.17	1.08
Fluency-Figural	.72	11	.67	6	.12	.13	1.20	9.00	30.67	3.41*
Flexibility-Figural	.50	11	.44	6	.11	.10	.23	9.27	20.58	2.22
Originality-Figural	.39	11	.25	6	.22	.18	.70	83.00	89.67	1.08
Figural Elaboration	.47	11	-.45	6	1.48	.64	3.92	287.73	228.33	.79

* p < .05.

of the study. Although the number of subjects is so small that heritability ratios are suspect, the findings deserve brief comment. The Torrance Test of Creativity (1966), another buffer test, is given in a relaxed, casual manner and does not demand too much attention and concentration. The subject is asked to state the causes of an illustrated event, guess about the consequence of an event, suggest ways to improve a toy, and think of unusual uses for cardboard boxes and tin cans. Several subtests are direct modifications of Guilford's work. Other subtests are adaptations of earlier tests of drawing completion. Altogether there are seven subtests, four verbal and three figural, named to match the factors Guilford identified as fluency, flexibility, originality, and elaboration.

Heritability ratios for the Torrance Test are shown in Table XV–I. One of the seven subtests, figural fluency, yields a significant within-pair variance F ratio. Minimal significance should be attached to these findings not only because of the small number of twins involved but also because of the author's comments concerning figural fluency: "The impulsive thinker, the banal thinker, and even the 'non-thinker' can achieve rather easily high scores. . . . More meaning may perhaps be attached to low than to high scores" (Torrance, 1966, p. 74).

The Revised Beta Examination, a short nonverbal intelligence test, was also given to the subjects in the EEG study. The Beta was first developed during World War I for testing draftees unable to read and write. The revised edition is suitable for use with most of the lower- and middle-ability ranges of the general population (Table XV–J). The within-pair variance F ratio is statistically significant for the Beta IQ beyond the .01 level. With such small numbers, only a sampling accident could have yielded such a highly significant F ratio.

The Minnesota Multiphasic Personality Inventory is the last test to be considered (Table XV–K). The within-pair variance ratios for the clinical scales are suspiciously high. However, only the Depression scale suggests that the variance accounted for by heredity is more significant than that accounted for by environment. Within-pair variance ratios for four other scales, Hypochondriasis, Hysteria, Paranoia, and Hypomania, approach significance, but none was found to be significant in a much

Table XV–J

Heritability Coefficients for the *Revised Beta Examination* for Black and White Twins—IQ

Variable	MZ		DZ		T(Cor)	Heritability Ratios		Within-pair Variances		
	r	N	r	N		H	HR	MZ	DZ	F
IQ	.91	13	.11	6	2.16	.90	1.76	17.62	92.92	5.28*

* $p < .01$.

Table XV-K

Heritability Coefficients for the *Minnesota Multiphasic Personality Inventory* for Black and White Twins—T-scores

Variable	MZ		DZ			Heritability Ratios			Within-pair Variances		
	r	N	r	N	T(Cor)	H	HR	MZ	DZ	F
Hypochondriasis (Hs)	−.20	11	−.12	6	−.11	−.07	.75	100.59	243.08	2.42
Depression (D)	.76	11	−.33	6	1.99	.82	2.87	37.68	283.83	7.53*
Hysteria (Hy)	.19	11	.10	6	.14	.10	.95	62.23	125.92	2.02
Psychopathic deviate (Pd)	.10	11	.72	6	−1.21	−2.26	−13.05	68.91	47.42	.69
Masculinity-femininity (Mf)	.63	11	.42	6	.43	.36	.67	37.32	24.08	.65
Paranoia (Pa)	.53	11	−.43	6	1.55	.67	3.64	64.18	132.50	2.06
Psychasthenia (Pt)	.39	11	−.06	6	.70	.42	2.32	98.05	165.83	1.69
Schizophrenia (Sc)	.35	11	.17	6	.29	.22	1.03	120.45	224.08	1.86
Hypomania (Ma)	.56	11	.06	6	.84	.53	1.77	40.14	110.33	2.75
Social introversion (Si)	.48	11	.13	6	.58	.41	1.46	65.68	98.00	1.49

* $p < .01$.

170

larger twin study by Gottesman (1963). Despite claims to the contrary, personality factors whether measured by the Minnesota Multiphasic Personality Inventory, the Cattell Junior High Personality Questionnaire, or other personality tests seem to show that environment causes more variance than heredity.

The short reports presented in this chapter are offered to round out the analysis of psychological tests given in the twin project. Investigators wishing to explore more fully the tests described here or in other chapters will find the necessary raw data in the Appendix.

XVI

Concluding Remarks

In this final chapter we attempt to bring together the major findings reported in the previous chapters and to relate the evidence to the primary goals and purposes of the study. The nature of twins automatically restricts the number of prospective participants and limits considerably the experimental ideal of numbers of subjects neatly balanced by age, race, sex, and zygosity. Occurring only once in about every 88 live births, twins are easily identified by their teachers, friends, and parents, but both twins of a set do not always volunteer in the desired numbers or types for an experiment, especially an experiment which involves blood-typing and psychological testing, requirements which undoubtedly discourage some prospective volunteers. Because of these practical reasons and because of the ever increasing number of local, state, and federal restrictions on the use of human subjects in experiments involving psychological tests, the data were collected over an eight-year period.

For some reason not known, black male DZ twins did not volunteer for the study in the same proportion as black female DZ's nor as white male DZ's. The black-white proportion, however, of the total group was not appreciably different from the 1970 U.S. census.

No doubt, other aspects of the experimental design may be faulted by J. M. Thoday (1973) who may invoke "environmental factor X" to explain the findings and by Richard Lewontin who believes "it is a waste of taxpayer's money to study IQ, heredity, or other genetic components of human personality" ("We're all the same under the skin," 1976).

Despite the less than ideal experimental conditions, the new and positive aspects of the twin study should not be overlooked. Excepting the Scarr-Salapatic study (1971) in which zygosity was estimated from group data rather than being directly determined by blood tests, this study contains the largest sample of black American twins reported to date.

172

Anwar Riad A. Rhiem of Minia, Egypt, is at present attempting to replicate our work with Egyptian school children.

Blood-typing for zygosity diagnosis was performed by one of the most highly regarded blood banks in the United States, War Memorial Blood Bank, Minneapolis, Minnesota. Psychological tests in all cases were administered by expert psychometrists according to standard published instructions. To rule out the possibility of examiner bias, approximately one-third of the subjects in the Georgia sample were tested by black examiners. To insure reliability, biometric measurements were made three separate times. The average was used for zygosity determination.

Reliability of the psychological measurements is attested by the significantly high split-half reliability coefficients for both subtests and factor IQ's of the Basic Battery. Reliabilities of the Primary Mental Abilities Test and Cattell's Culture Fair Intelligence Test meet standards for published group IQ tests.

Validity of mental measurements was determined in two ways: 1) by correlating tests of unreported validity with standardized tests of known validity; for example, subtests and total score of the Basic Battery were correlated with the Primary Mental Abilities IQ; and 2) by correlating Cattell's Culture Fair Intelligence Test and the Primary Mental Abilities Test with measures of school achievement—spelling and arithmetic. In all cases validity coefficients compare favorably with those of published standardized IQ tests such as the Wechsler or Binet.

The socio-economic status of the twins tested in Georgia reflects the cross-section of the State, representing rural areas, small industrial towns, and large metropolitan areas. Since the Kentucky sample was also drawn from public school volunteers, there is no reason to expect it does not reflect a cross-section of the population of that state.

The test battery was designed to make it possible to compare the motivation of black and white twins on tests of different levels of difficulty. Performance on tests requiring mental concentration and attention was compared with the results of nonverbal buffer tests which do not demand a high degree of mental capacity. Black students performed as well on the difficult verbal reasoning tests as they did on the simple repetitive tasks. In the ability range represented by our sample, IQ's 68 to 135, the level of test difficulty does not appear to impair the motivation of black twins.

Cultural bias of psychological test items is frequently cited as an explanation of performance differences between blacks and whites. The possibility of culture bias of tests in the Twin Study was examined in two ways. Included in the Basic Battery was a broad spectrum of difficult mental ability tests reflecting school learning and verbal reasoning and also easy nonverbal tests requiring only attention and cooperation. If, as claimed by some, the tests are biased in favor of the white middle-class subject, tests scores of blacks should be relatively higher on the latter than on the former. This is not the case. Black performance is as high and in some cases higher on the culturally loaded tests as on the culture free tests. The idea of cultural bias of test items was also examined in another way. Cattell's Culture Fair Intelligence Test was administered as part of the Twin Study Battery. In the case of the CCFIT, results are even more convincing that standardized mental ability tests are not unfair to blacks. Despite the fact that *all* items on the CCFIT are nonverbal and all are novel and no subject has specialized training that would transfer to the test, the black-white performance difference was greater on the Cattell Culture Fair Intelligence Test than on any other test in the battery, the difference sometimes approaching 20 IQ points.

Leon Kamin was not the first to claim and to attempt to demonstrate with *post hoc* correlations a strong effect of age on the IQ of twins. A. L. Stinchcombe (1969) suggested that environments accumulate much as interest does when compounded. By carefully selecting twin studies for review and calculating age—IQ correlations based on groups of seven, three, nine, and three pairs of twins while ignoring groups of 14 and 24 pairs, Kamin (1974) concludes, "The data seem to indicate, however, either that our leading I.Q. tests are very badly standardized, or that general population norms do not apply to twins, or that the twin samples studied by psychologists are bizarre—or all three" (p. 65). Any prudent first year graduate student would reject these conclusions out of hand. The serious reader interested in the age-IQ relationship and the related literature is referred to Chapter XI, Stablility of IQ. The IQ is stable not only for the total group of twins in the study but for both types of twins even when analyzed by race and sex.

Prenatal environment of twins, birth order, and Rh incompatibility are sometimes cited as factors contributing to low mental test performance of minorities. These factors, along with malnutrition and infantile lead poisoning, are beyond the scope of this study.

Regardless of the efforts of the investigator, there is no defense against what one might call the Bodmer paralogism. W. F. Bodmer (1972) has concluded that the difference in average IQ between American blacks and whites "could be explained by environmental factors, many of which we still know nothing about" (p. 112). Peter Urbach (1974) replies: "Professor Bodmer is of course right; everything in the world can be explained by factors about which we know nothing" (p. 253, Part 2).

In spite of the many weaknesses in the twin method, human twins provide the best subjects available for the study of genetic-environmental interactions. The four primary purposes of the present study were stated in Chapter IV and are restated here: 1) to determine the difference in average performance of U.S. blacks and whites on a wide variety of intelligence (IQ) tests; 2) to examine the proposition that differences in variance in general intelligence are essentially the results of inherited differences; 3) to determine if there are differences between U.S. blacks and whites in heritability of general intelligence; and 4) to make available raw test data, biometric measures, and blood test results for the 496 pairs of twins in the study.

Findings related to the first goal of the Twin Study are summarized in Figure XVI–1 in which means and standard deviations are shown for blacks and whites for the nine IQ tests which were derived from 22 different cognitive tests, representing the full range for both verbal

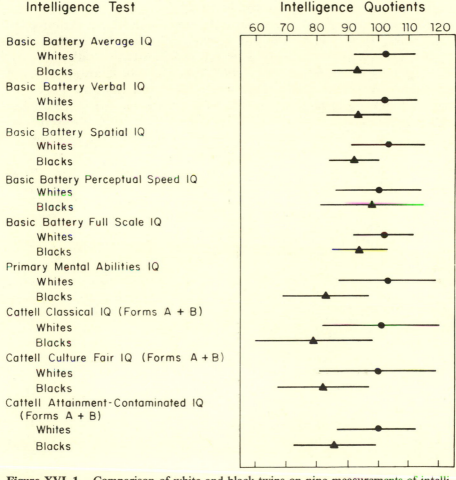

Figure XVI–1. Comparison of white and black twins on nine measurements of intelligence. The mean and standard deviation for each group are shown. Horizontal lines represent ±1 standard deviation.

and nonverbal measurements of the primary mental abilities. The pattern of mean differences is remarkably consistent regardless of the nature of the test. The results do not differ appreciably from reports of Shuey (1966), Jensen (1969), Loehlin *et al.* (1975), nor from data reported in the National Longitudinal Study (Levinsohn, Lewis, Riccobono, & Moore, 1976), and the HEW report, Equality of Educational Opportunity (1966). "The basic data are well known: on the average, Negroes test about 1 standard deviation (15 IQ points) below the average of the white population in IQ" (Jensen, 1969, p. 81). The differences represent overlaps of approximately 15%; that is, 15% of the black twins reached or exceeded the mean of whites.

To examine the proposition that differences in variance in general intelligence are essentially the results of inherited differences, 120 sets of the three classical heritability ratios were computed for various subpopulations as well as for the total group. Following the method used by Nichols (1969) in his analysis of 100 different twin studies, all MZ and DZ intraclass correlations for the 120 heritability ratios are brought together in Figure XVI–2. Subtest intraclass correlations are shown as closed circles; IQ intraclass correlations are represented as open circles.

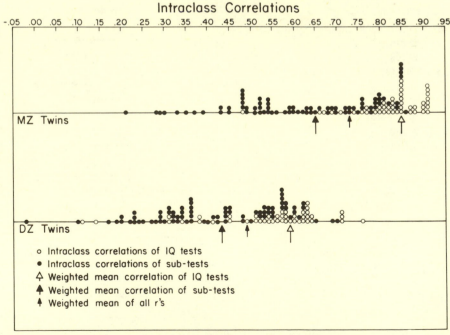

Figure XVI–2. Intraclass correlations of various mental ability dimensions from each substudy for MZ (identical) and DZ (fraternal) twins.

Table XVI-A
Comparison of the Heritability of Intelligence of Black and White Twins

Intelligence Tests	Heritability Ratios		Within-pair Variances			
	H	HR	MZ	DZ	F	U[a]
Basic Battery Average IQ						
White	.61	.54	14.1	35.7	2.53**	
Black	.75	.85	10.6	31.3	2.95**	1.48
Basic Battery Full Scale IQ						
White	.62	.58	15.5	36.6	2.36**	
Black	.70	1.15	14.8	47.8	3.22**	.73
Basic Battery Factor IQ						
Own Racial Group						
White	.58	.50	3517.4	9335.4	2.65**	
Black	.79	.73	1619.3	6398.3	3.95**	.31
Opposite Racial Group						
White	.58	.50	2839.1	7696.9	2.71**	
Black	.79	.77	1955.7	7340.8	3.75**	.62
Total Group						
White	.58	.50	3302.0	8822.3	2.67**	
Black	.79	.76	1838.9	7049.7	3.83**	.47
Primary Mental Abilities IQ						
White	.37	.52	86.5	106.5	1.23	
Black	.42	.61	57.4	118.0	2.06*	.169
Cattell Classical IQ (Forms A + B)						
White	.71	1.08	67.1	161.7	2.41**	
Black	.19	.24	129.6	154.1	1.19	1.88
Cattell Culture Fair IQ (Forms A + B)						
White	.65	.98	86.8	110.8	1.28	
Black	.38	.40	62.4	63.5	1.02	.61
Cattell Attainment-Contaminated IQ (Forms A + B)						
White	.70	1.07	38.8	66.2	1.71	
Black	.32	.46	52.2	74.5	1.43	.37

* $p < .05$.
** $p < .01$.
[a] difference in U's. Paulson's statistic for determining the significance of differences in F's.

From the figure it is clear that the range of intraclass r's is wide, indicating a variation in heritability among tests of the battery. However, when only the longer, more reliable IQ tests are considered (open circles) variation among the tests is greatly reduced, particularly for MZ's. Intraclass r's for IQ tests are generally high and all are positive, showing that both types of twins tend to be alike on the wide range of mental abilities represented in the study. MZ's in virtually all cases are more alike than DZ's. Arrows on the figure indicate weighted average intraclass correlations for subtests and for IQ's for the two types of twins. The difference in intraclass r's between fraternal and identical twins for IQ is .26, which is interpreted as indicating that one-half to three-fourths the variation in mental abilities measured in this study is due to genetic factors. Our estimates are statistically conservative since no h^2s have been corrected for attenuation. Errors of measurement normally make up about 5 to 10 percent of total phenotypic variance. Numerous other investigators have reported similar findings for Caucasians.

Our relatively large sample of black twins enables us now to compare the heritability estimates of IQ's of blacks and whites. The classical heritability ratios for the nine different IQ's are brought together in Table XVI–A. IQ's derived from all types of mental tests are represented ranging from the Attainment-Contaminated IQ of Cattell's scale to the 12-test IQ derived from the Basic Battery. Patterns of heritability ratios for blacks and whites are remarkably congruent, with the longer, more reliable tests yielding the most convincing heritability ratios. In no case are the black-white differences in within-pair variance F ratios significant. Even the short, nonverbal Cattell scales show insignificant between-race differences in F ratios. We interpret these findings as indicating that black and white twins have essentially the same pattern of mental test (IQ) heritability; that is, about one-half to three-fourths of the variance of both ethnic groups is due to genetic factors. While the existence of similar heritability patterns of blacks and whites might be considered self-evident, the fact that it can be demonstrated statistically is of major importance for studies of genetic-environmental interactions.

The fourth goal of the study, to provide all raw data to investigators interested in verifying the findings and examining unreported relationships among the variables, was accomplished by providing Appendixes A through H. Tapes of the appendixes are available from the author.

Appendix A

Appendix A is a guide to Appendixes B through H.

Appendix B identifies all variables which are listed in Appendixes C through H. The methods of obtaining anthropometric measurements, blood tests, and physical observations used to determine zygosity in the Twin Study are described. Although many of the psychological and other examinations are well-known, they are all described briefly and identified by author and publisher in Appendix B. Also included are reproductions of the SES rating scale and the Modified Project Talent Twin Questionnaire (Twin Survey Questionnaire).

Appendixes C through G identify the 123 Twin Study variables and list individual scores and measurements of the twins on the various psychological tests and other variables. For convenience, the variables are grouped to place similar results in the same appendix. For example, blood group genes are shown in Appendix C; all biometric measures are given in Appendix D.

The test raw scores for each twin are reported in the event investigators wish to verify reported findings or to examine new relationships.

In the tables found in the appendixes, rows represent twins identified by their unique numbers while columns refer to individual tests, biometric, and other variables. Column variables are identified in the text and in the appendixes.

Appendix H summarizes the data available in Appendixes C through G for the 496 pairs of twins in the Twin Study.

In the following table, all variables in Appendixes C through H are identified by column number and appendix:

Column #	Group	Appendix
1	Identification number: first three digits identify twin sets; fourth digit identifies twins within a set.	C–H
2	Sex: 1 = Male; 2 = Female	C–H
3	Race: 1 = White; 2 = Black	C–H
4	Age in years (last birthday)	C–H

Column #	Group	Appendix
5	Zygosity: M = MZ; D = DZ, same sex; U = DZ, unlike sex	C–H
6–19	Blood group genes	C
20–34	Biometric measurements, physical observations, and socio-economic status	D
35–66	Psychological tests, except personality	E
67–99	Psychological tests, personality	F
100–123	EEG Battery	G
124–133	Summary of data listed in Appendixes C through G	H

Appendix B

In Appendix B all Twin Study variables are identified or described. The first five variables identify the twins by sex, race, age, and zygosity. The next 28 variables describe the procedures used to obtain blood tests, anthropometric measurements, and physical observations used for zygosity determination. Variable 34 describes the socio-economic index used in this study. Next the psychological tests are identified by author and publisher. Finally, data from the EEG battery and summary variables are listed. Each variable is identified by a unique column number which is constant for all entries for that variable in all appendixes. Appendix B also contains a reproduction of the SES rating scale and the Modified Project Talent Twin Questionnaire (Twin Survey Questionnaire).

Scores or measurements for all variables described in this appendix have been listed in Appendixes C through H.

Column #	Variable
1	Identification number: first three digits identify twin sets; fourth digit identifies twins within a set.
2	Sex: 1 = Male; 2 = Female
3	Race: 1 = White; 2 = Black
4	Age in years (last birthday)
5	Zygosity: M = MZ; D = DZ, same sex; U = DZ, unlike sex.
6–19	Blood Group Genes
	Serological Tests: Group, M, N, S, s, P_1, D, C, E, c, Le^a, K, Fy^a, Jk^a.
	Reference: Serological tests were performed at the Minneapolis War Memorial Blood Bank, Minneapolis, Minnesota.
20	Face length
	Measurement: Distance in millimeters from trichion to gnathion measured with a sliding compass.
	Reference: M. F. Ashley Montagu, *An Introduction to Physical Anthropology.* Charles C. Thomas: Springfield, Illinois, 1951.

Column #   *Variable*

21   Maximum head length
        Measurement: The distance in millimeters between the glabella
        and the farthest point on the midline on the back of the head
        measured with a spreading caliper.
        Reference: M. F. Ashley Montagu, *(op. cit.)*

22   Maximum head breadth
        Measurement: The greatest transverse distance in millimeters of
        the head (usually found over each parietal bone) measured with
        a spreading caliper.
        Reference: M. F. Ashley Montagu, *(op. cit.)*

23   Head circumference
        Measurement: The distance in millimeters from the area between
        the eyebrows around the maximum projection of the occiput mea-
        sured with steel tape.
        Reference: M. F. Ashley Montagu, *(op. cit.)*

24   Standing height
        Measurement: Inches in stocking feet.

25   Weight
        Measurement: Pounds in street clothes without shoes.

26   Nose length
        Measurement: Distance in millimeters between nasion and subna-
        sale measured with a sliding compass.
        Reference: M. S. Ashley Montagu, *(op. cit.)*

27   Color blindness
        Score: Number of correct responses to Dvorine Pseudo-Isochro-
        matic Plates.
        Reference: George A. Peters, Jr. "The New Dvorine Color Percep-
        tion Test." *The Optometric Weekly,* Nov. 11, 1954, 1801–1803.

28   Handedness
        Code: The subject's preferred hand for writing and throwing was
        coded: R = right; L = left; A = ambidextrous.
        Reference: M. F. Ashley Montagu, *(op. cit.)*

29   Eye color (self-reported)
        Code: (1) brown; (2) blue; (3) green, including blue-green; (4)
        hazel (light brown or yellowish brown); (5) other; (·) no data.

30   Hair color (self-reported)
        Code: (1) black; (2) brown, including all shades; (3) blond, includ-
        ing dishwater blond; (4) red, including auburn and reddish brown;
        (·) no data.

31   Difference in hair color (self-reported)
        Code: (1) no difference; (2) different shade of same color; (3)
        different color; (·) no data.

32   Other hair differences (self-reported)
        Code: (1) no "other" differences; (2) "other" differences noted;
        (·) no data.

33   Mistaken Identity (self-reported)
        Code: If three of five statements relative to mistaken identity were

Column #   *Variable*

marked frequently or occasionally, the subject was given a score
of 1; if less than three, a score of 2.
Reference: Modified Project Talent Twin Questionnaire (Twin
Survey Questionnaire) items 11–15.

34   Socio-economic status
Score: Range of 4 to 28 based on parents' education and occupa-
tion.
Reference: W. L. Warner, M. Meeker, and K. Eells, *Social Class
in America: A Manual of Procedure for the Measurement of Social
Status.* Science Research Associates: Chicago, 1949.

35   Calendar Test
Score: Number right — number wrong
Reference: C. Remondino. Calendar Test. *Revue de Psychologie
Appliquee,* 1962, *12,* 62–81.

36   Cube Comparisons Test
Score: Number right — number wrong (total score).
Reference: From Kit of Reference Tests for Cognitive Factors
by J. W. French, Ruth B. Ekstrom, and Leighton A. Price, 1963.
Published by Educational Testing Service, Princeton, New Jersey.

37   Simple Arithmetic Test
Score: Number right — ¼ number wrong (total score).
Reference: B. N. Mukherjee. *Simple Arithmetic Test.* Unpublished
Ph.D. thesis, University of North Carolina, 1963.

38   Wide Range Vocabulary Test—Part I
Score: Number right — ¼ number wrong.
Reference: From Kit of Reference Tests for Cognitive Factors
by J. W. French, Ruth B. Ekstrom, and Leighton A. Price, 1963.
Published by Educational Testing Service, Princeton, New Jersey.

39   Surface Development Test
Score: Number right (total score).
Reference: From Kit of Reference Tests for Cognitive Factors
by J. W. French *et al., (op. cit.)*

40   Form Board Test
Score: Number right (total score).
Reference: From Kit of Reference Tests for Cognitive Factors
by J. W. French *et al., (op. cit.)*

41   Self-Judging Vocabulary Test—Part II
Score: Number right — ⅕ number wrong.
Reference: A. W. Heim, "Self-Judging Vocabulary Test." *Journal
of General Psychology,* 1965, *72,* 285–294.

42   Paper Folding Test
Score: Number right — ¼ number wrong (total score).
Reference: From Kit of Reference Tests for Cognitive Factors
by J. W. French *et al., (op. cit.)*

43   Object Aperture Test
Score: Number right — ¼ number wrong (total of Forms A and
B).

Column #   *Variable*

Reference: P. H. DuBois and G. Gleser, "Object Aperture Test."
American Psychologist, 1948, *3,* 363.

44   Identical Pictures Test
Score: Number right − ¼ number wrong (total score).
Reference: From kit of Reference Tests for Cognitive Factors by
J. W. French *et al., (op. cit.)*

45   Newcastle Spatial Test
Score: Number right (total score).
Reference: I. McFarlane Smith and J. S. Lawes, *Newcastle Spatial
Test.* Bedford England: Newnes Educational Publishing Company,
Ltd., for the National Foundation for Educational Research in
England and Wales, 1959.

46   Spelling Achievement Test
Score: Number right.
Reference: R. D. Allen *et al. Spelling Achievement Test; Metropoli-
tan Achievement Test.* Yonkers on Hudson: World Book, 1946.

47–48   Mazes Test
Scores: Number of half blocks completed; number of errors.
Reference: "A Twin Study of Spatial Ability," by Steven S. Vandenberg, University of Louisville School of Medicine, Report No.
26, April, 1967.

49   Inference Test—Part I for twins #01–48; total for twins #500–
875.
Score: Number right − ¼ number wrong.
Reference: From Kit of Reference Tests for Cognitive Factors
by J. W. French *et al., (op. cit.)*

50   Mooney Faces Test
Score: Number right.
Reference: C. M. Mooney, "Age in the Development of Closure
Ability in Children." *Canadian Journal of Psychology,* 11:219–
226, 1957.

51   Logical Reasoning Test
Score: Number right + ¼ number omitted.
Reference: Alfred F. Hertzka and J. P. Guilford, 1955. Sheridan
Psychological Services, Inc., P.O. Box 6101, Orange, California.

52   Whiteman Test of Social Perception
Score: Number right − ⅓ number wrong.
Reference: M. Whiteman, "The Performance of Schizophrenics
on Social Concepts." *Journal of Abnormal and Social Psychology,*
49:266–271, 1954.

53   Cancellation Test
Score: Number right.
Reference: Steven S. Vandenberg, "A Twin Study of Spatial Abil-
ity," University of Louisville School of Medicine, Report No. 26,
April, 1967.

Column #	Variable

54   Card Rotation Test
Score: Number right − number wrong (total score).
Reference: From Kit of Reference Tests of Cognitive Factors by
J. W. French *et al., (op. cit.)*

55   Ship Destination Test
Score: Number right + ⅕ number omitted.
Reference: Paul R. Christensen and J. P. Guildford, 1958. Sheridan
Psychological Services, Inc., P.O. Box 6101, Orange, California.

55–60   Primary Mental Abilities Test
Scores: Five quotient scores—verbal meaning, number facility,
reasoning, spatial relations, total.
Reference: Science Research Associates, Inc., 259 East Erie Street,
Chicago, Illinois.

61–66   IPAT Culture Fair Intelligence Test (both Forms A & B administered)
Scores: Form A—Classical IQ, Culture Fair IQ, Attainment Contaminated IQ. Form B—(same as Form A).
Reference: The Institute for Personality and Ability Testing, 1602–
04 Coronado Drive, Champaign, Illinois.

67–85   How Well Do You Know Yourself?
Scores: 19 raw scores—irritability, practicality, punctuality, novelty-loving, vocational assurance, cooperativeness, ambitiousness,
hypercriticalness, dejection, general morale, persistence, nervousness, seriousness, submissiveness, impulsiveness, dynamism, emotional control, consistency, test objectivity.
Reference: Executive Analysis Corp., 50 East 42nd Street, New
York, New York.

86–99   High School Personality Questionnaire—Form A
Scores: 14 factor raw scores—reserved vs. warmhearted, dull vs.
bright, affected by feelings vs. emotionally stable, undemonstrative
vs. excitable, obedient vs. assertive, sober vs. enthusiastic, disregards rules vs. conscientious, shy vs. adventurous, tough-minded
vs. tender-minded, zestful vs. circumspect individualism, self-assured vs. apprehensive, sociable group-dependent vs. self-sufficient,
uncontrolled vs. controlled, relaxed vs. tense.
Reference: The Institute for Personality and Ability Testing, *(op.
cit.)*

100   EEG Visual Evoked Response
See text for explanation.

101   EEG Diagnostic Impression
See text for explanation.

102   Revised Beta Examination
Score: IQ
Reference: The Psychological Corporation, 304 East 45th Street,
New York, New York.

Column #	*Variable*

103–116   Minnesota Multiphasic Personality Inventory (T scores)
Scores: Four validity scales—?, L, F, K; ten clinical scales—Hs, D, Hy, Pd, Mf, Pa, Pt, Sc, Ma, Si.
Reference: The Psychological Corporation, *(op. cit.)*

117–123   Torrance Tests of Creative Thinking, Research Edition
Scores: Seven scores—verbal fluency, verbal flexibility, verbal originality, figural fluency, figural flexibility, figural originality, elaboration.
Reference: Personnel Press, Education Center, P.O. Box 2649, Columbus, Ohio.

124   Summary of Blood Group Genes
Codes: C = complete data; blank = no data.
Reference: Appendix C.

125   Summary of biometric measurements (examiner reported)
Codes: C = complete battery; P = partial battery; blank = no data.
Reference: Appendix D.

126   Summary of biometric variables (self-reported)
Codes: C = complete battery; P = partial battery; blank = no data.
Reference: Appendix D.

127   Socio-economic index
Codes: C = available; blank = no data.
Reference: Appendix D.

128   Summary of psychological tests—Basic Battery
Codes: C = complete battery; P = partial battery; blank = no data.
Reference: Appendix E.

129   Summary of psychological tests—Secondary Battery
Codes: C = complee battery; P = partial battery; blank = no data.
Reference: Appendix E.

130   Summary of psychological tests—Culture Fair Battery
Codes: C = complete data; blank = no data.
Reference: Appendix E.

131   Summary of personality questionnaire—How Well Do You Know Yourself?
Codes: C = complete data; blank = no data.
Reference: Appendix F.

132   Summary of personality questionnaire—High School Personality Questionnaire
Codes: C = complete data; blank = no data.
Reference: Appendix F.

133   Summary of EEG Battery
Codes: C = complete data; blank = no data.
Reference: Appendix G.

TWIN STUDY
Socio-economic Status (after Warner *et al.,* 1949)

SES is the total of four weights: father's occupation, mother's occupation, father's education, and mother's education. If one parent is not employed or if the information concerning the occupation or education of a parent is not available, the total is prorated.

1. Education of mother (see code below).
2. Education of father (see code below).
3. Occupation of mother.
4. Occupation of father.
   Code for Education:
   1 = Professional or graduate school.
   2 = 1–4 years college.
   3 = High school, 11 or 12 years.
   4 = One or two years of high school.
   5 = Eight years.
   6 = Four to seven years.
   7 = Three years.
   0 = Missing data.

TWIN SURVEY QUESTIONNAIRE

Name (Please print)_____

Address_____
              (Street)   (City)   (State)

Date of birth_____

School_____ Grade_____

1. Do you have a twin? Yes_____ No_____
2. What is the natural color of your hair?_____
3. If your hair is different in any of the following ways from that of your twin please describe these differences.
   Color:_____
   Rate of Growth:_____
   Hairline or pattern of growth:_____
   Thickness or texture:_____
   Curliness:_____
   Other (Please specify):_____
4. What is the color of your eyes?_____
5. If your eye color is different from that of your twin please describe the difference.
   _____
6. How tall are you? _____ft._____in.
7. What is the difference in your height and that of your twin?
   I am_____inches (taller, shorter). Circle one
8. How much do you weigh? _____pounds
9. What is the difference in your weight and that of your twin?
   I am_____pounds (lighter, heavier). Circle one

10. If you know your blood type and Rh factor indicate them here.

_____

11. As a young child did your parents ever mistake you for your twin? (check one)
          _____Yes, frequently
          _____Occasionally
          _____Rarely or never

12. Have your parents mistaken you for your twin *recently?* (check one)
          _____Yes, frequently
          _____Occasionally
          _____Rarely or never

13. Have your teachers ever mistaken you for your twin? (check one)
          _____Yes, frequently
          _____Occasionally
          _____Rarely or never

14. Have *close* friends ever mistaken you for your twin? (check one)
          _____Yes, frequently
          _____Occasionally
          _____Rarely or never

15. Have casual friends ever mistaken you for your twin? (check one)
          _____Yes, frequently
          _____Occasionally
          _____Rarely or never

16. Do you and your twin look alike? Please explain in what ways.

_____
_____

17. Describe those physical features which most closely resemble those of your twin. (Give details)

_____
_____

18. Describe those physical features most unlike those of your twin. (Give details)

_____
_____

19. Do you know whether you are a fraternal or identical twin?
          _____I don't know whether I am an identical or fraternal twin.
          _____I think I am a fraternal twin.
          _____I know for sure that I am a fraternal twin.
          _____I think I am an identical twin.
          _____I know for sure that I am an identical twin.

20. If you know whether you are fraternal or identical, indicate how and by whom it was determined.

_____
_____

21. If you had any major illnesses or accidents that your twin did not have, please indicate the nature of the illness or accident and your age when it occurred.

_____
_____

22. If you were ever separated from your twin for more than a month at a time before age 18 years, please indicate where each of you was living, what you were doing, and your age at the time.

_____

_____

23. Have you had any important experiences or training that your twin has not had? Please explain.

_____

_____

24. Did you go to any school after high school? Please explain briefly.

_____

_____

25. If you have a paid job:
    a)   What is this job called?_____

    b)   What do you do on it?_____

_____

Appendix C

The results of blood group gene tests. Serological test results are available for 48 pairs of twins, including three pairs of boy-girl twins.

The column numbers in the following table correspond to the column headings in the Appendix C printout, where a "+" is to be interpreted as the presence of the indicated blood group gene and a "−" as the absence of the blood group gene.

Column Number	Blood Group Genes
6	Group
7	M
8	N
9	S
10	s
11	P_1
12	D
13	C
14	E
15	c
16	Le^a
17	K
18	Fy^a
19	Jk^a

OBS	ID	SEX	RACE	AGE	ZYG	_6	_7	_8	_9	_10	_11	_12	_13	_14	_15	_16	_17	_18	_19
1	11	1	2	17	M	A1													
2	12	1	2	17	M	A1													
3	21	2	2	17	D	A1													
4	22	2	2	17	D	A1													
5	31	1	1	14	D	A2													
6	32	1	1	14	D	A2													
7	41	2	1	18	M	A2													
8	42	2	1	18	M	A2													
9	51	1	1	17	M	A1													
10	52	1	2	17	M	A1													
11	61	2	2	17	M	B													
12	62	2	2	16	M	B													
13	71	2	2	14	O	O													
14	72	2	1	14	M	B													
15	81	1	2	14	C	O													
16	82	2	2	15	M	O													
17	91	2	2	15	M	O													
18	92	1	1	17	M	O													
19	101	2	2	16	M	O													
20	102	2	2	16	D	O													
21	111	2	1	16	D	A1													
22	112	2	1	15	D	A1													
23	121	2	2	17	M	A1													
24	122	2	2	16	M	O													
25	131	1	1	16	D	A1													
26	132	1	1	15	D	O													
27	141	1	1	15	D	A1													
28	142	1	1	17	D	O													
29	151	2	1	18	D	O													
30	152	2	2	18	D	O													
31	161	2	2	17	M	A1													
32	162	2	2	17	M	A1													
33	171	2	1	14	M	A2													
34	172	2	1	14	D	O													
35	181	1	1	14	D	O													
36	182	1	2	14	D	C													
37	191	2	2	15	M	O													
38	192	2	1	15	M	O													
39	201	1	2	14	M	A1													
40	202	1	1	14	M	A1													
41	211	1	1	14	D	A1													
42	212	1	1	14	D	A1													
43	221	2	2	17	D	A1													
44	222	2	2	14	D	O													
45	231	2	2	17	D	O													
46	232	2	2	15	D	C													
47	241	2	1	15	M	A1													
48	242	2	1	13	M	A1													
49	251	2	2	14	M	A1													
50	252	2	1	14	M	A1													
51	261	2	1	17	M	A2													
52	262	2	1	17	M	A2													
53	271	2	1		M														
54	272	2	1		M														

CAS	ID	SEX	RACE	AGE	ZYG	_6	_7	_8	_9	_10	_11	_12	_13	_14	_15	_16	_17	_18	_19
55	281	1	1	13	D	D	-	+	+	+	+	+	+	-	+	-	-	+	+	+
56	282	1	1	13	D	D	+	-	+	+	+	+	+	-	+	-	+	+	+	+
57	291	2	1	15	U	C	+	+	+	+	+	+	+	-	+	-	+	+	+	-
58	292	1	1	15	U	C	+	+	+	+	-	-	-	-	+	-	+	+	-	+
59	301	2	1	17	U	A2	+	+	-	+	+	+	+	-	+	-	+	+	+	+
60	302	1	1	17	U	A2	+	+	+	+	+	+	+	-	+	-	+	-	+	+
61	311	2	2	17	D	C	+	+	+	+	+	+	+	-	+	-	+	+	+	+
62	312	2	2	17	D	C	+	+	+	-	+	+	+	-	+	-	+	+	+	+
63	321	2	1	16	M	C	-	+	+	+	+	+	-	-	-	-	+	+	-	+
64	322	2	1	16	M	C	-	+	+	-	+	+	-	-	-	-	+	+	-	-
65	331	1	1	17	M	A1	-	-	+	+	+	-	-	-	-	-	+	+	-	-
66	332	1	1	17	D	A1	-	-	+	+	+	-	-	-	-	+	-	-	-	-
67	341	2	2	15	D	A1	-	-	-	-	+	-	-	-	-	+	-	-	+	-
68	342	2	2	15	M	A2	+	+	+	+	+	+	+	+	-	+	-	+	+	+
69	351	2	2	16	M	C	+	+	+	+	+	+	+	+	-	+	-	+	+	+
70	352	1	2	16	M	C	+	+	+	+	+	+	+	+	+	+	+	+	+	+
71	361	1	1	14	D	C	-	-	+	-	-	-	+	-	-	+	-	-	-	+
72	362	1	1	14	D	A1	-	-	+	-	-	-	+	-	-	+	-	-	-	+
73	371	1	1	18	M	C	+	+	+	+	+	+	+	+	+	+	+	+	+	+
74	372	1	1	18	M	C	+	+	+	+	+	+	+	+	+	+	+	+	+	+
75	381	2	2	15	M	A1B	+	+	+	+	+	+	+	-	-	+	-	-	-	+
76	382	2	2	15	M	A1B	+	+	+	-	+	+	+	-	-	+	-	-	-	+
77	391	2	1	15	M	C	+	+	+	-	+	+	+	+	+	+	-	-	-	+
78	392	2	1	15	M	C	+	+	+	-	+	+	+	+	+	+	-	-	-	+
79	401	2	2	16	D	C	+	+	+	+	+	+	+	+	+	+	-	-	+	+
80	402	1	2	16	D	C	+	+	+	+	+	+	+	+	+	+	-	-	+	+
81	411	2	2	14	D	A1	-	-	+	-	+	-	-	-	+	+	-	-	-	+
82	412	2	2	14	D	A1	-	-	+	-	-	-	+	-	+	+	-	-	-	+
83	421	1	1	15	M	A1	-	+	-	+	-	-	+	+	-	+	-	-	-	+
84	422	1	1	15	M	A1	+	+	-	+	-	-	+	+	-	+	-	-	-	+
85	431	2	2	14	D	A1	-	+	+	-	+	+	+	+	+	+	-	-	+	+
86	432	2	2	14	D	B	-	+	+	-	+	+	+	+	+	+	-	-	+	+
87	441	2	1	16	D	B	-	+	+	-	+	+	+	+	+	+	-	-	+	+
88	442	2	2	16	D	A1B	-	+	+	-	+	-	+	+	-	+	-	-	-	+
89	451	2	2	16	M	A1	-	-	+	-	-	-	+	-	-	+	-	-	-	+
90	452	2	1	16	D	A1	-	+	+	-	+	+	+	+	-	+	-	-	+	+
91	461	2	2	15	D	B	-	-	+	-	-	+	+	+	-	+	-	-	-	+
92	462	1	2	15	D	C	+	+	+	-	+	+	+	+	-	+	-	-	+	+
93	471	1	1	18	D	C	-	+	+	-	+	+	+	+	-	+	-	-	+	+
94	472	2	1	18	D	C	-	+	+	-	+	+	+	+	-	+	-	-	+	+
95	481	1	1	16	D	C	+	+	+	-	+	+	+	+	-	+	-	-	+	+
96	482	1	1	16	D	C	+	+	+	-	+	+	+	+	-	+	-	-	+	+

N=96

Appendix D

The biometric measurements and physical characteristics used for zygosity determination in the Twin Study. Also included is the socio-economic index. The column numbers in the following table correspond to the column headings on the Appendix D printout.

Since not all data are available for all twins, the Appendix D printout is divided into two parts. A full discription of each variable reported in the printout can be found in Appendix B.

Column #

20	Face length (millimeters)
21	Head length (millimeters)
22	Head breadth (millimeters)
23	Head circumference (millimeters)
24	Standing height (inches)
25	Weight (pounds)
26	Nose length (millimeters)
27	Color blindness: number of correct responses to Dvorine Pseudo-Isochromatic Plates.
28	Handedness: the subject's preferred hand for writing and throwing was coded right, left, or ambidextrous.
29	Self-reported eye color Code: (1) brown; (2) blue; (3) green, including blue-green; (4) hazel (light brown or yellowish brown); (5) other; (·) no data.
30	Self-reported hair color Code: (1) black; (2) brown, including all shades; (3) blond, including dishwater blond; (4) red, including auburn and reddish brown; (·) no data.
31	Self-reported difference in hair color. Code: (1) no difference; (2) different shade of same color; (3) different color; (·) no data.

32   Other hair differences (self-reported). Code: (1) no "other" differences; (2) "other" differences reported; (·) no data.

33   Mistaken identity (self-reported): If three of five statements (items 11 through 15 on the Modified Project Talent Twin Questionnaire) were marked frequently or occasionally, the subject was given a score of 1; if less than three, a score of 2.

34   Socio-economic status (SES)
            Score: Range of 4 to 28, based on parents' education and occupation. (SES rating scale is included in Appendix B).

OBS	ID	SEX	RACE	AGE	ZYG	_20	_21	_22	_23	_24	_25	_26	_27	_28
1	11	1	2	17	M	186	191	142	538	68	142	58	14	R
2	12	1	2	17	M	188	192	143	540	69	153	56	13	L
3	21	2	2	17	D	182	176	137	513	67	97	42	13	L
4	22	2	2	17	D	191	180	139	529	66	102	43	14	R
5	31	1	1	14	D	187	195	148	551	70	117	51	14	R
6	32	1	1	14	D	198	199	151	569	71	127	52	14	R
7	41	2	1	18	M	178	172	139	514	64	100	47	14	R
8	42	2	1	18	M	180	178	138	523	65	100	45	14	L
9	51	1	1	17	M	172	181	144	537	75	170	45	14	R
10	52	1	1	17	M	179	185	141	534	75	174	46	14	L
11	61	2	2	17	M	186	174	138	470	65	116	61	13	R
12	62	2	2	17	M	188	171	142	480	65	130	62	12	L
13	71	2	2	16	D	195	195	138	551	68	148	45	14	R
14	72	2	2	16	D	198	192	136	541	67	137	47	14	R
15	81	2	1	14	M	170	178	138	521	66	135	44	14	R
16	82	2	1	14	M	160	184	143	538	66	134	44	14	R
17	91	1	2	14	D	181	185	141	530	68	112	42	14	R
18	92	1	2	15	M	179	188	138	530	69	113	42	14	R
19	101	2	2	15	M	186	183	133	534	65	105	45	14	R
20	102	2	2	15	M	185	189	133	543	68	104	42	14	R
21	111	2	2	17	M	186	182	148	538	63	106	49	14	R
22	112	2	2	17	M	187	185	146	542	64	106	47	14	R
23	121	2	2	16	M	188	182	143	545	65	124	47	14	R
24	122	2	1	16	D	185	185	140	544	67	126	48	14	R
25	131	1	1	16	C	186	192	141	537	70	138	51	14	R
26	132	1	1	16	D	197	188	147	535	68	130	50	14	R
27	141	1	1	15	D	190	201	146	559	73	147	48	14	L
28	142	1	1	15	M	194	204	145	573	72	160	49	14	R
29	151	1	1	17	D	185	193	145	542	74	171	48	14	R
30	152	1	1	17	M	185	196	139	554	71	173	50	6	R
31	161	2	1	18	M	167	185	134	540	63	110	53	13	R
32	162	2	1	18	D	167	174	139	512	60	106	53	14	R
33	171	2	2	17	O	177	184	140	544	61	112	37	14	L
34	172	2	2	17	U	183	182	138	513	61	112	40	14	L
35	181	1	1	14	J	184	175	146	533	66	135	49	14	R
36	182	1	1	14	M	184	174	138	537	66	115	47	14	R
37	191	1	2	15	M	194	185	145	511	66	126	44	14	R
38	192	1	1	15	D	187	199	147	539	68	114	46	14	R
39	201	2	1	14	M	180	188	146	570	64	109	46	14	R
40	202	1	2	14	D	182	188	136	560	66	110	46	13	R
41	211	1	1	14	O	179	193	138	530	66	169	42	14	R
42	212	1	1	14	C	190	190	137	549	70	145	46	14	R
43	221	2	1	14	O	184	193	138	557	68	120	48	14	R
44	222	2	2	14	D	191	202	143	566	67	137	46	14	R
45	231	1	2	17	O	189	184	141	552	64	152	51	14	R
46	232	2	1	17	O	186	186	135	536	69	128	48	14	R
47	241	2	1	15	M	187	186	140	536	65	122	43	14	R
48	242	2	1	15	M	180	187	140	523	63	97	44	14	R
49	251	2	2	13	M	174	190	136	536	62	96	45	14	R
50	252	2	1	13	M	178	188	139	548	68	132	45	14	R
51	261	2	1	14	M	179	188	139	539	67	132	44	12	R
52	262	2	1	17	M	180	172	139	506	59	114	40	12	R
53	271	2	1	17	M	181	175	137	507	60	104	43	14	R

OBS	ID	SEX	RACE	AGE	ZYG	_20	_21	_22	_23	_24	_25	_26	_27	_28
55	281	1	1	13	D	171	185	139	514	63	108	46	14	R
56	282	1	1	13	D	170	186	143	521	62	109	43	14	R
57	291	2	1	15	D	191	185	135	532	65	113	49	14	R
58	292	1	1	15	D	197	200	147	563	71	134	49	0	K
59	301	2	1	17	D	185	187	150	549	63	111	48	14	R
60	302	1	2	17	D	196	199	153	566	68	152	49	14	R
61	311	2	2	17	C	172	182	134	521	62	114	41	14	R
62	312	2	2	17	C	184	191	138	549	64	130	39	14	R
63	321	2	1	16	M	182	187	133	537	69	125	47	14	L
64	322	2	1	16	M	178	183	136	535	68	121	49	14	R
65	331	1	1	17	M	.	.	.	.	.	.	.	.	
66	332	1	1	15	M	198	193	150	569	71	138	51	14	R
67	341	2	2	15	D	184	183	140	528	59	94	43	14	R
68	342	2	2	16	M	190	182	135	529	61	115	41	14	R
69	351	2	2	16	M	201	192	135	558	63	118	46	14	R
70	352	2	2	14	M	204	193	150	552	63	126	44	14	R
71	361	1	1	14	M	182	197	150	560	69	120	46	14	R
72	362	1	1	18	D	180	194	151	563	69	120	47	14	R
73	371	1	1	18	M	190	197	152	572	76	169	54	14	R
74	372	1	2	15	D	186	194	154	571	71	139	53	14	R
75	381	2	2	15	M	205	195	144	572	65	175	51	14	R
76	382	2	2	15	M	202	198	141	567	66	196	48	14	L
77	391	2	1	15	M	175	176	146	531	67	123	43	14	L
78	392	2	1	16	M	193	177	145	522	67	115	42	14	R
79	401	2	2	16	M	196	186	151	549	66	131	44	14	R
80	402	2	2	14	M	185	185	150	550	64	120	45	14	R
81	411	2	1	14	D	176	183	138	527	64	128	43	14	R
82	412	2	1	15	D	175	185	139	528	64	135	40	14	R
83	421	1	2	15	C	161	180	143	530	68	102	44	14	R
84	422	1	2	14	D	163	185	151	536	65	110	41	14	R
85	431	1	1	14	C	186	182	135	524	62	95	43	14	R
86	432	1	1	14	M	195	186	136	520	66	85	45	14	R
87	441	2	2	16	M	184	181	138	540	66	123	58	14	R
88	442	2	2	16	D	183	182	143	533	65	124	57	14	R
89	451	2	2	16	D	187	183	147	539	63	140	44	14	R
90	452	2	1	15	D	182	185	149	554	64	131	44	13	R
91	461	2	2	15	D	175	194	142	555	63	99	42	14	R
92	462	2	2	18	D	187	188	145	552	66	100	41	14	R
93	471	2	1	18	D	195	187	142	521	63	128	57	14	R
94	472	2	1	16	D	185	188	144	526	66	147	57	14	L
95	481	1	1	16	D	190	193	150	566	71	175	54	0	L
96	482	1	1	16	D	181	201	149	578	67	170	56	0	R

N=96

196

OBS	ID	SEX	RACE	AGE	ZYG	_20	_21	_22	_23	_24	_25	_26	_27	_28	_29	_30	_31	_32	_33	_34
1	2001	1	1	16	D	173	178	156	548	67	186	53	14	R	2	1	1	1	2	12
2	2002	1	1	16	D	183	180	150	530	67	155	57	14	R	2	2	1	1	1	12
3	2011	2	2	16	M	141	184	138	535	64	107	47	14	R	4	1	.	1	1	12
4	2012	1	1	16	M	140	181	133	534	63	106	46	13	R	4	2	1	1	1	12
5	2021	1	1	16	U	189	190	150	559	69	148	48	10	R	2	3	1	2	2	9
6	2022	1	1	16	U	178	185	143	542	62	117	51	13	L	2	1	1	1	2	9
7	2031	1	1	16	U	187	194	157	572	69	162	51	14	L	3	1	1	1	2	13
8	2032	2	1	17	U	173	191	143	550	63	103	44	14	R	1	2	1	1	1	13
9	2041	1	1	17	D	202	203	148	580	71	144	54	2	R	1	1	1	1	1	5
10	2042	1	1	16	M	222	205	146	583	72	149	57	3	R	1	1	1	1	2	5
11	2051	2	2	16	M	183	192	146	576	64	112	48	11	R	2	3	1	1	2	19
12	2052	2	2	15	U	179	179	142	532	61	105	47	10	R	2	1	1	1	2	19
13	2061	2	1	15	U	185	198	145	574	64	132	50	14	R	1	3	1	2	2	7
14	2062	1	1	15	M	183	183	144	583	63	126	53	14	R	2	1	1	1	2	7
15	2071	1	2	16	D	171	181	138	539	58	100	43	13	R	2	4	1	1	1	19
16	2072	2	2	15	D	191	181	136	522	58	105	45	14	R	1	1	1	2	2	19
17	2081	1	2	16	U	181	193	145	565	73	135	52	14	R	5	2	1	1	1	18
18	2082	2	2	15	U	183	199	146	573	64	132	40	14	R	1	1	1	1	1	18
19	2091	1	1	15	D	179	201	142	574	73	157	48	14	R	2	3	1	2	1	14
20	2092	2	1	13	D	167	184	135	530	62	131	46	14	A	1	2	1	1	2	16
21	2101	2	1	13	U	174	181	136	519	63	115	53	14	R	1	2	3	1	1	16
22	2102	2	1	17	M	170	183	137	533	63	107	50	14	R	1	2	1	2	2	24
23	2111	2	2	15	U	187	198	141	578	64	158	45	14	A	1	2	3	1	1	13
24	2112	2	1	15	M	183	201	148	589	65	160	47	14	R	1	3	1	1	2	13
25	2121	2	2	16	D	188	187	141	544	67	122	54	13	R	2	2	1	1	2	18
26	2122	2	1	16	D	169	185	146	550	66	119	49	12	A	1	2	1	2	1	18
27	2131	2	1	17	D	194	195	145	568	67	124	60	11	R	2	2	2	1	2	12
28	2132	1	1	17	U	177	193	144	563	71	152	50	12	R	2	4	1	1	2	12
29	2141	1	1	17	U	169	192	146	565	67	191	53	14	R	2	2	1	1	2	12
30	2142	1	1	17	U	164	192	150	570	66	223	54	13	R	2	3	1	1	2	10
31	2151	1	1	14	D	189	206	152	596	75	180	55	14	L	2	2	2	1	1	14
32	2152	1	2	18	U	177	188	148	569	67	142	50	14	R	1	1	3	2	1	14
33	2161	1	1	18	U	171	195	146	568	69	140	48	12	R	3	4	1	1	2	16
34	2162	2	2	17	D	194	182	138	527	67	125	44	14	A	5	2	1	2	1	16
35	2171	2	1	14	M	165	179	139	532	63	156	48	14	R	3	2	2	1	1	16
36	2172	2	2	16	M	177	185	150	552	65	177	58	14	L	1	2	3	1	1	9
37	2181	1	1	18	U	194	195	146	551	74	150	62	14	R	1	2	1	2	1	9
38	2182	1	1	17	U	195	190	142	550	72	142	51	14	L	2	2	1	1	1	22
39	2191	1	1	14	M	190	200	152	589	74	214	49	14	R	2	2	1	2	2	22
40	2192	1	1	16	M	179	196	154	573	70	162	51	14	A	3	2	2	1	2	13
41	2201	1	1	14	M	179	195	149	568	54	168	44	14	R	3	2	1	1	2	13
42	2202	1	1	16	D	162	181	135	537	63	105	49	14	R	3	3	2	1	1	13
43	2211	1	1	16	D	177	192	147	560	68	132	45	2	L	1	1	.	1	1	15
44	2212	1	1	16	M	173	191	148	566	73	127	57	13	L	2	2	2	2	1	15
45	2221	2	1	15	U	169	179	136	530	61	98	52	13	R	2	2	1	1	2	19
46	2222	2	2	15	U	177	189	140	543	62	97	53	13	R	3	2	1	1	2	19
47	2231	2	2	15	U	181	187	146	572	69	109	48	13	L	1	1	.	1	1	21
48	2232	1	1	15	M	202	204	149	590	73	155	48	14	R	2	2	1	2	1	21
49	2241	1	1	15	M	189	200	147	587	71	134	55	14	R	2	2	1	2	2	21
50	2242	1	1	15	M	184	192	157	576	62	144	48	14	L	2	2	1	1	1	21
51	2251	2	1	15	M	157	181	135	528	62	108	45	14	P	2	2	2	1	2	21
52	2252	2	1	15	M	158	177	136	520	66	126	44	14	R	2	4	1	1	2	21
53	2261	1	1	15	D	182	191	144	554	66	121	53	14	R	2	3	.	2	2	15
54	2262	1	1	15	D	173	181	144	535	66	121	47	14	R	3	2	2	1	2	15

APPENDIX D – PART 2

OBS	ID	SEX	RACE	AGE	ZYG	_20	_21	_22	_23	_24	_25	_26	_27	_28	_29	_30	_31	_32	_33	_34
55	2271	2	1	14	U	166	174	148	553	65	131	43	14	R	1	4	.	.	2	17
56	2272	1	1	14	U	180	180	153	558	69	152	51	14	R	1	4	.	.	2	17
57	2281	1	1	16	D	176	178	143	537	71	129	52	13	A	1	1	3	1	1	14
58	2282	1	1	16	D	171	139	139	544	66	100	53	12	R	3	2	2	.	1	14
59	2291	2	1	16	M	165	193	141	551	64	116	45	14	L	2	3	.	2	1	15
60	2292	1	1	16	M	200	190	141	547	64	110	44	14	R	2	2	1	2	1	15
61	2301	1	1	16	U	165	207	147	583	65	135	61	13	L	4	3	1	2	1	8
62	2302	1	1	15	D	197	206	150	591	65	146	58	14	R	4	2	2	.	1	8
63	2311	1	1	15	U	169	185	142	545	62	120	47	13	R	2	3	1	1	2	12
64	2312	2	1	17	U	152	178	137	532	63	112	42	12	L	4	3	3	2	2	12
65	2321	2	1	17	M	168	185	141	543	62	107	54	13	R	3	2	.	.	1	12
66	2322	2	1	17	D	168	185	137	540	62	95	47	14	L	2	2	2	.	1	12
67	2331	2	1	16	D	171	173	136	520	63	110	51	14	L	3	2	2	1	2	13
68	2332	2	1	16	M	172	181	131	526	62	126	50	13	A	3	2	3	1	1	13
69	2341	2	1	15	U	188	192	138	550	66	116	53	14	R	1	2	.	.	1	12
70	2342	2	1	15	U	191	194	139	547	66	121	48	14	R	3	2	1	1	2	12
71	2351	1	1	16	U	174	197	141	566	70	179	49	13	R	1	2	.	1	2	10
72	2352	1	1	16	U	188	195	158	578	75	177	52	12	R	3	2	2	1	2	10
73	2361	1	1	16	U	191	193	160	594	69	185	50	14	R	1	4	2	1	2	8
74	2362	2	1	16	D	181	189	142	557	62	125	49	13	R	1	2	.	.	2	8
75	2371	2	1	17	D	175	183	144	540	62	112	53	13	R	3	2	2	1	2	19
76	2372	2	1	17	M	164	178	137	529	60	99	45	13	R	3	3	1	1	2	19
77	2381	2	1	17	D	161	185	151	556	64	131	45	13	L	1	2	.	.	1	12
78	2382	2	1	17	U	159	184	146	547	62	112	42	13	R	1	2	1	1	2	12
79	2391	2	1	16	M	165	182	134	527	60	94	50	12	R	2	2	.	.	1	12
80	2392	1	1	16	D	160	182	134	532	61	97	47	12	L	4	2	3	2	2	12
81	2401	1	1	15	U	186	195	155	565	68	132	55	13	R	4	2	3	2	2	14
82	2402	1	1	15	M	179	187	142	543	68	130	51	13	R	1	4	1	1	2	14
83	2411	2	2	15	U	184	194	143	560	67	106	51	14	R	1	1	.	.	1	12
84	2412	2	2	15	U	180	187	137	542	67	116	54	13	R	2	2	1	2	2	12
85	2421	2	2	16	D	183	191	134	538	64	90	54	12	R	2	2	1	1	1	15
86	2422	2	2	16	D	166	186	143	546	65	111	43	13	R	4	2	2	2	2	15
87	2431	2	2	16	M	185	193	137	578	62	149	48	13	R	1	1	.	.	1	24
88	2432	2	2	13	U	178	187	146	567	63	130	48	14	R	1	1	1	1	1	24
89	2441	2	2	13	U	187	190	138	573	66	102	52	14	R	3	1	.	.	2	20
90	2442	2	2	14	U	181	188	147	577	64	98	44	11	A	3	1	1	1	1	20
91	2451	2	2	14	D	173	186	140	579	64	107	47	13	R	3	1	.	.	2	16
92	2452	1	1	14	U	172	185	140	547	64	119	46	13	R	3	1	1	2	2	16
93	2461	2	1	13	M	161	175	149	580	63	133	44	14	L	1	2	.	.	1	19
94	2462	2	2	13	M	162	173	135	556	63	130	55	14	A	5	1	2	1	2	19
95	2471	2	2	13	M	161	183	137	593	65	133	44	14	R	4	2	.	.	1	23
96	2472	2	2	13	U	166	183	142	584	62	93	45	14	R	1	1	1	1	2	23
97	2481	1	2	13	U	188	198	138	574	61	93	53	6	R	1	1	2	1	2	16
98	2482	1	1	18	D	181	200	155	577	69	182	47	11	A	2	1	2	1	2	16
99	2491	1	1	18	U	187	187	138	568	60	87	48	14	L	3	2	1	1	1	13
100	2492	2	1	13	M	173	184	146	543	69	125	46	14	A	3	2	1	.	2	13
101	2501	2	1	18	M	190	193	146	565	69	121	46	14	R	3	2	.	.	1	8
102	2502	2	1	16	U	181	188	145	563	62	123	47	14	R	3	2	2	2	2	14
103	2511	2	1	16	D	167	198	143	570	62	127	44	14	R	2	2	3	1	1	14
104	2512	1	1	15	O	170	195	142	566	67	124	47	14	L	2	1	2	1	2	11
105	2521	2	1	15	D	177	197	142	561	69	113	44	14	A	3	2	.	.	1	11
106	2522	1	1	13	M	172	190	137	536	60	86	43	14	R	2	3	1	1	2	12
107	2531	1	1	13	M	171	186	138	547	61	96	46	14	R	2	3	1	1	1	12
108	2532	2	1	13	M	171	188	138	547	61	96	46	14	R	2	3	1	1	1	12

APPENDIX D — PART 2

OBS	ID	SEX	RACE	AGE	ZYG	_20	_21	_22	_23	_24	_25	_26	_27	_28	_29	_30	_31	_32	_33	_34
109	2541	2	1	16	D	158	187	143	556	63	114	47	14	R	1	2	2	1	2	13
110	2542	2	1	16	D	160	179	136	527	65	118	46	14	R	2	2	2	1	2	13
111	2551	1	1	14	D	180	189	139	548	67	126	51	14	R	2	3	.	2	2	6
112	2552	1	1	14	D	172	192	150	572	64	154	52	14	R	3	3	3	2	2	6
113	2561	2	1	13	D	167	183	143	551	61	111	45	13	R	2	4	3	1	2	17
114	2562	2	1	13	D	173	176	136	524	61	85	50	14	R	1	2	1	1	1	17
115	2571	1	1	16	M	182	187	151	567	54	117	50	14	R	2	1	1	1	1	14
116	2572	1	1	16	M	182	188	150	548	64	118	49	14	R	1	1	1	2	1	14
117	2581	1	1	16	M	191	189	140	548	68	122	48	14	R	1	1	2	1	1	9
118	2582	1	1	17	M	189	187	140	542	58	113	45	13	R	1	2	1	.	1	9
119	2591	2	2	17	M	177	174	142	550	60	94	46	13	R	1	1	1	1	1	18
120	2592	2	2	15	D	177	175	135	552	59	93	46	14	R	1	2	1	2	1	18
121	2601	1	2	15	D	167	188	142	559	67	97	51	13	L	1	1	1	1	2	15
122	2602	1	2	14	P	190	195	139	593	66	130	46	13	R	3	2	1	1	1	15
123	2611	1	2	14	M	182	192	136	582	69	126	51	13	R	1	2	2	1	1	13
124	2612	1	2	15	M	186	187	134	577	59	44	44	12	R	1	2	1	1	1	13
125	2621	2	2	15	D	172	190	141	571	65	139	41	14	R	1	1	1	2	2	12
126	2622	2	2	14	D	176	186	149	588	62	184	43	13	R	1	1	2	1	1	12
127	2631	2	2	14	M	185	185	135	552	64	94	46	14	R	1	1	1	1	2	13
128	2632	1	2	14	M	188	196	144	584	67	114	47	14	R	1	1	1	1	1	16
129	2641	2	2	14	U	169	178	135	543	63	99	44	7	R	1	1	2	1	1	16
130	2642	2	2	14	F	160	182	135	544	62	96	46	13	R	5	1	1	2	2	7
131	2651	2	2	14	D	174	184	135	538	63	98	44	14	R	1	1	2	1	2	7
132	2652	2	2	14	I	184	184	143	565	65	139	48	14	R	1	1	2	2	1	9
133	2661	2	2	14	M	180	189	145	599	63	115	50	13	R	1	2	1	1	1	9
134	2662	2	2	14	M	180	182	149	587	64	117	50	14	R	1	1	1	1	1	12
135	2671	2	2	14	M	179	186	137	565	59	84	45	14	R	1	1	2	2	1	12
136	2672	1	2	14	D	174	187	135	569	59	89	48	13	R	1	1	1	1	2	8
137	2681	2	2	14	D	189	187	137	556	67	91	49	14	R	1	1	1	1	2	8
138	2682	2	2	17	M	183	185	137	544	66	93	44	11	R	1	1	1	2	2	16
139	2691	2	2	17	U	170	183	144	543	64	103	46	14	L	1	1	1	1	1	16
140	2692	2	2	14	U	170	190	143	554	64	107	45	13	R	1	1	2	1	1	13
141	2701	2	1	14	D	168	181	140	562	58	102	45	14	R	5	1	1	2	2	13
142	2702	2	1	14	M	159	187	133	556	57	121	39	13	R	1	2	3	1	1	13
143	2711	2	1	17	D	174	208	142	592	72	167	48	14	R	2	2	2	1	2	24
144	2712	1	1	16	D	188	191	153	557	63	118	51	13	A	2	3	2	1	1	22
145	2721	2	2	14	O	174	191	146	596	64	118	45	10	R	2	3	1	2	1	12
146	2722	1	1	14	D	163	182	143	582	62	102	48	11	R	2	2	2	1	2	12
147	2731	2	1	14	I	164	180	143	539	64	108	45	13	A	2	3	1	1	1	13
148	2732	2	1	14	M	191	184	157	545	69	113	46	13	R	5	3	2	2	2	13
149	2741	1	1	14	D	168	199	143	587	64	145	51	13	R	5	1	.	1	1	24
150	2742	1	1	16	D	177	191	155	556	66	93	45	13	R	1	1	1	1	2	24
151	2751	1	2	14	D	168	185	155	567	65	119	43	14	L	1	1	1	1	1	17
152	2752	2	2	14	O	193	193	146	559	62	131	48	14	R	1	1	2	1	1	17
153	2761	1	1	14	D	170	199	142	598	63	164	46	14	R	1	1	1	1	2	21
154	2762	2	1	14	I	177	185	139	590	64	168	44	13	L	4	1	1	2	1	21
155	2771	1	1	14	M	182	192	143	551	64	118	44	9	A	4	1	1	1	1	8
156	2772	2	2	14	M	182	190	143	561	69	119	48	13	R	4	1	1	1	1	8
157	2781	1	1	16	M	180	185	143	557	64	127	49	14	R	1	2	.	2	2	8
158	2782	2	1	16	M	186	188	149	564	69	126	57	14	R	1	2	2	1	1	8
159	2791	2	1	17	H	199	197	141	555	70	134	57	3	L	1	1	1	1	2	17
160	2792	2	1	17	M	186	197	141	562	68	135	57	14	R	1	2	.	2	1	8
161	2801	1	2	17	H	199	197	149	562	68	135	57	14	L	4	2	1	2	2	17
162	2802	2	2	17	M	191	199	144	580	69	130	51	14	R	1	2	1	1	1	17

OBS	ID	SEX	RACE	AGE	ZYG	_20	_21	_22	_23	_24	_25	_26	_27	_28	_29	_30	_31	_32	_33	_34
163	2811	1	2	13	U	186	191	145	574	61	100	45	14	R	1	1	.	.	2	13
164	2812	2	2	13	U	178	195	141	570	63	117	43	14	L	1	2	.	.	2	13
165	2821	2	2	14	D	164	183	131	551	66	122	39	5	R	1	1	.	1	2	16
166	2822	2	2	14	O	177	187	134	545	65	115	41	13	R	1	1	1	1	2	16
167	2831	1	2	17	U	189	186	136	545	65	104	58	14	R	1	1	1	1	2	13
168	2832	2	2	17	U	177	190	128	553	53	119	53	13	R	5	1	3	.	2	13
169	2841	2	2	15	D	180	190	125	534	62	94	45	14	L	5	1	3	2	2	27
170	2842	2	2	15	O	177	183	132	538	61	104	41	14	R	1	2	3	.	2	13
171	2851	1	2	14	R	175	175	145	543	62	102	46	11	R	1	1	2	2	1	27
172	2852	1	2	14	R	170	179	146	546	63	103	37	12	R	1	2	2	1	1	28
173	2861	1	2	14	O	166	186	143	559	65	144	45	13	R	1	2	2	.	1	28
174	2862	1	2	14	X	156	185	145	571	67	139	43	13	L	1	2	3	2	1	17
175	2871	1	2	14	M	193	185	144	557	65	100	48	14	R	1	1	1	1	1	13
176	2872	1	2	14	X	180	173	145	561	64	95	43	13	R	1	2	2	1	1	13
177	2881	2	2	16	R	178	194	156	547	66	114	53	14	R	1	2	3	2	2	16
178	2882	2	2	16	R	168	185	144	569	66	104	49	13	R	5	2	3	2	2	16
179	2891	2	2	15	D	193	194	138	553	60	125	46	14	R	1	1	3	1	2	21
180	2892	2	1	15	D	168	185	137	553	63	98	44	13	R	1	2	3	1	2	16
181	2901	1	2	18	U	187	182	151	550	69	159	58	14	R	1	1	2	1	1	21
182	2902	1	2	17	F	179	185	151	566	70	168	51	14	R	5	2	1	2	1	10
183	2911	1	1	17	Z	182	195	152	609	68	140	40	14	R	1	1	1	1	1	10
184	2912	1	2	13	D	183	198	140	620	68	140	38	12	R	5	2	2	2	1	5
185	2921	2	2	13	O	147	194	140	559	67	129	46	13	R	1	1	2	2	2	5
186	2922	2	2	14	O	153	190	139	559	65	113	47	10	R	1	2	2	2	2	16
187	2931	2	2	14	U	197	199	136	564	71	130	60	13	R	5	2	3	1	2	15
188	2932	2	2	14	D	186	190	134	565	63	114	46	14	R	1	2	.	1	2	12
189	2941	2	2	15	O	173	173	137	528	59	114	45	11	R	1	1	2	1	2	12
190	2942	2	2	15	U	159	173	132	510	59	90	36	13	L	1	2	2	1	2	11
191	2951	2	2	16	D	190	190	.	572	68	141	54	14	R	1	2	3	1	2	11
192	2952	2	2	15	O	178	178	137	550	62	105	43	13	R	1	4	.	2	1	.
193	2961	2	2	15	O	187	184	130	549	67	108	49	14	R	1	1	2	1	1	7
194	2962	2	2	15	M	177	184	146	536	61	163	48	10	R	1	1	2	2	2	7
195	2971	2	2	15	E	181	202	181	599	72	199	52	13	R	1	1	3	1	1	.
196	2972	2	2	16	J	190	195	147	603	71	160	53	14	R	1	1	1	1	2	19
197	2981	2	2	15	D	174	184	135	573	71	126	48	12	R	4	1	2	1	1	19
198	2982	2	2	16	O	180	188	129	543	64	113	44	14	R	4	1	2	.	1	12
199	2991	1	2	17	M	197	199	137	558	65	196	43	13	R	1	1	1	2	2	17
200	2992	1	2	13	D	203	186	145	583	63	114	50	14	R	5	1	1	2	2	17
201	3001	2	2	13	O	197	199	145	583	65	100	51	14	R	5	4	1	1	1	12
202	3002	2	2	18	O	193	186	146	578	67	109	52	13	R	5	1	3	1	1	17
203	3011	1	2	18	M	174	192	140	578	64	145	37	14	R	1	1	1	2	1	17
204	3012	1	2	17	F	172	185	152	598	66	162	38	14	R	1	1	2	1	2	23
205	3021	2	2	17	O	176	182	133	543	61	94	51	13	R	1	1	2	2	1	16
206	3022	2	2	14	O	180	185	140	548	63	130	51	14	R	1	4	1	1	2	23
207	3031	2	2	14	D	174	179	139	540	64	102	46	12	R	1	1	1	1	2	16
208	3032	2	2	15	O	170	175	145	547	64	108	46	14	R	1	1	1	1	2	16
209	3041	1	2	16	M	197	192	142	565	66	131	45	13	R	1	1	1	1	2	16
210	3042	1	2	15	U	164	182	142	568	66	115	44	14	R	1	1	1	1	2	16
211	3051	1	2	14	D	191	193	147	593	63	138	40	13	R	1	1	1	2	2	14
212	3052	1	2	14	O	195	195	146	599	64	140	43	14	R	1	1	1	1	2	14
213	3061	2	2	13	M	182	187	145	555	66	197	50	13	R	1	1	1	1	2	16
214	3062	2	2	16	D	190	186	142	554	66	144	45	14	R	2	1	1	1	2	16
215	3071	2	2	16	O	167	177	139	532	64	94	46	14	R	1	2	2	.	2	17
216	3072	2	2	16	M	175	179	134	540	65	97	46	11	R	1	2	.	.	1	17

OBS	ID	SEX	RACE	AGE	ZYG	_20	_21	_22	_23	_24	_25	_26	_27	_28	_29	_30	_31	_32	_33	_34
217	3081	2	2	15	M	185	190	133	552	65	95	50	14	R	1	2	.	.	1	15
218	3082	2	2	15	M	190	188	134	549	65	98	52	12	L	1	2	.	.	1	15
219	3091	2	1	17	D	170	183	148	555	65	122	46	12	R	1	2	2	1	2	15
220	3092	2	1	17	D	171	198	142	557	75	155	49	12	L	1	2	1	2	2	15
221	3101	1	2	16	D	202	195	151	573	69	174	60	14	R	1	2	2	1	2	15
222	3102	2	1	16	D	174	191	142	558	69	136	49	11	R	3	2	.	2	2	.
223	3111	2	1	14	U	191	188	136	555	61	100	50	14	R	1	2	.	1	2	.
224	3112	1	2	16	U	189	181	140	554	65	101	54	12	L	1	1	1	2	2	19
225	3121	2	1	16	U	183	185	149	550	64	113	54	14	R	2	1	2	1	2	19
226	3122	2	1	16	U	177	176	148	536	63	125	43	13	R	2	1	1	1	2	13
227	3131	2	1	13	U	167	180	135	525	61	86	46	11	L	2	3	3	1	2	13
228	3132	2	2	13	U	158	188	137	517	66	106	47	14	R	1	3	3	1	2	16
229	3141	2	2	13	M	180	190	130	533	63	93	43	14	A	1	1	1	1	1	17
230	3142	1	2	15	M	182	182	138	544	65	106	50	13	R	1	2	.	2	2	17
231	3151	2	2	17	R	182	185	144	562	65	108	46	14	R	1	2	.	2	1	16
232	3152	1	2	17	M	190	181	145	568	67	98	53	14	R	1	2	2	1	2	16
233	3161	2	1	14	U	168	200	151	580	67	134	59	14	R	1	2	2	1	1	16
234	3162	2	1	17	D	190	198	146	578	66	125	54	14	R	4	2	2	1	2	12
235	3171	2	1	14	O	168	180	126	522	60	111	47	14	L	2	2	2	2	2	12
236	3172	2	1	14	D	175	179	180	532	63	125	50	14	R	1	1	2	1	2	13
237	3181	2	1	18	O	161	179	141	544	61	120	47	14	R	4	2	2	2	1	13
238	3182	1	1	18	O	163	170	134	520	61	104	50	14	R	2	1	2	1	2	13
239	3191	1	2	18	O	204	191	135	555	57	113	56	13	R	1	1	1	1	1	16
240	3192	1	2	13	O	199	195	143	556	68	114	51	14	R	1	2	2	2	2	19
241	3201	2	2	13	D	192	185	146	550	60	100	40	13	K	5	2	1	1	2	19
242	3202	2	2	14	U	183	184	144	559	64	148	45	14	R	1	4	3	2	2	7
243	3211	1	2	14	M	179	180	144	543	62	90	38	13	R	1	2	3	.	1	16
244	3212	1	2	14	U	185	180	141	542	63	96	45	14	R	1	3	3	2	2	16
245	3221	2	1	14	M	197	195	143	573	66	121	57	12	R	3	1	3	.	1	12
246	3222	2	1	15	D	178	180	133	527	60	86	51	14	K	2	1	.	1	2	21
247	3231	1	1	15	O	173	175	147	548	70	142	52	14	R	1	1	1	2	2	21
248	3232	1	1	16	D	175	185	138	561	63	146	57	14	R	2	1	1	1	1	20
249	3241	2	2	16	O	197	181	145	540	66	95	51	13	L	1	1	.	2	2	20
250	3242	2	2	17	O	172	176	145	545	66	109	40	14	R	1	2	1	2	2	20
251	3251	1	2	16	D	178	184	146	566	67	137	54	11	L	1	1	1	2	2	16
252	3252	2	1	18	M	181	181	155	574	71	120	45	14	R	1	1	2	1	1	16
253	3261	2	2	16	U	182	195	145	572	67	155	51	14	R	5	1	.	1	1	17
254	3262	2	2	18	O	174	188	144	560	67	122	50	13	R	2	1	2	2	1	17
255	3271	2	2	16	D	198	199	151	567	68	135	43	14	R	1	1	1	2	2	17
256	3272	2	2	16	M	170	185	141	534	63	127	44	12	L	1	1	2	1	1	17
257	3281	1	2	18	M	149	177	131	528	50	99	42	13	R	1	3	1	.	1	17
258	3282	1	2	16	D	163	173	137	560	60	101	50	14	R	1	1	.	2	1	17
259	3291	2	1	14	D	178	197	150	547	69	116	45	13	R	5	3	2	1	1	11
260	3292	2	1	14	O	173	186	135	550	68	110	46	9	R	2	2	2	1	1	12
261	3301	1	1	17	D	182	181	139	547	60	91	51	14	R	1	1	1	1	1	12
262	3302	2	1	17	O	196	181	135	550	60	94	50	14	R	1	1	.	1	1	11
263	3311	2	1	14	D	181	195	142	570	64	108	52	14	L	1	3	2	2	1	12
264	3312	1	1	14	M	176	200	138	575	61	102	44	14	R	3	2	.	2	2	12
265	3321	2	2	14	D	170	190	142	546	61	90	52	14	R	1	2	1	1	1	12
266	3322	2	2	13	M	170	184	134	523	60	80	49	14	R	1	2	1	2	2	24
267	3331	1	1	13	O	173	176	139	522	58	78	50	14	R	3	4	3	2	1	24
268	3332	2	1	13	D	172	186	139	545	63	130	54	14	R	2	2	1	1	2	24
269	3351	2	2	14	O	187	189	140	540	69	140	45	14	R	5	2	3	1	1	20
270	3352	1	2	15	M	183	186	140	547	69	134	53	14	R	5	1	.	1	1	20

OBS	ID	SEX	RACE	AGE	ZYG	_20	_21	_22	_23	_24	_25	_26	_27	_28	_29	_30	_31	_32	_33	_34
271	3361	2	1	15	D	177	190	136	556	62	131	48	14	A	2	4	3	.	2	8
272	3362	2	1	15	D	182	180	136	535	65	109	53	14	R	2	2	3	.	2	8
273	3371	2	2	12	M	197	191	140	560	60	90	51	14	R	1	2	.	1	1	9
274	3372	2	2	12	M	200	190	139	560	60	90	54	14	R	3	2	.	1	1	9
275	3381	1	1	15	M	182	195	142	571	70	138	49	14	R	3	4	.	.	1	14
276	3382	1	1	15	M	189	189	144	568	71	145	57	13	R	4	1	.	2	1	14
277	3391	1	2	14	M	192	188	144	567	70	126	56	12	R	5	1	1	.	1	16
278	3392	1	2	14	U	189	188	142	566	69	118	48	12	R	5	1	1	2	1	16
279	3401	2	2	15	U	184	183	133	545	66	115	55	13	R	5	1	1	.	1	10
280	3402	2	2	15	U	183	178	137	535	64	103	49	14	R	1	1	1	.	1	16
281	3411	2	2	16	D	194	195	147	575	65	135	51	14	R	1	1	1	2	2	20
282	3412	2	2	16	O	179	139	150	565	63	170	49	14	R	1	1	.	2	2	20
283	3421	2	2	14	R	172	180	145	563	63	112	53	13	R	1	2	2	1	1	17
284	3422	2	2	14	M	182	182	143	544	63	107	47	12	L	1	1	.	.	1	.
285	3431	2	2	15	U	169	169	137	535	62	82	49	13	R	1	1	1	2	1	16
286	3432	2	2	15	D	193	205	148	604	67	131	52	14	R	5	1	.	2	2	16
287	3441	2	2	13	U	195	196	138	575	64	124	43	13	R	5	1	2	1	2	16
288	3442	2	2	13	O	187	199	146	590	68	120	50	13	R	5	1	2	1	1	16
289	3451	2	2	16	M	185	185	139	540	65	107	47	14	R	5	2	.	2	2	16
290	3452	2	2	16	O	181	178	137	541	67	112	50	14	R	1	2	1	1	1	16
291	3461	2	1	14	M	171	173	153	545	65	110	50	3	R	1	2	.	2	2	18
292	3462	2	1	14	U	184	181	149	535	68	121	50	14	R	1	2	1	1	1	18
293	3471	2	1	14	U	189	166	137	516	61	108	44	14	R	2	2	2	.	1	18
294	3472	2	1	14	D	180	179	141	532	63	112	54	14	R	3	2	3	2	1	18
295	3481	1	1	16	O	194	197	154	580	67	135	54	11	L	1	1	1	2	1	12
296	3482	1	1	16	D	169	181	150	556	63	124	47	14	R	1	2	.	1	1	12
297	3491	2	2	13	O	180	186	140	532	58	72	52	14	R	2	2	.	2	2	17
298	3492	2	2	13	M	180	175	139	530	61	84	47	12	R	3	1	2	2	1	17
299	3501	1	2	18	D	194	202	142	558	67	233	46	13	R	5	1	.	1	2	12
300	3502	1	2	18	O	179	199	143	543	66	137	47	14	R	1	2	.	2	1	17
301	3511	1	1	17	M	185	186	150	550	67	165	56	13	R	1	2	2	1	1	17
302	3512	1	1	17	O	194	190	144	550	70	159	57	14	R	1	2	2	.	2	12
303	3521	2	1	15	D	179	188	148	565	70	125	51	14	R	4	2	2	1	1	10
304	3522	2	1	15	O	181	190	145	560	69	124	55	14	R	1	1	2	2	2	13
305	3531	2	1	17	M	184	183	140	539	64	119	52	13	R	1	2	2	1	2	10
306	3532	2	1	17	O	186	190	146	565	69	118	55	14	R	1	1	1	.	1	13
307	3541	2	2	14	D	190	188	129	533	69	120	50	12	L	2	1	1	2	2	16
308	3542	2	2	14	O	179	194	144	555	71	136	45	6	R	4	1	.	1	2	16
309	3551	1	2	14	M	180	191	141	557	66	115	50	13	R	1	1	2	1	2	12
310	3552	1	2	16	D	168	192	142	540	64	110	46	13	R	1	3	3	2	2	11
311	3561	1	1	16	O	181	181	146	544	64	108	51	13	R	4	3	.	1	2	12
312	3562	1	1	15	O	154	137	144	554	64	116	42	12	R	2	4	.	1	2	11
313	3581	1	1	17	M	182	181	134	538	63	115	45	14	R	1	2	2	2	2	17
314	3582	1	1	17	O	191	192	147	564	63	121	42	13	R	4	3	2	1	1	10
315	3591	1	1	14	M	177	138	141	550	66	105	51	14	R	2	2	.	1	1	10
316	3592	1	1	14	M	183	180	141	543	65	110	49	13	R	3	2	1	1	1	8
317	3601	2	1	15	O	199	193	145	560	64	105	49	14	L	1	3	2	2	2	8
318	3602	2	1	15	O	175	136	143	552	64	108	57	14	R	4	1	.	1	2	17
319	3611	2	2	13	D	196	187	147	570	65	122	44	13	R	1	2	3	.	2	17
320	3612	2	2	13	O	185	180	149	545	61	108	39	14	R	1	4	.	1	1	11
321	3621	1	1	17	O	164	185	135	534	57	70	44	14	R	1	2	2	.	2	12
322	3622	1	2	13	D	180	193	127	535	60	80	55	13	R	1	2	2	1	1	11
323	3631	1	1	18	O	195	199	142	569	74	144	54	14	R	1	1	.	.	1	15
324	3632	1	1	18	M	203	198	140	560	73	135	57	13	R	1	1	1	1	1	15

OBS	ID	SEX	RACE	AGE	ZYG	_20	_21	_22	_23	_24	_25	_26	_27	_28	_29	_30	_31	_32	_33	_34
325	3641	1	1	14	D	162	183	145	539	61	88	40	14	R	2	3	2	1	2	19
326	3642	1	1	14	D	173	184	144	540	50	87	50	14	L	2	2	2	1	2	19
327	3651	1	1	14	D	191	195	156	583	69	168	52	14	R	1	2	2	2	2	11
328	3652	1	1	14	M	182	185	154	570	69	132	51	13	L	2	2	1	1	2	11
329	3661	2	1	14	M	148	175	148	530	52	98	40	14	R	4	2	1	1	1	13
330	3662	2	1	14	D	160	177	147	535	62	98	46	14	R	3	3	2	.	1	13
331	3671	1	1	13	C	200	197	144	575	71	136	52	14	R	2	3	1	1	1	15
332	3672	1	1	13	M	183	196	144	574	69	124	44	11	R	2	1	.	2	1	15
333	3681	2	2	16	M	187	181	140	544	64	111	50	9	L	1	4	2	.	1	17
334	3682	2	2	16	M	179	184	136	545	62	91	45	14	R	1	2	1	2	2	17
335	3691	1	1	14	U	180	190	142	555	65	112	50	12	R	1	2	1	1	1	11
336	3692	2	1	14	U	186	175	139	525	66	114	51	14	R	1	1	1	1	2	16
337	3701	1	2	14	M	176	190	130	525	64	115	45	14	R	1	2	.	1	2	16
338	3702	1	1	14	M	186	191	137	554	68	96	46	14	R	1	2	3	.	1	7
339	3711	2	2	13	D	178	189	138	551	67	116	45	13	R	1	1	2	2	1	7
340	3712	2	2	13	D	192	201	150	566	67	112	46	14	R	1	1	2	2	2	21
341	3721	2	2	13	D	189	184	142	588	62	154	52	12	R	1	1	.	.	2	21
342	3722	2	2	13	D	179	181	137	566	65	131	45	14	L	2	2	.	2	1	12
343	3731	2	2	13	M	176	187	145	592	67	113	45	14	R	1	2	2	2	2	12
344	3732	2	2	13	C	170	187	130	580	65	107	46	13	R	1	2	2	2	1	17
345	3741	2	2	13	D	168	195	143	564	61	97	43	14	R	2	2	.	2	1	17
346	3742	2	2	13	D	178	186	136	554	62	90	42	14	L	1	1	.	.	1	12
347	3751	2	2	17	C	171	203	146	547	62	116	57	14	R	2	4	3	2	1	12
348	3752	2	1	17	C	188	185	148	537	61	124	51	13	R	1	2	.	.	1	12
349	3761	1	2	13	D	206	183	145	549	65	159	47	14	R	1	1	.	2	1	16
350	3762	2	2	13	D	186	188	140	615	66	174	48	14	R	1	1	.	2	1	16
351	3771	2	2	13	M	171	196	139	551	64	199	47	14	R	1	1	2	1	2	17
352	3772	2	2	15	M	192	202	141	543	65	114	48	13	R	1	1	2	1	2	17
353	3781	2	2	16	M	184	205	139	564	63	117	49	14	R	1	1	.	.	1	13
354	3782	1	2	16	M	204	195	140	583	70	120	48	13	R	1	1	.	2	1	13
355	3791	2	2	16	M	208	203	141	586	70	141	49	14	R	5	1	3	.	1	11
356	3792	2	2	16	U	197	184	143	565	64	133	54	14	R	1	5	.	2	1	11
357	3801	2	2	16	M	198	176	145	587	71	111	55	14	R	1	1	.	2	2	25
358	3802	1	2	16	U	175	189	143	520	64	140	51	11	L	1	1	.	.	2	25
359	3811	2	2	14	M	176	184	132	521	64	147	52	14	R	1	1	1	.	1	10
360	3812	2	2	15	M	195	176	135	540	63	88	45	14	R	1	1	3	.	1	10
361	3821	2	2	15	M	182	195	135	539	64	87	47	14	R	1	1	1	.	1	16
362	3822	2	2	13	D	172	181	146	563	64	112	53	13	R	5	1	.	2	1	16
363	3831	2	2	13	M	188	136	150	556	63	91	46	14	R	1	1	.	.	2	17
364	3832	2	2	13	M	191	184	151	551	64	100	45	14	R	1	1	1	2	2	17
365	3841	2	2	15	M	184	183	135	548	65	89	50	14	R	1	1	1	1	2	20
366	3842	1	2	14	D	179	177	137	556	64	97	49	14	R	1	1	.	1	2	20
367	3851	1	2	13	M	195	198	140	543	62	90	50	14	R	1	1	.	2	1	12
368	3852	2	2	13	M	179	184	138	536	61	102	57	14	R	1	1	1	.	1	12
369	3861	2	2	13	M	181	177	137	499	60	99	51	14	R	1	1	1	2	1	12
370	3862	2	2	15	U	189	179	137	501	62	110	48	14	R	1	1	3	.	1	12
371	3871	2	2	14	D	170	198	142	578	62	111	49	14	R	1	1	1	2	1	13
372	3872	2	2	14	M	173	185	146	582	65	111	43	13	R	1	1	.	.	1	13
373	3881	2	2	14	M	190	173	143	554	65	118	51	10	R	1	2	1	1	2	16
374	3882	2	2	14	M	189	198	146	525	65	111	49	14	R	1	1	.	1	1	16
375	3891	2	2	14	M	170	185	143	525	65	118	43	13	R	1	1	1	.	1	16
376	3892	2	2	14	U	173	193	147	567	66	180	51	10	R	1	2	1	1	2	16
377	3901	1	2	14	U	190	185	140	555	61	94	60	14	R	1	1	3	.	2	16
378	3902	1	1	13	U	191	185	140	555	61	94	60	14	R	1	1	3	.	2	16

OBS	ID	SEX	RACE	AGE	ZYG	_20	_21	_22	_23	_24	_25	_26	_27	_28	_29	_30	_31	_32	_33	_34
379	3911	1	2	15	U	185	194	137	564	66	115	46	14	R	1	2	2	2	2	19
380	3912	2	2	15	U	185	196	140	546	62	114	47	13	R	1	2	.	.	2	19

N=380

Appendix E

The test scores for all twins who took part or all of the psychological tests (except personality tests) in the Basic (Cols. 35–48, inc.), Secondary (Cols. 49–55, inc.), and Culture Fair (Cols. 56–66, inc.) batteries. All twins did not take every test in all three batteries. A decimal character (·) in Appendix E indicates no data available for the test listed. A zero represents an earned score of zero. For some multiple-choice tests, a negative score is possible when the correction for guessing is applied. In the following table, the column numbers correspond to the column heading in the printouts.

Since no subject took all psychological tests, the printout for Appendix E is divided into two parts. Part 1 lists scores for twins who took the Basic and Secondary batteries; Part 2, the Basic and Culture Fair batteries. A full description of each variable reported in the printout can be found in Appendix B.

Column #	Name of Test
35	Calendar
36	Cube Comparisons
37	Simple Arithmetic
38	Wide Range Vocabulary
39	Surface Development
40	Form Board
41	Self-Judging Vocabulary
42	Paper Folding
43	Object Aperture
44	Identical Pictures
45	Newcastle Spatial
46	Spelling Achievement
47	Mazes-number of half blocks completed
48	Mazes-number of errors
49	Inference (Part I only for twins #01–48; total for twins #500–875)

Column #	*Name of Test*
50	Mooney Faces
51	Logical Reasoning
52	Whiteman Test of Social Perception
53	Cancellation
54	Card Rotation
55	Ship Destination
56	PMA-verbal meaning
57	PMA-number facility
58	PMA-reasoning
59	PMA-spatial relations
60	PMA-total
61	IPAT Culture Fair-Form A-Classical IQ
62	IPAT Culture Fair-Form A-Culture Fair IQ
63	IPAT Culture Fair-Form A-Attainment Contaminated IQ
64	IPAT Culture Fair-Form B-Classical IQ
65	IPAT Culture Fair-Form B-Culture Fair IQ
66	IPAT Culture Fair-Form B-Attainment Contaminated IQ

OBS	ID	SEX	RACE	AGE	ZYG	_35	_36	_37	_38	_39	_40	_41	_42	_43	_44	_45	_46	_47	_48	_49	_50	_51	_52	_53	_54	_55
1	11	1	1	17	M	4	-11	74	6	15	2	36	0	1	56	13	32	25	46	-1	14	5	10	174	53	9
2	12	1	2	17	M	10	-6	25	0	6	2	42	-1	-5	47	18	27	14	25	-1	13	5	10	176	10	11
3	21	2	2	17	D	0	-8	24	-3	5	1	22	0	-1	54	22	31	24	4	-0	10	0	4	239	62	10
4	22	2	2	17	D	2	-2	49	1	17	10	38	18	-5	76	33	41	24	4	3	17	6	13	238	112	8
5	31	1	1	14	D	25	35	104	6	59	26	63	11	29	91	94	41	48	5	1	11	14	12	228	130	44
6	32	1	1	14	D	27	28	119	13	58	22	73	20	71	90	36	29	48	4	7	11	15	9	295	160	46
7	41	2	1	18	M	2	-3	17	0	16	14	39	14	9	48	4	31	24	2	6	4	9	5	223	142	9
8	42	2	1	18	M	10	12	47	5	16	9	40	8	2	47	31	47	21	1	0	12	13	3	69	145	6
9	51	1	1	17	M	24	16	133	10	33	9	70	5	5	70	77	58	21	5	2	12	16	5	299	143	36
10	52	1	1	17	M	20	10	123	14	26	10	72	7	7	50	77	57	15	1	4	12	16	16	163	122	32
11	61	2	2	17	M	13	0	15	0	16	2	8	-2	-5	38	25	28	15	14	1	6	4	-4	148	50	7
12	62	2	2	16	M	0	-4	48	0	14	1	33	-1	31	31	20	15	22	14	5	3	8	8	157	32	13
13	71	2	2	16	M	0	-2	48	0	6	1	8	-1	-5	48	19	39	11	5	0	6	8	8	221	28	7
14	72	2	2	16	M	-4	-12	32	4	9	7	30	10	-1	57	40	32	20	7	7	7	10	10	120	36	10
15	81	2	1	14	D	7	-6	61	2	20	13	25	8	-4	58	22	22	17	11	0	6	8	13	213	150	13
16	82	2	1	14	D	8	8	65	-3	30	16	45	8	6	54	68	30	22	8	-1	7	10	13	239	137	28
17	91	2	1	14	M	9	0	70	10	46	6	62	3	5	43	37	37	6	6	-1	13	9	11	213	103	12
18	92	2	1	14	M	16	-4	74	4	10	5	62	-2	3	44	70	28	28	6	-2	11	9	11	223	101	34
19	101	2	1	15	M	-1	-9	5	-2	10	3	-4	-1	-1	48	25	17	17	14	0	3	3	5	203	52	12
20	102	2	1	15	M	-6	-6	5	0	16	1	16	0	-1	16	0	0	48	22	0	5	1	5	205	76	9
21	111	2	1	17	M	10	-2	86	3	22	12	61	2	9	78	71	51	44	6	6	9	12	13	313	141	10
22	112	2	1	17	M	18	-5	89	7	28	5	55	4	7	71	55	46	45	6	5	9	14	14	295	153	27
23	121	2	1	16	M	16	16	53	4	23	5	55	1	7	49	50	55	29	21	1	13	13	14	214	86	13
24	122	1	2	16	M	26	20	65	6	31	17	60	12	7	50	64	58	27	7	4	16	12	14	230	166	36
25	131	2	1	16	M	17	18	46	6	46	7	57	12	20	69	81	37	26	1	6	13	14	14	209	115	44
26	132	2	1	16	M	16	20	72	4	28	26	57	13	13	66	35	35	42	13	5	16	11	10	217	146	42
27	141	2	1	15	D	12	9	51	6	14	13	45	8	6	63	36	41	33	7	3	11	9	9	246	71	32
28	142	1	1	15	D	9	9	123	5	19	9	25	8	-1	51	46	15	7	1	0	10	9	10	172	99	13
29	151	1	1	17	M	23	8	112	10	36	19	68	13	14	61	84	46	30	7	5	12	10	12	247	107	36
30	152	1	1	17	M	28	13	140	13	44	19	74	14	75	85	81	50	45	9	8	14	16	15	228	121	44
31	161	2	2	18	M	27	13	140	10	37	19	72	15	15	85	91	52	42	5	9	12	17	12	321	157	42
32	162	2	2	18	M	28	12	133	3	41	10	70	10	80	80	50	50	46	8	7	14	17	12	260	184	32
33	171	2	2	17	D	-2	-2	67	5	20	13	31	0	0	60	45	23	20	5	1	9	10	11	209	110	12
34	172	2	2	17	D	9	-9	39	3	20	5	44	9	6	44	44	48	48	6	0	7	11	13	335	174	30
35	181	1	1	14	U	17	14	57	5	16	11	50	9	5	39	41	48	40	23	-0	11	11	3	295	130	6
36	182	1	1	14	M	6	-0	23	0	9	7	45	7	-7	48	29	40	40	12	1	8	3	8	257	137	11
37	191	2	1	14	M	6	-3	30	1	11	13	40	3	1	71	42	10	24	4	-1	15	6	6	136	43	7
38	192	2	1	15	M	20	3	70	3	11	17	50	4	3	38	50	25	26	1	-1	13	7	10	75	79	7
39	201	2	1	15	D	14	26	70	11	47	15	67	13	6	89	74	37	48	18	5	14	14	12	333	185	32
40	202	2	1	14	D	12	23	87	13	53	23	52	10	8	87	74	48	48	6	6	15	15	12	333	174	27
41	211	2	1	14	M	11	10	57	7	14	11	52	6	0	66	42	10	32	7	0	4	14	11	260	137	9
42	212	2	1	14	M	8	11	89	3	23	14	26	13	-2	44	34	17	32	2	2	10	11	8	179	8	10
43	221	1	1	17	D	22	11	111	5	29	14	60	11	11	59	74	32	46	7	6	12	13	12	194	95	33
44	222	2	1	17	D	15	8	71	8	28	28	57	13	14	68	68	46	32	10	3	13	14	13	222	129	15
45	231	2	1	15	M	15	14	95	6	19	34	64	11	65	75	34	54	46	17	3	19	8	13	307	162	11
46	232	2	1	15	M	18	24	81	3	28	21	57	18	71	68	72	38	32	8	-1	8	13	12	218	155	13
47	241	2	2	17	D	15	5	45	8	25	21	48	-0	-5	50	46	46	28	9	-1	13	10	10	207	95	17
48	242	2	2	13	D	-4	-4	7	-1	13	5	2	-2	-3	27	15	1	17	50	0	4	16	16	153	81	8
49	251	2	2	13	M	1	4	12	1	14	2	7	-1	-0	46	31	26	26	11	-0	6	10	10	229	59	7
50	252	2	2	14	M	21	10	91	4	22	9	55	10	4	64	38	20	20	2	6	6	12	12	223	90	11
51	261	2	2	14	M	10	0	84	5	13	8	55	2	-3	50	24	41	17	11	2	7	10	12	218	78	12
52	262	2	2	14	M	16	20	60	2	23	21	42	12	14	61	70	31	27	16	1	18	9	14	292	149	11
53	271	2	1	17	M	20	12	48	3	26	19	51	10	13	58	64	42	32	3	-1	16	11	8	267	174	6

207

OBS	ID	SEX	RACE	AGE	ZYG	_35	_36	_37	_38	_39	_40	_41	_42	_43	_44	_45	_46	_47	_48	_49	_50	_51	_52	_53	_54	_55
55	281	1	1	13	D	18	-8	89	0	43	20	40	7	73	78	30	48	17	3	0	13	14	290	147	35
56	282	1	1	13	D	3	-6	69	4	17	14	38	6	49	46	26	30	20	2	13	6	10	234	173	3
57	291	2	1	15	U	4	-1	108	-2	20	7	32	-2	61	53	43	48	8	-1	15	9	9	274	140	10
58	292	2	1	15	U	16	10	106	3	20	17	40	9	61	54	50	35	17	1	19	9	194	23	11	
59	301	1	2	17	U	32	16	130	13	56	29	68	18	74	90	55	42	2	8	15	15	293	150	37	
60	302	2	2	17	U	21	17	118	16	34	16	66	12	77	83	41	42	16	6	14	14	278	153	45	
61	311	2	2	17	D	2	-9	24	-2	28	5	26	10	47	29	35	28	16	-2	15	10	13	279	79	16
62	312	2	2	17	C	0	3	73	-1	16	5	32	0	68	29	17	42	13	1	14	10	10	387	72	12
63	321	2	2	16	M	11	6	21	-1	16	10	30	-2	60	40	17	20	3	0	12	10	10	147	146	7
64	322	2	2	16	M	2	2	14	1	14	7	38	3	63	40	17	12	7	3	12	10	8	204	156	5
65	331	1	1	17	M	18	16	75	8	42	20	54	14	74	90	53	36	4	0	9	12	9	292	154	34
66	332	1	1	17	M	13	14	67	8	40	16	50	19	75	79	52	33	24	5	14	12	13	306	180	22
67	341	2	2	15	D	13	-3	33	9	19	12	21	20	60	21	32	24	18	-2	15	12	13	266	48	7
68	342	2	2	15	M	12	-1	72	2	13	8	39	8	46	48	39	23	15	-2	12	11	8	259	118	13
69	351	2	2	16	M	11	-7	75	-2	13	12	19	-3	51	37	15	35	22	1	11	8	13	286	166	13
70	352	2	2	16	D	11	-3	73	3	13	9	26	-5	48	54	13	22	4	0	17	8	8	242	154	12
71	361	1	1	14	M	8	7	98	-1	34	27	34	6	62	81	37	34	9	1	15	12	11	213	124	15
72	362	1	1	14	M	10	8	92	1	40	28	43	10	68	67	35	41	30	2	10	15	12	208	139	8
73	371	1	1	18	O	26	19	120	12	53	21	76	18	71	89	44	48	20	0	14	11	13	280	101	28
74	372	1	1	18	M	19	16	46	5	29	14	63	24	66	74	38	48	28	5	11	13	15	252	180	28
75	381	2	2	15	D	14	10	34	1	18	14	18	9	35	30	24	19	12	0	13	6	6	191	129	7
76	382	2	2	15	D	8	1	55	-1	19	9	40	4	46	36	39	18	4	3	15	11	11	247	71	15
77	391	1	1	15	M	19	-14	62	5	36	33	33	4	71	61	35	48	14	2	10	13	13	289	88	21
78	392	1	1	15	M	13	8	34	1	25	9	19	9	52	63	10	28	22	1	14	10	10	242	101	5
79	401	2	2	16	D	26	4	53	7	17	21	46	14	54	56	42	14	17	3	10	14	14	253	145	5
80	402	2	2	16	M	15	3	57	1	9	4	50	3	54	45	48	24	14	4	14	4	10	256	125	6
81	411	2	2	16	D	8	0	12	-1	13	10	4	0	76	9	0	0	48	4	5	7	4	232	78	11
82	412	2	2	14	D	5	7	7	1	9	14	19	-3	47	20	28	46	44	0	5	5	4	242	15	7
83	421	1	1	15	D	6	-6	47	3	8	8	51	5	40	20	21	16	23	1	8	7	3	230	78	7
84	422	1	1	14	D	3	12	16	6	3	1	-9	2	28	22	21	18	35	0	8	7	1	120	-7	7
85	431	1	2	14	O	3	-3	4	13	9	7	7	0	34	34	2	19	10	-1	7	3	117	53	7	
86	432	1	2	16	M	12	-3	7	1	6	3	6	-2	29	36	6	19	4	0	4	4	82	37	10	
87	441	2	2	16	M	24	5	74	8	23	9	69	8	82	56	50	24	13	5	19	10	14	341	109	31
88	442	2	2	16	M	24	91	10	20	10	66	6	84	54	48	35	14	-1	24	16	16	314	94	31	
89	451	1	1	16	D	9	110	12	22	23	44	-3	52	27	27	39	9	5	18	13	9	117	156	4	
90	452	1	2	16	D	13	31	3	42	10	70	15	63	84	43	40	2	0	15	14	12	220	174	12	
91	461	1	1	15	M	3	18	4	10	6	40	-1	53	26	40	22	6	-1	15	15	2	237	96	5	
92	462	1	2	15	M	17	121	18	23	24	26	-1	37	59	45	50	3	0	11	2	156	63	17		
93	471	2	2	18	D	16	17	53	37	69	61	87	0	71	87	51	27	7	-2	15	10	10	333	168	30
94	472	2	2	18	D	10	22	2	40	9	32	8	63	65	47	30	14	0	12	12	6	306	208	27	
95	481	1	1	16	D	22	76	37	50	14	8	76	72	38	42	14	14	11	13	10	218	109	19		
96	482	1	1	16	D	72	40	10	48	10	47	38	46	46	3	12	12	14	246	140	19			
97	5001	2	2	15	D	0	-6	72	11	40	14	50	10	38	61	52	38	46	1	14	14	11	162	17	17
98	5011	2	2	15	D	17	12	48	7	31	8	34	4	47	28	24	26	8	3	12	13	16	296	72	17
99	5002	1	1	18	M	15	5	77	22	8	27	54	12	59	68	26	40	19	1	11	15	14	301	84	34
100	5012	1	1	18	M	3	-1	81	7	33	10	44	3	46	47	49	32	13	-1	11	10	14	220	74	14
101	5021	2	2	14	O	5	2	33	7	10	3	5	0	40	12	12	9	19	3	12	6	7	216	52	16
102	5022	2	2	13	M	3	27	3	3	3	13	0	42	8	30	7	0	7	7	8	163	12	9		
103	5031	2	2	13	M	7	-3	20	18	17	8	4	6	66	28	32	23	7	-2	12	6	6	158	28	16
104	5032	2	2	16	D	4	3	37	14	8	19	36	3	33	33	44	21	7	0	10	12	10	127	-8	6
105	5041	1	1	16	O	20	3	68	15	12	6	47	6	38	44	31	40	24	5	11	13	6	215	99	28
106	5042	1	1	17	D	21	11	54	12	39	16	70	11	71	27	48	22	15	8	12	15	10	300	180	13
107	5051	2	1	17	M	16	2	88	9	36	10	62	13	82	63	48	48	22	8	16	17	14	276	154	21

OBS	ID	SEX	RACE	AGE	ZYG	_35	_36	_37	_38	_39	_40	_41	_42	_43	_44	_45	_46	_47	_48	_49	_50	_51	_52	_53	_54	_55
109	5061	2	1	14	D	5	19	72	6	32	7	38	10	6	49	61	48	32	4	4	6	16	15	212	147	33
110	5062	2	1	14	D	19	-1	68	4	15	6	31	9	4	42	49	33	25	5	5	13	12	16	197	86	17
111	5071	2	1	17	D	11	16	62	3	19	22	37	9	5	57	50	13	44	5	4	12	13	13	267	88	9
112	5072	2	1	17	D	17	-5	62	0	21	12	17	5	0	44	52	18	30	12	3	8	12	13	270	74	12
113	5081	1	1	17	M	15	15	79	10	34	26	53	11	21	41	41	40	32	5	0	15	9	14	232	15	28
114	5082	1	1	17	M	15	15	65	4	42	6	37	10	4	27	43	39	43	6	4	13	8	14	238	169	33
115	5091	2	1	13	D	20	13	49	3	31	12	40	4	11	48	48	40	29	16	6	18	9	14	259	114	31
116	5092	2	1	13	M	20	2	57	10	23	24	46	11	-2	66	65	36	38	13	3	18	14	12	254	94	37
117	5101	2	1	14	D	5	-1	14	4	12	3	-2	-4	-2	43	32	3	2	0	4	9	5	5	85	-1	10
118	5102	2	1	14	D	5	1	11	2	9	2	-1	3	-3	46	28	8	12	13	0	11	1	1	51	-4	12
119	5111	2	1	15	D	13	6	50	4	13	14	34	10	8	53	•	33	32	12	2	14	12	12	154	89	24
120	5112	2	1	15	D	14	5	50	5	32	13	20	5	9	50	•	26	28	7	1	10	11	11	155	56	26
121	5131	1	1	20	D	14	5	50	4	20	13	32	6	2	56	•	41	48	6	2	13	6	10	248	140	22
122	5132	1	1	20	M	16	25	46	2	34	10	19	6	-4	42	38	28	32	7	1	16	0	8	168	130	12
123	5141	1	1	15	D	16	11	47	2	19	10	38	6	-5	46	37	37	27	6	-2	14	2	16	194	179	6
124	5142	1	1	15	M	18	14	61	6	17	7	45	4	-4	23	35	47	34	1	1	8	5	13	213	176	10
125	5151	1	1	17	D	8	14	72	1	15	4	45	9	5	47	41	50	18	7	-3	15	11	11	247	110	19
126	5152	2	1	17	D	5	4	70	4	25	16	20	6	2	45	47	8	24	1	3	2	12	8	279	110	11
127	5161	2	1	13	D	8	5	40	3	22	16	17	8	7	38	48	10	21	5	1	7	10	10	158	87	16
128	5162	2	1	13	M	8	-3	47	6	30	13	50	4	5	47	62	18	38	19	-1	9	9	8	156	83	15
129	5171	2	1	17	D	18	-3	61	3	19	13	50	8	3	48	48	41	22	5	1	7	7	10	222	157	18
130	5172	2	1	13	D	9	2	56	3	14	10	19	3	1	49	59	25	16	3	0	3	9	22	228	127	9
131	5181	2	1	13	M	9	2	76	2	25	11	35	5	6	43	47	47	29	11	5	14	13	13	231	74	18
132	5182	2	1	13	D	14	-1	73	8	25	9	37	7	2	45	51	32	32	15	1	11	12	5	155	123	10
133	5191	2	1	13	D	14	-4	51	5	8	3	10	6	2	36	26	22	22	17	-1	7	7	5	136	-24	5
134	5192	2	1	13	M	7	2	61	2	24	6	17	3	3	27	27	28	31	2	-2	18	8	12	172	42	15
135	5201	1	1	15	D	2	0	17	1	3	5	16	8	•	35	35	22	18	13	0	7	8	6	137	57	11
136	5202	1	1	15	D	4	4	24	3	12	4	22	2	6	83	83	27	22	18	-2	0	8	11	96	66	16
137	5211	2	1	13	M	2	0	46	1	14	5	11	0	4	30	35	32	20	7	0	3	4	9	213	•	13
138	5212	2	1	13	D	11	3	53	3	19	2	22	5	1	22	22	30	24	14	3	7	7	9	245	•	12
139	5221	2	1	13	M	9	8	42	3	15	2	11	7	0	43	29	41	16	3	4	0	10	9	169	63	23
140	5222	2	1	13	D	9	8	38	3	14	10	21	9	5	56	49	30	22	4	1	13	9	9	132	49	14
141	5231	1	1	16	D	14	13	72	4	18	3	51	7	1	50	50	39	46	15	-2	12	9	10	249	163	16
142	5232	1	1	16	M	15	17	64	8	18	6	50	5	-5	48	59	43	36	21	0	14	7	10	367	156	23
143	5241	2	1	14	D	5	0	35	2	22	3	10	-1	1	48	•	8	18	8	-2	12	5	8	106	-5	13
144	5242	2	1	14	M	8	0	29	2	20	3	38	-1	-5	41	41	5	26	8	0	8	8	17	169	8	18
145	5251	2	1	13	D	18	8	44	7	14	23	15	6	7	73	56	31	32	3	3	15	0	14	194	117	16
146	5252	2	1	13	D	11	0	37	1	17	4	54	8	-1	57	45	33	34	12	-1	10	11	14	221	83	24
147	5261	1	1	16	D	26	27	78	8	59	19	54	13	17	82	73	49	48	14	1	16	17	9	316	218	33
148	5262	1	1	16	M	5	29	82	13	52	31	55	15	15	83	73	51	34	8	3	7	9	13	417	210	42
149	5271	2	1	16	D	6	-5	51	4	13	3	1	1	3	40	23	28	24	33	-1	14	6	14	241	40	18
150	5272	2	1	16	M	5	12	54	4	21	11	11	8	7	57	40	22	16	8	0	16	9	9	202	-6	19
151	5281	2	1	17	D	15	12	80	3	27	3	34	13	3	74	46	41	20	8	6	9	12	17	282	180	27
152	5282	2	1	17	M	22	22	89	17	24	11	35	12	7	56	59	44	18	3	4	18	13	14	215	163	31
153	5291	2	1	18	D	14	13	71	3	17	6	28	5	5	53	53	46	22	19	3	8	12	14	232	142	23
154	5292	2	1	13	M	3	7	51	0	17	6	13	5	3	44	46	41	30	18	-1	12	6	12	161	111	12
155	5301	1	1	13	D	7	8	59	11	35	18	35	8	4	54	63	30	27	18	-3	5	13	12	145	129	11
156	5302	1	1	13	D	-1	7	63	4	15	13	46	8	4	48	37	20	18	1	3	13	12	12	179	4	10
157	5311	1	1	14	D	8	-3	9	1	9	2	3	-2	0	36	22	10	10	2	-1	4	2	7	180	11	11
158	5312	1	1	14	M	7	3	46	1	10	4	8	9	3	43	42	30	30	15	-3	6	11	13	230	98	12
159	5321	2	1	16	D	13	12	58	8	30	12	28	11	6	57	52	44	28	6	1	6	10	13	252	102	14
160	5322	2	1	16	M	12	10	42	3	33	14	18	8	3	52	52	34	34	3	3	6	13	11	232	110	23
161	5331	1	1	17	D	8	0	49	4	23	16	50	8	-3	52	52	18	26	0	-1	15	6	12	191	96	12
162	5332	2	1	17	M	13	0	55	7	23	16	55	5	2	54	39	22	24	5	5	16	13	14	199	115	28

OBS	ID	SEX	RACE	AGE	ZYG	_35	_36	_37	_38	_39	_40	_41	_42	_43	_44	_45	_46	_47	_48	_49	_50	_51	_52	_53	_54	_55
163	5341	2	1	13	D	6	-8	45	4	17	5	3	2	-6	41	32	27	22	19	-1	15	5	10	147	37	8
164	5342	2	1	13	D	6	4	43	14	14	7	4	0	-1	.	31	21	.	.	6	6	5	0	.	35	11
165	5351	2	1	16	D	16	36	43	3	29	19	20	10	2	53	74	25	38	.	8	2	16	16	270	124	24
166	5352	2	1	16	D	22	12	59	5	26	20	13	13	6	39	78	51	25	3	16	4	16	14	226	116	29
167	5361	1	1	17	M	14	14	53	4	43	20	5	10	3	50	74	30	26	6	15	6	15	12	238	168	34
168	5362	1	1	17	M	.	-3	58	5	12	5	33	5	-6	41	67	22	24	1	18	0	5	14	179	168	34
169	5371	1	1	17	D	8	-3	90	5	12	7	38	3	2	38	35	45	23	18	0	5	13	14	193	160	24
170	5372	1	1	13	D	12	-1	88	8	11	16	9	3	-6	32	43	28	24	18	7	0	14	12	216	124	29
171	5381	1	1	13	D	6	-3	18	2	15	4	2	11	-3	25	25	8	23	10	-2	11	2	11	139	22	19
172	5382	1	1	15	D	15	7	18	2	11	2	6	5	-3	38	54	34	24	9	0	0	12	13	208	107	33
173	5391	2	1	15	M	18	8	52	5	19	24	24	11	2	54	59	48	30	11	5	11	13	12	315	148	18
174	5392	2	1	15	D	18	1	105	5	38	14	63	6	0	73	59	53	.	30	5	16	13	11	346	171	17
175	5401	2	1	14	D	10	11	117	-1	17	20	.	3	7	70	55	.	.	.	-2	6	11	11	242	-28	7
176	5402	2	1	14	D	10	13	27	4	14	2	-1	.	1	45	45	1	38	23	-1	10	5	12	234	111	12
177	5411	1	1	12	M	5	1	26	4	17	2	12	15	-5	36	44	24	26	4	-1	11	8	12	192	24	14
178	5412	2	1	12	D	13	1	26	3	9	5	9	4	-5	32	32	19	22	4	-1	3	7	12	184	38	4
179	5421	2	1	15	D	4	3	23	0	14	5	.	-1	-4	27	40	10	10	8	-8	13	9	7	.	58	14
180	5422	1	1	15	M	0	2	28	5	25	9	22	1	-4	26	61	5	28	20	1	10	6	10	149	58	19
181	5431	1	1	14	D	3	4	43	6	9	3	11	3	-3	31	26	24	20	12	-2	4	6	5	98	65	15
182	5432	1	1	14	M	4	3	33	-1	49	8	15	-3	-1	26	.	28	18	10	4	3	2	16	109	99	8
183	5441	1	1	14	D	13	14	51	3	24	16	13	13	4	48	.	13	48	20	-2	14	5	13	215	124	25
184	5442	1	1	14	D	13	13	67	9	28	16	11	11	3	46	59	28	29	13	5	12	16	.	232	108	29
185	5451	2	1	18	M	14	12	77	8	20	9	41	7	0	60	52	47	26	15	4	14	10	13	250	135	25
186	5452	2	1	18	M	20	10	72	10	20	5	49	8	9	56	52	48	32	32	13	14	13	13	222	150	26
187	5461	1	1	17	M	20	11	94	13	11	7	49	10	9	59	46	58	28	54	11	10	12	17	226	95	24
188	5462	1	1	17	M	3	2	83	17	16	5	74	8	7	52	38	58	28	6	0	6	14	14	177	76	37
189	5471	2	1	16	D	3	-2	26	1	10	7	79	7	8	38	34	34	33	27	5	13	6	9	239	17	11
190	5472	2	1	16	D	3	30	35	6	16	7	21	3	0	.	39	24	14	4	3	13	10	11	73	.	13
191	5481	1	1	17	M	3	30	109	6	48	23	46	16	20	52	86	33	42	4	10	18	10	11	321	146	39
192	5482	1	1	17	M	22	29	86	10	47	27	60	13	20	80	80	35	28	4	3	15	13	14	251	154	43
193	5491	1	1	14	M	9	5	26	6	16	2	17	6	13	42	.	23	22	6	-3	11	6	5	145	65	20
194	5492	1	1	14	M	11	6	10	6	15	1	15	13	16	37	.	15	10	6	0	16	5	11	128	81	19
195	5511	2	2	15	M	10	11	59	3	39	17	.	13	9	50	71	33	32	10	2	15	4	10	236	155	17
196	5512	1	2	13	M	13	6	43	8	26	23	3	16	13	34	85	4	30	6	9	9	5	12	143	87	20
197	5521	2	2	13	M	13	5	35	15	3	10	8	5	5	32	33	16	22	10	3	6	12	12	177	44	10
198	5522	2	1	13	D	24	-2	34	-1	8	3	11	-1	1	29	29	16	18	18	-2	10	14	2	177	42	9
199	5532	2	1	16	D	8	8	91	8	7	13	36	7	9	56	61	53	22	50	2	8	8	11	242	136	32
200	5532	2	1	16	D	17	8	97	3	19	14	15	10	7	30	61	24	15	4	5	15	8	2	191	97	19
201	5541	1	1	16	M	14	14	87	3	24	36	15	9	7	38	63	24	34	3	4	8	13	11	178	114	23
202	5542	1	1	16	M	17	4	77	7	37	15	15	13	9	53	40	15	15	20	9	15	8	13	191	104	30
203	5551	1	1	17	D	15	2	49	2	13	15	7	4	3	40	53	24	24	19	3	5	8	10	103	36	21
204	5552	1	1	17	D	15	5	57	3	11	7	1	4	18	36	40	8	26	2	8	6	8	8	130	57	31
205	5571	1	1	15	M	8	-3	41	2	5	4	24	9	-2	24	15	37	24	6	3	6	7	9	223	45	11
206	5572	2	1	15	M	12	5	58	6	1	11	28	4	13	38	18	42	26	19	2	10	6	13	237	65	24
207	5581	2	1	15	M	12	8	62	1	34	14	14	12	-2	48	48	26	24	8	3	12	8	10	225	151	30
208	5582	2	1	16	D	7	10	22	3	25	11	10	13	13	46	63	17	26	8	3	8	6	13	233	143	33
209	5591	1	1	15	D	11	11	57	2	46	22	23	10	10	55	66	23	35	6	2	6	6	11	254	131	28
210	5592	1	1	16	M	11	32	84	5	44	30	23	20	13	62	85	22	32	14	4	17	11	11	290	182	23
211	5601	2	1	16	D	-4	-2	60	4	22	17	28	17	10	53	74	40	44	16	3	9	11	12	192	17	13
212	5602	2	1	15	D	10	31	58	13	32	5	13	10	-7	.	.	23	23	11	-1	10	11	9	134	84	16
213	5611	2	1	17	D	19	-3	98	2	16	13	52	7	10	57	82	16	27	50	4	17	11	13	291	107	16
214	5612	1	1	17	D	14	10	78	8	35	24	56	5	5	47	75	49	25	7	4	13	10	11	228	85	38
215	5621	2	1	16	M	15	7	13	20	14	11	10	5	51	54	56	16	2	4	13	10	12	152	77	17
216	5622	2	1	16	M	11	5	68	3	26	13	18	1	3	43	56	45	14	4	3	13	14	14	241	108	11

OBS	ID	SEX	RACE	AGE	ZYG	_35	_36	_37	_38	_39	_40	_41	_42	_43	_44	_45	_46	_47	_48	_49	_50	_51	_52	_53	_54	_55
217	5631	2	2	14	M	-9	-8	28	7	9	0	11	1	-6	.	17	16	.	.	3	4	6	9	.	14	8
218	5632	2	1	14	N	0	-8	33	4	18	11	11	3	4	45	7	10	24	24	-1	2	5	12	153	4	7
219	5641	2	1	13	D	11	2	20	-2	18	12	15	6	3	35	18	30	16	16	5	11	5	14	159	-2	12
220	5642	2	1	13	D	.	2	36	0	21	19	25	11	10	48	41	37	16	8	6	12	15	15	182	61	29
221	5661	2	1	13	M	11	31	110	17	42	27	74	10	10	83	59	24	44	19	6	12	15	16	245	146	42
222	5662	2	1	17	M	22	20	97	14	30	12	76	4	13	72	68	56	42	8	8	13	15	12	220	133	35
223	5671	2	1	13	D	4	7	13	4	5	8	9	9	4	43	14	9	20	15	0	4	7	4	129	32	8
224	5672	2	1	13	D	7	-7	29	2	20	8	6	4	1	37	14	17	20	20	-1	4	7	4	218	-16	7
225	5681	1	1	15	D	4	3	70	4	18	6	8	9	6	64	40	11	31	28	-2	13	7	14	224	18	32
226	5682	1	1	15	M	2	.	57	1	24	6	3	5	6	63	40	34	22	22	2	6	11	14	197	20	31
227	5691	1	1	17	M	16	15	93	5	31	8	8	9	24	52	51	39	30	3	13	11	14	16	269	89	33
228	5692	1	1	17	D	20	13	87	2	45	18	41	9	18	49	68	40	28	11	1	6	10	14	264	67	33
229	5701	1	1	13	D	15	1	32	8	32	20	51	7	8	51	80	42	29	24	0	5	13	14	181	65	28
230	5702	2	1	13	D	13	5	71	2	15	11	36	1	8	48	57	45	23	10	5	4	13	10	173	133	23
231	5711	1	1	16	D	15	5	32	1	29	5	45	1	7	70	82	43	18	16	6	5	13	14	322	104	23
232	5712	1	1	15	M	2	6	67	3	23	8	1	2	2	48	64	28	45	19	-1	13	12	11	291	79	41
233	5721	1	1	15	D	11	11	48	3	13	7	35	2	5	37	39	3	16	3	0	7	10	14	101	116	30
234	5722	2	1	13	D	8	-2	13	-1	8	9	1	-1	5	42	16	15	8	-1	0	10	10	8	100	118	16
235	5731	2	2	13	D	16	6	52	0	14	5	8	5	1	50	36	36	2	2	1	5	10	11	135	38	17
236	5732	2	2	15	D	9	3	38	4	17	11	6	9	1	47	27	16	18	13	-5	5	7	7	178	27	11
237	5741	2	1	15	D	4	.	0	0	8	3	-2	3	5	27	0	13	17	-1	5	5	2	7	75	18	8
238	5742	2	1	15	D	1	-6	7	10	10	6	4	7	7	75	2	6	28	2	6	5	6	13	183	140	30
239	5751	1	1	13	M	12	9	59	7	23	23	54	8	1	49	27	26	34	13	4	4	14	11	167	104	29
240	5752	2	1	13	M	24	9	74	4	21	45	14	8	5	55	22	34	22	-1	4	7	11	14	214	16	16
241	5761	1	1	13	M	6	1	69	10	15	14	6	0	0	62	43	31	40	27	5	0	11	11	186	82	22
242	5762	2	1	16	D	5	-6	51	6	25	23	15	5	1	50	35	24	37	21	7	10	14	0	192	33	12
243	5771	2	1	16	D	-7	-4	48	3	14	7	23	5	0	48	24	24	28	19	0	12	13	2	137	98	15
244	5772	2	1	16	D	18	3	79	9	13	6	39	1	-3	46	80	43	36	1	4	15	12	13	247	140	37
245	5781	1	1	17	D	12	15	102	5	36	11	62	13	12	52	55	55	48	29	6	5	13	17	260	156	34
246	5782	1	1	17	M	21	8	107	8	40	16	48	15	11	53	73	53	30	7	5	11	12	16	286	177	31
247	5791	2	2	17	M	10	13	86	6	35	18	53	18	8	53	80	54	24	3	-1	10	11	13	259	169	32
248	5792	2	1	18	D	20	13	94	5	31	8	39	8	-4	61	60	51	16	7	3	13	11	10	214	87	10
249	5801	2	1	18	M	8	1	58	19	14	5	15	-4	5	53	30	47	30	3	0	10	11	178	98	5	22
250	5802	2	1	18	D	5	3	73	5	37	3	25	1	-1	51	49	50	24	7	1	15	14	13	241	160	30
251	5811	2	1	18	D	1	-1	30	0	19	9	12	5	-2	51	55	23	25	8	2	8	8	10	202	70	19
252	5812	2	1	15	D	5	18	79	7	14	4	49	6	0	43	38	12	27	13	1	16	13	6	173	79	7
253	5821	1	1	15	M	14	16	77	-1	37	5	25	2	3	44	38	37	38	15	0	13	13	10	193	99	9
254	5822	1	1	15	M	15	10	60	0	19	3	12	6	3	51	42	28	28	10	1	11	12	5	148	84	16
255	5841	2	1	15	D	-5	9	61	-1	11	7	50	6	-3	24	32	25	23	2	4	2	6	14	192	28	11
256	5842	2	1	15	D	14	0	32	6	52	24	37	11	16	54	88	35	36	17	0	16	10	5	263	153	33
257	5861	2	1	17	D	13	13	48	1	47	37	13	8	10	65	83	37	32	8	0	19	9	14	271	206	36
258	5862	2	2	18	M	13	13	50	12	16	8	22	4	8	43	45	5	26	18	1	18	5	14	191	121	19
259	5871	2	1	18	M	11	10	83	8	21	5	13	4	8	56	48	12	36	2	0	14	10	7	204	109	25
260	5872	2	1	18	M	9	15	38	2	29	13	17	10	5	44	60	44	48	17	1	15	8	12	252	163	20
261	5881	1	1	16	M	13	13	67	6	22	12	45	7	9	38	48	41	24	26	1	11	8	13	218	129	15
262	5882	2	2	16	D	14	10	76	8	27	16	29	6	7	58	64	39	28	28	2	11	11	13	258	78	21
263	5892	2	1	16	M	15	13	56	6	37	9	29	0	6	72	66	46	26	26	4	13	13	13	235	68	21
264	5892	2	1	17	D	21	14	70	13	20	12	50	12	0	43	63	50	25	26	6	5	13	16	178	111	30
265	5901	2	1	17	M	5	14	68	2	27	17	57	13	11	58	69	51	26	23	3	6	14	13	202	107	30
266	5902	2	1	17	M	19	0	88	3	30	16	45	14	10	33	66	48	22	5	.	12	13	14	326	197	9
267	5921	2	1	14	D																					25
268	5922	2	1	14	M																					
269	5931	2	1	16	D																					
270	5932	1	1	16	D																					

OBS	ID	SEX	RACE	AGE	ZYG	_35	_36	_37	_38	_39	_40	_41	_42	_43	_44	_45	_46	_47	_48	_49	_50	_51	_52	_53	_54	_55
271	5941	2	1	15	M	14	6	92	8	9	7	53	10	2	51	46	52	22	3	4	8	10	13	280	148	26
272	5942	2	1	15	M	15	8	89	9	18	4	49	.	5	45	45	53	28	1	7	14	12	13	243	152	28
273	5951	1	1	13	D	18	.	46	1	19	4	-2	0	-1	32	20	10	10	11	1	4	4	4	179	114	32
274	5952	1	1	13	D	11	0	49	2	12	5	23	1	-2	44	20	15	19	6	1	10	8	14	141	40	24
275	5961	1	1	15	D	15	0	89	1	15	5	27	1	-1	57	45	36	35	6	2	1	11	6	175	89	16
276	5962	2	2	15	D	7	.	67	3	26	6	4	5	5	59	63	10	18	15	1	12	11	10	216	133	14
277	5971	1	1	16	M	13	13	51	3	16	10	35	7	5	48	64	45	18	5	4	14	13	13	288	142	10
278	5972	2	2	16	M	12	12	70	4	13	13	42	3	6	38	58	52	15	5	5	10	15	13	269	115	13
279	5981	2	2	18	M	20	2	44	7	35	4	53	10	14	23	64	54	26	9	4	17	11	10	192	100	31
280	5982	2	2	18	M	25	12	47	7	46	9	58	1	12	41	63	43	22	8	2	6	13	12	241	105	23
281	5991	1	1	14	D	8	4	63	9	24	16	43	8	4	52	40	42	8	0	4	9	14	7	204	46	13
282	5992	1	1	14	D	18	4	67	7	18	13	49	7	5	40	63	46	14	0	5	9	14	17	212	86	17
283	6001	1	1	15	D	18	25	81	3	40	17	45	11	1	63	61	21	48	10	5	16	8	12	290	202	32
284	6002	1	1	16	D	14	0	59	3	34	9	17	1	8	45	28	46	34	8	3	17	7	16	243	93	29
285	6011	1	1	16	D	8	-2	55	5	16	5	31	4	45	35	26	34	8	0	13	7	8	130	47	16	
286	6012	2	1	16	D	8	-5	8	6	14	5	-3	4	53	35	0	32	12	-1	11	8	3	148	58	6	
287	6021	1	1	16	D	10	-14	55	8	11	10	50	-1	49	38	10	26	3	4	3	11	3	194	5	17	
288	6022	2	2	16	M	9	-3	66	8	11	9	13	5	58	47	37	31	10	5	6	9	13	213	-10	20	
289	6031	1	1	16	M	22	15	107	6	32	14	51	5	2	69	47	51	33	13	1	14	14	13	260	146	31
290	6032	2	2	16	M	18	18	101	1	34	14	45	10	10	69	59	54	28	3	6	2	15	16	254	128	31
291	6041	1	1	13	D	17	12	72	4	34	16	29	12	2	46	69	34	27	6	4	15	10	10	243	132	36
292	6042	1	1	13	D	10	12	64	2	29	29	5	10	9	46	55	17	35	1	10	9	9	14	240	132	28
293	6051	1	2	15	D	10	-14	40	5	7	11	11	9	46	25	35	14	6	1	10	5	12	212	87	12	
294	6052	2	2	16	M	11	-1	61	2	5	7	50	10	2	49	23	42	22	6	1	5	5	10	193	58	7
295	6061	1	1	16	M	11	-2	72	8	30	16	41	10	3	49	23	50	22	6	1	13	12	13	290	166	26
296	6062	2	1	16	D	25	16	95	6	32	10	54	11	3	77	84	52	32	3	3	14	8	12	379	201	19
297	6071	1	1	15	D	1	-1	54	1	18	5	35	-5	5	29	32	25	20	12	0	14	11	10	109	84	4
298	6072	1	1	15	D	12	3	55	8	20	7	24	-5	4	44	46	20	30	10	2	10	8	9	183	147	33
299	6081	1	2	15	M	8	-3	39	3	10	9	13	7	8	23	23	27	26	10	1	6	6	5	131	-10	25
300	6082	2	2	14	M	10	5	24	6	9	.	24	8	3	34	19	19	34	11	8	8	5	5	182	107	15
301	6101	1	1	14	D	6	10	56	1	4	.	13	11	4	59	29	31	20	9	1	10	8	7	178	81	20
302	6102	2	1	14	D	9	6	71	3	25	44	44	1	41	54	45	24	10	0	4	10	14	191	71	20	
303	6111	1	1	16	M	10	-5	34	4	5	3	16	1	9	58	48	10	25	5	1	6	5	12	159	105	18
304	6112	2	2	14	D	9	-5	40	2	17	5	13	3	2	55	47	14	25	10	0	4	6	10	125	57	18
305	6121	1	1	16	M	26	27	85	8	24	18	34	3	9	50	44	49	20	9	6	16	8	12	257	114	9
306	6122	2	1	16	M	21	15	67	3	23	18	38	1	5	48	62	49	36	2	5	17	13	11	261	120	13
307	6131	1	1	13	D	12	-1	74	0	21	7	34	5	1	48	52	42	22	9	2	13	12	11	225	117	10
308	6132	2	1	13	D	20	-2	80	3	19	34	8	3	49	52	49	29	10	1	10	11	11	218	77	15	
309	6141	1	1	16	M	19	3	43	3	25	10	54	8	8	66	46	16	25	9	6	12	12	14	253	101	41
310	6142	2	1	16	M	16	5	54	6	24	58	58	8	3	46	56	27	26	4	9	12	9	14	214	99	36
311	6151	1	1	15	M	4	9	38	5	16	9	25	10	2	35	54	50	26	8	6	5	6	10	228	107	16
312	6152	1	1	16	D	9	8	41	5	13	6	28	3	1	41	43	43	40	25	5	11	9	11	256	107	12
313	6161	1	1	16	M	16	13	63	9	9	8	36	11	5	54	24	47	24	4	11	11	11	242	69	20	
314	6162	1	2	16	M	20	1	50	5	12	12	41	9	45	45	31	33	11	1	18	14	16	251	70	17	
315	6171	1	1	19	D	13	-2	52	3	44	31	20	14	19	45	31	44	27	9	9	14	9	12	245	150	19
316	6172	2	1	19	D	9	-2	57	8	38	20	26	12	17	40	37	47	25	18	1	18	7	16	267	143	20
317	6181	2	2	18	M	11	-2	51	8	24	26	74	0	40	52	40	18	7	9	15	10	13	294	65	16	
318	6182	1	1	18	M	6	0	69	6	16	6	66	8	1	54	40	44	24	8	3	18	13	14	294	69	7
319	6191	2	1	18	D	6	4	68	-2	15	7	43	1	62	31	44	34	-2	0	16	13	13	178	136	9	
320	6192	2	2	18	D	15	4	93	6	19	4	47	1	61	55	31	34	9	2	16	10	12	207	65	27	
321	6201	2	2	15	M	15	13	27	3	32	9	12	6	61	22	55	22	10	6	8	12	12	177	20	20	
322	6202	2	2	15	M	14	-2	30	2	20	8	26	10	56	27	27	26	17	3	12	11	11	177	26	28	
323	6211	2	2	15	D	14	3	66	11	26	11	34	13	0	48	43	28	26	2	6	14	8	13	374	65	11
324	6212	1	1	15	D	14	2	92	0	14	4	45	10	2	54	64	33	30	12	1	17	11	11	137	174	15

OBS	ID	SEX	RACE	AGE	ZYG	_35	_36	_37	_38	_39	_40	_41	_42	_43	_44	_45	_46	_47	_48	_49	_50	_51	_52	_53	_54	_55
325	6221	2	1	14	D	5	19	44	7	13	4	26	4	0	49	23	25	23	16	0	5	3	5	173	27	17
326	6222	2	1	14	D	6	9	36	2	16	6	31	11	1	43	42	41	28	8	-1	9	6	8	197	51	10
327	6231	1	1	17	D	5	-2	52	12	9	20	64	12	12	39	56	51	20	8	0	2	11	13	191	60	22
328	6232	1	1	17	D	12	11	37	5	2	6	43	5	7	30	36	41	21	2	1	5	11	10	221	100	25
329	6241	1	1	17	D	18	27	89	5	52	25	39	10	12	58	81	47	34	8	1	17	14	13	237	157	36
330	6242	1	1	17	D	5	2	58	5	38	17	40	10	2	59	82	35	39	29	3	19	11	14	278	174	15
331	6251	1	1	15	M	15	5	64	3	20	11	20	8	-3	49	54	16	20	9	3	2	7	12	254	127	17
332	6252	1	1	15	M	15	5	69	2	24	5	25	5	-3	48	52	22	20	12	5	11	10	17	243	115	18
333	6261	1	1	16	M	17	22	68	3	27	8	41	11	12	71	82	27	20	10	1	16	12	17	250	178	32
334	6262	1	1	16	M	24	26	73	7	15	23	46	10	7	61	67	34	37	6	9	16	9	13	243	196	27
335	6271	2	1	15	M	20	0	89	-1	12	2	32	1	1	46	26	44	16	21	4	3	10	8	161	70	9
336	6272	2	1	15	M	8	6	87	7	15	7	49	6	-4	36	24	48	16	48	6	12	13	13	197	20	6
337	6281	2	1	14	D	23	13	72	5	39	11	30	6	12	47	45	45	36	13	3	16	12	12	243	139	22
338	6282	2	1	14	D	26	21	79	5	55	22	40	0	-5	46	94	54	32	1	2	12	18	12	256	168	37
339	6291	2	2	14	M	-1	-17	1	0	0	-1	6	0	-18	14	14	0	1	9	0	1	6	-2	38	-6	9
340	6292	2	2	14	M	-1	-6	6	-4	10	1	6	-1	-39	37	23	1	5	14	6	7	1	16	158	-1	12
341	6301	1	1	17	D	18	-2	95	4	35	7	47	6	3	65	37	38	22	4	1	0	7	16	273	109	30
342	6302	1	1	17	D	8	-3	92	-3	14	9	22	6	0	63	38	45	9	22	1	12	10	10	279	13	7
343	6311	1	1	19	M	2	-3	24	3	16	13	0	9	1	55	57	3	40	33	3	8	6	9	174	110	22
344	6312	1	1	19	M	7	4	28	0	11	5	6	7	-6	47	44	3	28	12	0	8	14	3	287	136	12
345	6321	1	1	18	D	25	6	31	11	14	9	72	7	-5	60	34	50	42	6	5	13	10	14	239	81	31
346	6322	1	1	18	D	20	15	117	13	36	22	72	2	-3	70	68	51	42	3	4	16	12	14	266	194	37
347	6331	1	1	15	D	15	15	43	6	18	2	18	2	15	50	66	19	32	11	2	12	12	14	218	76	37
348	6332	1	1	15	D	10	2	31	3	16	10	20	8	10	48	69	26	32	12	5	14	10	12	185	108	25
349	6341	1	1	16	D	16	9	52	4	18	15	19	6	-3	45	53	25	20	12	3	13	10	12	323	108	9
350	6342	1	1	16	D	18	13	49	3	18	15	28	0	-3	51	48	27	20	7	1	12	4	8	251	180	12
351	6351	1	1	16	D	8	-7	53	3	16	5	25	5	-2	52	37	32	24	2	2	1	9	14	186	128	13
352	6352	1	1	16	D	8	-4	34	1	11	5	26	5	0	46	39	17	32	13	2	5	9	11	167	79	19
353	6361	1	1	15	D	5	-5	47	0	16	9	-1	2	1	34	36	22	22	4	-1	4	12	12	224	44	9
354	6362	1	1	15	D	4	-4	16	6	9	9	8	3	-3	49	45	29	24	11	0	4	5	2	232	-2	17
355	6371	1	1	16	D	13	11	57	6	13	5	27	3	7	32	45	50	26	9	4	9	12	12	161	38	19
356	6372	1	1	16	D	11	11	96	3	26	9	39	9	-1	38	41	44	21	6	2	8	11	14	212	125	13
357	6381	1	1	15	D	14	13	85	3	22	7	50	9	-3	49	64	44	13	13	4	10	12	9	214	103	19
358	6382	1	1	15	D	8	10	73	2	37	7	35	13	4	51	67	40	17	5	7	11	9	13	234	104	40
359	6391	1	1	18	D	17	-7	87	12	16	6	32	3	8	62	46	27	16	5	1	11	14	14	133	66	37
360	6392	1	1	18	D	8	-1	69	4	13	4	13	5	-1	57	52	29	28	6	2	4	8	8	272	88	12
361	6401	2	2	18	D	6	4	100	1	10	6	37	2	-6	48	34	28	28	7	0	8	11	16	272	72	16
362	6402	2	2	18	D	10	1	71	4	22	6	37	1	-4	49	45	45	34	6	0	14	13	10	212	63	9
363	6411	2	1	14	D	16	17	86	6	29	9	54	10	9	58	77	51	30	7	5	15	11	11	140	148	38
364	6412	2	1	14	D	19	17	95	5	32	8	28	3	3	42	59	51	30	10	6	15	15	15	262	181	40
365	6431	1	1	17	D	14	9	72	2	48	19	66	14	15	62	77	46	28	1	6	9	8	16	297	202	26
366	6432	1	1	17	D	8	21	27	6	27	12	41	13	11	51	77	24	36	18	5	17	9	8	215	77	4
367	6441	2	1	15	D	9	5	33	0	28	12	12	10	-0	59	44	20	24	14	5	11	11	12	188	30	33
368	6442	2	1	15	D	6	4	41	3	19	8	28	1	1	44	50	14	16	10	5	15	8	6	235	116	18
369	6451	1	1	15	M	22	23	36	3	11	8	27	0	-1	52	53	32	28	0	0	12	7	12	208	79	17
370	6452	1	1	15	M	13	-8	41	3	19	2	2	14	0	44	46	14	9	8	2	11	9	14	215	77	15
371	6461	1	1	15	M	11	-1	51	1	17	21	19	10	-1	52	65	45	45	13	-3	12	11	14	276	151	7
372	6462	2	1	15	M	8	6	61	6	30	40	28	6	-1	56	46	37	26	6	4	19	11	6	239	134	25
373	6471	1	1	16	M	25	18	77	2	20	15	28	6	5	63	47	45	31	13	5	15	7	16	229	142	23
374	6472	1	1	16	M	2	8	80	6	18	7	40	11	6	31	43	39	36	6	0	9	12	12	213	-36	21
375	6481	1	1	14	M	8	7	54	2	27	4	40	3	10	48	48	43	37	13	3	7	10	16	225	72	22
376	6482	2	1	14	M	11	7	63	7	16	7	36	5	9	47	46	43	11	6	6	9	9	12	213	71	21
377	6491	1	1	14	D	18	8	96	9	13	12	46	6	8	65	59	55	27	11	8	16	12	16	273	94	21
378	6492	2	1	14	D																					

213

OBS	ID	SEX	RACE	AGE	ZYG	_35	_36	_37	_38	_39	_40	_41	_42	_43	_44	_45	_46	_47	_48	_49	_50	_51	_52	_53	_54	_55
379	6501	1	1	17	M	16	11	98	12	43	11	68	12	15	78	75	44	25	3	7	15	15	12	278	144	36
380	6502	1	1	17	M	15	1	108	16	42	11	73	13	13	63	76	48	27	4	7	13	14	16	280	157	29
381	6511	1	1	15	M	9	23	61	4	29	7	18	6	8	47	61	38	36	8	2	16	6	8	261	96	24
382	6512	1	1	15	M	7	7	66	4	31	8	19	10	3	53	51	23	40	22	2	9	7	4	240	88	28
383	6521	1	2	15	M	21	12	81	6	43	13	46	12	3	36	68	39	38	10	3	15	9	14	229	80	35
384	6522	1	2	15	M	22	12	89	2	23	15	32	10	-6	50	63	35	29	5	4	16	13	16	216	79	42
385	6531	1	2	15	D	-1	2	80	14	14	9	20	2	-1	14	16	9	31	37	1	13	4		193	30	6
386	6532	2	1	16	D	0	-5	45	-3	17	4	10	-1	-3	35	16	9	.	.	-2	1	0		169	-1	12
387	6541	1	1	16	D	0	3	85	2	23	4	36	11	13	49	42	24	26	4	-2	6	7	12	192	122	26
388	6542	1	1	16	D	6	9	83	2	24	9	6	8	-3	39	36	17	18	1	4	8	7	12	176	115	34
389	6551	2	1	17	M	14	17	95	6	36	12	72	8	-3	66	68	50	48	3	8	13	16	17	258	203	31
390	6552	2	1	17	M	11	11	87	7	31	21	75	4	13	53	70	53	22	7	7	16	12	12	257	136	16
391	6561	1	1	14	M	20	7	94	3	27	13	43	12	13	42	78	52	38	2	6	3	11	11	204	136	34
392	6562	1	1	14	M	23	15	99	3	12	14	58	0	-7	46	80	49	39	7	6	11	10	10	242	110	37
393	6571	1	1	17	M	16	9	57	7	12	29	29	0	-3	58	29	48	39	24	6	13	8	8	250	85	7
394	6572	1	1	17	M	24	11	85	9	42	28	69	10	0	67	53	47	40	8	8	16	14	11	305	114	18
395	6581	1	2	17	M	20	10	62	2	37	9	29	10	5	52	51	50	26	19	8	15	14	14	244	140	31
396	6582	2	2	16	D	23	23	108	8	27	14	50	11	1	72	71	53	23	11	8	14	14	16	276	188	33
397	6591	1	1	16	D	14	14	103	6	15	10	40	6	6	54	83	38	37	6	3	17	14	-3	307	81	38
398	6592	1	1	17	D	4	4	90	2	23	8	25	9	5	48	64	14	48	39	0	9	9	13	245	102	22
399	6601	2	2	13	D	7	3	42	11	11	24	17	5	6	31	35	36	19	13	1	17	7	10	47	88	10
400	6602	2	2	13	D	10	10	62	3	24	20	20	5	5	51	46	50	32	16	10	16	13	14	180	123	24
401	6611	2	2	18	D	18	-5	89	4	18	10	65	3	5	53	51	52	32	20	8	13	11	12	170	29	29
402	6612	2	2	18	D	13	13	82	1	23	13	60	7	6	83	54	50	44	20	1	14	14	12	247	-14	8
403	6621	2	2	16	D	14	14	53	3	10	13	66	4	4	54	54	54	20	6	5	12	12	13	283	104	27
404	6622	2	2	18	D	4	0	49	7	14	6	30	4	3	73	19	53	24	9	2	10	9	9	188	81	9
405	6631	1	1	14	M	-1	-1	16	1	6	0	6	1	8	38	.	17	18	13	-1	7	7	11	90	28	11
406	6632	2	2	14	M	9	9	20	2	0	1	10	6	-2	29	83	28	18	11	-1	6	6	5	98	52	6
407	6641	1	1	19	D	7	0	50	0	14	1	13	0	-1	31	39	24	22	16	-1	4	5	8	150	16	9
408	6642	1	1	19	D	9	0	35	0	7	7	27	0	2	70	.	0	0	3	0	.					
409	6651	1	1	18	M	7	9	68	8	23	8	65	7	2	49	56	46	24	16	9	13	13	13	264	138	23
410	6652	1	1	18	M	10	9	72	18	18	8	66	7	0	45	49	45	28	16	6	13	13	13	258	129	31
411	6661	1	1	18	M	25	16	111	8	58	13	65	19	19	97	97	50	36	9	17	4	19	14	276	195	44
412	6662	1	1	18	M	24	23	108	1	40	21	21	11	18	47	65	55	34	6	16	13	15	15	323	147	42
413	6671	2	1	15	M	8	8	77	6	44	13	40	13	4	49	75	49	21	1	8	8	11	15	221	131	28
414	6672	2	1	15	M	15	10	88	2	27	6	16	5	4	33	44	26	26	4	4	11	11	15	233	91	24
415	6681	2	1	13	D	5	12	55	4	18	3	26	4	5	47	52	45	14	0	-1	10	10	8	186	27	28
416	6682	2	1	13	D	3	1	49	4	22	10	15	5	6	47	.	22	28	2	6	12	12	8	199	49	27
417	6691	2	1	17	M	18	11	92	12	21	18	72	6	3	42	66	45	28	1	3	13	12	12	207	142	20
418	6692	2	1	17	M	16	17	70	2	24	23	54	9	8	52	60	45	32	9	9	3	18	13	240	147	14
419	6701	1	1	15	D	14	17	78	9	22	22	31	9	6	55	55	38	36	16	6	14	4	14	324	170	18
420	6702	1	1	15	D	18	4	23	12	12	22	31	8	3	52	75	13	28	21	7	13	3	5	201	77	30
421	6711	1	1	13	M	5	2	36	4	9	8	14	9	9	80	29	13	28	16	0	17	11	7	150	48	14
422	6712	1	1	13	M	4	4	49	1	16	3	23	1	-1	29	32	15	24	12	1	17	6	7	172	101	19
423	6721	1	1	14	M	11	11	44	0	24	3	27	3	-3	49	34	39	34	13	-2	11	11	11	193	80	16
424	6722	1	1	14	M	-5	-5	57	5	16	6	27	3	3	38	33	31	32	13	0	10	14	13	196	112	12
425	6731	1	1	16	D	8	0	77	1	19	6	34	5	4	48	52	52	28	8	3	12	12		220	39	24
426	6732	1	1	16	D	15	10	62	3	15	26	56	6	3	36	84	45	28	12	3	13	13	13	215	69	11
427	6741	2	1	13	M	27	28	123	9	46	28	69	18	20	77	49	54	44	12	6	15	13	13	289	172	43
428	6742	1	1	17	D	26	15	104	7	54	28	65	20	20	82	86	51	46	17	4	9	15	16	309	206	41
429	6751	1	1	15	D	13	6	88	6	11	6	43	6	-6	51	53	42	48	31	9	4	14	13	266	115	23
430	6752	2	1	15	D	5	-1	67	3	29	4	27	12	2	53	53	43	38	23	6	4	14	16	252	175	23
431	6771	1	1	17	D	1	-6	35	1	11	3	10	-1	4	47	40	12	23	20	-1	4	4	13	22	108	18
432	6772	1	1	17	D			10	2	25	2	8	4	2	41	2	2	23	0	12	0			109	37	14

OBS	ID	SEX	RACE	AGE	ZYG	_35	_36	_37	_38	_39	_40	_41	_42	_43	_44	_45	_46	_47	_48	_49	_50	_51	_52	_53	_54	_55
433	6781	1	1	14	D	11	-4	5	-5	7	8	4	10	4	34	35	8	22	16	-1	12	7	5	222	95	9
434	6782	1	1	14	D	12	6	39	3	3	8	40	9	5	35	50	19	18	-1	1	15	2	12	185	12	13
435	6791	2	1	16	D	13	13	36	-2	37	8	17	6	5	46	36	11	48	17	0	11	6	12	172	58	7
436	6792	2	1	16	M	4	5	38	-1	28	8	43	5	12	45	36	25	48	13	2	11	16	12	174	60	12
437	6801	2	1	15	M	12	5	58	7	14	8	48	7	12	54	29	49	44	41	5	10	16	14	259	52	28
438	6802	2	1	15	M	17	5	94	8	17	14	48	9	25	53	44	49	32	15	1	15	16	14	275	80	24
439	6811	2	1	16	M	27	4	86	3	14	14	56	8	16	54	54	32	32	12	3	12	9	17	226	100	13
440	6812	2	1	16	M	14	0	66	3	23	4	60	9	10	63	50	42	30	13	3	6	7	17	226	123	19
441	6841	2	1	13	D	12	-4	30	1	24	3	8	6	7	50	46	31	22	12	0	9	10	11	160	27	33
442	6842	2	1	13	D	13	6	45	2	37	2	15	4	19	37	77	31	30	13	3	9	12	11	205	109	14
443	6851	2	1	15	D	-4	-4	29	3	16	5	20	4	-14	40	34	27	18	11	3	14	3	-1	31	-3	14
444	6852	2	1	15	M	10	5	35	6	10	-1	17	3	4	40	69	27	18	6	4	8	1	-1	152	36	11
445	6861	2	1	16	M	11	5	76	4	30	7	44	7	58	66	48	45	25	8	2	15	14	14	217	119	33
446	6862	1	2	16	M	14	15	62	8	23	12	34	4	7	36	67	48	28	5	1	13	11	12	214	111	32
447	6871	1	2	19	M	11	2	70	3	15	11	19	5	5	59	48	41	16	6	1	17	14	12	180	153	25
448	6872	1	1	16	M	16	6	88	8	26	13	13	9	7	76	67	46	16	2	3	12	14	9	132	108	23
449	6881	1	1	14	M	4	6	26	2	21	10	11	4	5	47	49	15	23	8	1	11	11	10	234	·	18
450	6882	1	1	14	M	5	1	16	0	8	16	14	3	5	31	48	9	18	13	3	13	8	5	161	·	23
451	6891	2	1	13	M	15	21	29	4	15	4	27	10	9	57	76	7	32	0	0	4	8	8	146	58	31
452	6892	2	1	13	M	8	0	46	7	8	9	14	6	16	61	45	13	30	2	7	9	11	9	209	·	9
453	6901	2	1	13	M	9	4	61	4	15	11	17	7	9	62	68	40	48	26	0	14	5	12	260	45	22
454	6902	2	1	14	M	10	-2	22	3	32	2	14	2	6	52	76	7	40	10	2	9	4	6	290	78	23
455	6911	2	1	14	M	7	-3	37	6	11	16	27	2	5	52	74	13	48	7	5	10	5	7	123	116	20
456	6912	2	1	17	D	19	16	43	3	28	4	17	4	9	45	45	30	22	4	1	13	6	9	123	67	32
457	6921	2	1	15	D	11	12	30	9	8	14	48	4	2	46	35	43	16	3	3	16	16	16	192	122	25
458	6922	2	1	15	D	2	7	72	4	37	14	46	4	4	49	38	53	28	9	-1	13	5	14	232	158	14
459	6931	2	1	15	M	2	6	65	3	12	20	44	6	2	57	26	35	32	6	-1	13	8	14	283	114	25
460	6932	1	1	16	M	13	12	65	5	15	14	29	8	6	67	57	26	46	21	-2	8	8	14	216	123	9
461	6941	1	1	16	M	18	10	17	-1	17	17	8	10	5	47	62	17	2	24	0	13	11	12	194	96	14
462	6942	1	1	15	M	3	2	32	2	8	15	11	6	1	32	45	3	46	6	2	16	6	10	207	81	25
463	6951	2	1	15	D	2	5	43	4	11	2	16	4	0	29	23	0	31	9	1	9	5	7	116	33	8
464	6952	2	1	15	M	8	8	37	2	8	4	14	1	5	23	20	14	31	29	2	7	5	7	116	15	11
465	6961	2	1	13	M	2	5	20	-4	8	5	14	0	2	32	20	9	12	18	-2	2	6	5	138	-5	12
466	6962	2	2	13	D	-1	8	11	2	16	2	16	1	3	26	23	31	24	3	1	2	5	5	94	-2	10
467	6971	2	2	14	D	4	0	46	4	18	4	19	4	3	41	35	2	28	21	0	3	6	5	169	20	10
468	6972	2	1	17	D	11	-1	29	1	11	5	11	2	-4	25	20	15	9	17	2	16	7	5	52	86	16
469	6981	1	1	17	M	8	3	10	0	16	5	19	8	4	33	27	24	4	23	-1	14	11	-2	156	114	10
470	6982	1	1	15	M	18	11	71	2	19	0	8	8	6	36	35	4	28	21	-1	13	8	12	227	151	12
471	6991	2	2	15	D	11	7	66	2	31	6	41	5	0	39	·	46	25	17	2	15	10	14	226	226	29
472	6992	2	2	15	M	17	7	55	1	12	12	30	3	9	40	47	49	42	9	-1	15	13	14	178	120	19
473	7001	2	2	15	D	8	12	58	2	29	9	32	0	4	61	58	42	17	0	1	8	10	13	67	130	15
474	7002	2	2	16	M	8	0	56	4	21	7	43	-5	0	42	53	46	18	34	2	13	8	11	90	59	12
475	7011	2	1	15	D	8	3	28	4	3	3	5	8	4	42	15	18	15	27	-1	6	8	8	120	2	8
476	7012	2	1	15	D	8	4	52	3	21	7	23	5	7	52	·	8	26	16	-1	14	8	6	154	47	12
477	7021	2	1	15	M	7	-4	30	5	13	3	14	1	5	49	42	39	16	12	1	13	11	5	102	-2	10
478	7022	2	1	15	M	17	11	61	5	32	17	39	8	-1	37	53	37	26	5	3	15	4	12	260	142	·
479	7031	1	1	17	M	20	0	99	3	28	5	29	9	5	55	42	24	24	11	4	10	13	14	273	167	14
480	7032	1	1	17	D	1	-3	112	3	13	8	31	8	-1	55	53	37	5	3	3	15	5	12	279	82	25
481	7041	2	1	15	D	4	11	96	6	20	6	33	9	2	65	53	50	16	1	5	10	13	13	300	145	29
482	7042	2	1	15	M	10	3	79	2	11	7	36	3	9	45	53	46	18	8	3	11	10	12	118	61	19
483	7061	2	1	16	M	21	7	62	7	16	2	13	12	5	66	66	24	18	15	3	3	13	12	175	126	20
484	7062	2	1	15	D	12	10	78	-2	42	12	46	13	17	24	45	47	32	11	4	12	12	13	230	155	21
485	7071	1	1	18	M	26	11	72	6	12	12	11	1	24	38	·	38	21	5	14	15	13	269	109	22
486	7072	1	1	18	M	19	11	62	3	38	12	44	12	15	·	·	47	48	28	5	14	15	·	·	·	·

OBS	ID	SEX	RACE	AGE	ZYG	_35	_36	_37	_38	_39	_40	_41	_42	_43	_44	_45	_46	_47	_48	_49	_50	_51	_52	_53	_54	_55
487	7081	2	1	14	D	6	-3	39	2	19	4	32	3	-4	52	55	48	32	15	4	10	9	13	160	40	10
488	7082	2	1	14	D	15	-4	38	6	28	14	22	7	2	52	49	4	26	15	1	7	13	14	172	18	15
489	7091	1	1	15	M	1	12	35	3	28	10	6	0	1	47	·	4	24	15	-1	2	6	10	153	94	13
490	7092	1	1	15	M	20	0	50	6	46	22	25	8	12	45	·	34	22	17	3	11	5	12	176	140	31
491	7101	2	1	15	D	18	0	58	12	50	9	50	5	0	51	34	46	35	27	5	11	11	16	265	107	25
492	7102	2	1	17	D	14	3	57	6	21	5	42	9	0	58	50	46	28	19	5	8	6	16	201	96	23
493	7111	2	1	17	M	22	28	106	7	53	13	44	9	3	50	80	41	26	4	4	14	12	16	262	60	23
494	7112	2	1	17	M	23	13	126	9	38	9	62	12	15	65	92	49	46	15	8	16	17	16	256	110	29
495	7121	2	1	15	D	14	9	65	4	35	17	25	10	-7	42	38	46	26	16	3	6	8	10	268	85	25
496	7122	2	1	15	D	13	10	61	8	51	22	17	7	0	72	38	46	23	16	3	11	11	10	263	149	10
497	7131	2	1	15	D	17	25	96	4	35	14	41	10	-6	64	83	43	40	6	4	12	14	14	201	210	36
498	7132	2	1	15	D	9	10	55	8	16	11	41	12	-7	50	72	41	24	13	2	7	10	12	179	20	11
499	7141	1	1	13	M	13	3	·	3	13	11	0	6	-2	39	10	36	20	15	-1	7	9	11	179	90	14
500	7142	1	1	13	M	0	-3	38	0	13	3	17	5	-1	27	27	39	23	8	2	8	7	11	138	42	15
501	7151	2	1	13	D	12	-1	35	2	13	1	2	3	-1	25	29	16	21	10	1	7	6	3	188	11	17
502	7152	2	1	13	D	5	22	88	0	27	4	-6	8	3	34	57	18	17	7	4	6	9	7	178	134	13
503	7161	2	1	16	M	10	22	96	2	22	9	55	6	0	40	47	18	26	21	6	14	12	9	221	134	8
504	7162	2	1	16	M	17	22	82	5	38	9	42	3	0	56	71	56	32	5	0	13	13	11	240	171	20
505	7171	2	1	15	M	11	14	89	4	33	20	52	11	8	48	39	39	32	21	0	12	17	16	242	122	17
506	7172	2	1	15	M	11	-1	65	6	29	23	40	4	6	54	62	35	28	5	0	11	17	14	258	132	21
507	7191	1	1	13	M	25	14	78	4	24	15	58	9	5	54	64	41	25	8	2	10	10	10	259	94	23
508	7192	1	1	13	M	18	22	56	6	29	15	56	1	4	61	41	36	36	19	6	6	8	13	259	101	22
509	7201	1	1	17	M	19	12	72	4	18	17	54	5	5	61	41	43	34	45	8	10	9	6	207	102	16
510	7202	1	1	17	M	21	16	78	12	29	17	17	4	-7	43	57	36	36	5	1	3	8	8	227	38	21
511	7221	1	1	15	D	-8	11	78	3	32	14	49	9	-1	57	68	46	25	8	17	17	14	8	227	123	23
512	7222	1	1	15	D	16	9	50	2	40	20	17	7	12	43	81	19	26	7	2	10	14	12	260	149	26
513	7231	1	1	16	D	16	27	54	6	47	20	22	6	3	52	27	27	34	8	3	14	12	16	242	110	33
514	7232	1	1	16	D	13	25	84	2	15	5	24	3	-1	46	62	22	28	5	11	12	11	9	274	130	29
515	7241	2	1	16	D	14	4	82	4	11	21	37	10	0	42	47	40	22	5	6	6	9	14	108	·	21
516	7242	2	1	16	M	25	14	68	2	51	44	33	5	0	52	53	47	20	0	5	5	14	13	88	·	0
517	7251	1	1	15	M	18	22	73	4	15	21	44	12	-8	48	89	38	22	8	9	9	7	13	194	133	39
518	7252	2	1	15	D	21	16	64	6	51	21	33	10	13	56	63	36	22	0	5	8	9	9	169	184	37
519	7271	2	2	18	D	15	27	134	12	40	13	57	13	3	63	63	53	20	4	12	14	13	16	274	208	28
520	7272	2	2	18	M	15	31	113	14	23	14	55	1	1	51	60	51	20	18	13	13	13	13	224	190	35
521	7281	1	1	17	D	20	6	83	3	38	14	31	13	13	43	50	39	26	8	4	14	15	13	245	135	12
522	7282	2	1	17	D	3	1	88	12	39	14	47	4	4	53	71	40	0	9	0	3	9	16	207	77	8
523	7291	1	2	16	D	3	17	35	9	8	6	11	0	0	44	·	12	22	8	6	0	9	7	177	65	12
524	7292	1	2	16	M	17	21	40	7	18	11	7	6	-1	41	·	15	23	7	13	3	14	6	207	67	11
525	7301	1	1	16	D	18	8	57	2	39	4	10	4	20	37	·	16	37	20	9	1	13	14	207	130	17
526	7302	1	1	14	M	7	4	62	4	30	12	24	0	11	38	·	32	41	29	1	14	7	14	232	203	16
527	7311	1	1	18	M	3	1	62	4	26	16	13	0	0	50	14	24	24	5	4	8	·	9	280	·	9
528	7312	2	1	15	M	18	8	75	4	15	21	44	3	3	48	28	49	28	8	0	8	7	9	189	124	22
529	7321	1	1	15	M	8	6	75	2	15	11	55	7	3	53	66	49	28	8	8	10	10	12	243	89	25
530	7322	2	2	13	M	4	5	65	2	21	14	50	1	4	47	26	15	10	9	5	9	11	15	281	117	28
531	7331	2	1	13	M	6	-9	28	0	8	2	15	2	-8	37	15	5	12	12	16	3	9	10	180	-8	10
532	7332	2	1	15	M	10	-1	31	1	15	5	2	4	2	31	12	10	11	11	0	0	11	8	125	-9	·
533	7341	1	1	15	D	10	1	71	3	17	7	22	7	1	25	54	9	18	12	13	13	12	8	152	63	33
534	7342	1	1	17	D	16	3	75	11	24	11	41	11	0	50	61	9	32	15	1	2	11	12	167	113	29
535	7351	1	1	17	D	15	13	48	9	41	13	65	8	20	39	42	48	34	19	3	5	12	14	200	175	17
536	7352	1	1	17	D	13	2	44	10	16	12	10	10	10	40	21	42	14	15	12	5	14	14	216	125	18
537	7361	1	1	14	M	1	1	14	2	16	4	13	0	-5	30	16	21	10	6	5	2	-2	-2	108	28	7
538	7362	1	1	14	M	6	3	35	3	17	10	8	0	3	39	10	16	26	2	0	5	5	9	37	27	8
539	7371	2	2	16	M	18	18	68	2	38	29	28	8	8	59	41	41	22	6	4	7	15	7	287	178	29
540	7372	2	1	16	M	15	16	46	3	42	29	22	11	14	55	89	45	31	6	2	12	13	16	209	130	27

216

OBS	ID	SEX	RACE	AGE	ZYG	_35	_36	_37	_38	_39	_40	_41	_42	_43	_44	_45	_46	_47	_48	_49	_50	_51	_52	_53	_54	_55
541	7381	2	1	13	D	7	-2	50	0	29	9	13	5	-2	44	43	24	17	5	3	7	9	11	228	97	26
542	7382	2	1	13	D	5	1	74	2	25	14	7	7	1	46	28	36	22	12	1	4	11	9	186	50	17
543	7391	1	2	16	D	.	-2	28	5	18	6	29	4	1	41	23	16	16	11	1	7	4	9	176	0	13
544	7392	1	1	16	D	1	-6	39	3	8	3	40	-2	2	20	26	29	27	12	1	14	4	8	200	-8	16
545	7411	2	1	14	D	8	-1	48	3	18	8	18	0	10	32	7	33	15	4	4	9	11	8	300	37	10
546	7412	2	1	16	M	12	-12	67	8	7	8	38	3	-3	23	8	44	24	9	5	10	14	8	162	1	9
547	7421	2	1	16	M	17	12	86	12	27	2	59	7	1	43	48	51	9	9	4	7	12	14	234	145	16
548	7422	2	1	14	M	25	3	83	20	20	2	54	6	-2	44	48	30	18	6	5	10	12	14	221	161	33
549	7431	2	1	14	M	15	4	87	-1	16	10	28	5	-1	44	28	18	22	8	-1	15	5	10	203	105	18
550	7432	2	1	14	M	15	-12	80	-1	10	4	25	7	2	40	34	34	20	17	-2	13	2	6	228	72	8
551	7441	1	1	16	M	5	5	61	1	3	8	6	3	0	34	16	0	22	10	-2	5	5	4	236	2	16
552	7442	1	1	16	M	7	-7	55	9	16	9	7	5	0	30	33	.	.	1	1	12	6	6	214	30	16
553	7451	1	1	14	M	16	17	55	16	38	10	44	11	17	35	79	37	32	11	8	16	17	12	211	60	30
554	7452	1	1	14	M	18	24	78	12	40	16	50	16	19	50	64	49	36	19	9	3	11	12	237	111	38
555	7461	2	1	16	M	14	-3	57	6	32	14	41	15	4	50	66	49	27	7	7	17	11	12	235	90	33
556	7462	2	2	16	M	16	17	64	6	37	14	63	11	19	53	79	43	24	2	1	14	11	17	271	159	35
557	7471	2	1	17	M	12	13	72	3	17	15	43	9	16	54	43	38	28	4	6	8	10	16	236	89	20
558	7472	2	1	17	M	6	5	47	11	14	9	36	9	9	50	50	31	29	11	2	9	9	11	177	76	32
559	7481	2	1	14	M	5	5	45	5	19	5	29	-1	4	44	22	40	16	13	-1	8	11	11	160	35	15
560	7482	2	2	14	D	21	15	59	0	13	6	36	2	1	48	21	40	13	10	3	8	8	14	160	78	.
561	7491	2	1	18	D	21	15	101	7	30	9	39	2	0	55	55	45	36	10	7	3	12	17	358	182	35
562	7492	2	1	18	M	22	11	108	8	44	6	61	10	11	53	63	52	36	13	13	16	16	16	262	152	40
563	7501	1	1	14	D	12	14	60	4	18	5	52	8	3	43	44	41	32	9	10	14	8	11	170	108	23
564	7502	1	1	14	M	20	14	74	2	34	7	41	12	2	47	37	37	34	11	5	13	11	11	233	143	26
565	7521	1	1	17	M	16	3	69	8	29	16	40	8	-9	47	70	16	43	21	1	6	11	6	151	134	15
566	7522	2	1	17	D	16	9	69	7	26	20	21	6	6	72	62	6	42	16	17	11	14	14	236	159	27
567	7531	1	1	18	D	16	9	61	5	29	5	50	5	5	49	38	40	30	8	1	9	15	12	239	51	27
568	7532	1	2	18	D	13	4	58	7	13	2	44	11	8	50	55	49	23	6	5	10	14	12	203	99	18
569	7541	1	1	16	M	16	6	84	12	12	12	52	8	8	62	60	52	34	12	0	14	13	12	240	147	9
570	7542	2	1	16	D	16	10	64	4	27	17	52	13	1	46	76	56	24	3	6	17	12	10	284	136	12
571	7551	1	1	17	M	23	12	93	12	23	7	68	22	1	40	60	46	29	5	0	13	13	13	225	148	22
572	7552	1	1	17	M	13	-13	78	7	7	9	44	0	0	40	23	51	16	7	6	10	12	14	192	48	24
573	8751	1	1	18	M	20	25	94	13	36	10	76	14	-18	55	86	49	31	12	3	11	14	13	232	168	40
574	8752	1	1	18	M	23	15	90	12	51	15	62	9	8	36	79	51	26	1	1	6	11	14	249	145	36

N=574

217

OBS	ID	SEX	RACE	AGE	ZYG	_35	_36	_37	_38	_39	_40	_41	_42	_43	_44	_45	_46	_47	_48	_56	_57	_58	_59	_60	_61	_62	_63	_64	_65	_66
1	2001	1	1	16	D	12	14	70	20		9	73	4	2	84	71	52	23	3	129	122	107	119	125	103	96	97	94	91	94
2	2002	1	1	16	D	21	25	78	24	8	16	75	13	2	69	80	53	23	0	118	120	119	108	119	94	91	94	111	105	104
3	2011	2	1	16	M	2	-2	61	8	2	15	39	12	0	91	78	37	20	0	100	99	93	73	80	81	84	89	94	91	94
4	2012	2	1	16	U	17	2	50	3	1	15	38	0	7	92	61	38	20	3	77	69	93	115	95	103	96	97	81	84	89
5	2021	1	1	16	J	16	2	90	37	18	16	64	11	9	86	84	45	25	0	107	124	109	124	103	103	96	97	127	133	122
6	2022	2	1	16	J	0	-12	64	14	15	12	63	5	2	75	53	46	26	2	115	120	109	92	103	116	113	127	94	91	94
7	2031	1	1	16	J	0	5	42	14	6	12	52	10	5	66	47	36	29	2	103	93	100	96	86	78	81	87	78	81	87
8	2032	2	1	16	J	3	5	33	15	3	0	46	1	1	94	47	35	18	1	114	79	100	81	86	78	81	87	99	94	96
9	2041	1	1	17	M	20	30	93	56	9	37	76	19	21	95	92	45	48	0	134	131	133	119	139	145	159	139	127	133	122
10	2042	1	1	17	M	40	36	159	57	15	34	68	21	21	81	92	45	48	0	141	118	130	106	135	145	150	145	159	159	139
11	2051	2	1	16	J	5	0	5	15	5	4	4	3	1	26	9	1	11	13	74	82	68	73	58	58	70	54	64	66
12	2052	2	1	16	J	21	12	24	41	27	19	66	15	11	96	78	48	29	21	82	88	65	61	37	64	64	57	64	64	57
13	2061	1	1	15	M	17	12	82	34	19	18	69	4	11	92	67	39	26	1	130	132	127	115	134	123	127	118	123	127	118
14	2062	2	1	15	M	-3	-2	57	19	13	5	15	0	0	90	67	33	23	5	115	120	116	83	115	127	133	122	111	105	104
15	2071	2	1	15	D	7	-2	46	19	8	7	23	4	-8	73	40	30	17	6	83	81	89	90	76	85	86	91	85	86	91
16	2072	2	2	15	D	4	-4	19	18	3	6	23	1	-6	34	34	39	12	5	95	80	89	97	84	85	72	81	89	88	92
17	2081	2	1	16	D	7	6	24	19	4	4	18	12	-6	74	61	47	30	8	87	80	82	90	84	78	81	87	78	81	87
18	2082	2	1	16	D	9	5	80	44	5	20	61	18	18	87	65	47	28	0	107	108	115	90	107	110	103	102	116	113	109
19	2091	1	1	15	J	21	21	72	22	9	19	60	9	-4	83	67	47	14	4	123	103	127	123	115	110	103	102	127	133	122
20	2092	2	1	15	J	3	21	31	29	1	4	38	1	3	45	26	33	22	0	85	87	102	78	107	88	89	93	116	113	109
21	2101	2	1	15	M	13	19	40	16	6	31	26	1	3	53	26	26	14	2	85	71	87	78	82	88	84	97	98	94	96
22	2102	2	1	13	M	12	21	41	27	5	10	23	1	11	44	47	33	16	1	77	93	102	103	89	88	88	92	93	92	95
23	2111	1	1	17	M	0	11	40	29	9	20	26	9	1	16	47	34	19	3	80	85	85	101	89	103	84	97	81	84	89
24	2112	2	1	17	M	10	11	43	27	5	10	46	15	-4	51	41	34	22	3	80	93	101	87	91	101	88	89	99	88	96
25	2121	1	1	15	D	15	7	66	24	4	25	46	5	4	52	41	34	17	3	96	96	102	104	99	81	84	89	89	88	92
26	2122	2	2	15	D	11	7	57	26	4	9	39	7	-4	50	31	32	18	3	94	99	98	105	91	85	86	91	111	105	104
27	2131	1	1	16	D	11	12	40	25	3	7	40	7	2	55	55	32	21	6	88	100	98	105	99	103	86	91	85	86	91
28	2132	2	1	16	D	17	10	93	28	9	11	56	11	7	62	77	40	18	1	88	122	118	121	120	116	113	109	99	94	96
29	2141	2	1	17	J	8	7	81	29	8	10	43	3	8	86	51	32	32	1	91	94	94	94	91	91	91	94	99	94	96
30	2142	2	1	17	J	12	12	71	13	5	19	45	6	4	48	55	43	30	2	91	101	103	104	98	110	103	102	99	94	96
31	2151	1	1	17	J	15	-8	54	27	4	9	48	8	4	77	55	43	18	9	95	101	98	130	108	108	102	97	94	91	94
32	2152	2	1	17	J	21	4	60	15	2	7	63	6	1	57	46	31	22	1	123	101	102	103	109	145	120	113	116	113	109
33	2161	1	1	15	J	16	10	53	23	5	28	56	13	7	70	77	41	36	5	118	108	118	118	125	127	133	122	116	105	104
34	2162	2	1	14	J	18	3	85	29	8	21	68	5	8	85	65	48	48	5	118	122	123	118	123	122	122	133	133	140	127
35	2171	2	2	14	D	10	-12	48	13	2	3	20	-1	-3	29	22	26	14	10	96	69	88	84	77	78	81	87	42	64	57
36	2172	2	1	14	D	4	10	41	25	2	3	20	2	1	45	40	26	31	0	85	85	88	90	90	78	94	96	94	94	96
37	2181	1	1	18	M	17	10	51	41	16	26	62	16	20	87	89	30	48	0	105	111	113	113	109	133	140	127	106	100	99
38	2182	2	1	18	M	14	10	61	47	24	16	61	11	15	78	78	22	37	0	105	98	101	99	96	119	120	113	116	113	109
39	2191	1	1	17	D	15	10	69	24	9	16	61	12	12	86	64	30	26	3	103	86	104	73	86	103	103	102	116	120	109
40	2192	2	1	17	D	3	-1	42	21	8	9	56	8	1	74	64	27	33	0	95	100	98	105	98	103	97	97	99	94	96
41	2201	1	1	14	J	12	-7	42	16	1	8	36	3	-3	78	60	25	26	0	84	83	78	73	85	63	64	76	68	72	81
42	2202	2	2	14	J	19	8	65	21	5	17	36	8	-3	78	74	25	36	3	93	105	97	103	86	103	96	97	89	88	92
43	2211	1	1	16	M	15	8	61	24	5	43	43	9	7	82	74	22	45	3	82	101	94	85	86	63	64	76	119	120	113
44	2212	2	1	16	M	16	5	53	24	6	18	20	14	0	72	65	23	39	12	103	94	94	97	97	116	113	109	100	100	99
45	2221	1	1	15	J	10	20	69	30	7	16	43	16	5	61	61	23	42	10	103	100	114	122	108	103	96	97	94	91	94
46	2222	2	2	15	J	12	6	56	36	10	16	52	-4	6	68	52	23	38	5	105	122	114	107	108	113	103	109	106	91	94
47	2231	1	1	15	J	12	6	42	10	3	2	29	0	0	33	40	39	18	5	83	95	94	112	95	84	84	89	73	76	84
48	2232	2	1	15	M	4	-19	27	9	0	13	15	-1	0	41	12	28	13	11	75	71	84	81	81	81	64	73	56	64	68
49	2241	1	1	15	U	17	12	72	11	6	13	46	-6	0	48	66	36	31	10	109	84	105	116	91	61	100	89	89	88	96
50	2242	2	1	15	M	10	9	64	26	8	22	43	8	10	64	66	36	25	8	103	103	103	112	112	81	103	102	89	88	92
51	2251	1	1	15	M	17	12	77	17	9	10	37	9	0	69	63	33	36	10	114	101	105	98	98	61	100	103	94	94	96
52	2252	2	2	15	M	14	10	61	26	7	10	44	11	11	53	54	20	32	3	102	114	103	116	114	116	103	109	103	96	97
53	2261	1	1	15	D	19	9	68	17	2	10	64	9	5	54	54	33	31	8	117	114	109	109	114	113	105	105	103	96	97
54	2262	1	1	15	D	13	8	72	42	10	13	72	17	18	65	90	49	31	3	130	108	114	116	116	133	140	127	99	94	96

OBS	ID	SEX	RACE	AGE	ZYG	_35	_36	_37	_38	_39	_40	_41	_42	_43	_44	_45	_46	_47	_48	_56	_57	_58	_59	_60	_61	_62	_63	_64	_65	_66
55	2271	2	1	14	U	9	1	69		23	8	32	1	2	45	39	34	21	5	98	91	119	76	91	89	38	92	81	84	89
56	2272	1	1	14	U	14	0	61	5	24	23	19	5	6	45	64	23	26	1	87	87	99	99	94	78	81	87	103	96	97
57	2281	1	1	16	D	11	10	63	7	24	19	55	7	4	62	67	40	32	23	113	116	107	104	113	94	91	105	119	120	113
58	2282	2	1	16	D	13	12	77	7	25	18	58	4	7	61	66	50	28	4	113	108	98	104	101	94	105	105	103	96	97
59	2291	2	1	16	M	12	2	87	3	25	18	42	11	8	37	66	47	24	1	95	108	98	106	101	94	106	105	111	105	104
60	2292	2	1	16	M	17	0	99	3	21	21	61	15	8	84	63	29	25	1	113	122	119	106	111	106	100	99	119	120	113
61	2301	1	1	16	E	17	0	73	11	39	13	69	15	-1	92	86	29	32	10	125	94	105	116	98	103	96	97	85	86	91
62	2302	1	1	16	U	20	7	0	2	35	19	36	5	-2	67	70	29	38	0	86	108	102	92	118	88	88	92	73	113	84
63	2311	2	1	15	U	7	-8	49	3	15	5	50	3	8	70	38	27	32	5	109	95	84	92	89	89	38	105	91	76	94
64	2312	2	1	15	I	13	10	85	8	23	14	50	17	8	70	35	42	30	5	118	121	106	122	113	113	105	105	111	105	104
65	2321	2	1	17	M	14	0	94	15	43	26	73	13	11	82	71	56	29	5	118	122	110	92	122	113	107	109	105	104	104
66	2322	2	1	16	D	17	14	118	15	45	13	72	4	8	76	76	56	26	0	137	126	123	88	112	116	113	109	111	105	104
67	2331	1	1	16	D	18	-4	108	15	15	11	76	8	-1	87	32	44	28	1	115	98	123	139	139	120	120	109	111	105	113
68	2332	2	1	16	D	13	-4	72	4	15	10	66	4	-1	51	32	44	14	1	115	98	106	86	95	73	76	84	68	72	81
69	2341	2	1	15	M	-1	16	75	4	20	5	36	5	-2	67	59	15	23	6	80	81	94	93	97	73	81	87	81	84	89
70	2342	2	1	16	D	-2	16	97	7	29	6	37	5	2	51	59	22	23	8	102	88	103	93	106	85	74	91	85	86	91
71	2351	2	1	16	I	20	-4	95	5	51	6	49	9	-3	95	59	38	33	1	121	118	125	141	136	119	127	113	116	113	109
72	2352	1	1	16	X	19	20	110	12	51	27	61	10	5	96	65	53	32	8	117	124	109	99	129	118	118	113	119	120	113
73	2361	2	1	16	U	15	19	87	11	32	11	68	14	5	59	80	58	32	2	117	137	141	99	112	119	127	113	119	120	113
74	2362	2	1	17	U	11	-6	75	7	17	16	67	10	-4	79	49	47	24	10	125	99	100	105	92	89	88	92	119	120	113
75	2371	2	1	17	D	11	7	83	4	17	16	59	8	9	50	49	42	26	0	104	87	93	105	96	94	94	96	85	86	92
76	2372	2	1	17	U	20	6	104	12	16	16	43	18	-9	66	49	47	24	0	111	99	105	122	127	99	96	96	85	86	91
77	2381	2	1	16	I	20	16	89	11	55	16	69	14	11	53	80	45	36	0	119	122	126	122	127	123	133	118	127	133	122
78	2382	2	1	17	M	20	0	68	5	22	6	54	4	-1	68	57	48	32	2	127	100	109	86	92	85	86	91	150	150	133
79	2391	2	1	15	U	15	0	81	8	16	6	66	9	6	61	61	52	42	6	111	88	90	90	98	92	86	91	89	88	92
80	2392	2	1	16	U	3	6	98	5	18	15	63	4	4	82	59	42	22	1	94	102	93	105	96	98	88	96	73	76	84
81	2401	1	2	16	H	-5	1	69	12	56	15	58	6	15	47	32	52	32	4	109	102	95	88	104	113	107	105	97	81	84
82	2402	1	1	15	D	33	27	124	5	41	34	75	14	13	82	88	52	42	6	132	144	144	138	149	123	133	118	123	127	118
83	2411	1	2	17	H	18	13	118	8	21	26	70	3	-3	72	66	50	32	2	136	138	134	143	143	127	127	118	116	113	109
84	2412	1	2	16	D	10	9	63	3	29	26	48	3	5	56	35	53	25	2	97	105	105	101	98	79	79	96	103	96	97
85	2421	1	2	16	U	34	6	125	8	29	18	60	13	6	54	61	55	48	3	111	111	126	128	126	140	140	127	103	96	97
86	2422	2	2	16	U	-6	9	23	7	11	18	3	13	-1	83	23	36	30	50	59	70	79	85	59	75	79	96	66	68	79
87	2431	2	1	16	M	8	-0	71	3	15	10	20	9	-6	45	23	29	19	50	74	70	77	85	59	70	64	66	66	64	76
88	2432	2	1	13	M	4	-1	27	0	12	0	24	1	-3	30	44	29	13	22	107	124	113	108	114	113	113	66	63	64	103
89	2441	2	1	13	H	11	-3	66	3	12	7	33	-1	0	57	35	34	19	19	85	91	107	77	108	108	104	103	108	104	103
90	2442	2	1	13	H	-6	-6	39	2	12	6	16	-1	3	24	31	20	26	2	76	69	85	77	107	89	104	103	102	97	98
91	2451	2	1	14	U	5	-6	18	1	3	5	5	4	1	14	19	20	16	3	88	74	73	84	68	73	64	92	63	64	62
92	2452	1	2	14	D	3	-6	14	-2	20	6	13	5	-2	14	14	26	11	50	100	95	90	88	82	64	97	112	98	94	96
93	2461	1	2	13	U	10	-6	28	-2	18	3	7	6	5	41	35	32	16	13	77	84	94	78	70	84	97	92	94	94	96
94	2462	2	2	13	D	7	-6	15	-2	11	8	10	1	-1	18	41	28	10	50	82	102	82	94	82	97	118	92	105	100	100
95	2471	2	2	15	O	0	-6	0	0	13	5	8	4	-1	45	18	11	16	50	77	57	63	93	73	70	73	92	72	76	84
96	2472	2	2	13	D	7	-5	15	0	11	5	10	-1	-6	18	21	11	16	50	82	91	97	77	73	44	66	59	76	76	84
97	2481	1	2	13	H	5	-11	21	3	13	9	10	3	-6	47	21	11	28	5	85	91	93	94	101	88	84	93	88	89	93
98	2482	2	2	13	H	-5	0	77	3	13	0	33	4	-3	30	31	34	19	3	85	91	82	94	75	88	88	93	81	84	89
99	2491	2	1	18	D	16	0	58	1	19	5	32	1	-0	53	31	27	26	5	76	82	94	94	94	73	76	84	75	79	86
100	2492	2	1	13	H	20	21	96	1	36	14	44	7	6	35	74	35	27	5	120	106	123	86	78	74	78	84	99	94	96
101	2501	2	1	13	U	20	21	96	36	19	14	50	5	0	67	74	35	23	7	113	115	120	120	111	144	154	116	117	118	112
102	2502	1	2	13	H	15	-2	93	-3	21	29	64	18	9	96	89	38	22	8	105	98	127	108	129	156	177	103	131	136	124
103	2511	2	1	16	I	23	24	98	6	43	64	64	14	11	77	89	33	32	4	102	115	108	128	123	103	103	151	133	140	127
104	2512	1	1	16	D	10	10	106	5	31	28	68	14	12	51	76	35	28	1	99	109	123	103	112	103	103	97	106	100	99
105	2521	2	1	15	M	12	29	83	4	41	23	60	12	12	83	61	37	38	7	105	111	87	103	106	116	113	109	94	91	94
106	2522	2	1	15	D	15	29	41	1	39	22	68	4	4	51	72	35	31	3	96	111	94	92	92	83	83	81	88	89	93
107	2531	1	1	13	A	10	-2	15	-1	14	16	16	7	1	40	51	13	31	7	96	101	87	92	84	73	74	83	88	89	93
108	2532	2	1	13	M	10	-2	19	-1	14	9	2	1	1	40	37	8	21	6	82	84	94	92	84	73	83	83	96	95	97

219

OBS	ID	SEX	RACE	AGE	ZYG	_35	_36	_37	_38	_39	_40	_41	_42	_43	_44	_45	_46	_47	_48	_56	_57	_58	_59	_60	_61	_52	_63	_64	_65	_66
109	2541	2	1	16	D	12	10	108	0	29	22	36	10	4	59	44	42	27	0	97	94	112	111	106	123	127	118	103	96	97
110	2542	2	1	16	D	14	-5	59	2	19	2	43	13	6	56	56	38	39	5	94	102	119	100	100	99	94	96	103	96	97
111	2551	1	1	14	D	9	16	56	2	26	10	44	9	-1	46	68	23	43	20	91	122	119	106	111	99	94	96	89	88	92
112	2552	1	1	14	D	8	6	69	7	11	18	40	11	1	57	53	24	25	4	85	104	105	105	101	81	94	86	85	86	91
113	2561	2	1	13	D	8	2	49	4	21	10	21	4	-1	69	46	15	25	12	88	75	112	110	101	94	91	94	89	86	92
114	2562	2	1	13	D	12	-1	37	3	13	0	30	2	0	53	35	25	27	3	106	99	105	91	90	89	92	92	78	81	87
115	2571	1	1	16	M	16	-1	47	1	20	16	56	7	2	58	55	29	24	3	105	99	132	96	98	103	105	97	106	100	99
116	2572	1	1	16	M	16	15	84	3	24	19	63	3	5	45	55	37	24	6	105	99	107	113	98	113	96	97	100	94	99
117	2581	1	1	16	M	17	16	87	4	38	16	53	7	2	66	55	37	34	5	99	118	121	98	98	103	97	97	99	94	96
118	2582	1	1	17	M	13	16	93	5	46	24	54	16	15	95	90	31	44	7	99	118	121	113	108	113	107	105	116	113	109
119	2591	2	2	17	D	8	0	27	3	4	3	6	0	15	54	32	10	14	0	82	62	57	82	56	73	76	84	66	68	79
120	2592	2	2	15	D	-5	-5	22	0	20	0	12	6	-3	49	32	7	14	7	82	56	57	85	56	73	76	84	66	68	79
121	2601	1	2	17	D	4	-7	20	2	17	17	5	12	16	42	66	10	21	7	68	62	78	94	82	81	72	81	58	64	71
122	2602	1	2	14	D	15	4	39	3	44	6	55	0	16	68	37	0	0	12	90	85	94	94	99	99	94	96	89	88	92
123	2611	2	2	14	M	8	3	79	1	12	5	32	6	50	50	28	26	21	5	105	103	91	97	104	106	113	113	106	100	99
124	2612	2	2	14	M	7	4	60	3	17	6	26	12	16	47	38	41	18	12	90	100	86	102	95	99	120	91	85	96	91
125	2621	2	2	15	D	14	3	76	4	25	10	32	-1	1	55	39	42	22	1	86	90	91	107	104	106	100	99	103	91	97
126	2622	2	2	14	U	13	11	91	7	26	10	58	7	0	73	41	41	18	2	110	90	102	102	104	75	79	86	94	74	94
127	2631	2	2	15	U	12	-3	66	4	25	0	38	-1	-7	55	55	38	30	10	102	95	102	112	108	113	113	109	70	74	83
128	2632	1	2	14	U	20	0	90	2	38	0	29	10	0	73	35	41	27	0	116	91	102	116	108	116	102	86	103	96	97
129	2641	2	2	14	M	4	-2	15	-1	3	3	6	0	-8	26	22	38	13	50	103	105	73	73	61	75	62	62	50	64	62
130	2642	2	2	14	D	1	3	45	-1	11	1	14	0	-6	45	25	24	27	48	81	87	76	76	61	50	64	84	58	64	71
131	2651	2	2	14	M	19	-3	91	1	11	0	55	7	-4	66	51	24	13	28	116	116	112	118	119	85	73	92	89	88	92
132	2652	2	2	14	D	20	0	84	3	29	5	66	5	-2	45	43	54	47	17	101	101	121	122	126	119	76	81	116	88	109
133	2661	2	2	14	M	7	-3	66	1	16	5	37	3	-12	58	40	32	24	5	95	87	96	115	103	78	81	87	103	96	97
134	2662	2	2	14	D	5	1	56	7	24	3	48	8	-1	64	31	35	28	3	88	99	99	88	88	42	64	89	81	84	62
135	2671	2	2	14	D	6	9	80	0	25	10	28	5	0	65	47	33	10	9	95	101	89	102	96	75	73	86	87	74	88
136	2672	2	2	14	M	6	6	79	4	20	3	40	3	-4	56	40	27	10	37	99	103	101	103	96	23	76	83	85	88	92
137	2681	1	2	14	D	8	21	73	5	22	2	34	1	5	48	24	40	39	0	96	114	89	101	93	75	79	81	70	76	84
138	2682	2	1	14	D	16	-16	68	6	12	11	18	2	-6	31	42	20	33	26	111	87	105	86	91	81	64	86	116	79	86
139	2691	2	2	14	M	-1	3	43	14	14	4	14	-2	4	35	24	21	20	17	102	78	73	73	61	23	73	75	75	64	76
140	2692	2	2	14	D	2	-1	32	-1	28	1	28	1	-8	51	33	15	15	50	79	82	75	81	106	64	64	63	63	79	89
141	2701	2	2	17	D	5	-1	54	7	31	0	14	3	-1	41	38	36	9	8	104	78	107	94	101	75	79	86	81	84	89
142	2702	1	2	13	D	7	-7	10	1	35	5	33	5	0	43	19	21	15	8	89	89	88	84	106	23	86	83	50	64	62
143	2711	2	2	13	D	21	11	65	8	24	14	9	11	-5	57	68	25	31	41	102	102	88	84	80	64	94	81	119	120	113
144	2712	1	2	16	D	14	14	81	7	10	7	41	8	0	29	79	34	14	6	70	122	113	102	101	64	64	94	94	91	94
145	2721	2	1	14	M	2	2	33	0	7	2	67	7	2	55	20	28	10	8	80	89	85	91	117	75	72	85	85	86	83
146	2722	2	2	14	D	9	4	69	1	15	7	15	4	0	65	19	10	18	0	88	78	91	98	81	81	84	86	70	88	92
147	2731	2	2	14	M	7	0	37	4	25	13	25	5	-14	42	60	14	39	12	89	96	97	97	91	78	89	89	89	113	109
148	2732	1	2	14	D	2	3	48	15	6	10	35	12	5	95	72	28	33	8	96	105	91	94	110	84	87	87	116	91	94
149	2741	2	2	14	D	4	1	62	6	26	4	44	4	5	65	43	39	20	12	104	113	114	105	117	75	81	103	103	91	109
150	2742	1	1	14	M	0	-1	8	14	14	13	-4	5	-4	38	54	34	10	8	90	116	116	86	72	81	94	87	37	64	94
151	2751	2	2	16	D	-2	1	66	1	18	-4	30	0	7	42	20	33	20	15	93	121	121	85	69	46	64	57	31	64	57
152	2752	2	1	14	D	6	-8	72	1	17	4	67	1	-1	48	43	0	21	3	85	80	128	98	91	81	64	89	73	76	57
153	2761	2	2	14	M	2	3	59	7	22	11	15	2	5	42	54	21	21	12	94	93	92	93	91	84	84	87	76	89	84
154	2762	2	2	16	M	4	1	69	4	18	4	25	5	1	47	33	39	12	3	122	113	107	94	91	81	89	92	103	96	97
155	2771	1	1	16	M	6	-3	69	1	11	7	31	4	-1	41	42	33	24	70	70	80	90	86	110	106	92	99	106	100	99
156	2772	2	2	14	D	2	0	98	7	28	11	24	3	1	41	39	31	40	3	88	89	90	84	86	89	92	92	106	100	94
157	2781	2	2	14	D	20	21	89	5	31	18	31	9	-12	47	92	64	40	4	109	133	129	94	83	89	88	133	111	105	104
158	2782	2	1	14	M	18	0	98	5	35	4	35	15	45	65	41	0	48	3	139	147	124	107	130	139	150	113	139	150	133
159	2791	2	1	14	M	17	21	80	10	41	10	73	12	18	78	65	31	30	4	107	132	100	133	122	119	120	122	133	140	127
160	2792	1	2	16	M	27	27	107	8	24	2	50	9	78	83	31	30	34	10	129	102	102	111	139	120	133	122	89	88	92
161	2801	1	1	17	D	-2	-2	21	0	2	2	1	2	2	41	41	0	34	2	106	69	63	84	84	54	64	66	70	74	83
162	2802	1	2	17	M	4	22	33	15	1	5	2	5	4	60	0	32	32	6	71	86	111	106	99	99	96	96	99	94	96

OBS	ID	SEX	RACE	AGE	ZYG	_35	_36	_37	_38	_39	_40	_41	_42	_43	_44	_45	_46	_47	_49	_56	_57	_58	_59	_60	_61	_62	_63	_64	_65	_66
163	2811	1	2	13	U	10	4	40	3	10	2	18	5	-2	50	42	10	40	14	77	91	103	96	94	103	96	97	94	91	94
164	2812	2	2	13	U	11	-16	44	5	14	2	22	3	-5	59	33	11	16	5	92	99	95	98	93	68	72	81	73	76	84
165	2821	2	2	14	D	5	-1	19	-1	14	0	4	1	-2	3	1	1	18	0	90	67	72	65	65	37	64	81	46	64	57
166	2822	2	2	14	D	5	12	18	7	1	1	6	3	-6	41	22	8	18	15	87	87	63	76	64	75	79	86	66	68	79
167	2831	1	2	17	U	3	12	40	13	13	9	19	8	-1	58	39	1	28	18	86	85	85	85	77	81	84	89	106	100	99
168	2832	2	2	17	U	12	-4	82	18	18	2	26	0	1	38	40	36	20	6	91	97	80	89	81	89	88	92	99	94	96
169	2841	2	2	15	D	4	-2	16	-1	1	2	2	4	0	54	27	3	12	6	75	81	78	74	62	66	68	79	75	79	86
170	2842	2	2	14	D	-1	-5	42	4	12	2	13	0	-1	52	30	0	6	12	75	81	81	83	69	61	64	83	58	72	71
171	2851	1	2	14	M	6	-2	12	-1	15	2	6	0	4	45	37	0	34	13	88	101	91	94	88	73	76	84	68	72	81
172	2852	2	2	14	D	-1	1	15	1	20	6	13	0	1	48	37	0	26	0	80	85	81	88	88	81	34	89	89	88	92
173	2861	1	2	14	D	3	2	11	-2	1	4	-2	4	-5	26	26	3	12	3	93	78	78	76	66	81	34	89	68	72	81
174	2862	2	2	14	O	-2	-1	17	2	15	3	13	5	-1	52	36	7	20	5	81	67	67	66	66	81	64	76	66	68	79
175	2871	1	2	14	O	10	-8	22	11	20	3	6	-1	-1	52	40	37	26	1	91	80	80	79	79	63	64	91	85	76	91
176	2872	1	2	14	M	10	16	43	6	2	3	39	0	-1	41	36	33	30	0	85	93	78	85	85	85	86	92	73	76	84
177	2881	2	2	16	M	4	20	20	21	11	3	6	11	1	45	40	26	14	10	94	91	80	104	95	89	38	91	73	74	83
178	2882	2	2	15	M	-4	-4	56	8	26	9	20	-1	-1	53	41	27	30	10	82	80	64	99	96	81	74	83	70	76	97
179	2891	2	2	15	U	8	0	31	1	12	3	33	-1	0	68	47	38	32	3	90	64	65	81	100	70	84	89	68	72	81
180	2892	1	2	15	U	6	0	84	8	23	8	1	0	7	69	68	16	16	1	95	91	99	96	102	81	84	103	103	96	113
181	2901	2	1	18	M	24	6	15	7	14	14	49	11	12	95	54	16	38	1	75	81	98	110	109	79	96	97	68	88	92
182	2902	1	1	18	M	16	74	73	28	20	49	53	9	13	54	52	32	44	7	103	78	92	114	113	91	100	105	119	120	113
183	2911	1	1	17	M	11	13	39	18	64	11	67	14	16	68	71	35	32	0	107	100	99	105	99	106	107	122	116	113	109
184	2912	2	1	17	M	14	14	57	8	18	8	21	14	14	60	77	26	29	2	93	92	96	97	127	127	133	106	100	100	99
185	2921	2	2	13	D	-5	13	81	7	21	5	17	-2	-8	65	34	20	20	0	97	99	95	97	81	60	66	71	70	73	82
186	2922	2	2	14	D	-4	14	67	5	5	4	5	3	3	54	35	20	18	8	88	101	99	90	97	81	84	89	76	79	86
187	2931	1	2	14	D	2	-5	21	-1	3	2	22	0	-3	46	35	0	32	7	92	83	101	107	90	54	64	66	89	64	68
188	2932	2	2	14	D	7	-2	55	9	9	2	9	0	-1	49	51	39	14	15	87	73	70	85	85	100	100	66	56	64	92
189	2941	2	2	15	D	2	-8	6	5	11	9	18	-2	0	32	31	14	16	50	69	76	78	63	63	23	72	57	56	64	68
190	2942	2	2	15	D	4	0	45	4	23	2	26	1	-3	41	28	22	34	15	80	87	87	94	76	81	81	81	94	94	94
191	2951	2	2	16	U	5	18	63	3	19	9	2	-2	0	60	51	50	22	15	87	94	94	120	120	123	127	118	99	94	96
192	2952	2	2	15	U	13	14	89	4	23	7	51	11	-1	76	53	27	28	8	93	77	115	115	97	68	72	81	89	76	84
193	2961	2	2	16	U	7	2	26	8	2	2	29	0	4	48	17	0	7	33	110	103	77	98	50	23	64	57	73	64	57
194	2562	2	2	17	U	3	13	60	2	7	10	38	-1	2	13	40	10	10	8	83	74	50	74	74	64	64	37	151	168	145
195	2971	1	2	14	U	15	14	68	8	35	5	35	2	3	54	70	38	30	30	96	103	106	122	103	127	140	122	106	100	99
196	2972	2	2	15	U	7	15	15	4	24	10	13	3	0	47	51	9	16	4	82	88	102	102	107	127	133	106	78	81	87
197	2981	1	2	16	O	2	7	48	2	13	5	7	2	-2	58	53	16	20	28	78	88	78	89	83	50	64	62	58	64	71
198	2982	2	2	17	O	5	-3	14	1	18	2	27	-1	-1	33	16	20	16	6	90	79	67	90	64	81	84	89	70	74	83
199	2991	2	2	17	M	4	2	30	8	5	7	10	4	2	82	23	10	18	3	83	75	75	74	70	58	64	70	70	70	83
200	2992	2	2	13	M	-3	3	25	1	4	0	7	-1	-1	86	36	18	14	13	64	79	75	63	63	66	68	70	70	74	66
201	3001	1	2	18	M	12	0	4	2	4	1	0	1	-1	36	23	0	3	3	85	86	61	77	76	106	100	99	54	79	86
202	3002	1	2	18	O	8	0	50	0	4	19	-1	4	1	44	18	0	40	16	93	91	82	80	75	63	64	70	75	73	84
203	3011	2	2	18	O	6	0	26	7	8	0	0	5	-1	67	50	10	20	21	86	86	87	76	58	54	54	70	73	76	87
204	3012	2	2	17	D	4	0	8	8	10	0	8	0	2	30	35	0	12	5	83	55	57	73	63	66	66	70	78	81	83
205	3021	2	2	17	D	3	0	28	2	5	1	3	-1	1	51	34	0	10	22	82	73	73	58	58	66	68	73	75	73	84
206	3022	2	2	14	D	-2	2	27	3	19	1	25	2	-1	45	32	10	6	12	90	81	95	82	82	66	88	75	56	58	68
207	3031	1	2	14	D	2	-11	11	3	3	3	15	2	4	38	16	0	16	50	80	80	36	95	84	61	64	78	75	94	86
208	3032	2	2	14	M	-11	-1	55	6	19	4	4	4	-1	30	32	2	9	18	92	90	75	75	72	75	76	73	56	64	68
209	3041	1	2	15	M	10	-10	76	-3	12	9	27	4	4	69	36	26	32	10	92	90	80	72	72	76	64	84	94	91	94
210	3042	2	2	14	D	-6	7	31	1	16	2	27	-4	0	68	42	26	48	8	69	91	91	91	104	75	74	83	63	64	76
211	3051	1	2	15	D	4	-1	80	3	23	6	24	-1	1	49	50	30	18	11	78	96	94	94	89	66	70	75	79	75	79
212	3052	2	2	14	D	11	-6	66	3	18	3	20	-6	-4	65	35	18	14	17	93	96	95	94	43	68	68	79	79	79	86
213	3061	2	2	13	D	4	8	66	0	18	5	29	1	-1	53	35	26	16	2	103	96	87	77	77	70	74	88	76	79	86
214	3062	2	2	13	O	-8	5	97	2	14	2	20	-1	-6	65	54	47	22	17	77	91	87	77	78	78	81	81	76	105	104
215	3071	1	2	16	O	6	11	119	-1	21	5	29	7	-4	73	53	40	16	2	87	80	95	101	97	78	81	88	111	105	104
216	3072	2	2	16	M	17	-7	101	2	23	8	33	7	-4	92	54	48	20	20	99	99	102	108	102	107	96	97	103	96	97

OBS	ID	SEX	RACE	AGE	ZYG	_35	_36	_37	_38	_39	_40	_41	_42	_43	_44	_45	_46	_47	_48	_56	_57	_58	_59	_60	_61	_62	_63	_64	_65	_66
217	3081	2	2	15	M	5	-18	50	4	6	6	16	-1	-3	47	15	17	12	5	68	81	82	74	65	46	64	57	70	74	83
218	3082	2	2	15	M	3	4	33	2	2	4	10	3	-1	44	35	13	12	50	90	85	82	92	82	63	64	76	63	64	76
219	3091	2	2	17	D	14	4	66	14	14	14	8	8	-5	66	56	44	32	8	88	82	95	101	90	116	113	109	103	96	97
220	3092	2	1	17	D	16	11	95	6	21	12	60	5	0	39	43	26	32	4	102	100	98	100	97	94	85	86	91	96	97
221	3101	1	1	16	J	11	-2	22	7	23	14	25	-2	-5	41	34	18	22	8	91	56	78	96	82	58	64	70	68	72	81
222	3102	2	2	16	J	16	-17	79	2	3	13	45	2	-1	44	45	18	22	8	100	69	76	73	76	78	81	87	81	84	89
223	3111	2	2	14	J	3	0	11	5	14	13	46	4	2	49	47	40	14	1	98	111	88	107	99	106	100	99	99	94	96
224	3112	2	2	16	J	7	0	22	5	4	2	20	3	-1	46	34	10	16	1	109	60	78	76	75	63	64	76	94	94	94
225	3121	1	1	16	J	3	0	24	-1	-2	21	11	-1	-5	42	26	0	16	21	66	75	73	73	75	68	72	81	61	64	73
226	3122	2	2	16	J	9	12	24	12	14	2	10	10	-1	72	53	10	16	5	80	75	93	98	86	103	96	97	106	100	99
227	3131	2	1	13	J	0	-1	0	-2	-1	1	11	10	-1	18	17	0	36	5	55	51	93	78	50	46	64	61	57	64	66
228	3132	2	2	13	D	12	-4	10	-4	-4	4	33	0	0	13	8	6	24	11	55	50	50	78	54	54	54	54	54	127	66
229	3141	1	2	13	M	4	2	7	3	13	5	-3	0	1	54	46	26	24	36	119	87	117	88	96	89	88	92	123	127	118
230	3142	1	2	13	D	4	9	9	4	10	5	-2	-4	0	50	12	1	24	40	113	77	87	91	90	24	66	74	32	66	59
231	3151	2	2	15	M	9	17	78	3	40	11	52	10	1	70	72	56	30	10	105	100	112	114	111	127	133	122	94	91	94
232	3152	2	2	15	D	12	79	79	5	22	6	66	1	2	76	61	46	32	2	111	111	96	125	103	123	133	122	127	133	122
233	3161	1	1	17	D	12	51	51	7	20	5	60	1	4	42	43	40	40	2	111	119	96	103	104	75	79	86	85	86	91
234	3162	2	1	17	D	17	77	77	5	19	3	52	3	-8	74	66	30	40	9	109	119	110	116	106	106	100	111	105	105	104
235	3171	1	1	14	D	8	-2	18	4	18	10	22	1	-8	67	27	14	16	26	87	71	90	90	37	64	64	42	64	64	57
236	3172	2	2	14	D	7	32	32	7	20	10	31	3	-7	76	32	36	16	5	101	77	89	75	77	72	72	81	99	94	96
237	3181	1	1	18	D	19	17	53	3	39	22	61	8	-1	96	47	47	16	4	102	99	99	102	99	123	127	116	116	113	109
238	3182	2	1	18	D	28	17	83	37	37	15	46	9	16	93	55	37	34	3	105	98	109	91	97	127	133	122	139	150	133
239	3191	1	2	18	M	7	7	52	6	17	17	46	8	9	52	55	37	16	3	90	93	98	100	97	93	94	96	123	127	118
240	3192	1	2	18	D	10	17	60	8	16	13	43	10	7	51	45	18	38	5	90	100	92	119	100	106	94	103	96	97	97
241	3201	1	2	13	J	10	2	64	-1	6	5	34	4	-2	38	25	37	26	11	90	99	92	85	90	84	87	91	112	111	108
242	3202	2	2	13	D	5	2	64	4	5	5	24	1	-3	48	24	37	24	7	103	91	102	78	89	98	94	94	117	118	112
243	3211	1	1	14	D	8	4	14	8	12	6	12	-2	-3	61	32	11	24	8	76	67	76	90	76	75	79	86	66	68	79
244	3212	2	2	14	M	1	-1	14	1	8	3	18	-2	-1	71	32	16	18	10	84	67	81	76	67	85	86	73	81	84	76
245	3221	1	1	14	D	3	9	6	1	8	0	16	3	-5	28	45	16	20	3	94	96	106	104	73	92	84	89	73	76	84
246	3222	1	1	15	J	-2	0	90	-3	11	4	51	5	-8	53	27	45	32	3	99	71	106	106	100	81	91	89	103	96	97
247	3231	2	1	15	D	12	0	28	4	15	12	13	1	-1	66	27	10	16	1	83	81	96	75	90	68	68	94	116	113	109
248	3232	1	1	16	M	4	0	24	4	28	5	26	2	0	49	49	17	18	40	87	81	96	73	90	86	91	94	94	91	94
249	3241	2	2	16	D	12	-8	24	6	8	8	21	-1	-1	47	24	24	20	8	72	75	82	72	72	74	68	79	68	72	81
250	3242	2	2	14	D	4	6	34	8	4	2	10	0	0	-4	29	23	20	5	90	80	66	73	56	42	64	57	23	64	57
251	3251	1	1	15	J	-1	6	11	3	6	5	38	1	-1	59	13	24	16	5	75	119	87	84	76	66	64	79	70	74	71
252	3252	2	1	15	D	11	6	41	0	8	0	56	1	-1	43	38	15	22	50	107	82	86	88	76	61	64	87	58	64	57
253	3261	1	2	16	J	13	5	51	5	12	7	70	13	0	46	51	47	21	8	87	84	91	88	83	42	81	89	89	88	92
254	3262	2	2	16	D	5	5	81	7	8	9	19	-1	-4	44	24	20	21	9	84	76	73	88	83	89	88	92	111	105	104
255	3271	1	1	16	M	20	7	84	3	18	12	14	2	-3	47	38	13	32	5	84	78	71	92	93	89	88	92	111	105	104
256	3272	2	1	16	M	6	-8	50	5	5	9	39	-1	-1	47	26	16	16	5	98	87	71	92	81	46	64	57	46	64	57
257	3281	2	2	16	J	11	0	55	7	5	0	9	-2	-1	46	27	10	22	8	93	81	102	73	102	61	103	57	103	74	83
258	3282	2	2	16	M	13	9	69	2	15	17	37	10	-1	65	31	19	14	8	100	75	86	88	76	110	103	102	106	100	99
259	3291	1	1	14	M	13	-9	12	6	13	3	28	10	-5	50	18	16	21	17	84	90	91	93	83	118	103	97	78	81	87
260	3292	2	1	17	D	4	0	12	4	3	11	14	12	0	46	13	47	32	8	84	78	73	112	93	89	88	92	111	105	104
261	3301	1	1	17	D	6	-6	1	3	17	3	30	-1	-1	47	13	16	32	1	83	75	71	92	81	46	64	57	46	64	57
262	3302	2	1	14	M	8	0	43	7	21	5	44	8	1	38	16	21	48	40	88	75	89	92	81	61	64	57	42	64	57
263	3311	1	2	13	D	18	3	71	14	15	19	51	-2	10	94	71	11	31	8	128	105	119	120	122	110	118	111	116	100	99
264	3312	2	2	14	M	15	16	84	13	31	17	48	3	-3	95	41	43	43	15	108	114	117	117	118	110	103	102	106	100	97
265	3321	1	1	14	D	14	16	72	2	26	17	43	-1	-1	64	41	41	32	9	108	93	124	109	112	103	96	97	106	100	99
266	3322	2	1	14	D	8	4	42	2	2	4	13	-2	-1	48	25	15	32	3	100	87	100	91	90	103	96	97	103	96	97
267	3331	1	1	13	J	9	-2	38	1	18	4	12	-1	2	52	31	18	24	27	103	87	90	90	89	81	94	89	73	79	86
268	3332	2	1	13	M	3	-4	10	-2	13	3	16	-1	-3	48	25	18	26	19	109	95	90	90	89	64	64	89	54	76	84
269	3351	2	2	15	D	6	-1	20	2	19	3	12	2	0	48	8	8	24	13	86	77	78	74	66	64	64	62	54	64	66
270	3352	1	1	15	M	3	-6	30	4	13	18	18	0	1	46	16	16	14	7	86	77	78	74	66	50	64	63	63	64	76

OBS	ID	SEX	RACE	AGE	ZYG	_35	_36	_37	_38	_39	_40	_41	_42	_43	_44	_45	_46	_47	_48	_56	_57	_58	_59	_60	_61	_62	_63	_64	_65	_66
271	3361	2	1	15	D	2	4	30	22	22	1	11	-1	-1	84	23	16	22	15	87	99	95	75	79	70	74	83	68	72	81
272	3362	2	2	15	D	0	-4	24	5	2	2	1	-3	-3	90	14	12	24	17	105	81	71	87	79	61	64	73	54	64	66
273	3371	2	2	12	M	4	2	20	5	11	2	16	1	-6	47	17	12	22	25	93	101	87	79	80	77	77	85	58	53	69
274	3372	2	2	12	M	-6	2	31	-1	1	8	8	1	3	45	17	12	32	23	93	109	108	96	89	54	64	65	88	89	93
275	3381	1	1	15	M	13	-3	81	4	12	10	57	10	5	45	60	33	19	4	111	109	108	105	108	94	94	96	103	96	97
276	3382	1	2	15	M	-4	-7	64	-4	4	14	57	14	5	58	56	27	6	4	105	103	116	115	116	113	113	116	113	113	109
277	3391	1	1	15	M	12	-3	16	5	23	9	20	6	-3	54	39	27	29	16	76	89	88	85	73	78	81	87	89	88	92
278	3392	1	2	14	M	11	4	22	5	14	1	27	9	5	51	36	12	20	8	91	93	80	89	73	79	79	86	70	74	83
279	3401	1	2	15	D	8	13	30	7	5	8	49	0	1	59	45	39	20	3	99	95	88	99	90	75	79	86	81	79	89
280	3402	2	2	15	D	0	0	20	2	3	15	50	5	-1	59	48	35	32	10	103	95	100	105	106	106	64	62	70	74	86
281	3411	2	2	16	D	8	0	61	2	20	15	58	14	-3	71	39	46	20	11	105	85	79	81	94	50	99	92	75	79	96
282	3412	2	2	16	D	4	-1	74	5	3	3	16	-3	-1	47	31	32	16	9	105	64	82	105	81	106	88	99	106	100	99
283	3421	2	2	14	D	17	7	28	5	20	3	37	-1	-1	43	26	27	16	4	94	102	88	88	85	89	74	83	94	91	94
284	3422	2	2	14	D	-6	-5	26	3	25	4	32	-5	-3	54	31	29	16	4	81	93	88	86	79	73	64	86	81	84	89
285	3431	2	2	15	D	4	3	12	-1	14	1	8	-2	-1	43	17	16	30	15	102	103	75	74	87	54	64	66	68	68	72
286	3432	1	2	13	D	11	3	16	0	17	2	21	-5	5	37	24	17	20	14	107	71	102	92	92	75	79	86	66	91	94
287	3441	2	1	13	D	6	0	18	0	23	0	16	6	0	80	29	25	12	14	87	95	99	122	109	110	100	102	99	94	96
288	3442	1	1	16	D	2	-3	21	2	21	2	16	-1	-3	46	24	22	14	14	83	84	83	73	73	70	91	83	85	86	91
289	3451	2	2	16	D	6	-10	32	2	21	2	33	-5	2	43	20	33	18	11	93	84	83	84	73	54	54	66	78	81	87
290	3452	2	2	16	D	7	-5	39	2	21	14	13	1	-3	44	10	10	11	7	87	90	90	73	82	64	64	86	78	81	87
291	3461	2	2	14	D	8	-5	39	1	19	20	21	-3	-3	65	32	10	32	7	101	90	95	75	70	79	79	86	63	64	76
292	3462	2	2	14	D	5	-3	30	2	4	5	18	1	-3	48	24	8	13	9	90	73	98	76	70	85	86	94	111	105	104
293	3471	2	1	14	D	5	1	30	2	22	5	7	1	2	41	32	8	8	4	87	87	101	76	76	86	86	94	111	105	104
294	3472	2	2	14	D	8	-3	42	2	13	5	73	10	2	41	43	48	13	8	110	107	120	125	131	116	113	109	116	113	109
295	3481	1	1	16	D	17	0	84	12	38	8	57	12	15	66	86	40	26	14	114	107	107	114	139	139	107	111	111	113	109
296	3482	1	2	16	D	21	0	54	2	37	9	32	3	0	58	58	32	36	8	114	107	107	90	88	150	133	96	111	105	104
297	3491	2	2	13	M	-8	-5	26	-2	17	4	24	1	-7	48	31	31	14	8	88	91	99	78	88	98	94	96	78	81	82
298	3492	2	2	13	M	-8	11	49	8	11	5	15	1	1	93	35	23	11	1	70	97	84	78	72	81	81	96	70	73	94
299	3501	1	2	18	M	9	8	96	8	41	7	48	-1	-1	96	35	19	20	1	93	111	111	93	90	116	113	109	94	91	94
300	3502	1	1	17	M	11	8	93	11	9	7	56	-7	1	24	39	51	19	0	93	109	110	85	90	99	94	62	103	96	97
301	3511	1	1	17	D	9	-8	21	3	17	7	-4	9	-1	46	32	19	22	12	80	64	66	73	46	50	64	62	58	64	71
302	3512	1	2	17	M	0	-4	10	10	3	10	-1	0	11	64	25	25	32	2	77	93	93	101	83	83	133	122	139	150	133
303	3521	1	1	15	M	21	25	86	10	48	10	-1	-2	9	71	86	47	32	1	114	132	132	117	123	127	133	102	139	150	133
304	3522	1	2	14	D	23	17	41	7	21	23	64	13	13	74	86	50	32	28	112	134	132	125	133	110	103	122	133	140	127
305	3531	1	1	17	D	15	19	102	1	25	7	55	12	15	48	37	29	26	1	120	107	93	92	91	99	94	96	78	81	87
306	3532	1	2	14	D	2	19	64	12	16	23	67	12	11	48	37	44	33	6	120	107	109	95	96	116	113	109	58	64	71
307	3541	2	2	14	D	-6	-6	70	-3	-2	12	29	5	10	35	16	10	26	7	104	80	96	81	79	73	76	84	58	64	76
308	3542	1	1	14	D	-8	-7	70	-3	16	6	26	-4	-7	49	32	19	26	6	103	96	96	77	90	63	76	70	63	64	76
309	3551	1	1	14	D	4	25	30	4	14	9	23	1	-2	56	19	19	13	4	90	85	86	89	96	58	88	102	70	74	83
310	3552	2	2	14	D	10	-13	46	15	18	7	43	-5	-2	61	19	29	12	6	99	98	101	77	96	109	94	99	70	74	83
311	3561	1	1	15	D	0	-4	46	4	21	6	46	-1	11	58	30	21	44	2	94	102	109	91	79	110	103	84	84	94	96
312	3562	2	2	13	D	-4	-1	29	1	14	6	25	1	-4	53	20	30	12	1	94	80	96	81	76	73	76	84	81	86	89
313	3581	1	2	15	M	3	-1	51	1	-1	3	41	9	2	90	13	19	26	2	83	90	86	95	76	63	84	89	75	79	86
314	3582	2	1	15	M	14	-10	54	-4	12	14	54	-1	-1	41	67	44	26	7	117	122	112	116	81	81	113	109	111	105	104
315	3591	2	2	17	D	4	-5	94	4	39	19	62	-4	-5	70	45	47	12	10	126	120	102	100	94	96	91	94	89	88	92
316	3592	2	2	17	D	16	-10	100	9	8	14	63	12	6	70	60	60	26	9	110	107	99	100	99	94	91	94	106	100	99
317	3601	1	1	14	D	-5	-2	82	4	9	8	42	-1	5	54	32	32	40	3	123	93	112	107	77	113	113	137	106	100	99
318	3602	2	2	14	D	16	-5	78	11	29	8	61	-2	-3	90	49	35	23	18	87	103	86	89	85	89	88	92	81	84	86
319	3611	2	2	15	D	7	-3	84	1	21	5	34	-2	4	41	29	21	23	17	94	85	89	89	85	103	96	97	64	74	76
320	3612	2	2	15	D	0	-4	69	0	22	11	16	-1	-6	42	21	20	26	1	94	91	91	95	91	78	78	88	81	79	89
321	3621	2	2	14	D	2	-2	44	1	24	11	16	1	1	34	21	20	23	4	81	71	91	78	81	73	84	87	76	79	86
322	3622	2	2	13	D	11	21	78	-1	24	19	33	6	1	50	54	16	32	4	115	96	118	91	115	116	87	88	98	94	96
323	3631	1	2	13	D	21	28	28	2	24	19	31	7	0	50	25	16	30	6	90	106	104	91	88	113	116	113	109	106	99
324	3632	1	1	18	M	16	10	44	5	20	15	48	13	0	56	70	23	34	3	97	109	104	104	102	94	94	96	119	120	113

OBS	ID	SEX	RACE	AGE	ZYG	_35	_36	_37	_38	_39	_40	_41	_42	_43	_44	_45	_46	_47	_48	_56	_57	_58	_59	_60	_61	_62	_63	_64	_65	_66
325	3641	1	1	14	D	8	2	68	5	4	7	39	3	-2	67	37	34	48	21	113	87	98	113	106	94	91	94	85	86	91
326	3642	1	1	14	D	9	-6	8	7	4	5	31	-1	-1	48	47	26	40	1	90	100	83	93	88	89	88	92	89	88	92
327	3651	1	1	14	D	8	0	45	5	11	5	45	8	-4	82	52	24	37	13	95	100	94	94	88	94	88	94	89	111	104
328	3652	1	1	14	D	4	9	7	0	13	3	?	2	?	40	14	6	22	11	61	73	72	83	62	63	64	76	70	74	83
329	3661	2	1	14	M	18	10	73	3	35	12	45	13	-3	54	50	46	36	15	108	104	131	128	124	94	91	94	119	120	113
330	3662	2	1	14	M	15	10	80	5	35	16	55	6	-1	48	62	44	24	9	104	102	119	121	124	110	92	95	116	116	109
331	3671	1	1	13	D	6	12	49	4	5	6	24	3	7	70	50	33	24	3	103	102	111	119	99	93	92	95	98	94	96
332	3672	1	1	13	D	4	-4	59	4	0	12	12	7	7	53	62	33	22	4	104	102	111	107	103	93	74	83	84	87	91
333	3681	2	2	16	D	4	-2	69	4	20	7	38	3	5	70	50	20	18	50	97	84	78	88	72	70	74	83	85	86	86
334	3682	2	2	16	D	6	-3	43	3	16	0	40	3	5	82	17	50	16	5	87	81	80	88	81	89	88	92	75	79	86
335	3691	2	1	14	M	25	-3	54	4	16	10	51	6	4	94	61	38	33	10	120	114	110	108	114	89	88	92	94	91	94
336	3692	2	1	14	M	13	-4	47	4	13	8	52	1	-3	37	44	34	26	3	113	102	110	101	103	81	84	89	78	81	87
337	3701	2	2	14	J	-2	-1	17	1	6	5	10	-3	-3	26	12	8	31	10	61	111	52	76	70	63	84	76	58	68	71
338	3702	1	2	14	J	-5	-2	29	4	3	1	2	-1	-4	24	23	8	13	10	82	83	73	85	70	73	76	84	66	64	79
339	3711	2	2	14	M	5	1	51	-1	3	16	10	1	0	95	11	4	8	31	102	98	77	77	76	61	64	73	61	64	73
340	3721	2	2	13	D	5	-2	20	0	2	0	2	-5	0	63	22	11	35	26	85	89	92	78	76	81	84	89	78	65	83
341	3722	2	2	13	D	7	-5	29	1	11	6	13	-2	-5	23	26	28	11	37	88	91	88	93	76	88	76	93	78	66	77
342	3731	2	2	13	D	10	-1	63	2	11	5	34	-2	-4	43	31	12	21	6	93	73	94	93	87	72	76	84	68	70	80
343	3732	2	2	13	D	8	-3	76	2	7	0	18	-2	-1	67	30	16	20	3	96	73	80	95	80	81	84	89	88	89	93
344	3741	2	2	13	D	6	8	51	-2	13	0	19	-2	0	45	18	16	20	4	85	85	90	77	75	68	72	81	58	64	71
345	3741	2	2	13	D	2	8	59	0	2	8	8	0	-9	95	21	13	20	22	72	75	73	77	62	70	74	81	58	64	71
346	3742	2	2	17	M	4	8	145	11	23	11	8	11	9	87	21	13	31	1	105	109	98	88	82	99	94	96	89	88	92
347	3751	2	1	17	D	17	-1	135	0	34	61	52	-1	0	87	82	47	28	2	109	116	110	90	102	110	103	102	99	94	96
348	3752	2	1	17	D	14	-1	-2	2	2	8	2	-2	3	-4	87	48	25	3	109	91	85	78	79	68	70	80	65	66	77
349	3761	1	1	13	D	6	1	66	-2	20	10	10	0	-3	69	29	21	43	9	100	109	110	90	114	88	103	80	99	96	77
350	3762	1	1	13	D	5	2	117	0	17	2	21	-2	0	95	50	21	16	3	103	91	89	78	89	81	70	93	65	92	95
351	3771	2	2	13	D	-6	0	25	0	17	5	3	3	-5	95	23	9	16	2	94	89	77	77	74	68	72	81	63	64	76
352	3772	2	2	13	D	0	0	26	0	19	6	7	0	1	47	13	6	25	1	76	89	69	77	68	66	68	79	63	76	76
353	3781	2	2	15	M	9	0	51	1	19	15	13	3	1	82	39	8	15	6	115	70	75	85	70	78	81	87	73	76	84
354	3782	2	2	16	M	6	-7	45	10	11	11	54	-1	-1	54	27	13	18	2	92	94	81	86	82	68	72	81	75	76	86
355	3791	1	1	16	D	4	-3	45	4	11	2	34	3	-3	35	41	16	21	6	97	84	81	90	82	81	72	89	81	84	89
356	3792	1	1	16	D	6	-4	44	5	10	4	31	9	0	34	39	25	21	6	106	84	89	86	86	66	68	79	70	84	83
357	3801	1	2	16	D	13	-2	41	4	11	21	33	1	-1	79	39	24	20	1	94	80	94	86	84	80	84	89	84	87	97
358	3802	1	2	16	D	-2	3	93	3	11	0	46	4	4	70	78	40	18	2	103	99	101	103	100	99	94	89	103	96	99
359	3811	2	1	16	D	-1	-3	33	-1	18	8	18	9	4	96	49	23	17	2	87	76	75	89	89	81	68	79	85	100	91
360	3812	2	1	16	D	-1	3	48	3	8	7	31	1	4	48	49	23	20	13	94	83	83	94	89	66	68	79	73	76	84
361	3821	1	1	14	M	-5	-1	80	-1	6	10	17	1	-1	83	23	22	17	13	95	83	79	94	88	78	81	87	63	64	76
362	3822	2	2	14	M	5	-6	98	0	1	4	22	-3	1	66	23	35	48	13	90	86	86	83	94	73	84	84	98	87	96
363	3831	2	2	15	D	3	-4	81	0	13	4	4	-4	-3	78	14	18	48	50	85	80	75	81	72	63	64	76	63	64	76
364	3832	2	2	13	D	3	-7	74	0	4	8	8	-1	-3	39	10	13	22	22	93	70	66	80	64	23	64	46	46	57	62
365	3841	1	1	13	D	3	-5	7	4	4	1	14	4	4	19	26	1	32	2	88	77	50	78	60	42	64	57	50	64	62
366	3842	2	1	13	D	6	0	43	1	15	2	58	-4	-5	91	22	19	14	8	119	109	118	95	67	37	67	91	54	64	66
367	3851	1	2	13	M	1	3	114	8	14	5	55	-2	1	42	47	42	24	4	103	95	105	95	97	84	87	91	98	87	91
368	3852	2	2	13	M	34	0	114	5	14	7	43	4	-1	35	49	41	20	14	106	93	105	84	94	94	91	94	84	96	97
369	3861	2	2	13	D	24	12	51	5	18	4	40	4	1	41	58	42	16	4	91	93	116	95	98	94	91	94	103	96	97
370	3862	2	2	15	D	10	9	99	4	13	5	51	10	5	42	62	37	10	8	100	85	86	90	87	81	86	94	103	96	97
371	3871	2	2	15	D	4	4	76	2	6	5	39	2	2	30	35	42	10	5	91	71	86	84	84	73	76	84	78	81	87
372	3872	2	2	14	D	10	-3	76	1	12	1	33	-1	2	89	49	42	16	6	93	90	84	84	76	85	86	97	75	79	86
373	3881	2	2	14	D	14	-8	130	21	16	33	39	-5	-5	92	49	34	33	6	94	101	106	101	103	102	86	97	78	81	87
374	3891	2	2	14	D	10	-3	106	3	12	2	3	0	-1	95	52	34	16	6	94	103	103	101	103	85	86	96	111	105	104
375	3892	2	2	14	D	-6	-8	22	2	16	4	17	0	-1	54	32	28	14	14	87	67	83	96	69	37	64	57	61	64	73
376	3893	2	2	14	M	5	0	52	-1	12	2	25	-2	-5	90	30	20	33	50	90	78	99	96	93	103	96	97	89	88	92
377	3901	2	2	13	J	5	0	68	-2	12	2	3	-4	-2	68	19	20	13	22	87	78	72	78	72	52	66	63	76	79	86
378	3902	2	1	13	J	8	-13	11	-3	6	4	4	-2	-5	44	14	0	15	6	95	51	60	85	62	48	66	59	63	66	74

APPENDIX E - PART 2

OBS	ID	SEX	RACE	AGE	ZYG	_35	_36	_37	_38	_39	_40	_41	_42	_43	_44	_45	_46	_47	_48	_56	_57	_58	_59	_60	_61	_62	_63	_64	_65	_66
379	3911	1	2	15	U	8	10	34	2	14	3	28	3	6	51	44	17	14	2	98	100	99	95	91	73	76	84	70	74	83
380	3912	2	2	15	U	20	18	88	5	27	5	48	11	7	83	75	46	19	0	98	108	104	93	97	103	96	97	106	100	99

N=380

Appendix F

The raw scores for all twins who took either of the personality questionnaires, *How Well Do You Know Yourself?* or *High School Personality Questionnaire.*

In the following table, the column numbers correspond to the column headings in the Appendix F printouts.

Since each twin took only one of the two personality tests, the printout for Appendix F is divided into two parts. A full description of each variable reported in the printout can be found in Appendix B.

Column #	*HOW WELL DO YOU KNOW YOURSELF?*
67	Irritability
68	Practicality
69	Punctuality
70	Novelty-loving
71	Vocational assurance
72	Cooperativeness
73	Ambitiousness
74	Hypercriticalness
75	Dejection
76	General morale
77	Persistence
78	Nervousness
79	Seriousness
80	Submissiveness
81	Impulsiveness
82	Dynamism
83	Emotional control
84	Consistency
85	Test objectivity

HIGH SCHOOL PERSONALITY QUESTIONNAIRE

86	Reserved vs. warmhearted
87	Dull vs. bright
88	Affected by feelings vs. emotionally stable
89	Undemonstrative vs. excitable
90	Obedient vs. assertive
91	Sober vs. enthusiastic
92	Disregards rules vs. conscientious
93	Shy vs. adventurous
94	Tough-minded vs. tender-minded
95	Zestful vs. circumspect individualism
96	Self-assured vs. apprehensive
97	Sociable group-dependent vs. self-sufficient
98	Uncontrolled vs. controlled
99	Relaxed vs. tense

OBS	ID	SEX	RACE	AGE	ZYG	_67	_68	_69	_70	_71	_72	_73	_74	_75	_76	_77	_78	_79	_80	_81	_82	_83	_84	_85
1	11	1	2	17	M	14	19	16	30	17	29	20	17	7	9	24	7	24	14	7	14	14	12	16
2	12	1	2	17	M	26	21	22	23	19	27	17	19	7	15	18	19	18	7	9	19	15	4	21
3	21	2	2	17	D	15	15	14	17	18	21	9	14	14	13	15	9	12	13	7	11	13	6	25
4	22	2	2	17	D	11	15	21	17	17	20	16	15	4	16	14	7	8	15	9	16	13	5	22
5	31	1	1	14	D	13	14	19	22	15	18	13	12	3	21	17	9	10	16	11	17	12	2	28
6	32	1	1	14	D	8	16	19	19	15	15	12	12	8	15	18	11	14	11	9	13	15	11	29
7	41	2	1	18	D	7	12	17	25	26	22	10	7	4	22	20	10	17	24	8	13	16	5	25
8	42	2	1	18	M	10	14	20	21	17	23	17	6	5	14	17	8	13	16	14	15	16	1	26
9	51	1	1	17	M	13	17	11	13	14	20	19	9	10	16	17	12	13	16	8	16	16	0	30
10	52	1	1	17	M	11	17	23	15	19	23	11	13	11	14	13	15	17	26	11	17	15	20	15
11	61	2	2	17	M	17	11	4	25	21	22	11	11	18	16	14	19	12	6	16	21	10	11	17
12	62	2	2	16	M	15	18	11	9	15	11	7	6	4	18	18	15	13	18	15	18	4	11	15
13	71	2	1	16	M	14	16	16	26	16	25	22	18	9	13	21	19	12	6	9	20	8	4	21
14	72	2	2	14	D	15	16	20	18	17	26	16	11	4	16	18	3	18	18	10	15	16	5	24
15	81	2	1	14	M	9	16	18	25	17	23	13	11	5	11	21	11	12	15	8	14	14	11	25
16	82	2	2	14	M	6	23	18	28	15	28	15	5	5	24	18	7	9	21	7	18	18	7	23
17	91	1	1	14	M	14	24	20	20	19	23	16	13	4	11	23	6	18	17	22	22	24	9	25
18	92	2	2	15	M	11	21	27	19	16	27	16	18	5	25	17	20	16	19	15	15	14	17	9
19	101	2	2	16	M	12	16	12	19	21	19	12	21	2	17	24	13	17	10	20	21	16	20	21
20	102	2	1	15	M	9	18	17	24	24	20	16	11	8	24	17	13	13	22	11	18	16	7	16
21	111	2	1	17	M	10	15	12	19	18	24	11	6	1	17	14	5	12	13	28	20	10	6	21
22	112	2	2	16	M	16	16	21	22	21	25	21	8	0	16	21	6	18	17	4	13	12	11	17
23	121	2	2	16	D	10	17	17	25	24	24	13	11	6	21	18	5	13	7	11	10	11	4	17
24	122	2	2	16	M	20	15	18	22	21	17	12	13	6	24	18	8	5	5	1	14	23	11	25
25	131	1	1	16	M	11	14	10	25	18	24	17	16	4	25	15	9	15	7	12	14	19	4	28
26	132	1	1	15	M	12	15	17	22	16	17	13	6	1	17	14	10	11	5	12	15	16	6	25
27	141	1	1	17	D	9	15	18	19	21	18	13	9	7	13	16	9	16	7	12	16	10	6	19
28	142	1	1	17	D	11	18	15	18	15	26	17	14	10	16	23	8	18	18	10	15	16	8	25
29	151	1	2	14	M	18	12	15	26	21	15	9	4	4	17	13	7	8	12	15	21	15	2	29
30	152	1	2	17	M	13	15	21	23	19	21	12	14	2	16	15	8	10	13	13	16	18	4	27
31	161	1	1	18	M	9	15	11	25	23	24	14	5	1	19	10	9	16	10	12	18	13	4	26
32	162	1	1	17	D	12	16	17	27	22	24	13	10	1	18	15	5	14	14	11	17	13	4	20
33	171	1	1	17	D	11	19	20	22	24	29	18	12	7	18	23	10	12	12	11	18	18	4	21
34	172	1	2	14	J	11	18	23	26	27	25	22	12	2	19	24	4	13	7	8	22	14	4	23
35	181	1	2	14	M	9	18	21	21	19	24	22	11	3	16	19	10	18	16	9	13	14	8	25
36	182	1	2	15	M	8	20	15	26	22	30	21	17	1	13	15	4	5	15	23	18	12	3	17
37	191	2	1	14	M	22	21	20	29	17	21	15	16	13	14	16	19	21	7	19	13	14	3	18
38	192	2	2	15	M	9	24	24	23	22	12	20	18	2	25	20	13	14	16	11	18	14	3	29
39	201	2	2	14	D	20	21	22	27	26	19	21	13	15	20	23	11	18	15	9	22	10	3	26
40	202	2	1	15	D	9	14	12	18	22	21	20	10	7	15	20	4	11	11	6	19	9	11	19
41	211	1	1	14	M	14	20	24	23	20	21	20	11	11	18	19	12	8	16	15	12	17	7	20
42	212	1	2	14	M	20	13	12	23	18	12	16	16	5	18	16	7	18	18	11	18	11	1	27
43	221	1	1	14	D	12	18	23	19	23	24	16	13	7	20	13	12	14	12	12	12	12	6	27
44	222	2	2	14	D	22	18	20	23	18	20	13	18	9	19	14	14	11	10	14	18	8	5	30
45	231	2	1	17	M	14	12	17	17	10	18	13	9	4	15	11	21	12	10	14	21	13	7	24
46	232	2	1	15	M	14	15	16	23	13	14	7	16	7	15	13	14	13	15	10	10	12	6	27
47	241	2	1	13	M	10	10	19	17	17	15	6	7	12	18	12	21	18	11	14	14	8	5	27
48	242	2	1	13	M	14	13	24	21	17	19	8	16	4	16	13	14	11	10	14	18	13	7	11
49	251	2	2	14	M	16	17	18	24	13	23	9	17	6	15	11	13	18	15	12	16	10	13	12
50	252	2	2	14	M	10	23	22	24	18	27	22	17	2	19	21	11	13	11	14	21	12	12	10
51	261	2	1	14	M	24	11	11	24	23	24	15	17	6	20	20	11	18	21	10	11	13	10	18
52	262	2	1	17	M	19	18	25	25	18	22	23	14	6	20	16	9	17	20	17	21	15	8	23
53	271	2	1	17	M	11	15	15	21	18	24	23	10	5	20	24	9	13	18	6	19	15	11	27
54	272	2	2	17	M	18	21	8	20	16	22	14	9	4	19	15	8	9	16	12	19	18	4	27

228

OBS	ID	SEX	RACE	AGE	ZYG	_67	_68	_69	_70	_71	_72	_73	_74	_75	_76	_77	_78	_79	_80	_81	_82	_83	_84	_85
55	281	1	1	13	D	17	15	16	24	19	20	23	13	8	16	18	11	19	18	11	17	12	3	29
56	282	1	1	13	D	15	21	20	26	20	23	28	11	8	17	15	10	17	23	10	23	13	9	22
57	291	2	2	15	D	15	17	18	24	19	23	17	9	16	19	13	12	18	16	15	15	14	8	28
58	292	2	1	15	U	11	17	16	26	22	22	20	6	4	24	24	6	12	18	16	21	19	1	23
59	301	1	1	17	U	15	15	16	23	26	24	22	11	3	21	21	6	19	14	10	11	14	5	22
60	302	2	1	17	U	13	17	25	22	21	24	14	13	8	16	9	9	16	18	13	15	24	5	28
61	311	2	2	17	U	6	15	18	20	17	21	12	9	5	15	14	6	10	12	12	19	12	3	20
62	312	2	2	17	D	18	21	20	21	17	27	15	12	11	17	13	15	14	10	10	19	15	7	24
63	321	2	1	16	D	9	10	19	23	28	25	19	13	4	21	15	5	14	11	10	10	21	6	27
64	322	2	1	16	M	5	15	15	22	22	20	13	11	7	15	17	8	10	19	7	16	16	5	15
65	331	1	1	17	M	17	17	18	24	18	25	22	14	8	18	25	2	11	8	7	21	15	11	21
66	332	1	2	15	M	9	21	15	25	22	22	22	3	1	21	23	18	21	14	10	17	19	5	21
67	341	1	2	15	D	17	12	18	28	18	25	18	14	8	16	15	12	18	21	14	8	14	14	20
68	342	2	2	16	D	10	22	20	28	23	22	21	3	7	17	23	13	15	12	9	18	15	12	21
69	351	2	2	16	M	13	23	22	27	21	21	18	18	4	22	21	7	19	14	14	17	14	13	25
70	352	2	1	14	M	18	16	22	23	19	21	21	10	6	18	10	11	18	13	9	16	14	6	27
71	361	1	1	14	M	18	9	20	17	11	18	12	11	8	17	13	9	16	20	12	15	12	7	28
72	362	2	1	18	D	3	22	15	22	23	20	18	8	3	18	20	6	18	22	11	17	24	5	22
73	371	2	1	18	D	14	16	16	25	19	23	19	6	6	20	16	9	24	17	26	13	16	7	24
74	372	2	1	18	M	13	20	20	27	18	26	20	17	6	17	20	16	23	13	15	22	17	5	24
75	381	1	2	15	D	7	19	17	21	26	22	23	15	5	16	21	7	19	12	10	12	13	7	21
76	382	2	2	15	M	12	17	15	15	12	16	13	9	7	15	14	17	12	13	18	16	17	1	28
77	391	2	1	15	F	18	14	18	21	13	15	16	11	11	13	11	19	17	13	14	17	12	4	28
78	392	2	1	16	F	15	23	15	24	24	26	19	10	4	11	19	8	22	16	4	17	17	8	22
79	401	2	2	16	M	13	21	22	19	25	25	18	10	11	18	21	6	21	21	20	17	17	5	22
80	402	2	2	14	D	20	16	19	24	18	26	21	8	4	22	18	17	20	17	4	27	14	15	18
81	411	2	2	14	D	9	15	8	19	15	15	20	15	13	20	12	8	9	10	9	9	13	18	18
82	412	2	2	15	D	13	17	17	20	21	20	5	12	8	22	18	11	16	17	4	21	23	13	27
83	421	1	1	15	M	16	15	17	19	17	21	18	18	6	20	12	8	12	12	11	9	14	11	24
84	422	1	1	14	M	12	15	17	20	14	14	14	11	11	15	15	15	12	12	15	21	10	19	13
85	431	2	2	14	D	6	16	7	16	25	19	16	13	4	19	19	0	18	22	26	25	18	11	23
86	432	1	2	16	D	12	20	19	25	14	26	27	12	9	16	13	10	18	12	15	16	16	4	26
87	441	2	2	16	M	17	16	19	22	25	21	21	13	8	15	21	13	18	12	10	17	16	3	19
88	442	2	2	16	M	22	18	28	24	23	26	19	6	9	18	24	16	18	18	18	22	10	8	20
89	451	1	2	16	M	20	23	24	29	25	22	14	12	0	15	16	20	18	15	5	15	15	12	22
90	452	2	2	15	D	14	21	23	27	23	22	12	9	5	16	9	15	14	16	10	14	14	2	20
91	461	2	2	15	D	14	12	15	16	17	22	18	14	17	15	14	16	21	16	20	13	14	2	22
92	462	2	2	18	D	8	18	23	25	26	25	10	8	0	13	20	11	19	16	9	19	19	1	20
93	471	2	1	18	D	8	20	23	30	16	26	25	18	11	23	18	4	18	18	6	22	12	20	24
94	472	1	1	16	O	15	14	12	24	22	22	21	14	1	21	16	11	13	14	7	19	19	9	25
95	481	1	1	16	M	12	17	17	23	16	17	17	12	5	16	18	7	12	10	12	14	14	3	28
96	482	2	1	15	M	11	14	14	23	14	19	13	14	7	15	13	11	10	14	13	15	0	0	27
97	5001	2	1	18	M	13	12	22	20	21	22	14	13	4	17	15	0	12	12	8	18	18	4	0
98	5002	2	1	18	M	13	16	19	25	0	24	14	12	5	17	19	7	10	14	16	18	12	10	29
99	5011	2	1	14	O	16	12	16	17	20	18	14	16	10	15	13	13	16	22	6	22	14	10	29
100	5012	2	1	13	D	3	19	21	24	21	25	14	8	6	18	21	10	20	15	16	20	20	9	24
101	5021	2	2	16	M	16	16	16	27	22	29	8	12	6	21	24	16	19	21	6	0	20	5	14
102	5022	2	1	16	M	15	18	21	23	24	24	18	13	1	16	25	11	17	18	18	28	10	8	18
103	5031	2	2	14	D	18	16	16	26	16	12	19	19	10	14	16	13	20	19	20	22	16	1	20
104	5032	2	1	13	D	3	10	21	25	16	24	9	8	6	21	19	16	17	24	6	20	16	8	26
105	5041	1	2	16	O	16	18	18	26	24	25	7	12	1	20	27	11	20	19	18	28	16	5	18
106	5042	2	1	16	D	16	19	16	25	16	12	19	13	10	14	16	11	17	18	20	22	16	1	20
107	5051	1	1	17	M	15	19	10	25	24	24	9	13	1	14	19	5	20	19	20	22	16	26	18
108	5052	2	2	17	M	17	14	13	21	19	24	11	11	1	13	12	5	17	17	12	20	0	5	27

OBS	ID	SEX	RACE	AGE	ZYG	_67	_68	_69	_70	_71	_72	_73	_74	_75	_76	_77	_78	_79	_80	_81	_82	_83	_84	_85
109	5061	2	1	14	D	12	11	21	23	15	20	24	11	4	19	11	8	10	13	13	18	13	3	29
110	5062	2	1	14	D	11	20	18	25	19	24	21	12	5	21	15	13	14	18	9	22	15	5	28
111	5071	2	1	17	D	12	20	21	22	22	25	16	14	5	14	20	13	15	20	5	25	17	10	22
112	5072	1	1	17	D	7	19	24	24	19	26	25	13	7	19	20	19	23	21	10	19	20	8	25
113	5081	1	1	17	M	11	15	19	19	20	22	12	8	6	15	12	8	14	13	12	19	22	5	25
114	5082	1	1	17	M	13	10	20	20	16	18	11	9	6	16	13	8	11	9	16	15	15	2	25
115	5091	2	1	13	M	10	12	13	21	14	23	27	7	6	15	22	7	11	11	15	12	11	4	0
116	5092	2	1	14	D	18	11	12	17	13	15	12	0	12	13	16	11	11	9	14	11	14	0	30
117	5101	2	1	14	D	14	13	17	29	12	14	17	9	13	11	23	2	11	17	13	11	21	7	17
118	5102	2	1	15	D	17	22	11	23	23	23	27	21	23	18	16	14	24	11	13	29	11	11	11
119	5111	1	1	15	D	16	12	24	21	15	15	16	10	6	13	19	9	13	26	8	16	11	9	30
120	5112	1	1	20	D	7	14	21	27	24	19	11	11	6	23	17	6	16	26	13	22	18	11	19
121	5131	1	1	15	D	8	15	13	18	18	24	15	10	10	13	13	15	20	14	20	18	19	6	28
122	5132	1	1	20	D	16	11	16	25	20	20	14	10	6	22	19	9	10	12	14	16	15	6	27
123	5141	1	1	15	D	14	14	13	17	12	13	10	11	7	12	13	8	8	12	15	16	13	3	29
124	5142	2	2	17	M	12	11	16	19	13	17	9	13	3	13	16	7	9	16	13	16	11	5	27
125	5151	2	2	17	M	10	21	19	30	14	21	10	12	4	12	14	8	10	10	15	12	16	9	21
126	5152	2	2	13	M	18	18	15	26	25	18	12	9	9	16	20	6	9	13	14	15	17	10	0
127	5161	1	1	13	D	19	12	14	24	16	19	12	9	9	17	20	15	15	20	12	18	16	9	29
128	5162	1	1	17	D	11	15	16	25	15	27	15	14	13	20	16	17	20	10	14	18	13	10	23
129	5171	2	2	13	M	22	18	15	19	0	22	10	23	6	21	21	16	13	14	13	16	15	8	26
130	5172	2	2	13	M	17	12	19	22	26	24	17	16	15	24	14	16	16	20	14	17	15	6	21
131	5181	2	2	16	D	14	17	23	25	23	26	20	13	8	21	14	13	10	14	14	24	21	8	26
132	5182	2	2	14	D	13	12	19	22	21	18	13	13	6	18	21	14	12	10	14	14	11	6	29
133	5191	1	1	13	D	17	12	16	13	14	17	7	14	10	5	15	13	19	12	12	18	0	0	23
134	5192	1	1	13	D	17	12	20	28	19	26	27	14	15	18	23	16	12	19	7	16	16	9	20
135	5201	1	1	15	D	9	16	19	24	18	15	10	7	14	18	19	13	13	10	18	14	12	14	19
136	5202	1	1	15	M	4	13	14	29	27	27	18	17	4	25	18	9	18	20	15	21	24	10	10
137	5211	2	1	13	M	11	22	15	24	18	20	8	12	3	12	20	7	12	14	13	19	13	20	20
138	5212	2	1	13	D	8	8	16	20	16	23	11	8	1	17	12	8	12	9	11	13	16	2	20
139	5221	1	1	18	C	14	19	16	24	22	20	13	17	5	23	16	10	20	15	7	14	11	6	18
140	5222	1	1	13	M	13	18	18	22	23	24	19	16	5	18	21	11	13	20	9	16	20	9	20
141	5231	2	2	14	M	12	21	27	27	20	25	17	16	3	16	20	8	11	20	8	21	15	0	29
142	5232	2	2	14	M	11	19	23	19	23	26	20	19	12	22	17	8	11	19	14	20	14	9	22
143	5241	1	1	14	D	11	21	20	27	19	18	14	14	2	16	21	16	11	17	16	16	17	11	20
144	5242	1	1	13	D	20	19	23	19	24	17	21	10	5	22	24	5	15	13	7	13	9	18	20
145	5251	2	1	13	D	21	20	20	23	26	23	24	14	8	14	10	16	20	14	18	19	14	10	25
146	5252	2	1	16	M	13	15	20	20	15	14	21	10	11	19	18	12	17	15	15	16	11	6	26
147	5261	2	1	16	M	12	19	19	16	23	22	12	14	6	18	13	13	15	20	13	20	18	4	28
148	5262	2	1	16	M	11	18	16	20	15	24	21	14	4	17	24	12	18	14	11	21	18	5	28
149	5271	1	1	16	D	19	14	18	16	13	20	15	9	11	11	10	13	13	13	9	17	11	7	24
150	5272	1	1	17	D	9	19	16	25	27	27	21	16	6	14	18	9	18	13	11	14	20	5	24
151	5281	2	2	17	D	13	12	18	17	17	22	15	16	4	15	14	11	17	16	11	16	13	8	27
152	5282	2	2	18	M	16	11	12	20	18	20	12	12	15	12	16	12	15	13	7	14	11	6	24
153	5291	1	1	18	D	16	16	19	24	19	25	9	13	19	19	15	11	18	11	9	16	17	8	27
154	5292	1	1	13	D	13	21	12	24	17	22	13	9	14	14	24	12	17	17	7	23	13	8	17
155	5301	1	1	13	M	16	22	21	24	22	25	15	17	24	21	20	7	15	11	8	22	20	12	27
156	5302	1	1	14	M	13	9	20	24	14	15	13	14	2	11	7	13	18	17	14	11	20	12	25
157	5311	2	2	14	M	12	8	19	24	14	13	0	10	0	15	7	9	22	9	17	8	12	9	28
158	5312	2	2	14	M	15	15	14	19	12	22	13	17	0	19	18	0	4	8	12	19	11	4	4
159	5321	2	2	16	M	22	16	15	27	18	23	13	10	12	14	15	13	13	17	15	9	9	12	0
160	5322	2	2	17	M	14	16	18	17	16	23	21	11	5	15	14	20	20	16	13	19	13	9	25
161	5331	2	1	16	M	14	0	14	0	21	23	14	11	15	15	14	9	17	14	18	18	12	12	27
162	5332	2	1	17	M	10	16	14	14	19	20	12	9	5	19	8	8	16	14	12	13	14	6	27

OBS	ID	SEX	RACE	AGE	ZYG	_67	_68	_69	_70	_71	_72	_73	_74	_75	_76	_77	_78	_79	_80	_81	_82	_83	_84	_85
163	5341	2	2	13	D	18	16	20	27	12	25	12	10	9	19	12	3	3	13	10	19	14	8	20
164	5342	2	1	13	D	.	.	.	.	.	.	.	.	.	.	.	.	.	.	.	.	.	.	.
165	5351	2	1	16	D	16	13	25	29	26	23	22	4	8	14	11	12	16	17	13	10	11	4	24
166	5352	2	1	16	D	11	16	21	25	23	19	16	9	5	18	11	9	12	18	10	18	17	6	25
167	5361	1	1	17	M	19	12	15	19	16	21	18	15	7	17	20	11	18	11	12	17	16	15	27
168	5362	1	1	17	M	19	24	17	19	19	21	17	11	20	17	18	17	15	20	13	16	16	9	24
169	5371	1	1	17	D	13	18	21	24	13	21	17	11	2	12	17	8	15	10	10	12	16	6	27
170	5372	1	1	17	D	13	18	21	23	21	24	16	12	17	17	21	9	17	17	3	16	15	6	21
171	5381	1	1	13	M	.	.	.	.	.	.	.	.	.	.	.	.	.	.	.	.	.	.	.
172	5382	2	1	13	D	13	13	13	17	16	20	11	9	4	14	12	8	11	10	12	14	14	5	28
173	5391	2	1	15	M	13	15	15	21	13	17	9	12	7	15	12	11	9	8	9	13	14	2	29
174	5392	1	1	15	D	17	20	16	22	12	23	17	15	11	15	17	13	20	14	14	16	13	14	17
175	5401	1	1	14	D	16	18	16	27	18	22	19	11	12	14	11	12	9	12	11	12	18	24	21
176	5402	1	1	14	D	17	11	16	13	13	22	8	12	13	16	15	16	20	16	14	13	11	8	27
177	5411	2	1	12	D	9	12	10	15	13	16	13	11	17	14	15	16	16	20	10	13	10	0	0
178	5412	2	1	12	M	15	13	13	15	22	16	18	14	9	16	18	10	14	15	17	17	15	19	18
179	5421	1	1	15	O	15	12	17	15	12	13	11	7	13	15	10	10	16	13	13	13	13	10	27
180	5422	1	1	15	D	14	13	20	20	12	20	18	16	0	18	18	16	20	16	17	21	13	6	26
181	5431	1	1	14	M	14	20	22	22	16	21	18	17	6	15	14	20	18	15	12	17	21	0	21
182	5432	1	1	14	D	0	15	16	22	23	21	18	14	8	17	15	16	16	16	14	23	14	10	26
183	5441	1	1	14	M	23	16	14	19	14	19	14	18	10	16	13	16	18	12	16	17	12	0	0
184	5442	1	1	18	D	16	14	9	23	15	20	16	14	9	15	15	11	11	13	16	16	16	7	0
185	5451	1	1	17	M	11	21	0	23	20	17	24	12	4	18	21	15	15	14	11	16	14	12	30
186	5452	1	2	17	M	14	14	18	17	17	18	13	10	5	16	16	10	14	13	15	13	15	5	29
187	5461	1	1	16	M	14	13	17	23	20	18	20	12	7	19	17	7	14	16	0	25	16	1	28
188	5462	1	1	16	M	15	14	8	17	17	20	14	18	4	9	19	10	16	18	16	21	15	7	30
189	5471	2	1	17	M	10	13	16	23	23	21	21	18	10	12	21	12	0	0	15	17	13	5	26
190	5472	1	1	16	M	15	17	20	26	16	22	0	10	8	0	14	10	16	15	20	18	19	5	0
191	5481	1	1	17	M	14	0	24	20	0	23	13	14	0	18	0	0	15	13	17	20	17	4	0
192	5482	2	1	14	O	21	0	20	20	14	14	13	13	11	13	0	12	16	16	15	20	17	0	30
193	5491	2	1	14	D	15	13	26	15	20	18	15	9	8	12	18	9	16	18	12	15	14	8	24
194	5492	1	1	15	D	12	12	17	19	16	18	11	12	5	14	16	10	16	16	13	12	17	10	28
195	5511	1	1	15	M	15	18	13	27	16	27	11	13	16	18	18	13	18	18	12	19	16	5	17
196	5512	2	2	13	M	22	18	24	24	28	17	17	0	12	18	19	22	19	19	13	13	17	19	17
197	5521	2	2	16	M	14	0	22	22	15	26	12	14	2	10	17	13	11	11	15	13	22	25	26
198	5522	1	1	16	M	21	12	0	25	20	24	17	0	6	0	22	8	4	10	15	20	17	8	25
199	5531	2	1	16	M	14	14	22	25	13	26	16	8	12	15	9	18	10	16	11	10	8	8	22
200	5532	1	1	16	O	21	8	26	14	9	17	6	13	13	12	13	12	16	14	13	12	14	8	25
201	5541	2	1	17	D	12	16	17	0	20	17	17	10	11	14	18	13	18	16	18	15	9	14	0
202	5542	1	1	16	M	15	0	25	23	18	25	12	0	17	18	13	11	10	10	16	12	16	18	15
203	5551	1	1	16	D	15	8	15	23	18	28	17	14	11	18	15	4	8	11	11	13	16	10	0
204	5552	1	1	17	D	9	0	0	0	0	0	0	0	0	0	0	18	10	0	15	20	10	4	23
205	5571	2	1	15	M	12	8	9	29	21	20	12	8	12	10	12	18	11	15	13	10	18	18	18
206	5572	2	2	15	M	19	15	20	0	15	16	17	9	17	15	16	20	13	17	10	10	19	15	23
207	5581	1	1	16	M	16	17	20	13	21	20	15	12	14	22	12	9	14	13	20	19	20	24	24
208	5582	2	1	16	D	15	16	25	21	17	17	12	16	7	12	12	7	15	11	9	20	17	8	25
209	5591	1	1	16	M	11	15	18	21	19	18	12	3	8	12	13	10	15	13	13	14	8	8	24
210	5592	1	1	16	D	21	9	21	25	13	23	15	8	6	14	18	17	16	14	16	15	9	7	29
211	5601	1	1	15	D	12	0	11	14	20	18	12	13	7	17	19	8	18	10	12	12	7	11	21
212	5602	2	1	17	D	10	15	17	9	11	18	15	8	4	10	16	11	10	12	20	20	12	5	15
213	5611	2	1	17	M	16	9	16	17	23	26	19	13	5	16	19	13	16	12	14	14	19	7	29
214	5612	1	1	16	D	17	10	17	25	23	20	12	12	4	15	15	12	13	13	11	12	9	3	27
215	5621	1	1	16	M	17	12	16	22	23	0	14	14	5	15	16	11	12	11	13	19	9	6	27
216	5622	2	2	16	M	13	12	19	0	0	19	15	11	5	15	16	9	13	0	14	18	11	6	30

231

OBS	ID	SEX	RACE	AGE	ZYG	_67	_68	_69	_70	_71	_72	_73	_74	_75	_76	_77	_78	_79	_80	_81	_82	_83	_84	_85
217	5631	2	2	14	M	12	8	18	17	14	24	9	6	6	14	24	11	18	16	7	13	14	16	11
218	5632	2	2	14	M	7	13	11	25	20	26	12	7	13	17	0	15	16	24	12	24	15	0	16
219	5641	2	1	13	O	20	16	21	20	15	17	16	14	17	16	14	14	15	16	16	11	15	7	23
220	5642	2	1	13	M	17	16	17	20	24	24	22	14	8	20	17	18	16	10	9	22	17	3	24
221	5661	2	1	17	D	13	23	23	28	25	22	17	7	20	23	23	11	24	12	10	20	13	1	23
222	5662	2	1	17	M	15	16	18	25	19	18	15	11	5	15	12	6	15	17	19	13	15	4	28
223	5671	2	1	13	O	6	11	18	9	16	17	17	13	7	15	7	11	10	12	19	20	15	13	22
224	5672	2	1	13	D	12	13	16	15	13	12	12	13	13	15	12	13	9	11	15	13	14	6	23
225	5681	1	1	15	M	20	22	24	25	25	25	0	11	12	8	19	17	0	18	15	10	18	15	25
226	5682	1	1	15	M	16	24	26	25	22	17	16	20	15	19	22	7	25	14	17	21	16	15	22
227	5691	2	1	17	D	13	14	20	22	20	21	15	10	3	17	16	9	12	23	15	20	21	0	26
228	5692	2	1	17	D	0	19	16	19	19	24	15	13	1	18	15	14	8	16	17	20	18	4	0
229	5701	2	2	13	D	12	8	14	14	24	21	11	12	10	20	13	5	5	12	7	14	15	12	21
230	5702	2	1	13	D	12	11	20	19	21	17	21	14	5	16	19	9	9	11	18	10	13	0	28
231	5711	2	1	16	C	23	12	18	12	21	22	17	10	16	13	13	7	0	10	12	16	12	5	22
232	5712	2	1	15	D	10	14	14	14	14	17	9	0	8	15	11	6	9	12	15	15	13	0	28
233	5721	2	1	13	D	14	17	13	15	21	19	17	15	16	17	15	9	16	10	3	18	16	3	0
234	5722	2	1	13	D	11	20	14	17	13	16	16	13	11	14	11	10	14	0	9	13	11	12	25
235	5731	2	2	13	D	11	15	23	23	14	15	22	14	9	21	22	6	17	12	13	11	18	11	21
236	5732	2	1	15	D	16	18	17	20	16	17	14	14	7	17	15	9	14	13	10	15	14	14	15
237	5741	2	1	13	D	18	19	16	12	16	17	0	13	16	15	11	6	16	8	13	12	12	12	27
238	5742	2	1	15	D	13	12	0	10	17	16	16	12	18	21	20	18	13	18	14	14	13	8	25
239	5751	2	1	13	D	13	18	22	21	0	18	0	13	9	15	19	6	12	15	14	20	14	8	26
740	5752	2	1	13	M	14	17	18	13	20	15	15	12	6	22	16	13	10	15	16	14	14	8	26
241	5761	2	2	13	M	14	15	15	21	19	16	21	11	4	15	12	8	8	14	15	18	15	6	29
242	5762	2	2	13	D	14	16	16	24	17	22	13	13	6	18	19	9	12	18	21	21	17	3	29
243	5771	2	2	16	O	14	0	0	26	18	23	18	13	10	14	17	14	0	18	16	16	17	6	0
244	5772	2	1	16	M	7	14	18	29	23	18	12	9	6	16	11	13	12	15	9	15	15	1	22
245	5781	2	1	16	M	12	19	22	28	22	28	9	9	10	18	21	15	15	18	9	18	17	3	19
246	5782	2	1	16	D	13	15	19	13	22	14	19	9	1	14	21	12	14	19	15	10	20	1	30
247	5791	2	2	17	D	22	12	20	17	20	19	17	6	12	14	13	10	23	13	23	10	12	3	28
248	5792	2	1	17	D	14	17	19	17	15	20	11	12	13	16	18	10	16	18	10	21	16	3	27
249	5801	2	2	18	D	14	16	17	20	18	18	13	11	10	15	19	8	14	15	20	15	12	3	30
250	5802	2	2	18	D	15	19	17	23	21	19	16	15	4	16	13	7	10	12	10	11	16	2	26
251	5811	1	1	18	M	10	14	23	25	21	19	26	9	7	17	18	9	19	14	15	19	12	5	25
252	5812	1	1	18	M	14	13	18	14	14	18	11	10	9	18	11	15	8	20	9	17	13	5	26
253	5821	2	1	15	O	15	15	20	23	12	15	20	13	13	17	9	16	11	10	14	12	20	13	28
254	5822	2	2	15	D	10	12	25	18	17	21	16	0	11	18	13	11	10	14	15	16	11	4	26
255	5841	2	1	15	M	11	7	18	18	14	16	0	9	10	17	0	12	9	20	15	12	20	13	23
256	5842	2	1	15	M	10	11	14	15	12	16	10	13	1	16	13	10	4	10	11	16	11	5	29
257	5861	2	1	17	D	11	0	16	19	14	16	18	0	7	18	18	10	17	11	10	14	13	7	26
258	5862	2	1	18	M	12	20	30	19	16	21	14	13	12	20	24	10	23	11	10	21	14	5	27
259	5871	2	1	18	D	13	14	18	24	21	24	13	0	3	20	23	13	16	14	15	20	20	7	26
260	5872	2	2	16	O	13	16	0	24	18	0	11	11	9	21	18	8	18	13	10	15	20	4	29
261	5881	2	1	16	O	16	16	14	24	15	19	18	16	8	16	19	6	13	14	8	15	12	8	24
262	5882	2	2	16	D	11	10	15	20	16	19	13	15	4	14	12	6	17	11	12	16	14	0	0
263	5891	2	2	16	M	13	21	18	23	21	21	13	14	6	13	10	0	13	11	13	17	11	5	27
264	5892	2	1	17	M	16	13	20	22	19	21	13	14	6	18	16	11	17	18	13	18	13	9	29
265	5901	2	1	17	M	11	15	19	23	21	19	0	16	6	14	10	1	11	16	14	15	15	10	30
266	5902	2	1	14	M	21	17	27	18	14	21	14	16	10	16	10	8	14	19	14	14	12	5	28
267	5921	2	1	14	M	16	15	19	23	19	22	16	12	6	16	17	7	13	16	13	14	13	5	27
268	5922	2	1	14	D	14	14	19	23	17	19	16	13	9	14	16	9	14	15	13	13	15	5	0
269	5931	2	1	16	D	16	17	17	19	16	19	16	0	6	14	16	10	13	15	13	16	15	0	26
270	5932	1	1	16	D	6	20	21	17	17	23	14	12	5	20	17	8	13	9	13	16	17	4	26

OBS	ID	SEX	RACE	AGE	ZYG	_67	_68	_69	_70	_71	_72	_73	_74	_75	_76	_77	_78	_79	_80	_81	_82	_83	_84	_85
271	5941	2	1	15	M	0	16	18	19	16	16	15	11	6	13	18	11	17	11	9	12	13	3	0
272	5942	2	1	15	D	14	13	18	19	13	20	16	12	4	13	15	8	14	11	7	15	14	5	29
273	5951	1	1	13	D	11	16	19	27	17	19	19	14	10	18	18	10	16	15	15	18	19	6	28
274	5952	1	1	13	D	13	11	17	19	15	16	17	14	5	15	11	11	15	20	14	17	10	1	27
275	5961	2	1	15	D	13	22	22	27	20	23	24	14	12	14	18	12	14	20	14	17	15	6	24
276	5962	2	1	16	D	16	14	16	16	16	16	13	15	5	15	11	8	12	13	8	16	15	5	30
277	5971	2	1	16	D	14	11	17	26	22	26	15	16	11	19	19	4	13	13	11	14	14	3	28
278	5972	2	1	18	M	9	16	19	26	27	26	15	16	4	14	21	18	20	24	8	18	19	11	13
279	5981	2	1	18	M	6	17	23	24	22	24	22	16	8	20	18	10	22	13	9	14	17	2	20
280	5982	2	1	14	D	9	19	24	30	23	24	13	10	0	15	24	18	14	24	11	18	21	5	19
281	5991	1	1	15	D	13	22	28	23	23	22	14	20	7	23	17	13	12	15	14	13	10	6	28
282	5992	2	1	15	M	17	20	24	17	17	25	18	12	0	17	18	13	14	12	17	10	16	6	23
283	6001	1	1	16	D	16	14	19	18	15	19	19	10	7	18	15	16	11	15	11	16	0	9	28
284	6002	2	1	16	D	13	13	17	16	13	18	17	10	9	12	12	13	11	13	14	16	16	2	28
285	6011	2	1	16	M	0	17	14	0	8	17	17	12	8	12	15	16	10	13	14	0	0	10	0
286	6012	2	1	16	M	12	2	18	24	11	19	10	9	8	12	0	6	7	11	12	14	16	0	25
287	6021	1	1	16	D	17	12	13	13	18	12	7	15	1	22	12	12	10	10	22	8	24	11	20
288	6022	2	1	13	M	11	8	12	19	24	15	8	7	7	24	11	9	11	19	13	0	13	3	22
289	6031	2	1	15	M	8	17	20	14	19	20	9	12	5	14	18	10	12	11	14	15	12	5	26
290	6032	1	1	16	D	14	14	23	25	13	23	10	10	6	14	19	0	16	15	12	13	15	8	28
291	6041	1	1	16	D	14	18	19	19	21	18	11	12	7	21	19	15	12	18	18	22	22	7	25
292	6042	2	1	15	D	18	19	15	21	19	17	8	13	11	20	10	10	9	14	14	20	16	10	18
293	6051	2	1	16	D	21	16	13	26	18	25	27	7	4	11	17	17	11	16	17	24	14	8	27
294	6052	2	1	15	M	7	12	10	10	14	19	17	7	4	13	11	8	7	11	14	17	16	6	23
295	6061	1	1	16	M	10	15	20	22	15	20	15	13	7	12	11	9	13	10	17	12	21	1	28
296	6062	1	1	15	D	14	12	17	21	23	23	16	11	6	19	15	7	11	22	12	20	12	8	24
297	6071	1	1	15	D	12	16	21	21	27	26	17	5	6	20	22	9	17	5	19	14	14	5	16
298	6072	1	2	14	M	15	12	15	21	22	20	21	10	13	14	15	11	16	7	9	17	17	10	21
299	6081	2	1	14	M	15	0	16	15	17	18	17	13	8	17	18	9	13	10	20	21	11	6	29
300	6082	1	1	14	D	19	19	21	21	20	24	13	13	9	16	10	10	0	12	17	20	13	4	25
301	6101	2	2	16	M	15	16	17	19	15	18	5	15	7	14	13	20	15	11	20	17	16	12	25
302	6102	2	1	16	D	12	18	17	20	17	20	9	10	12	16	15	15	14	12	10	13	12	8	25
303	6111	1	1	13	M	23	11	21	18	18	17	18	18	11	17	16	9	19	11	19	18	13	6	29
304	6112	1	1	16	M	7	14	17	20	21	20	14	15	4	16	17	8	10	14	9	14	16	5	30
305	6121	2	1	16	M	13	18	17	22	21	18	17	10	6	16	13	11	19	12	11	18	12	6	29
306	6122	1	1	13	M	16	13	17	18	17	17	14	18	5	17	15	11	10	11	12	16	13	3	27
307	6131	1	2	16	D	16	15	20	24	25	23	17	18	5	20	17	15	19	14	11	13	13	9	27
308	6132	1	1	16	D	14	18	14	19	18	21	16	15	7	16	16	11	10	12	12	16	13	2	30
309	6141	1	1	15	M	16	18	23	24	25	23	13	15	8	15	14	8	18	14	12	16	11	5	28
310	6142	1	1	16	M	13	14	19	26	18	15	17	11	4	12	14	12	14	13	19	19	17	9	27
311	6151	1	1	16	M	14	17	18	18	11	19	13	11	7	17	18	11	14	14	12	23	11	4	28
312	6152	1	1	14	D	13	13	20	23	21	19	25	11	9	19	14	8	18	17	16	14	20	8	27
313	6161	2	1	16	M	22	15	15	25	20	22	17	18	4	17	17	12	13	17	9	11	13	4	24
314	6162	1	2	19	D	18	19	17	26	16	21	14	13	9	18	16	10	12	9	12	17	9	12	18
315	6171	1	1	18	M	11	15	17	15	15	22	6	14	2	14	13	7	10	10	14	20	20	11	21
316	6172	2	1	18	D	12	11	23	21	23	23	11	12	8	14	12	10	7	13	18	16	16	17	20
317	6181	1	1	18	D	20	14	19	25	17	20	12	15	3	17	16	6	10	23	13	15	15	4	29
318	6182	2	1	18	M	23	19	19	24	12	19	15	10	12	12	19	7	23	12	18	20	12	7	0
319	6191	2	1	18	M	7	17	10	20	13	21	18	13	4	17	19	27	12	10	14	14	16	5	21
320	6192	2	2	15	M	15	15	16	16	12	12	17	10	12	8	8	8	10	11	13	13	17	6	25
321	6201	2	2	15	D	10	10	18	18	13	11	18	11	12	9	12	12	8	18	7	18	17	8	25
322	6202	2	1	15	D	17	0	21	22	10	16	11	11	17	5	14	0	9	10	0	0	14	0	24
323	6211	2	1	15	M	17	16	18	24	15	16	13	11	12	21	17	6	8	15	21	13	12	2	23
324	6212	2	1	15	D	15	22	18	22	24	21	14	19	3	21	0	11	17	20	9	21	19	10	0

OBS	ID	SEX	RACE	AGE	ZYG	_67	_68	_69	_70	_71	_72	_73	_74	_75	_76	_77	_78	_79	_80	_81	_82	_83	_84	_85
325	6221	2	1	14	D	8	17	22	23	17	20	11	12	8	17	18	5	12	13	9	18	11	10	24
326	6222	2	1	14	D	14	15	17	18	17	16	16	13	9	14	14	10	12	13	14	18	12	7	30
327	6231	1	1	17	D	17	18	23	30	0	20	7	17	1	18	15	11	18	23	0	19	21	0	21
328	6232	1	1	17	D	12	21	6	24	25	19	15	0	20	16	16	9	10	8	6	19	18	6	22
329	6241	1	1	17	D	10	15	16	18	11	21	10	15	9	15	15	12	19	14	21	12	12	4	23
330	6242	1	1	17	M	9	14	28	24	14	17	16	0	12	16	18	10	19	16	13	23	12	0	26
331	6251	1	1	15	M	26	12	24	25	0	23	13	13	7	15	19	16	19	18	21	16	18	15	19
332	6252	1	1	15	M	18	0	0	0	15	22	21	12	6	0	22	10	14	11	13	13	21	18	25
333	6261	1	1	16	M	11	17	16	16	20	21	13	15	13	19	27	12	25	22	6	16	17	7	29
334	6262	1	1	16	M	12	13	25	24	20	21	18	11	9	15	21	15	21	22	11	20	18	5	30
335	6271	1	1	15	M	16	27	22	17	22	28	21	13	2	13	24	16	25	25	11	30	15	11	12
336	6272	1	1	14	D	24	21	20	22	16	7	15	20	8	16	16	16	14	9	16	16	14	11	22
337	6281	1	1	14	D	17	15	17	24	22	24	15	15	15	22	16	6	14	13	11	16	10	3	25
338	6282	2	1	14	D	12	13	15	26	22	21	15	11	8	15	16	6	14	15	13	23	15	21	26
339	6291	1	2	14	M	11	15	14	13	8	0	29	7	23	22	21	14	16	8	20	18	13	22	15
340	6292	1	2	17	D	19	12	0	16	21	0	0	11	0	16	7	12	0	12	16	9	15	5	0
341	6301	1	1	17	M	14	14	14	18	14	13	16	13	8	16	15	7	13	15	8	13	13	5	30
342	6302	1	1	19	M	14	16	15	25	17	17	18	14	8	16	15	8	17	19	6	22	15	0	22
343	6311	1	1	19	D	24	16	15	16	24	21	20	16	18	22	11	11	17	24	20	17	21	17	19
344	6312	1	1	18	D	11	19	15	21	13	20	12	13	19	18	12	13	16	15	10	16	13	16	24
345	6321	1	2	18	D	19	13	15	14	17	16	9	9	0	18	15	2	17	16	14	22	13	1	21
346	6322	1	2	18	M	7	16	24	26	15	22	22	14	7	14	12	10	26	23	10	15	11	6	25
347	6331	1	1	15	D	16	14	25	18	14	19	16	14	11	17	15	8	11	11	14	19	15	4	30
348	6332	1	1	15	M	14	12	17	21	19	16	16	14	3	13	13	9	8	14	12	21	16	5	26
349	6341	1	1	16	D	10	14	0	18	13	16	9	7	6	14	14	7	8	11	0	13	12	10	0
350	6342	2	1	16	D	9	11	19	19	15	22	20	8	3	15	19	12	14	11	13	12	13	0	26
351	6351	2	2	16	D	5	18	18	14	21	26	6	9	1	16	12	7	9	19	11	18	18	5	27
352	6352	2	2	16	D	11	12	16	13	18	24	7	3	12	16	15	6	14	18	12	13	13	11	17
353	6361	1	1	15	D	25	15	14	14	17	18	13	12	0	13	15	0	9	14	7	20	14	12	20
354	6362	1	1	16	D	11	9	12	28	15	16	16	11	8	14	11	22	0	11	8	16	6	0	18
355	6371	1	1	16	D	8	15	20	15	12	20	13	12	4	0	10	10	8	11	10	19	15	2	28
356	6372	1	1	16	D	11	19	18	23	16	18	10	11	15	14	17	8	12	14	11	16	13	6	26
357	6381	2	1	15	M	17	20	16	24	15	22	16	17	8	19	17	9	14	16	18	18	20	0	28
358	6382	2	1	18	M	14	19	21	20	14	18	10	5	5	18	17	13	15	18	11	18	22	4	27
359	6391	2	1	18	M	12	20	19	26	17	19	10	19	4	15	16	10	13	17	0	20	15	10	22
360	6392	2	1	18	M	3	9	14	29	22	25	10	20	0	17	23	12	21	20	14	20	8	6	25
361	6401	2	2	18	D	6	20	27	25	20	17	11	10	2	10	17	11	16	15	9	16	14	12	10
362	6402	2	2	14	D	18	21	14	30	19	20	4	0	4	13	23	9	21	20	12	23	12	13	20
363	6411	1	1	14	D	10	16	0	0	24	23	23	6	2	25	21	6	16	15	9	16	14	5	28
364	6412	1	1	14	D	9	20	16	16	19	23	17	4	4	19	21	5	16	18	12	18	13	9	25
365	6431	1	1	17	D	8	17	21	25	20	25	20	8	3	17	13	10	12	12	19	17	18	4	29
366	6432	2	1	17	D	11	16	20	19	16	21	14	9	4	15	20	5	19	11	14	19	22	5	24
367	6441	2	1	17	M	16	14	20	27	21	26	16	6	12	15	21	13	21	15	9	17	11	3	27
368	6442	2	1	15	D	13	18	17	16	21	18	16	8	7	12	16	7	18	12	17	13	13	0	24
369	6451	1	1	15	M	11	15	21	24	16	20	18	13	10	13	13	17	12	16	12	15	13	5	28
370	6452	2	2	15	M	16	10	16	26	16	18	16	16	6	14	15	11	10	12	16	10	15	5	23
371	6461	2	1	15	D	14	16	9	9	15	22	12	0	13	17	16	13	11	13	22	22	14	5	22
372	6462	2	1	16	D	15	14	17	18	16	18	8	9	15	13	10	17	16	9	10	18	14	10	25
373	6471	1	1	16	D	14	10	18	17	17	19	19	15	9	10	17	11	15	11	3	21	13	10	16
374	6472	1	1	16	D	12	14	27	20	17	27	27	19	0	18	21	5	14	19	12	13	13	0	26
375	6481	1	1	16	D	12	18	14	16	15	17	14	10	10	19	12	13	13	13	18	15	13	0	26
376	6482	1	1	14	D	15	13	16	22	17	18	15	7	0	18	16	12	14	8	12	17	10	8	16
377	6491	2	1	14	D	21	19	21	29	23	24	15	10	10	17	21	11	21	13	15	16	19	2	27
378	6492	2	1	14	D	10	14	21	24	22	26	14	10	2	20	20	8	13	15	15	22	14		

OBS	ID	SEX	RACE	AGE	ZYG	_67	_68	_69	_70	_71	_72	_73	_74	_75	_76	_77	_78	_79	_80	_81	_82	_83	_84	_85
379	6501	1	1	17	M	10	15	20	15	13	17	10	10	8	16	12	8	9	10	10	13	13	0	0
380	6502	1	1	17	M	3	13	19	24	22	22	13	9	0	23	15	7	9	16	9	20	20	4	19
381	6511	1	1	15	M	17	14	17	18	17	23	20	24	0	18	18	5	11	20	20	17	17	14	26
382	6512	1	2	15	M	15	14	13	22	17	20	11	11	11	15	18	13	13	11	14	11	10	10	29
383	6521	1	2	15	D	19	22	15	19	21	23	16	11	18	18	13	8	23	14	8	16	12	7	29
384	6522	2	1	15	D	11	15	25	23	22	20	10	10	5	17	14	12	15	14	9	25	15	5	27
385	6531	2	1	16	D	.	15	6	26	14	22	10	10	7	17	10	18	27	25	10	25	0	20	0
386	6532	2	1	16	D	.	.	.	.	.	.	.	.	.	.	.	.	.	.	.	.	.	.	.
387	6541	1	1	16	D	14	15	20	17	18	13	12	12	6	13	13	10	13	15	14	14	14	6	29
388	6542	1	1	16	M	.	17	12	22	20	0	20	0	5	17	13	10	12	12	14	14	11	11	0
389	6551	2	1	17	M	26	13	30	21	12	19	12	12	5	20	13	13	11	12	29	22	18	0	24
390	6552	2	1	17	M	12	18	24	28	22	21	18	7	6	16	15	15	14	10	13	20	22	5	27
391	6561	1	1	14	M	15	13	21	21	19	24	24	12	6	16	13	15	14	14	10	21	10	3	29
392	6562	1	1	14	M	16	18	19	25	18	25	15	14	11	19	9	11	17	14	8	15	11	7	17
393	6571	1	1	17	M	6	12	25	23	21	27	14	3	10	14	18	7	3	12	21	26	23	11	19
394	6572	1	1	17	M	17	12	24	16	23	22	14	15	14	14	26	4	20	6	10	22	16	6	23
395	6581	2	1	17	D	15	19	20	24	19	22	15	6	1	17	13	4	8	16	11	20	17	4	21
396	6582	2	1	17	D	16	13	18	21	16	23	14	14	3	18	15	4	12	16	12	11	15	2	28
397	6591	1	1	16	D	8	24	18	23	25	26	21	0	7	18	19	6	18	18	6	23	16	4	26
398	6592	1	1	13	D	14	11	15	18	14	18	13	14	3	23	15	4	12	8	0	15	14	6	23
399	6601	1	1	13	D	15	14	17	23	18	20	14	0	2	22	15	8	8	15	12	18	20	0	21
400	6602	2	1	13	M	10	0	20	24	19	22	23	15	2	19	20	7	20	24	10	25	17	4	28
401	6611	2	1	18	M	14	15	13	26	13	19	15	12	7	17	14	6	14	13	11	14	12	4	25
402	6612	2	1	18	D	16	17	23	19	21	22	19	9	3	17	12	8	10	12	16	19	14	4	25
403	6621	2	1	18	D	11	16	19	17	18	24	19	11	7	13	19	9	13	14	19	13	12	7	23
404	6622	2	1	18	D	16	16	14	22	18	20	5	11	11	19	13	9	16	16	17	17	12	25	25
405	6631	2	1	14	M	14	20	12	15	16	21	16	18	13	19	17	13	16	20	18	13	18	10	26
406	6632	2	1	14	M	20	21	18	18	13	17	20	18	19	19	15	12	16	11	13	15	20	15	26
407	6641	1	1	19	D	16	21	17	14	13	23	20	23	3	17	12	12	14	16	15	17	21	0	25
408	6642	1	1	19	D	23	22	22	0	0	22	15	18	5	13	12	12	20	14	13	15	12	0	26
409	6651	1	1	18	M	18	11	18	18	9	18	23	12	9	10	19	13	14	20	14	15	19	2	30
410	6652	1	1	18	M	12	22	22	17	9	19	19	9	5	18	16	12	20	12	15	17	14	5	29
411	6661	2	1	18	D	11	11	16	19	17	19	19	8	9	19	14	10	14	20	9	14	14	5	29
412	6662	2	1	18	D	14	20	14	21	17	20	19	12	5	16	12	9	20	14	12	15	12	3	27
413	6671	1	1	15	M	13	12	20	25	20	22	19	6	3	20	17	18	12	15	16	16	18	5	25
414	6672	1	1	13	M	19	13	16	26	20	22	23	14	16	13	20	7	12	23	16	15	13	3	28
415	6681	2	1	13	D	18	15	17	22	25	24	13	18	3	15	18	12	22	8	19	23	27	6	23
416	6682	2	1	15	D	13	18	23	23	14	19	17	10	11	21	16	9	13	16	12	15	19	3	21
417	6691	1	1	15	D	11	16	19	15	20	16	16	11	5	13	24	12	18	12	16	20	14	5	29
418	6692	1	1	13	D	9	18	19	18	19	25	12	10	10	14	15	14	8	13	13	12	18	6	24
419	6701	2	1	13	M	14	18	16	17	16	17	16	10	9	10	15	10	11	17	14	21	14	4	25
420	6702	2	1	13	M	21	12	16	29	18	21	23	12	3	15	20	12	18	22	15	20	18	0	0
421	6711	1	1	13	M	12	23	17	17	17	25	14	22	10	20	19	12	8	14	14	12	14	6	28
422	6712	1	1	14	M	12	13	16	22	18	21	12	14	3	18	13	5	11	15	12	21	18	7	21
423	6721	1	1	14	M	0	13	23	22	12	23	12	12	10	22	15	9	6	12	10	21	11	0	0
424	6722	1	1	16	M	12	19	17	27	15	23	11	11	3	18	17	11	11	15	17	13	11	6	22
425	6731	2	1	16	M	12	20	14	24	18	15	12	12	7	22	17	7	17	12	15	18	15	4	28
426	6732	2	1	16	D	10	15	23	26	21	22	12	12	5	16	13	6	13	14	10	17	16	3	29
427	6741	1	1	17	M	8	19	19	24	21	23	22	10	4	18	17	5	15	13	12	16	17	2	29
428	6742	1	1	17	M	14	17	22	26	24	23	12	13	3	15	20	7	13	14	7	15	12	7	19
429	6751	2	1	15	M	11	21	16	26	23	21	10	13	5	16	18	11	15	13	9	18	16	3	26
430	6752	2	1	17	D	16	0	21	26	16	19	19	12	4	16	20	11	17	15	6	13	15	12	22
431	6771	2	1	17	M	16	12	16	24	10	14	16	0	6	13	14	0	18	19	14	12	16	3	28
432	6772	1	1	17	D	.	.	.	.	.	.	.	.	17	13	14	0	18	19	.	12	16	7	28

OBS	ID	SEX	RACE	AGE	ZYG	_67	_68	_69	_70	_71	_72	_73	_74	_75	_76	_77	_78	_79	_80	_81	_82	_83	_84	_85
433	6781	1	1	14	D	18	15	15	14	18	20	18	20	22	16	12	9	15	12	16	17	20	21	20
434	6782	1	1	14	D	13	19	14	19	13	14	6	12	6	16	13	9	8	12	10	16	14	6	28
435	6791	2	1	16	M	14	10	11	23	19	20	0	17	3	17	19	10	15	12	8	21	9	8	25
436	6792	2	1	16	M	13	11	17	26	18	21	18	9	8	19	20	19	13	13	16	13	12	5	26
437	6801	1	1	15	M	19	16	11	23	14	16	13	13	15	14	13	11	12	0	16	17	11	10	27
438	6802	2	1	15	M	15	14	13	26	13	16	16	13	5	22	15	11	13	13	19	16	10	3	30
439	6811	2	1	16	M	18	13	23	0	13	29	19	15	0	15	26	17	20	5	8	19	18	6	20
440	6812	1	1	16	M	14	18	0	29	30	23	7	11	4	17	24	9	19	21	16	20	23	8	0
441	6841	1	1	13	D	17	12	17	20	17	21	19	9	13	15	18	8	19	21	11	20	17	10	28
442	6842	1	1	13	D	15	16	21	27	20	18	16	10	4	21	12	15	12	18	12	23	17	10	0
443	6851	1	1	15	M	23	18	17	28	20	26	30	10	8	22	19	15	23	12	4	22	11	18	29
444	6852	2	1	16	M	.	22	20	30	26	30	23	15	.	18	23	7	23	10	0	20	.	.	0
445	6861	1	2	16	M	16	27	18	24	28	27	13	13	4	19	22	16	23	10	6	18	25	12	18
446	6862	2	2	16	M	13	13	15	15	14	6	6	1	2	18	14	14	23	9	5	8	19	3	23
447	6871	1	1	19	M	21	0	10	24	14	25	17	8	6	15	19	13	12	17	0	16	13	4	0
448	6872	2	1	19	M	9	15	20	26	22	23	19	7	0	15	19	10	10	12	17	22	17	5	26
449	6881	1	1	14	M	12	13	25	24	26	23	10	7	4	17	21	12	20	13	15	22	17	16	21
450	6882	2	1	14	M	0	12	16	28	14	22	16	16	4	19	16	13	14	11	10	14	11	16	0
451	6891	1	1	13	D	11	18	14	25	17	20	13	12	5	15	20	6	13	13	13	19	14	5	0
452	6892	2	1	13	D	9	15	16	18	15	25	14	17	3	17	24	6	16	14	14	16	12	2	24
453	6901	2	1	13	D	11	15	18	26	14	23	14	16	5	18	19	4	16	14	14	20	13	4	18
454	6902	2	1	13	D	14	24	19	20	21	27	17	14	9	24	24	11	24	14	9	28	13	11	16
455	6911	2	1	14	M	18	10	14	16	12	14	16	16	8	18	20	21	23	17	8	25	10	4	27
456	6912	2	1	17	D	13	16	21	21	20	17	14	10	9	21	19	16	21	23	9	9	11	7	28
457	6921	2	1	17	D	12	10	26	22	19	23	16	13	8	18	21	14	20	10	16	14	10	5	27
458	6922	2	1	17	M	6	16	20	16	14	13	9	11	13	20	17	13	13	16	6	27	17	11	21
459	6931	2	1	15	M	14	14	0	23	21	23	19	0	7	12	13	10	10	14	11	18	12	18	25
460	6932	1	1	16	M	17	22	18	20	20	17	11	25	3	22	14	9	19	12	11	18	20	18	21
461	6941	1	1	16	M	15	22	15	24	20	20	12	0	0	0	19	14	10	14	12	18	15	0	21
462	6942	1	2	16	M	20	16	13	24	24	18	14	17	20	17	15	22	12	25	9	24	19	13	25
463	6951	2	2	15	M	12	21	0	23	15	3	3	0	0	0	25	22	21	25	0	19	16	0	0
464	6952	1	1	15	D	10	16	11	19	12	19	19	17	20	17	5	15	10	17	9	19	12	10	10
465	6961	2	2	13	D	13	21	12	20	19	7	7	12	14	16	0	17	20	16	21	17	15	12	0
466	6962	2	2	15	D	19	16	19	14	20	0	0	17	14	15	20	23	20	18	0	18	11	14	14
467	6971	2	2	15	D	11	24	14	21	20	22	5	17	22	22	17	13	11	13	21	15	10	14	22
468	6972	2	1	17	M	16	15	12	14	19	20	9	21	8	19	11	10	15	10	8	17	16	8	25
469	6981	2	1	17	M	14	9	15	20	15	19	5	12	17	14	14	9	10	11	13	8	12	26	18
470	6982	1	1	15	D	16	17	0	14	11	7	9	12	10	17	16	16	10	0	13	14	13	8	27
471	6991	2	1	15	M	9	0	15	20	20	18	10	8	17	14	17	5	8	15	10	18	14	5	0
472	6992	2	1	15	M	13	20	16	20	23	23	8	2	8	19	12	11	20	20	10	18	13	5	25
473	7001	2	1	16	M	8	16	20	19	18	22	18	9	4	14	13	12	18	15	12	15	14	5	28
474	7002	1	1	16	M	14	16	21	22	17	21	21	3	7	17	16	10	18	17	0	11	23	9	20
475	7011	1	2	15	M	0	16	16	16	20	24	0	13	17	14	15	11	12	0	8	17	14	8	0
476	7012	2	2	15	M	17	16	17	16	16	0	17	8	8	15	16	12	12	12	13	0	15	13	0
477	7021	1	1	17	M	11	10	14	19	0	19	13	13	9	12	17	15	12	10	15	14	13	15	0
478	7022	2	1	17	M	15	9	10	17	13	22	0	6	19	20	14	7	11	11	9	19	13	0	0
479	7031	1	1	17	D	13	13	14	21	23	17	15	13	10	14	17	9	11	12	12	10	23	9	29
480	7032	2	1	17	D	11	18	21	26	26	23	27	8	5	15	14	11	15	20	10	20	18	4	25
481	7041	1	1	15	M	15	15	15	23	21	12	23	10	9	12	21	14	16	12	12	19	15	5	27
482	7042	2	1	15	M	10	0	12	23	20	23	12	14	5	20	18	19	11	10	20	19	13	12	28
483	7061	2	1	15	D	13	18	19	23	20	20	13	11	9	17	17	14	15	9	12	20	18	4	29
484	7062	2	1	15	D	22	16	12	23	14	25	14	12	7	18	18	19	14	18	10	21	16	6	26
485	7071	1	1	18	M	18	16	21	24	19	18	25	13	6	14	17	11	18	10	12	24	14	8	26
486	7072	1	1	18	M	18	12	21	24	19	18	25	13	6	14	20	11	18	22	12	24	14	8	26

OBS	ID	SEX	RACE	AGE	ZYG	_67	_68	_69	_70	_71	_72	_73	_74	_75	_76	_77	_78	_79	_80	_81	_82	_83	_84	_85
487	7081	2	1	14	D	15	16	15	29	11	18	12	19	3	14	16	7	14	17	3	19	16	8	26
488	7082	2	1	14	D	19	15	17	27	17	21	6	8	0	23	15	6	12	12	10	20	21	16	20
489	7091	2	1	15	M	12	19	20	21	19	19	20	8	0	26	14	17	7	17	25	16	20	15	12
490	7092	1	1	15	M	13	17	22	23	19	23	22	13	3	18	19	5	13	17	23	23	19	9	23
491	7101	2	1	17	D	17	15	23	20	18	20	10	18	3	19	24	12	11	13	10	16	9	0	26
492	7102	2	2	17	D	17	20	23	22	24	27	17	10	7	18	20	15	19	19	8	17	11	7	25
493	7111	2	1	17	M	10	14	27	22	22	23	17	9	5	22	16	12	15	16	11	14	13	3	27
494	7112	2	1	17	M	17	13	16	22	21	22	9	12	7	20	17	11	13	20	14	14	14	8	30
495	7121	2	1	15	D	13	12	16	23	12	20	11	10	5	15	12	11	17	19	15	16	10	3	28
496	7122	2	1	15	D	12	16	21	27	21	22	10	12	6	14	12	2	15	23	6	19	16	3	27
497	7131	2	1	15	D	13	22	21	27	21	26	20	11	4	22	22	9	19	12	8	20	14	3	21
498	7132	1	1	13	M	19	15	23	27	19	24	14	5	16	16	20	13	13	15	11	12	17	3	25
499	7141	2	4	13	M	12	25	18	27	19	27	28	14	12	23	17	18	13	18	18	23	25	19	12
500	7142	1	1	13	M	16	17	13	27	14	24	23	13	20	14	17	14	20	12	17	16	15	8	21
501	7151	2	2	13	M	13	16	17	20	19	24	22	13	12	22	19	15	12	10	13	15	13	8	19
502	7152	2	2	16	M	13	12	10	13	16	14	16	13	11	14	11	15	10	11	11	10	12	5	25
503	7161	2	2	15	M	15	11	18	12	16	16	9	10	6	15	8	8	10	11	17	13	12	3	28
504	7162	2	1	15	M	14	15	20	23	16	22	8	15	5	10	12	12	10	8	11	13	12	3	26
505	7171	2	1	13	M	13	22	17	20	16	22	9	15	3	20	15	9	17	13	9	12	15	3	28
506	7172	2	1	13	M	14	27	24	25	27	25	11	15	7	19	23	8	15	14	0	18	20	6	26
507	7191	1	1	13	M	11	27	20	26	24	27	22	12	4	21	18	8	20	13	9	24	21	11	22
508	7192	1	1	17	M	14	24	22	24	20	29	23	15	3	16	15	8	21	15	0	28	17	2	24
509	7201	2	1	17	D	16	0	22	26	20	24	19	12	6	14	17	13	13	13	15	20	18	1	30
510	7202	2	2	15	D	21	17	0	24	12	17	10	11	0	17	14	10	13	15	12	19	12	11	26
511	7221	1	1	16	M	15	17	15	16	20	23	15	15	7	19	15	7	11	11	16	22	11	3	26
512	7222	1	1	18	M	18	22	21	18	23	17	13	12	3	13	17	11	16	18	15	13	12	14	27
513	7231	1	1	18	D	9	18	17	14	17	23	17	10	9	21	21	9	0	11	14	21	13	7	26
514	7232	2	1	16	D	9	16	16	19	20	24	17	20	5	16	13	0	16	12	11	12	12	4	27
515	7241	1	1	16	D	16	14	17	26	25	17	16	11	8	18	20	5	18	11	11	17	13	3	27
516	7242	1	2	15	D	16	21	19	28	24	28	21	12	7	17	0	6	15	13	10	22	17	4	27
517	7251	2	1	15	M	11	19	18	25	14	26	16	16	9	14	17	12	11	21	17	23	9	3	24
518	7252	2	1	18	M	22	13	19	24	20	20	20	10	0	24	13	9	12	12	16	12	12	2	29
519	7271	2	1	18	D	16	14	19	25	14	26	8	10	5	18	20	4	22	0	11	14	14	3	0
520	7272	2	1	17	D	14	24	25	30	22	26	24	14	0	14	17	9	14	10	10	14	13	11	18
521	7281	2	1	16	D	21	14	16	22	15	23	16	16	5	18	20	11	8	12	13	14	15	6	26
522	7282	2	2	14	D	19	14	0	5	17	15	10	16	6	14	17	26	10	13	14	16	14	2	23
523	7291	2	2	14	D	15	12	23	18	0	17	14	12	13	15	14	10	0	13	13	13	15	11	30
524	7292	1	1	18	D	17	7	12	14	17	20	11	8	11	18	6	0	10	11	14	16	5	12	0
525	7301	1	1	18	D	20	12	15	14	27	17	9	13	9	15	9	15	0	10	12	22	6	10	26
526	7311	1	2	15	M	12	7	23	19	20	25	19	20	5	0	13	4	12	15	15	18	20	9	12
527	7312	1	1	13	M	12	12	20	26	24	24	14	13	9	13	0	7	22	12	8	18	17	1	29
528	7321	1	1	15	M	11	16	21	23	20	18	18	12	8	17	10	6	14	11	9	17	0	6	29
529	7322	2	1	13	M	15	13	16	10	17	17	13	14	7	14	17	12	11	11	14	12	14	0	26
530	7331	1	1	13	M	12	13	16	20	10	15	16	11	8	13	11	9	9	12	13	13	13	3	30
531	7332	2	1	15	M	13	22	25	22	24	25	15	12	9	18	18	10	14	13	12	23	12	3	24
532	7341	2	1	17	M	14	16	20	5	16	0	13	18	12	9	8	7	20	12	23	21	14	10	18
533	7342	2	1	14	M	15	15	19	18	21	19	11	8	11	18	21	26	15	14	18	10	10	16	17
534	7351	2	1	16	M	13	13	21	22	12	22	5	10	7	12	20	10	14	22	4	13	16	11	15
535	7352	2	1	16	F	15	15	20	15	22	20	17	20	0	0	20	6	9	14	9	11	10	9	22
536	7361	1	1	16	M	12	13	20	16	22	20	9	0	8	18	17	13	16	22	23	19	11	11	0 |</table>

OBS	ID	SEX	RACE	AGE	ZYG	_67	_68	_69	_70	_71	_72	_73	_74	_75	_76	_77	_78	_79	_80	_81	_82	_83	_84	_85
541	7381	2	1	13	D	13	16	23	26	16	24	27	13	1	17	21	8	22	22	8	21	12	7	24
542	7382	2	1	13	D	13	11	18	15	13	13	10	13	10	16	12	8	10	12	15	12	11	5	26
543	7391	2	2	16	D	8	17	19	20	20	20	13	11	22	14	19	9	22	0	12	20	17	6	27
544	7392	1	2	16	D	7	19	25	27	25	25	10	6	9	26	14	4	16	17	14	19	15	19	11
545	7411	2	1	14	D	17	9	16	20	13	19	11	12	5	21	18	12	17	8	14	17	18	6	21
546	7412	2	1	16	D	15	15	15	16	16	19	8	5	5	11	13	12	9	11	6	13	19	3	23
547	7421	2	1	16	M	13	20	24	17	14	24	23	7	11	11	27	12	23	16	13	10	17	6	26
548	7422	2	1	16	M	23	22	23	24	21	23	8	10	9	19	24	11	18	12	9	11	9	3	22
549	7431	2	1	14	M	10	16	19	0	21	17	12	12	13	10	19	5	15	14	13	14	17	6	21
550	7432	2	1	14	M	11	12	12	14	10	16	10	12	14	13	16	0	14	18	15	12	9	19	20
551	7441	1	1	16	M	24	18	14	20	14	17	15	21	28	20	17	24	24	14	19	18	15	9	27
552	7442	1	1	16	M	12	22	18	25	23	19	25	21	14	15	17	8	16	24	19	26	13	13	10
553	7451	1	1	14	M	11	17	14	18	19	23	16	14	28	21	16	10	14	14	12	14	21	5	26
554	7452	1	1	14	M	11	17	14	24	19	17	15	14	6	11	14	13	16	14	15	16	16	5	0
555	7461	2	1	16	M	16	14	16	0	13	18	5	8	4	11	12	10	10	15	15	14	14	0	27
556	7462	2	1	16	M	11	12	19	28	15	16	4	15	17	11	14	11	16	11	12	18	19	5	28
557	7471	2	1	17	M	13	12	24	24	28	17	8	13	3	23	20	13	14	18	15	16	10	7	25
558	7472	2	1	17	M	13	22	24	18	27	20	10	2	2	24	20	7	10	17	12	16	18	3	20
559	7481	2	2	14	M	19	11	10	18	14	21	11	4	11	13	4	8	15	17	9	19	16	6	24
560	7482	2	2	14	M	14	21	13	26	18	27	13	14	14	16	10	7	10	7	16	19	17	3	18
561	7491	2	1	18	D	12	13	16	24	20	22	18	14	8	19	12	11	7	11	14	25	17	5	28
562	7492	2	1	18	D	15	13	16	23	23	22	16	17	8	15	15	12	18	18	14	17	16	2	28
563	7501	2	1	18	M	16	15	16	22	17	19	16	17	5	16	19	13	15	17	15	18	19	2	30
564	7502	2	1	14	D	11	18	20	20	17	15	16	17	2	10	20	13	12	7	11	16	13	0	23
565	7521	1	1	17	D	16	12	16	22	30	18	24	8	10	16	9	10	11	14	11	13	23	12	26
566	7522	1	1	17	D	9	11	10	18	19	19	13	17	1	16	13	12	11	11	13	16	14	7	23
567	7531	2	1	18	M	11	20	26	16	15	22	20	7	3	23	18	9	13	18	7	21	18	12	23
568	7532	2	1	18	M	17	16	22	18	19	21	8	6	1	17	21	6	16	13	18	16	16	5	25
569	7541	2	1	16	D	15	15	20	20	24	17	7	10	3	21	13	11	13	14	9	19	14	3	24
570	7542	2	1	16	M	21	19	23	24	21	25	10	12	5	14	18	17	16	9	18	16	16	5	23
571	7551	1	1	17	M	22	14	20	19	26	27	22	16	4	21	16	10	13	15	9	14	15	0	26
572	7552	1	1	17	M	14	16	17	21	17	20	17	11	6	9	14	19	18	15	12	15	13	6	24
573	8751	1	1	18	M	15	15	17	18	20	20	16	11	6	15	11	9	15	10	13	14	13	3	28
574	8752	1	1	18	M	15	15	20	23	20	20	11	12	5	17	13	8	15	10	12	13	11	3	30

N=574

APPENDIX F - PART 2

OBS	ID	SEX	RACE	AGE	ZYG	_86	_87	_88	_89	_90	_91	_92	_93	_94	_95	_96	_97	_98	_99
1	2001	1	1	16	D	4	8	13	9	12	5	14	4	8	11	6	11	13	10
2	2002	1	1	16	D	7	9	5	12	11	6	14	12	13	14	11	14	11	7
3	2011	2	1	16	M	9	7	9	13	11	7	10	4	13	8	12	7	12	8
4	2012	2	1	16	M	7	6	7	18	4	6	8	7	11	7	13	4	10	11
5	2021	1	1	16	J	7	8	9	10	8	6	12	7	8	8	8	13	14	14
6	2022	2	1	16	J	9	9	4	9	7	10	11	7	17	10	16	11	7	8
7	2031	2	1	16	J	10	8	10	10	7	11	12	14	8	9	15	6	11	17
8	2032	1	2	16	J	12	5	2	13	4	17	7	7	13	7	13	7	6	13
9	2041	1	1	17	M	12	10	10	11	10	10	16	8	5	11	13	15	10	8
10	2051	2	2	16	J	11	2	7	8	9	11	9	14	6	9	10	11	12	11
11	2052	2	2	17	J	10	8	10	11	12	8	10	9	8	8	5	10	9	6
12	2061	2	1	16	M	6	2	16	10	11	12	11	7	6	6	10	8	6	14
13	2062	2	1	15	M	14	8	7	10	9	16	14	9	14	8	9	8	5	8
14	2071	2	2	15	J	16	9	10	12	10	8	11	12	18	6	12	10	7	15
15	2072	2	2	16	D	10	5	9	12	9	7	9	10	10	11	11	6	8	17
16	2081	2	1	16	D	8	2	6	17	15	1	4	8	13	10	10	10	12	12
17	2082	2	2	15	D	10	3	4	12	10	10	12	10	9	14	11	11	11	9
18	2091	1	1	16	J	8	6	14	16	15	11	13	12	5	6	9	13	5	14
19	2092	2	2	15	J	9	9	15	18	10	8	13	4	11	10	16	10	9	18
20	2101	1	1	15	M	11	8	6	9	12	9	11	13	15	7	5	3	11	12
21	2102	2	2	13	M	14	8	3	14	5	7	8	6	14	7	13	10	14	12
22	2111	2	1	13	M	16	8	11	9	8	13	10	9	12	7	9	6	12	10
23	2112	2	2	17	D	11	6	7	9	6	11	5	6	6	8	9	11	13	13
24	2121	2	1	15	D	9	7	14	9	7	9	11	9	14	5	6	12	8	11
25	2122	2	1	16	D	14	5	7	6	13	7	8	10	14	4	6	4	14	8
26	2131	1	1	16	D	13	8	6	10	5	13	10	15	15	8	10	6	10	14
27	2141	1	1	16	J	8	9	7	10	8	14	14	6	11	6	10	15	8	10
28	2142	2	1	17	J	8	8	8	15	12	15	11	15	1	6	13	12	12	15
29	2151	2	1	17	J	14	9	12	14	13	8	15	11	8	4	7	11	10	7
30	2152	2	2	17	J	2	5	12	10	13	6	12	10	9	11	8	6	13	13
31	2161	1	1	15	J	6	9	10	9	7	4	4	5	20	14	10	12	15	9
32	2162	1	2	14	D	7	8	8	11	9	6	11	10	3	7	10	13	12	13
33	2171	2	2	14	D	5	4	11	12	2	13	11	5	20	9	10	11	9	16
34	2172	2	1	18	D	10	3	13	20	11	10	13	6	16	14	9	9	12	8
35	2181	2	1	18	M	10	6	14	7	12	9	18	16	18	11	2	5	19	11
36	2182	1	1	17	M	9	6	12	5	13	11	8	16	5	9	8	13	8	7
37	2191	1	1	14	J	14	7	12	11	11	8	10	11	2	11	9	11	15	10
38	2192	2	1	16	J	14	7	15	12	13	16	9	11	12	6	5	5	6	7
39	2201	2	1	15	D	13	7	15	11	10	16	6	12	12	1	8	8	4	10
40	2202	2	2	15	M	5	2	0	6	2	8	9	6	12	6	10	11	10	14
41	2211	1	1	16	J	12	5	7	15	13	12	10	10	12	8	8	8	8	6
42	2212	1	1	15	D	9	4	6	6	2	8	15	7	12	6	10	12	12	17
43	2221	2	2	15	J	13	4	9	20	13	9	11	10	10	9	8	10	10	12
44	2231	2	1	15	M	8	9	9	16	6	8	6	12	5	6	8	6	10	14
45	2232	1	1	15	M	10	3	6	11	11	7	11	13	6	9	15	8	6	12
46	2241	1	2	15	D	12	6	10	13	5	7	10	13	11	10	10	9	11	13
47	2242	2	2	15	D	14	5	11	9	9	9	10	9	5	9	11	7	16	14
48	2251	1	1	15	M	10	7	8	6	10	7	6	9	4	7	13	10	11	10
49	2252	1	1	15	M	10	9	5	12	9	9	5	5	11	9	11	9	11	14
50	2241	2	1	15	M	9	8	9	6	8	9	13	15	4	9	4	7	16	13
51	2251	2	1	15	M	15	9	5	12	5	9	13	7	15	9	5	8	11	6
52	2252	2	2	15	M	15	8	9	9	10	9	15	9	8	7	2	9	16	13
53	2261	2	1	15	D	15	9	9	9	12	9	15	12	4	7	5	8	10	9
54	2262	1	1	15	C	15	10	12	9	10	11	12	12	4	7	2	10	10	5

OBS	ID	SEX	RACE	AGE	ZYG	_86	_87	_83	_39	_90	_91	_92	_93	_94	_95	_96	_97	_98	_99
55	2271	2	1	14	U	11	7	3	9	10	4	11	5	16	4	15	9	7	15
56	2272	1	1	14	U	8	9	14	8	14	13	11	12	7	9	9	6	2	5
57	2281	1	1	16	D	13	9	9	16	10	13	4	9	5	8	10	14	10	15
58	2282	1	1	16	C	6	8	2	16	13	16	4	10	11	13	11	9	12	12
59	7291	2	1	16	C	13	7	4	15	7	10	11	8	11	12	13	1	8	17
60	2292	2	1	16	M	9	7	5	13	8	16	9	12	10	10	7	4	6	17
61	2301	1	1	16	M	12	10	13	12	12	14	8	15	9	10	3	6	12	9
62	2302	1	1	16	M	10	4	7	6	12	12	12	11	8	8	5	8	14	6
63	2311	1	1	15	U	11	6	10	10	9	10	13	6	15	4	9	4	11	9
64	2312	2	1	15	U	9	9	7	7	10	8	10	5	15	9	5	9	14	12
65	2321	2	1	17	M	2	9	10	13	7	9	8	4	16	6	9	7	13	13
66	2322	2	1	17	D	4	9	9	9	7	7	8	5	17	6	18	10	2	12
67	2331	2	1	16	M	15	8	3	13	4	11	18	4	14	12	8	3	16	11
68	2332	2	1	16	D	5	5	7	9	3	11	11	19	16	6	10	1	11	11
69	2341	2	1	15	O	12	9	13	13	5	7	9	7	16	9	11	5	11	11
70	2342	2	1	15	M	10	8	10	10	5	13	8	9	17	8	7	8	12	17
71	2351	2	1	16	U	9	6	9	9	10	14	9	15	5	15	3	5	10	7
72	2352	1	1	16	U	12	8	14	9	9	12	5	11	7	10	10	7	8	14
73	2361	2	1	16	U	11	6	10	8	8	11	8	13	13	6	5	4	17	4
74	2362	2	1	16	U	14	8	11	6	9	11	11	10	13	13	6	13	9	8
75	2371	2	1	17	O	8	10	13	4	7	11	10	3	13	11	11	14	8	11
76	2372	2	1	17	D	9	7	12	7	4	10	10	4	8	4	13	6	6	13
77	2381	2	1	17	M	15	8	8	10	7	11	10	8	16	7	8	7	4	14
78	2382	2	1	17	O	8	9	4	18	6	12	9	6	18	14	14	4	4	20
79	2391	2	1	16	D	6	7	4	18	6	10	12	2	18	10	7	2	12	16
80	2392	2	1	16	M	6	6	12	10	11	10	10	10	6	11	16	14	10	7
81	2401	2	1	15	O	5	5	6	10	12	9	10	9	18	7	7	13	8	9
82	2402	1	1	15	O	9	9	7	8	8	7	13	4	18	8	8	11	15	15
83	2411	2	2	15	M	18	9	14	12	6	9	11	18	13	12	14	6	8	14
84	2412	2	2	16	M	7	7	4	9	0	7	14	7	10	4	5	3	15	13
85	2421	2	2	16	U	8	8	2	8	10	8	13	12	13	10	7	2	10	8
86	2422	2	2	16	U	12	4	6	12	9	11	12	10	10	6	9	7	11	10
87	2431	2	2	13	D	12	4	10	14	8	7	10	12	13	9	10	7	13	18
88	2432	2	2	13	O	17	1	8	13	9	10	10	10	14	10	6	9	13	14
89	2441	2	2	14	O	11	5	6	16	6	7	8	13	0	6	8	7	13	13
90	2442	1	2	14	M	15	3	10	20	11	10	8	8	17	14	10	9	7	13
91	2451	2	2	13	M	9	5	8	12	8	8	11	8	9	3	11	8	9	14
92	2452	2	2	13	M	13	1	16	12	11	11	8	10	16	8	9	8	13	13
93	2461	2	2	13	M	7	5	8	12	10	6	9	12	13	10	6	5	9	16
94	2462	2	2	13	M	15	4	6	13	3	15	14	9	13	16	11	14	13	13
95	2471	2	2	13	M	8	6	6	8	5	7	15	8	18	16	9	12	10	16
96	2472	1	2	13	M	10	4	14	11	3	6	12	12	13	13	11	11	2	10
97	2481	1	1	18	O	8	6	9	12	14	13	10	9	5	2	5	8	10	12
98	2482	1	1	18	D	8	8	7	6	14	4	7	8	3	9	13	9	8	8
99	2491	2	1	13	M	13	5	13	9	12	4	7	2	8	7	7	4	12	12
100	2492	2	1	13	M	11	6	10	12	8	4	12	8	12	13	12	11	6	10
101	2501	2	1	13	U	14	8	9	13	9	19	13	8	15	10	10	6	12	10
102	2502	2	1	13	D	12	7	7	13	5	14	13	11	13	6	8	5	10	18
103	2511	2	1	16	D	5	7	9	16	11	10	12	10	6	2	10	10	11	13
104	2512	1	1	16	O	10	8	11	6	8	15	14	11	12	10	8	18	12	16
105	2521	1	1	15	O	5	9	7	7	8	5	10	12	11	7	6	13	14	10
106	2522	1	1	15	M	10	10	8	3	8	17	6	12	11	6	4	4	9	6
107	2531	2	1	13	M	11	5	8	14	8	7	13	8	10	10	8	6	12	16
108	2532	2	1	13	M	9	6	12	14	8	14	18	6	18	12	14	6	15	12

APPENDIX F - PART 2

CBS	ID	SEX	RACE	AGE	ZYG	_86	_87	_88	_89	_90	_91	_92	_93	_94	_95	_96	_97	_98	_99
109	2541	2	1	16	D	10	10	3	13	6	11	9	8	20	10	12	4	7	14
110	2542	2	1	16	D	10	7	6	9	0	7	10	6	16	7	11	5	7	16
111	2551	1	1	14	D	16	7	16	2	8	10	16	7	8	12	4	12	12	4
112	2552	2	1	14	D	3	7	8	6	10	9	4	6	8	10	12	8	9	11
113	2561	2	1	13	D	11	8	4	10	7	14	12	7	14	8	15	6	8	12
114	2562	2	1	16	D	13	7	5	14	5	17	6	6	18	7	14	12	9	13
115	2571	1	1	16	M	10	6	15	14	15	13	7	14	8	8	4	13	6	8
116	2572	1	1	16	M	6	9	8	14	8	12	10	5	4	5	10	9	14	14
117	2581	1	1	16	M	7	5	8	4	11	12	8	2	1	4	6	12	14	8
118	2582	1	1	16	M	10	10	14	2	10	12	7	17	0	6	8	14	12	0
119	2591	2	2	17	M	6	3	12	7	8	6	15	13	14	9	6	8	14	7
120	2592	1	2	17	M	7	2	10	15	5	8	13	14	12	8	8	7	12	11
121	2601	2	2	15	D	14	4	12	10	8	13	10	8	8	9	10	16	14	7
122	2602	2	2	15	D	8	10	7	14	11	14	7	8	4	11	11	5	7	15
123	2611	1	2	14	D	12	6	6	6	13	12	7	9	5	9	10	8	1	11
124	2612	2	2	15	M	12	8	15	14	13	12	8	8	3	8	12	9	12	12
125	2621	2	2	15	O	10	4	4	8	12	4	10	6	12	6	2	9	10	13
126	2622	2	2	15	D	9	9	14	8	7	8	8	7	15	8	7	9	15	12
127	2631	2	2	14	O	12	6	14	15	13	11	14	9	12	8	7	13	8	13
128	2632	2	2	14	J	12	5	11	10	7	10	12	7	15	7	12	10	9	12
129	2641	2	2	14	J	10	6	12	12	5	11	7	7	13	18	6	11	8	9
130	2642	2	2	14	M	18	4	8	10	14	8	14	8	16	12	14	14	8	12
131	2651	2	2	14	O	11	8	10	12	11	14	10	9	7	4	8	2	3	5
132	2652	2	2	14	O	15	10	9	14	10	12	13	10	7	6	14	10	11	12
133	2661	2	2	14	F	14	6	9	7	4	6	16	10	20	4	8	6	17	5
134	2662	2	2	14	M	17	6	5	9	11	9	8	8	14	6	9	4	8	12
135	2671	2	2	14	M	12	7	7	18	15	10	11	6	11	3	6	6	10	8
136	2672	2	2	14	M	16	8	13	15	7	12	15	7	9	14	12	10	7	13
137	2681	2	2	14	M	15	7	11	11	4	6	14	10	14	8	4	12	13	9
138	2682	2	2	14	M	13	6	5	14	7	2	2	9	16	12	9	11	11	14
139	2691	2	2	17	O	12	7	8	12	8	9	14	8	11	6	8	1	12	15
140	2692	1	2	13	D	10	5	7	5	12	5	13	11	17	8	4	7	18	17
141	2701	2	1	13	D	13	8	8	11	8	8	13	6	11	8	9	10	12	4
142	2702	2	2	16	O	10	3	6	7	12	14	17	12	18	5	8	1	11	8
143	2711	2	1	14	M	11	9	5	5	12	8	15	6	10	9	11	13	10	13
144	2712	2	2	14	O	10	4	7	6	12	14	16	12	4	5	6	11	11	12
145	2721	2	1	14	O	11	2	16	11	12	9	13	7	8	12	15	12	10	7
146	2722	2	2	14	D	12	5	10	9	7	6	9	11	10	12	7	8	9	9
147	2731	2	1	14	O	10	9	11	4	10	9	10	6	13	6	16	11	11	8
148	2732	1	1	14	O	13	5	7	8	11	19	12	16	16	9	15	12	9	12
149	2741	2	2	16	O	10	6	11	7	5	10	8	6	11	6	7	8	10	7
150	2742	2	2	14	D	13	5	8	6	15	19	12	16	13	9	5	11	8	9
151	2751	2	1	14	M	12	5	4	10	15	10	13	5	12	12	14	10	8	8
152	2752	1	2	14	O	9	1	10	6	7	12	8	11	15	17	12	5	8	15
153	2761	1	1	14	D	10	8	5	18	6	11	8	9	18	10	8	8	12	13
154	2762	2	2	14	D	9	3	7	10	3	3	14	11	13	7	10	10	12	15
155	2771	2	2	14	M	13	8	5	12	8	8	13	13	18	5	5	9	18	8
156	2772	2	2	14	M	9	5	5	12	11	6	15	14	10	8	2	13	15	12
157	2781	2	1	16	M	14	7	16	5	12	6	16	6	16	9	15	11	10	13
158	2782	1	1	16	M	7	9	11	4	13	12	15	13	16	8	5	13	11	15
159	2791	2	2	16	M	10	10	11	7	9	9	10	14	20	16	2	14	10	8
160	2792	2	1	16	M	10	12	4	12	13	10	15	15	7	16	15	10	13	12
161	2801	1	1	17	D	14	4	13	11	13	10	10	8	9	3	3	14	13	4
162	2802	2	2	17	M	15	5	16	4	13	10	7	8	13	12	8	9	4	10

OBS	ID	SEX	RACE	AGE	ZYG	_86	_87	_88	_89	_90	_91	_92	_93	_94	_95	_96	_97	_98	_99
163	2811	1	2	13	U	8	5	11	9	12	3	9	7	10	5	17	12	8	14
164	2812	2	2	13	U	15	3	13	8	13	4	9	11	15	11	3	9	13	8
165	2821	2	2	14	D	14	5	11	11	11	9	12	10	16	8	8	9	8	11
166	2822	2	2	14	U	9	4	9	13	10	8	11	13	11	12	13	14	12	17
167	2831	1	2	17	U	12	4	12	14	11	5	12	12	10	9	9	15	12	5
168	2832	2	2	17	U	14	6	8	14	15	6	14	10	15	8	12	11	10	15
169	2841	2	2	15	D	12	1	12	9	10	6	9	7	14	12	10	9	8	10
170	2842	2	2	15	D	15	5	8	10	11	9	13	16	11	2	4	10	10	11
171	2851	2	2	14	M	9	3	11	11	12	9	16	9	12	8	6	10	13	11
172	2852	2	2	14	M	7	5	11	10	10	8	12	14	10	6	7	11	12	12
173	2861	1	2	14	D	14	2	10	7	11	7	10	9	6	14	8	11	8	9
174	2862	1	2	14	D	12	2	12	10	10	13	13	11	10	10	10	8	11	11
175	2871	1	2	14	M	10	8	9	12	6	7	12	8	13	7	12	2	8	14
176	2872	2	2	14	M	12	7	10	12	8	9	10	12	12	12	10	7	10	12
177	2881	2	2	16	M	13	4	10	12	8	13	14	11	13	6	12	8	17	18
178	2882	2	2	16	M	12	5	17	8	8	6	16	8	12	12	12	9	14	9
179	2891	1	1	15	U	14	6	7	9	14	8	8	12	13	12	8	2	13	14
180	2892	1	2	15	U	10	3	8	9	13	6	13	7	12	10	7	7	9	8
181	2901	1	1	18	U	6	6	11	9	11	10	8	10	9	3	6	11	8	14
182	2902	1	2	18	D	1	7	14	9	12	7	7	7	1	11	9	9	7	13
183	2911	2	2	17	M	9	7	13	5	13	7	14	10	8	6	8	8	10	11
184	2912	2	2	13	M	7	8	14	9	18	7	9	9	10	3	6	10	8	5
185	2921	1	2	13	D	13	4	11	12	6	12	12	12	12	11	8	5	9	14
186	2922	2	2	14	D	10	6	10	11	5	8	9	6	6	6	6	9	12	11
187	2931	1	2	15	U	8	2	7	10	11	8	12	13	18	5	10	11	10	9
188	2932	2	2	15	U	13	5	8	12	9	10	12	6	12	7	9	10	10	10
189	2941	2	2	16	U	8	2	12	8	5	4	6	11	6	4	10	10	10	9
190	2942	1	2	16	D	12	4	12	10	15	11	11	11	18	10	8	13	14	12
191	2951	2	2	15	D	15	8	17	7	12	7	12	7	10	9	9	7	9	12
192	2952	2	2	15	U	10	5	8	10	4	2	11	4	14	6	12	12	12	12
193	2961	2	2	15	U	7	2	11	10	7	11	12	11	10	3	3	9	9	13
194	2962	2	2	15	D	10	8	10	16	11	17	6	15	0	11	13	0	8	15
195	2971	1	2	15	M	12	6	9	12	12	12	8	8	6	6	11	2	6	17
196	2972	1	2	16	M	10	5	11	11	10	17	7	12	7	6	11	9	14	14
197	2981	2	2	17	U	11	5	12	11	9	12	10	6	6	10	11	12	11	9
198	2982	2	2	17	U	12	6	4	11	4	11	9	5	13	14	11	15	7	18
199	2991	2	2	13	D	15	2	3	10	4	11	11	10	15	11	6	5	11	11
200	2992	1	2	13	D	9	5	2	14	7	4	5	8	12	2	6	4	8	9
201	3001	2	2	18	M	10	2	11	11	15	8	10	5	7	9	15	8	5	6
202	3002	2	2	18	M	11	4	7	8	10	14	11	8	6	6	9	11	12	12
203	3011	2	2	17	M	10	2	6	10	12	15	6	5	14	14	12	10	12	12
204	3012	2	2	17	D	10	3	10	12	6	6	7	6	12	7	9	13	11	13
205	3021	1	2	14	D	14	6	9	10	10	9	12	11	12	10	7	12	6	10
206	3022	1	2	14	M	14	4	9	8	8	10	5	2	10	10	8	11	8	4
207	3031	2	2	15	U	16	2	12	13	11	7	16	9	6	9	4	6	12	10
208	3032	2	2	14	U	6	5	11	11	10	10	4	15	7	7	10	9	13	6
209	3041	2	2	14	M	16	4	13	15	9	13	14	11	14	2	5	13	18	14
210	3042	2	2	15	M	13	5	16	10	9	1	16	13	10	4	2	10	10	7
211	3051	1	2	14	M	15	4	13	7	7	4	11	11	15	8	11	6	16	5
212	3052	2	2	14	D	8	5	14	11	5	7	8	9	7	7	9	13	12	8
213	3061	2	2	13	O	8	4	11	10	12	10	11	5	11	4	3	11	12	9
214	3062	2	2	13	M	17	9	11	9	7	6	16	13	13	7	4	10	18	5
215	3071	2	2	16	H	17	5	14	7	8	13	14	16	8	8	11	8	12	8
216	3072	2	2	16	M	17	5	14	11	12	13	14	16	8	8	4	6	13	11

OBS	ID	SEX	RACE	AGE	ZYG	_86	_87	_88	_89	_90	_91	_92	_93	_94	_95	_96	_97	_98	_99
217	3081	2	2	15	M	7	6	1	12	4	4	13	5	18	5	15	7	9	12
218	3082	2	2	15	M	8	7	7	13	10	7	13	8	15	11	13	13	9	11
219	3091	2	1	17	D	9	7	4	12	11	8	10	4	16	13	10	14	7	11
220	3092	2	1	17	D	10	8	6	8	13	5	16	5	19	9	11	11	10	13
221	3101	1	1	16	D	10	6	9	12	12	6	13	13	8	11	8	10	12	10
222	3102	2	2	16	D	5	8	6	8	7	3	16	13	18	9	9	11	12	8
223	3111	2	1	14	D	11	8	12	12	6	1	8	7	13	6	6	11	11	14
224	3112	2	2	14	D	14	4	16	13	4	0	17	13	12	5	5	13	12	7
225	3121	1	1	16	D	10	3	6	7	2	10	10	9	4	16	7	9	14	14
226	3122	2	1	16	D	19	4	13	15	7	12	12	10	20	4	11	7	9	14
227	3131	1	1	13	J	14	3	6	13	15	15	10	13	12	6	12	10	10	16
228	3132	1	1	13	U	10	4	5	4	10	4	5	12	8	3	12	6	15	8
229	3141	1	2	13	M	7	2	7	12	8	14	12	11	6	8	8	14	6	6
230	3142	2	2	13	M	8	4	15	10	12	11	17	10	6	10	3	7	16	7
231	3151	2	2	15	M	14	8	15	10	6	11	12	15	13	11	8	3	12	6
232	3152	1	1	17	J	9	9	15	13	6	7	9	4	11	7	3	9	9	9
233	3161	2	1	17	U	14	7	14	8	6	14	14	14	10	11	10	11	12	14
234	3162	1	1	14	D	16	2	14	18	6	13	9	5	11	4	2	2	9	7
235	3171	1	1	14	D	15	5	6	6	6	3	11	14	16	11	17	13	11	16
236	3172	2	1	18	C	6	6	10	13	11	10	15	5	12	6	4	7	16	5
237	3181	2	1	18	C	13	9	6	15	6	12	10	4	10	11	6	8	7	16
238	3182	2	1	18	C	6	10	15	14	12	10	17	11	17	4	6	11	10	13
239	3191	1	2	18	D	13	10	11	9	15	12	7	12	10	7	7	15	9	14
240	3192	1	2	13	D	14	5	7	11	11	6	9	4	11	4	8	10	12	11
241	3201	1	2	13	J	11	8	7	11	12	5	6	10	8	11	9	13	8	11
242	3202	1	2	14	M	11	6	10	15	10	11	10	11	13	10	9	10	11	13
243	3211	2	2	14	C	10	4	11	8	9	11	12	11	11	7	8	11	14	15
244	3212	1	1	14	J	7	5	7	15	12	9	9	9	10	12	13	13	6	8
245	3221	2	1	14	U	10	3	5	18	13	8	6	12	13	10	9	8	5	14
246	3222	2	2	15	U	8	6	10	11	13	5	6	5	2	8	6	11	9	16
247	3231	2	2	15	D	11	5	9	13	9	9	8	14	11	12	14	2	8	14
248	3232	1	1	16	M	12	6	7	14	10	9	11	9	7	6	9	9	9	15
249	3241	1	2	16	M	14	4	6	16	5	13	10	8	11	11	8	6	8	11
250	3242	2	2	16	C	12	5	12	10	6	12	8	8	9	17	10	7	15	10
251	3251	2	1	17	D	14	4	16	12	12	10	10	13	13	9	7	9	10	13
252	3252	1	2	17	M	8	8	11	9	9	3	15	8	11	11	16	6	7	12
253	3261	2	1	16	M	5	9	5	13	7	6	11	6	10	12	11	7	15	10
254	3262	1	1	16	C	11	7	11	12	11	12	15	8	10	9	9	9	15	6
255	3271	2	2	18	D	9	7	10	15	13	1	11	8	7	11	10	15	13	11
256	3272	2	2	18	M	13	7	9	14	10	5	13	3	14	9	7	8	12	16
257	3281	2	2	16	M	9	7	8	15	5	4	13	14	11	6	10	7	12	9
258	3282	2	2	16	C	12	7	6	9	6	8	10	7	13	4	5	10	13	12
259	3291	1	1	14	D	3	6	9	13	7	8	14	10	16	7	15	8	8	12
260	3292	2	2	17	M	4	3	8	9	2	8	9	9	13	11	10	12	13	10
261	3301	2	1	17	C	16	6	8	13	11	8	14	10	14	8	3	18	12	8
262	3302	2	2	14	D	14	5	8	9	9	2	9	5	13	12	15	6	9	4
263	3311	1	1	14	M	9	7	11	13	11	16	6	8	2	11	3	11	12	17
264	3312	2	2	14	M	15	7	12	10	13	14	13	15	10	4	9	6	10	13
265	3321	2	1	14	H	13	7	11	13	14	15	11	8	11	8	9	4	14	7
266	3322	2	2	13	O	8	8	12	11	6	9	12	6	9	4	8	8	15	13
267	3331	1	1	13	D	9	5	6	16	6	7	11	8	8	12	9	6	11	15
268	3332	2	2	13	M	10	4	10	6	7	11	12	8	13	5	12	9	10	4
269	3351	1	1	15	M	9	6	12	7	13	11	11	5	8	9	12	8	13	7
270	3352	1	2	15	M	10	6	10	7	13	9	10	16	6	8	12	12	13	7

OBS	ID	SEX	RACE	AGE	ZYG	_86	_87	_88	_89	_90	_91	_92	_93	_94	_95	_96	_97	_98	_99
271	3361	2	1	15	D	18	6	5	11	9	6	14	3	18	8	13	5	12	10
272	3362	2	1	15	D	12	4	8	13	9	10	14	9	10	13	10	14	8	7
273	3371	2	2	12	M	11	4	11	11	7	6	10	8	6	12	9	9	13	10
274	3372	2	2	12	M	11	3	9	13	6	9	8	9	8	7	12	14	14	13
275	3381	1	1	15	M	12	5	14	15	11	13	7	15	3	6	5	10	6	6
276	3382	1	1	15	M	4	8	11	13	8	11	6	7	5	9	9	14	10	11
277	3391	1	2	14	M	8	5	6	15	11	7	13	12	7	8	8	6	6	9
278	3392	1	2	14	U	7	5	5	14	8	6	10	11	8	10	14	4	10	15
279	3401	2	2	15	D	10	7	6	16	6	9	12	9	17	10	6	8	2	11
280	3402	1	2	15	D	8	6	6	15	8	12	9	14	8	11	6	7	4	11
281	3411	2	2	16	M	9	8	13	7	9	8	10	7	16	10	6	11	7	9
282	3412	2	2	16	D	15	6	12	14	6	6	10	7	13	7	9	14	12	10
283	3421	2	2	14	M	11	3	5	11	6	5	10	10	11	8	8	11	6	12
284	3422	2	2	14	M	14	8	7	11	6	3	10	11	14	6	9	12	10	9
285	3431	2	2	15	U	10	5	12	10	6	8	9	7	5	7	8	15	8	10
286	3432	2	2	15	U	9	4	10	14	10	8	9	11	13	8	9	14	9	14
287	3441	2	2	13	U	10	7	9	12	13	8	9	14	1	12	6	15	11	10
288	3442	2	2	13	U	4	10	14	12	11	14	6	7	10	13	7	5	17	9
289	3451	1	2	16	M	8	4	3	16	11	5	13	5	13	10	12	12	8	14
290	3452	2	2	16	U	11	5	11	15	11	4	7	11	11	9	14	12	10	10
291	3461	2	1	14	D	7	4	9	10	10	9	11	11	7	14	9	13	12	9
292	3462	1	1	14	D	18	3	9	10	14	8	17	11	10	13	8	10	13	15
293	3471	2	1	14	O	14	6	11	12	8	12	8	6	6	8	4	8	3	2
294	3472	1	1	14	U	12	5	12	10	8	12	9	4	12	10	1	12	14	6
295	3481	2	2	16	D	14	9	6	9	12	5	13	2	15	14	8	14	13	4
296	3482	1	2	13	U	10	9	7	10	6	11	9	10	8	8	10	12	8	16
297	3491	1	2	13	M	12	4	7	11	8	10	12	8	14	14	11	10	13	6
298	3492	1	2	18	D	12	3	7	7	12	7	13	8	12	15	11	5	8	16
299	3501	2	2	18	F	12	6	6	12	5	11	12	3	4	11	11	12	14	12
300	3502	1	1	17	F	11	4	9	16	11	11	9	11	8	8	11	5	8	10
301	3511	2	1	17	M	11	4	9	12	9	10	15	12	14	10	8	8	9	8
302	3512	2	1	15	D	10	9	13	12	4	8	12	13	12	6	4	14	12	8
303	3521	2	1	15	O	8	9	10	12	11	10	11	7	8	6	7	5	13	13
304	3522	2	1	15	D	14	7	6	11	6	10	15	3	14	6	4	9	16	7
305	3531	2	2	17	U	8	6	7	5	12	13	13	6	20	6	8	10	10	13
306	3532	1	1	17	U	14	8	15	13	14	10	16	12	8	15	6	9	11	6
307	3541	2	2	14	U	11	1	8	15	12	15	10	9	9	9	12	10	12	19
308	3542	2	2	14	D	12	6	8	9	9	9	5	7	7	4	11	5	11	6
309	3551	2	1	14	O	14	8	8	14	12	8	12	4	11	11	11	12	14	14
310	3552	2	2	16	P	14	7	11	9	7	6	18	10	12	6	11	8	14	13
311	3561	1	1	16	D	8	6	14	8	12	8	8	9	19	11	11	8	14	10
312	3562	2	2	15	O	10	4	8	7	6	10	15	7	10	5	10	8	8	17
313	3581	2	1	15	F	8	8	5	12	6	11	11	8	12	9	6	8	11	17
314	3582	2	2	17	M	15	9	8	8	6	8	11	3	13	6	5	10	11	12
315	3591	2	1	17	O	9	9	5	14	4	9	12	6	18	15	10	11	12	12
316	3592	2	1	14	D	6	7	11	13	14	10	14	12	6	11	7	14	14	13
317	3601	2	1	14	U	15	5	7	9	8	9	12	3	18	4	5	9	11	11
318	3602	2	2	15	D	11	7	7	6	10	9	16	6	12	10	10	11	16	6
319	3611	2	2	15	D	9	5	6	9	4	1	9	9	15	6	12	5	9	19
320	3612	2	2	13	P	17	3	17	6	13	12	16	6	20	3	11	4	12	14
321	3621	2	2	13	D	9	6	12	14	12	7	11	4	9	6	11	11	9	12
322	3622	1	1	18	M	9	8	12	10	12	11	11	10	8	3	10	13	11	12
323	3631	1	1	18	M	13	6	9	14	12	7	6	7	6	8	6	4	9	13
324	3632	2	1	18	M	9	8	11	12	12	15	4	3	12	15	10	10	10	15

CBS	ID	SEX	RACE	AGE	ZYG	_86	_87	_88	_89	_90	_91	_92	_93	_94	_95	_96	_97	_98	_99
325	3641	1	1	14	D	7	7	8	11	7	9	10	9	10	14	15	10	13	12
326	3642	1	1	14	D	12	5	8	11	11	14	8	3	10	9	8	5	10	14
327	3651	1	1	14	D	14	7	13	7	6	11	13	12	7	10	6	8	14	8
328	3652	1	1	14	D	5	4	10	8	11	4	12	12	4	11	7	15	15	14
329	3661	2	1	14	M	9	10	5	13	4	13	11	11	18	5	6	2	15	12
330	3662	2	1	14	M	9	8	5	11	6	8	11	14	20	11	10	8	8	15
331	3671	2	2	13	D	15	5	6	15	10	9	9	14	0	6	11	15	9	16
332	3672	1	1	13	D	11	5	12	6	8	8	13	18	1	6	2	8	4	8
333	3681	2	2	16	M	14	6	12	7	1	0	17	13	18	10	15	8	14	6
334	3682	2	2	16	M	13	6	12	11	15	6	10	11	12	6	1	8	10	8
335	3691	1	1	14	M	16	6	10	11	7	12	10	15	3	8	13	1	10	14
336	3692	1	1	14	M	15	6	12	12	10	11	10	16	4	10	4	7	10	15
337	3701	2	2	14	J	10	1	13	9	11	11	12	7	3	14	7	6	13	3
338	3702	1	2	14	M	4	2	9	12	8	3	12	9	14	7	11	12	13	13
339	3711	2	2	13	M	10	5	11	15	14	10	15	14	9	14	12	10	9	10
340	3712	2	2	13	M	10	5	14	8	7	4	15	8	11	8	8	17	12	14
341	3721	2	2	13	J	10	5	14	14	6	6	13	11	14	14	13	10	9	14
342	3722	2	2	13	J	11	7	5	8	7	10	7	4	14	9	11	17	10	9
343	3731	2	2	13	M	12	5	12	10	6	9	9	7	15	10	12	13	10	10
344	3732	2	2	13	D	11	6	13	13	3	4	8	11	16	10	12	12	11	8
345	3741	2	2	13	D	19	5	14	13	7	5	11	8	13	10	10	11	11	6
346	3742	2	2	13	D	16	9	14	14	7	8	14	8	14	9	10	2	16	10
347	3751	2	1	17	M	12	9	8	8	4	8	10	8	18	4	8	8	10	17
348	3752	2	1	17	M	14	3	8	12	9	7	18	3	15	6	6	11	9	11
349	3761	2	2	13	M	16	1	8	12	7	10	18	12	8	8	4	16	12	13
350	3762	2	2	13	M	14	3	14	11	11	5	13	9	9	11	6	8	12	14
351	3771	2	2	13	J	11	7	16	12	5	7	10	12	11	9	4	18	12	10
352	3772	2	2	13	J	6	3	10	11	15	11	12	12	10	10	10	8	6	14
353	3781	2	2	15	M	15	5	18	1	11	8	11	11	4	9	6	7	11	7
354	3782	2	2	16	M	11	6	6	8	11	10	8	3	9	12	8	10	3	14
355	3791	1	2	16	J	12	4	15	8	14	10	12	17	17	9	0	9	13	13
356	3792	2	2	16	J	17	7	17	7	12	10	11	19	5	7	13	12	12	6
357	3801	2	2	16	M	10	6	7	2	8	5	16	7	15	9	10	9	9	10
358	3802	2	2	16	M	12	4	9	9	16	8	15	12	3	14	8	12	10	12
359	3811	2	2	16	M	13	7	9	8	6	10	10	12	11	9	10	10	12	10
360	3812	2	2	16	M	17	3	14	4	16	8	10	12	3	6	2	8	14	10
361	3821	2	2	16	M	12	5	10	3	13	1	15	5	15	6	6	2	10	14
362	3822	2	2	14	M	8	7	7	14	4	5	12	7	14	8	8	12	13	15
363	3831	2	2	14	D	9	4	9	14	9	8	11	9	14	12	10	9	13	14
364	3832	2	2	15	D	7	2	13	15	14	10	11	10	9	7	9	7	13	15
365	3841	1	2	13	M	10	1	11	14	9	15	8	11	14	13	9	11	12	14
366	3842	1	2	13	M	7	7	12	11	14	7	13	11	17	14	7	14	7	13
367	3851	1	2	13	J	9	5	10	12	10	9	11	12	3	12	15	14	10	9
368	3852	2	2	13	J	7	6	14	10	12	5	16	15	4	9	6	12	11	8
369	3861	2	2	13	M	10	10	10	8	12	10	15	18	16	6	2	6	14	6
370	3862	2	2	15	D	18	5	14	9	11	4	17	15	13	4	8	7	12	9
371	3871	2	2	15	M	20	10	18	8	8	9	18	14	14	11	4	6	18	9
372	3872	2	2	14	M	16	5	10	10	6	4	15	8	17	6	7	8	10	12
373	3881	2	2	14	D	12	10	10	10	12	5	8	7	17	8	6	9	11	5
374	3882	2	2	14	M	12	5	11	13	9	7	13	8	11	6	9	6	11	10
375	3891	2	2	14	M	14	5	12	16	10	12	10	5	8	9	10	2	13	9
376	3892	2	2	14	J	5	4	12	11	4	9	9	4	14	6	10	1	4	6
377	3901	2	2	13	J	9	6	11	11	11	10	12	6	15	11	10	6	14	9
378	3902	1	2	13	J	14	3	10	11	9	13	7	15	13	3	10	10	7	8

OBS	ID	SEX	RACE	AGE	ZYG	_86	_87	_88	_89	_90	_91	_92	_93	_94	_95	_96	_97	_98	_99
379	3911	1	2	15	U	8	6	12	7	13	4	9	7	9	7	12	11	11	10
380	3912	2	2	15	U	16	8	5	6	2	0	18	10	20	12	6	13	16	8

N=380

246

Appendix G

Test scores for the small number (19 pairs) of twins given the EEG battery which not only includes two EEG parameters but also intelligence, personality, and creativity test results.

The column numbers in the following table correspond to the column headings in the Appendix G printout. A full description of each variable reported in the printout can be found in Appendix B.

Column # *EEG PARAMETERS*

100 Visual Evoked Response: latency to first significant negative peak measured in milliseconds on dominant side (see text)
101 EEG Diagnostic Impression: + sign indicates record available in text

102 *REVISED BETA EXAMINATION: I.Q.*

MINNESOTA MULTIPHASIC PERSONALITY INVENTORY

103 MMPI-validity scale ?
104 MMPI-validity scale L
105 MMPI-validity scale F
106 MMPI-validity scale K
107 MMPI-clinical scale Hs
108 MMPI-clinical scale D
109 MMPI-clinical scale Hy
110 MMPI-clinical scale Pd
111 MMPI-clinical scale Mf
112 MMPI-clinical scale Pa
113 MMPI-clinical scale Pt
114 MMPI-clinical scale Sc
115 MMPI-clinical scale Ma
116 MMPI-clinical scale Si

TORRANCE TEST OF CREATIVE THINKING-FORM A

OBS	ID	SEX	AGE	G	100	101	102	103	104	105	106	107	108	109	110	111	112	113	114	115	116	117	118	119	120	121	122	123
1	9011	1	18	M	239.1	+	126	50	60	68	53	47	80	51	55	73	65	54	69	55	71	98	48	101	25	20	45	63
2	9012	1	18	M	178.3	+	120	50	40	80	38	76	34	73	53	90	67	79	88	53	84	72	34	47	17	15	31	61
3	9021	2	20	M	190.3	+	120	50	50	46	59	50	51	59	55	55	33	71	74	48	55	81	35	73	18	17	22	59
4	9022	2	20	M	198.1	+	121	50	50	50	68	52	61	50	57	47	50	58	55	38	61	65	24	44	20	15	36	96
5	9031	2	22	M	214.7	+	128	.	.	.	.	.	.	.	.	.	.	.	.	.	.	.	.	.	.	.	.	.	.
6	9032	2	22	M	183.0	+	120	50	43	78	42	66	69	76	81	47	85	84	94	65	75	103	45	93	22	17	28	59
7	9041	2	18	M	190.0	+	116	50	53	62	42	52	61	57	64	49	65	71	74	81	54	55	35	31	16	13	16	82
8	9042	1	18	M	192.4	+	120	50	40	62	46	58	49	56	64	51	67	76	80	78	61	56	39	38	14	14	16	80
9	9051	2	16	M	220.3	+	105	50	43	58	49	42	42	45	46	55	65	56	64	68	51	61	22	36	19	18	26	95
10	9052	2	16	M	181.5	+	102	50	56	58	53	46	56	42	55	41	47	46	59	65	42	62	30	43	16	15	30	53
11	9061	1	18	M	172.3	+	105	50	46	60	46	41	50	55	46	53	50	50	57	60	39	38	22	26	18	14	24	13
12	9062	2	18	M	167.7	+	94	50	46	50	49	52	44	54	60	51	38	54	55	73	41	87	46	76	16	12	15	63
13	9071	1	15	M	201.6	+	101	50	53	53	61	47	39	54	71	63	50	51	55	60	56	89	45	82	15	10	23	83
14	9072	1	15	M	201.6	+	107	50	53	53	42	48	55	50	53	59	59	73	49	58	42	70	37	62	12	12	13	49
15	9081	2	19	M	226.0	+	113	56	53	60	53	48	40	58	60	57	57	51	55	58	56	76	33	60	15	15	15	32
16	9082	1	19	M	193.5	+	111	50	40	50	46	44	53	71	60	50	47	46	61	60	71	35	19	14	8	8	11	55
17	9091	1	11	M	192.8	+	85	50	43	53	49	59	72	44	50	47	57	66	50	68	60	31	21	19	8	6	11	21
18	9092	1	11	M	184.0	+	85	50	36	53	44	39	60	44	44	50	48	79	65	58	71	45	26	22	21	15	28	86
19	9101	1	18	M	210.8	+	109	62	43	58	57	41	44	44	44	60	57	36	43	58	56	94	48	88	29	24	61	108
20	9102	2	18	M	203.0	+	117	50	50	58	44	52	51	47	60	62	47	55	61	70	58	58	32	22	13	12	20	60
21	9111	1	11	M	165.3	+	85	.	.	.	.	.	.	.	.	.	.	.	.	.	.	.	.	.	.	.	.	.
22	9112	1	21	M	354.9	+	84	50	50	53	51	57	48	55	62	55	61	67	62	54	62	48	32	13	7	7	16	47
23	9121	1	21	M	216.5	+	135	50	43	48	42	36	46	49	43	55	56	56	54	51	43	36	21	27	9	9	19	54
24	9122	1	21	M	223.2	+	126	50	40	55	66	46	38	49	50	56	56	56	51	58	61	107	42	73	34	19	48	62
25	9131	1	19	M	264.8	+	107	50	50	66	53	46	44	49	49	50	66	57	53	58	56	113	43	87	15	9	23	69
26	9132	1	19	D	211.9	+	112	50	63	50	51	48	50	46	42	49	46	55	50	45	49	88	42	29	9	9	19	63
27	9141	2	11	D	178.0	+	102	50	53	55	64	44	38	54	54	49	50	59	56	53	44	107	42	73	34	19	48	62
28	9142	2	11	D	171.5	+	86	50	63	66	74	50	36	48	36	42	74	57	51	48	61	113	42	70	19	11	69	69
29	9151	2	15	D	220.0	+	109	50	63	80	42	50	92	95	92	91	93	57	50	58	56	88	43	87	15	14	23	63
30	9152	1	12	D	208.1	+	122	50	50	55	64	46	53	41	53	54	69	59	50	53	55	52	22	29	8	8	18	51
31	9161	1	12	D	216.8	+	97	50	50	80	74	41	46	41	32	53	53	57	73	86	78	52	21	29	17	22	43	48
32	9162	2	12	D	190.3	+	96	50	50	50	42	60	42	57	53	45	48	57	41	53	55	72	22	71	28	15	40	44
33	9171	1	18	D	188.9	+	103	50	63	80	42	48	53	41	64	53	69	57	70	86	60	59	37	13	17	12	20	40
34	9172	1	18	D	208.3	+	85	50	50	53	57	37	44	60	44	47	48	57	56	54	64	39	22	50	15	13	20	67
35	9181	1	18	D	200.9	+	106	50	50	58	38	57	38	48	53	45	64	55	44	41	32	64	31	42	17	12	22	42
36	9182	1	19	D	190.3	+	104	50	60	62	44	38	44	60	49	61	55	57	67	74	65	49	25	51	15	13	25	53
37	9191	2	19	D	183.3	+	93	50	43	44	44	44	44	60	53	50	64	37	47	41	60	61	22	41	7	6	11	37
38	9192	1	19	D	204.1	+	112	50	43	50	51	51	44	48	49	50	55	51	47	55	68	36	24	28	5	5	17	78

N=38

Appendix H

Not all tests were completed by both members of a twin set nor did all sets take identical test batteries. Virtually all twins, including 50 sets of boy-girl twins, completed the Basic Battery. However, only 19 sets of twins were given the EEG Battery. Appendix H shows at a glance the physiological, psychological, and sociological data available for each twin. All twins participating in the Twin Survey are identified by I.D. number, sex, race, age, and zygosity. A "C" opposite the I.D. number indicates the complete set of data is recorded for the variable indicated by the column heading. A "P" in the column indicates the data set is incomplete. If a subject missed one or more of the tests in the battery, he was given a "P", indicating partial battery. A decimal character (·) opposite the I.D. number indicates no data on the variable is available for that subject.

Column #

124	Blood group genes (Appendix C)
125	Biometric variables—examiner reported (Appendix D)
126	Biometric variables—self-reported (Appendix D)
127	Socio-economic status (Appendix D)
128	Psychological tests—Basic Battery (Appendix E)
129	Psychological tests—Secondary Battery (Appendix E)
130	Psychological tests—Culture Fair Battery (Appendix E)
131	Personality questionnaire—*How Well Do You Know Yourself?* (Appendix F)
132	Personality questionnaire—*High School Personality Questionnaire* (Appendix F)
133	EEG Battery (Appendix G)

OBS	ID	SEX	RACE	AGE	ZYG	_124	_125	_126	_127	_128	_129	_130	_131	_132	_133
1	11	1	2	17	M	0	0			0	0		0		
2	12	1	2	17	M	0	0			0	0		0		
3	21	2	2	17	D	0	0			0	0		0		
4	22	2	2	17	D	0	0			0	0		0		
5	31	1	1	14	D	0	0			0	0		0		
6	32	1	1	14	D	0	0			0	0		0		
7	41	2	1	18	D	0	0			0	0		0		
8	42	2	1	18	M	0	0			0	0		0		
9	51	1	1	17	M	0	0			0	0		0		
10	52	1	2	17	M	0	0			0	0		0		
11	61	2	2	17	M	0	0			0	0		0		
12	62	2	2	16	M	0	0			0	0		0		
13	71	2	2	16	M	0	0			0	0		0		
14	72	2	1	14	M	0	0			0	0		0		
15	81	2	2	14	M	0	0			0	0		0		
16	82	1	2	14	D	0	0			0	0		0		
17	91	1	1	15	M	0	0			0	0		0		
18	92	2	2	15	M	0	0			0	0		0		
19	101	2	2	17	M	0	0			0	0		0		
20	102	2	1	16	M	0	0			0	0		0		
21	111	2	2	16	M	0	0			0	0		0		
22	112	2	2	16	M	0	0			0	0		0		
23	121	1	2	16	M	0	0			0	0		0		
24	122	2	1	15	D	0	0			0	0		0		
25	131	1	1	16	D	0	0			0	0		0		
26	132	1	1	15	D	0	0			0	0		0		
27	141	1	2	15	D	0	0			0	0		0		
28	142	1	2	17	M	0	0			0	0		0		
29	151	1	1	18	M	0	0			0	0		0		
30	152	2	2	18	M	0	0			0	0		0		
31	161	2	2	17	M	0	0			0	0		0		
32	162	2	2	14	D	0	0			0	0		0		
33	171	2	1	14	D	0	0			0	0		0		
34	172	1	1	14	D	0	0			0	0		0		
35	181	2	2	15	M	0	0			0	0		0		
36	182	1	2	15	M	0	0			0	0		0		
37	191	1	1	14	M	0	0			0	0		0		
38	192	1	2	14	D	0	0			0	0		0		
39	201	2	2	14	D	0	0			0	0		0		
40	202	1	1	15	D	0	0			0	0		0		
41	211	1	1	14	D	0	0			0	0		0		
42	212	2	2	14	M	0	0			0	0		0		
43	221	2	1	14	D	0	0			0	0		0		
44	222	2	1	17	D	0	0			0	0		0		
45	231	2	1	17	D	0	0			0	0		0		
46	232	2	1	15	D	0	0			0	0		0		
47	241	2	1	15	D	0	0			0	0		0		
48	242	2	2	13	M	0	0			0	0		0		
49	251	2	2	13	M	0	0			0	0		0		
50	252	2	1	14	M	0	0			0	0		0		
51	261	2	1	14	M	0	0			0	0		0		
52	262	2	1	17	M	0	0			0	0		0		
53	271	2	1	17	M	0	0			0	0		0		
54	272	2	1	17	M	0	0			0	0		0		

251

OBS	ID	SEX	RACE	AGE	ZYG	_124	_125	_126	_127	_128	_129	_130	_131	_132	_133
55	281	1	1	13	D	C	C			C	C		C		
56	282	1	1	13	C	C	C			C	C		C		
57	291	2	1	15	U	C	C			C	C		C		
58	292	2	1	15	U	C	C			C	C		C		
59	301	2	1	17	U	C	C			C	C		C		
60	302	2	2	17	D	C	C			C	C		C		
61	311	2	2	17	D	C	C			C	C		C		
62	312	2	1	16	M	C	C			C	C		C		
63	321	2	1	16	M	C				C	C		C		
64	322	2	1	17	M	C	C			C	C		C		
65	331	1	2	17	D	C	C			C	C		C		
66	332	1	2	15	M	C	C			C	C		C		
67	341	2	2	15	M	C	C			C	C		C		
68	342	2	2	16	M	C	C			C	C		C		
69	351	2	2	16	D	C	C			C	C		C		
70	352	2	1	16	M	C	C			C	C		C		
71	361	1	1	14	D	C	C			C	C		C		
72	362	1	1	18	M	C	C			C	C		C		
73	371	1	2	18	M	C	C			C	C		C		
74	372	1	2	15	M	C	C			C	C		C		
75	381	2	1	15	M	C	C			C	C		C		
76	382	2	1	15	M	C	C			C	C		C		
77	391	2	2	16	M	C	C			C	C		C		
78	392	2	2	16	C	C	C			C	C		C		
79	401	2	2	14	D	C	C			C	C		C		
80	402	2	2	14	D	C	C			C	C		C		
81	411	2	1	14	C	C	C			C	C		C		
82	412	1	1	15	M	C	C			C	C		C		
83	421	1	2	15	M	C	C			C	C		C		
84	422	1	2	14	D	C	C			C	C		C		
85	431	1	2	14	D	C	C			C	C		C		
86	432	1	1	16	D	C	C			C	C		C		
87	441	2	1	16	D	C	C			C	C		C		
88	442	2	1	16	D	C	C			C	C		C		
89	451	2	1	16	D	C	C			C	C		C		
90	452	2	2	15	D	C	C			C	C		C		
91	461	2	1	15	C	C	C			C	C		C		
92	462	2	1	18	D	C	C			C	C		C		
93	471	2	1	18	M	C	C			C	C		C		
94	472	2	1	16	U	C	C			C	C		C		
95	481	1	1	16	U	C	C			C	C		C		
96	482	1	1	16	U	C	C			C	C		C		
97	2001	1	1	16	U	C	C	C	C	C	C	C	C	C	
98	2002	2	1	16	M	C	C	C	C	C	C	C	C	C	
99	2011	2	1	16	U		C	C	C	C	C	C	C	C	
100	2012	1	1	16	U		C	C	C	C	C	C	C	C	
101	2021	2	1	16	U		C	C	C	C	C	C	C	C	
102	2022	1	1	16	D		C	P	C	C	C	C	C	C	
103	2031	2	1	16	U		C	C	C	C	C	C	C	C	
104	2032	1	1	16	U		C	C	C	C	C	C	C	C	
105	2041	1	1	17	U		C	C	C	C	C	C	C	C	
106	2042	1	1	17	M		C	C	C	C	C	C	C	C	
107	2051	1	2	16	U		C	C	C	C	C	C	C	C	
108	2052	2	2	16	U		C	C	C	C	C	C	C	C	

OBS	ID	SEX	RACE	AGE	ZYG	_124	_125	_126	_127	_128	_129	_130	_131	_132	_133
109	2061	2	1	15	M		U	U	U	U		U		U	
110	2062	2	1	15	F		U	U	U	U		U		U	
111	2071	2	2	15	D		U	U	U	U		U		U	
112	2072	2	2	15	D		U	U	U	U		U		U	
113	2081	1	2	16	D		U	U	U	U		U		U	
114	2082	1	2	15	D		U	U	U	U		U		U	
115	2091	1	1	15	U		U	U	U	U		U		U	
116	2092	2	1	15	U		U	U	U	U		U		U	
117	2101	2	1	13	M		U	U	U	U		U		U	
118	2102	2	2	13	M		U	U	U	U		U		U	
119	2111	2	2	17	F		U	U	U	U		U		U	
120	2112	2	1	15	D		U	U	U	U		U		U	
121	2121	2	1	15	D		U	U	U	U		U		U	
122	2122	1	1	16	D		U	U	U	U		U		U	
123	2131	1	1	16	D		U	U	U	U		U		U	
124	2132	1	1	17	U		U	U	U	U		U		U	
125	2141	1	1	17	U		U	U	U	U		U		U	
126	2142	1	1	17	U		U	U	U	U		U		U	
127	2151	1	1	17	U		U	U	U	U		U		U	
128	2152	2	1	15	D		U	U	U	U		U		U	
129	2161	2	1	15	M		U	U	U	U		U		U	
130	2162	2	2	14	M		U	U	U	U		U		U	
131	2171	2	2	14	D		U	U	U	U		U		U	
132	2172	1	1	18	U		U	U	U	U		U		U	
133	2181	1	1	18	M		U	P	U	U		U		U	
134	2182	1	1	17	D		U	P	U	U		U		U	
135	2191	1	1	17	U		U	P	U	U		U		U	
136	2192	1	1	14	U		U	U	U	U		U		U	
137	2201	2	1	14	U		U	P	U	U		U		U	
138	2202	2	1	16	M		U	U	U	U		U		U	
139	2211	1	1	16	M		U	P	U	U		U		U	
140	2212	1	1	15	U		U	U	U	U		U		U	
141	2221	2	1	15	D		U	P	U	U		U		U	
142	2222	2	2	15	U		U	U	U	U		U		U	
143	2231	2	2	15	M		U	P	U	U		U		U	
144	2232	1	1	15	M		U	U	U	U		U		U	
145	2241	1	1	15	M		U	P	U	U		U		U	
146	2242	2	1	15	D		U	U	U	U		U		U	
147	2251	2	1	15	D		U	P	U	U		U		U	
148	2252	1	1	15	U		U	U	U	U		U		U	
149	2261	1	1	15	U		U	P	U	U		U		U	
150	2262	1	1	14	M		U	U	U	U		U		U	
151	2271	2	1	14	M		U	P	U	U		U		U	
152	2272	1	1	16	U		U	U	U	U		U		U	
153	2281	1	1	16	U		U	P	U	U		U		U	
154	2282	1	1	16	D		U	U	U	U		U		U	
155	2291	2	1	16	M		U	P	U	U		U		U	
156	2292	2	1	16	M		U	U	U	U		U		U	
157	2301	1	1	16	U		U	P	U	U		U		U	
158	2302	1	1	16	U		U	U	U	U		U		U	
159	2311	1	1	15	D		U	P	U	U		U		U	
160	2312	2	2	15	U		U	U	U	U		U		U	
161	2321	2	2	17	M		U	P	U	U		U		U	
162	2322	2	1	17	M		U	P	U	U		U		U	

APPENDIX H

OBS	ID	SEX	RACE	AGE	ZYG	_124	_125	_126	_127	_128	_129	_130	_131	_132	_133
163	2331	2	1	16	D		U	U	U	U		U		U	
164	2332	2	1	16	D		U	P	U	U		U		U	
165	2341	2	1	15	H		U	U	U	U		U		U	
166	2342	2	1	15	U		U	U	U	U		U		U	
167	2351	2	1	16	U		U	U	U	U		U		U	
168	2352	1	1	16	U		U	U	U	U		U		U	
169	2361	2	1	16	D		U	U	U	U		U		U	
170	2362	2	1	16	U		U	U	U	U		U		U	
171	2371	2	1	17	H		U	U	U	U		U		U	
172	2372	2	1	17	H		U	U	U	U		U		U	
173	2381	2	1	17	D		U	U	U	U		U		U	
174	2382	2	1	16	U		U	P	U	U		U		U	
175	2391	2	1	16	H		U	U	U	U		U		U	
176	2392	2	1	15	H		U	U	U	U		U		U	
177	2401	1	1	15	D		U	U	U	U		U		U	
178	2402	1	1	15	U		U	U	U	U		U		U	
179	2411	1	1	16	U		U	U	U	U		U		U	
180	2412	2	1	16	D		U	U	U	U		U		U	
181	2421	2	1	16	H		U	U	U	U		U		U	
182	2422	2	2	13	U		U	U	U	U		U		U	
183	2431	2	2	13	U		U	U	U	U		U		U	
184	2432	1	2	14	U		U	P	U	U		U		U	
185	2441	2	2	14	D		U	U	U	U		U		U	
186	2442	1	2	13	H		U	P	U	U		U		U	
187	2451	2	2	13	H		U	P	U	U		U		U	
188	2452	2	1	13	U		U	P	U	U		U		U	
189	2461	2	1	13	U		U	P	U	U		U		U	
190	2462	2	1	13	U		U	U	U	U		U		U	
191	2471	2	1	16	D		U	U	U	U		U		U	
192	2472	2	1	15	H		U	U	U	U		U		U	
193	2481	1	1	15	H		U	U	U	U		U		U	
194	2482	2	1	13	U		U	U	U	U		U		U	
195	2491	2	1	13	U		U	U	U	U		U		U	
196	2492	2	1	18	U		U	U	U	U		U		U	
197	2501	2	1	18	D		U	U	U	U		U		U	
198	2502	2	1	13	H		U	P	U	U		U		U	
199	2511	2	1	13	H		U	U	U	U		U		U	
200	2512	2	1	16	U		U	U	U	U		U		U	
201	2521	2	1	15	D		U	U	U	U		U		U	
202	2522	1	1	15	U		U	U	U	U		U		U	
203	2531	1	1	13	D		U	U	U	U		U		U	
204	2532	2	1	13	D		U	U	U	U		U		U	
205	2541	2	1	16	D		U	U	U	U		U		U	
206	2542	2	1	16	D		U	U	U	U		U		U	
207	2551	1	1	14	D		U	P	U	U		U		U	
208	2552	1	1	14	H		U	U	U	U		U		U	
209	2561	2	1	13	H		U	P	U	U		U		U	
210	2562	2	1	13	H		U	U	U	U		U		U	
211	2571	1	1	16	D		U	U	U	U		U		U	
212	2572	1	1	16	H		U	U	U	U		U		U	
213	2581	1	1	16	H		U	P	U	U		U		U	
214	2582	1	2	16	H		U	U	U	U		U		U	
215	2591	2	2	17	H		U	P	U	U		U		U	
216	2592	2	2	17	H		U	P	U	U		U		U	

CRS	ID	SEX	RACE	AGE	ZYG	_124	_125	_126	_127	_128	_129	_130	_131	_132	_133
217	2601	1	2	15	D										
218	2602	1	2	15	D										
219	2611	1	2	14	I										
220	2612	1	2	14	M										
221	2621	2	2	15	D										
222	2622	2	2	15	D										
223	2631	1	2	14	J										
224	2632	2	2	14	J										
225	2641	2	2	14	I										
226	2642	2	2	14	M										
227	2651	2	2	14	I										
228	2652	2	2	14	D										
229	2661	2	2	14	C										
230	2662	2	2	14	M										
231	2671	2	2	14	M										
232	2672	2	2	14	M										
233	2681	2	2	14	M										
234	2682	2	2	14	M										
235	2691	2	2	17	M										
236	2692	2	2	13	I										
237	2701	2	2	13	D										
238	2702	2	1	16	D										
239	2711	2	1	16	J										
240	2712	2	2	14	D										
241	2721	2	1	14	O										
242	2722	2	1	14	I										
243	2731	2	1	14	M										
244	2732	2	2	14	D										
245	2741	1	2	14	D										
246	2742	1	2	16	D										
247	2751	2	2	16	I										
248	2752	2	2	14	M										
249	2761	2	1	14	D										
250	2762	2	1	16	I										
251	2771	2	1	16	M										
252	2772	1	1	14	I										
253	2781	1	2	14	I										
254	2782	2	2	14	F										
255	2791	2	2	16	J										
256	2801	1	2	16	D										
257	2802	1	2	17	O										
258	2811	1	2	17	J										
259	2812	2	2	13	D										
260	2821	2	2	13	D										
261	2822	1	2	14	D										
262	2831	2	2	17	I										
263	2832	2	2	15	M										
264	2841	2	2	15	D										
265	2842	2	2	14	D										
266	2851	2	2	14	I										
267	2852	1	2	14	M										
268	2861	1	2	14	D										
269	2862	1	2	14	D										

OBS	ID	SEX	RACE	AGE	ZYG
271	2871	1	2	14	M
272	2872	1	2	14	M
273	2881	2	2	16	M
274	2882	2	2	16	U
275	2891	2	2	15	M
276	2892	1	2	15	M
277	2901	1	1	18	M
278	2902	1	1	18	M
279	2911	1	2	17	D
280	2912	1	2	17	D
281	2921	2	2	13	U
282	2922	2	2	13	U
283	2931	1	2	14	U
284	2932	2	2	14	D
285	2941	2	2	15	U
286	2942	2	2	15	U
287	2951	1	2	16	D
288	2952	2	2	16	U
289	2961	2	2	15	U
290	2962	2	2	15	D
291	2971	1	2	15	M
292	2972	1	2	15	U
293	2981	1	2	16	D
294	2982	2	2	16	U
295	2991	2	2	17	M
296	2992	2	2	17	U
297	3001	1	2	13	D
298	3002	1	2	13	M
299	3011	2	2	18	M
300	3012	2	2	18	M
301	3021	2	2	17	D
302	3022	1	2	17	M
303	3031	1	2	14	U
304	3032	1	2	14	M
305	3041	2	2	15	D
306	3042	2	2	14	M
307	3051	2	2	14	U
308	3052	2	2	13	M
309	3061	2	2	13	D
310	3062	2	2	16	M
311	3071	2	2	16	M
312	3072	2	2	15	M
313	3081	2	2	15	D
314	3082	2	1	17	D
315	3091	2	1	17	U
316	3092	1	1	17	U
317	3101	1	1	16	U
318	3102	1	1	16	U
319	3111	2	2	14	U
320	3112	1	2	14	U
321	3121	1	1	16	U
322	3122	1	1	16	U
323	3131	2	1	13	U
324	3132	2	1	13	U

OBS	ID	SEX	RACE	AGE	ZYG	_124	_125	_126	_127	_128	_129	_130	_131	_132	_133
325	3141	1	2	13	M		U	U	U	U		U		U	
326	3142	1	2	13	M		U	U	U	U		U		U	
327	3151	2	2	15	M		U	P	U	U		U		U	
328	3152	2	2	15	U		U	P	U	U		U		U	
329	3161	1	1	17	U		U	P	U	U		U		U	
330	3162	2	1	17	D		U	U	U	U		U		U	
331	3171	2	1	14	D		U	U	U	U		U		U	
332	3172	2	1	14	D		U	U	U	U		U		U	
333	3181	2	1	18	D		U	U	U	U		U		U	
334	3182	2	2	18	D		U	U	U	U		U		U	
335	3191	1	2	18	D		U	U	U	U		U		U	
336	3192	1	2	13	U		U	U	U	U		U		U	
337	3201	2	2	13	U		U	U	U	U		U		U	
338	3202	2	2	13	M		U	U	U	U		U		U	
339	3211	1	2	14	M		U	P	U	U		U		U	
340	3212	1	2	14	U		U	P	U	U		U		U	
341	3221	1	1	14	U		U	P	U	U		U		U	
342	3222	2	1	15	M		U	U	U	U		U		U	
343	3231	1	1	15	D		U	U	U	U		U		U	
344	3232	1	2	16	D		U	U	U	U		U		U	
345	3241	2	2	16	D		U	U	U	U		U		U	
346	3242	2	2	17	U		U	P	U	U		U		U	
347	3251	1	2	17	U		U	P	U	U		U		U	
348	3252	2	2	16	D		U	U	U	U		U		U	
349	3261	1	2	16	D		U	U	U	U		U		U	
350	3262	2	2	18	U		U	U	U	U		U		U	
351	3271	2	2	18	U		U	U	U	U		U		U	
352	3272	2	2	16	M		U	P	U	U		U		U	
353	3281	2	1	16	M		U	P	U	U		U		U	
354	3282	1	1	14	M		U	U	U	U		U		U	
355	3291	1	1	14	D		U	U	U	U		U		U	
356	3292	1	2	17	O		U	P	U	U		U		U	
357	3301	2	2	17	M		U	U	U	U		U		U	
358	3302	2	1	14	M		U	U	U	U		U		U	
359	3311	1	1	14	M		U	U	U	U		U		U	
360	3312	1	1	14	O		U	U	U	U		U		U	
361	3321	2	1	13	D		U	U	U	U		U		U	
362	3322	2	2	13	M		U	U	U	U		U		U	
363	3331	1	1	15	M		U	P	U	U		U		U	
364	3332	1	1	15	O		U	P	U	U		U		U	
365	3351	1	1	15	C		U	U	U	U		U		U	
366	3352	2	2	15	M		U	P	U	U		U		U	
367	3361	2	1	12	M		U	P	U	U		U		U	
368	3362	2	1	12	M		U	U	U	U		U		U	
369	3371	2	2	15	M		U	P	U	U		U		U	
370	3372	1	1	15	M		U	U	U	U		U		U	
371	3381	1	1	14	M		U	P	U	U		U		U	
372	3382	1	2	14	M		U	U	U	U		U		U	
373	3391	1	2	15	M		U	P	U	U		U		U	
374	3392	1	2	15	U		U	U	U	U		U		U	
375	3401	2	2	15	U		U	P	U	U		U		U	
376	3402	1	2	16	O		U	P	U	U		U		U	
377	3411	2	2	16	O		U	U	U	U		U		U	
378	3412	2	2	16	D		U	U	U	U		U		U	

APPENDIX H

OBS	ID	SEX	RACE	AGE	ZYG	_124	_125	_126	_127	_128	_129	_130	_131	_132	_133
379	3421	2	2	14	M		U	P	U	U		U		U	
380	3422	2	2	14	M		U	P	U	U		U		U	
381	3431	2	2	15	U		U	U	U	U		U		U	
382	3432	1	2	15	U		U	P	U	U		U		U	
383	3441	2	2	13	U		U	P	U	U		U		U	
384	3442	1	2	13	U		U	P	U	U		U		U	
385	3451	2	2	16	M		U	P	U	U		U		U	
386	3452	2	2	16	U		U	U	U	U		U		U	
387	3461	2	1	14	U		U	U	U	U		U		U	
388	3462	2	1	14	D		U	P	U	U		U		U	
389	3471	1	1	14	D		U	P	U	U		U		U	
390	3472	2	1	16	U		U	U	U	U		U		U	
391	3481	2	1	16	U		U	U	U	U		U		U	
392	3482	2	1	13	M		U	P	U	U		U		U	
393	3491	1	2	13	D		U	U	U	U		U		U	
394	3492	2	2	18	D		U	U	U	U		U		U	
395	3501	2	2	18	M		U	P	U	U		U		U	
396	3502	1	1	17	M		U	P	U	U		U		U	
397	3511	1	1	17	M		U	U	U	U		U		U	
398	3512	1	1	15	U		U	U	U	U		U		U	
399	3521	1	1	17	U		U	U	U	U		U		U	
400	3522	2	1	17	U		U	U	U	U		U		U	
401	3531	1	1	14	M		U	P	U	U		U		U	
402	3532	2	2	14	D		U	P	U	U		U		U	
403	3541	1	1	14	M		U	U	U	U		U		U	
404	3542	2	1	16	D		U	U	U	U		U		U	
405	3551	2	1	15	M		U	P	U	U		U		U	
406	3552	2	1	15	M		U	U	U	U		U		U	
407	3561	2	1	17	D		U	P	U	U		U		U	
408	3562	2	1	15	D		U	U	U	U		U		U	
409	3581	2	2	15	U		U	U	U	U		U		U	
410	3582	2	2	17	U		U	P	U	U		U		U	
411	3591	1	1	14	D		U	U	U	U		U		U	
412	3592	1	1	14	D		U	U	U	U		U		U	
413	3601	1	1	15	M		U	P	U	U		U		U	
414	3602	1	1	16	D		U	P	U	U		U		U	
415	3611	2	2	14	D		U	U	U	U		U		U	
416	3612	2	2	14	D		U	U	U	U		U		U	
417	3621	1	1	13	M		U	P	U	U		U		U	
418	3622	1	1	13	M		U	P	U	U		U		U	
419	3631	1	1	18	D		U	U	U	U		U		U	
420	3632	1	1	18	D		U	P	U	U		U		U	
421	3641	1	1	14	M		U	U	U	U		U		U	
422	3642	1	1	14	M		U	P	U	U		U		U	
423	3651	1	1	14	M		U	U	U	U		U		U	
424	3652	1	1	14	M		U	U	U	U		U		U	
425	3661	2	2	14	M		U	U	U	U		U		U	
426	3662	2	2	13	M		U	P	U	U		U		U	
427	3671	1	1	13	M		U	U	U	U		U		U	
428	3672	1	1	16	M		U	U	U	U		U		U	
429	3681	2	2	16	M		U	P	U	U		U		U	
430	3682	2	2	14	M		U	U	U	U		U		U	
431	3691	1	1	14	M		U	U	U	U		U		U	
432	3692	1	1	14	M		U	U	U	U		U		U	

CBS	ID	SEX	RACE	AGE	ZYG	_124	_125	_126	_127	_128	_129	_130	_131	_132	_133
433	3701	2	2	14	U		U	U	U	U		U		U	
434	3702	1	2	14	U		U	U	U	U		U		U	
435	3711	2	2	13	H		U	U	U	U		U		U	
436	3712	2	2	13	H		U	U	U	U		U		U	
437	3721	2	2	13	D		U	U	U	U		U		U	
438	3722	2	2	13	D		U	U	U	U		U		U	
439	3731	2	2	13	D		U	U	U	U		U		U	
440	3732	2	2	13	D		U	U	U	U		U		U	
441	3741	2	1	13	H		U	U	U	U		U		U	
442	3742	2	1	13	H		U	U	U	U		U		U	
443	3751	2	2	17	C		U	U	U	U		U		U	
444	3752	2	2	17	O		U	U	U	U		U		U	
445	3761	1	2	13	D		U	U	U	U		U		U	
446	3762	2	2	13	D		U	U	U	U		U		U	
447	3771	2	2	13	D		U	U	U	U		U		U	
448	3772	2	2	15	O		U	U	U	U		U		U	
449	3781	2	2	15	H		U	U	U	U		U		U	
450	3782	2	2	16	H		U	U	U	U		U		U	
451	3791	1	2	16	H		U	U	U	U		U		U	
452	3792	1	2	16	U		U	U	U	U		U		U	
453	3801	1	2	16	U		U	U	U	U		U		U	
454	3802	1	2	16	H		U	U	U	U		U		U	
455	3811	2	2	14	H		U	U	U	U		U		U	
456	3812	2	2	14	H		U	U	U	U		U		U	
457	3821	2	2	15	U		U	U	U	U		U		U	
458	3822	2	2	15	U		U	U	U	U		U		U	
459	3831	2	2	13	H		U	U	U	U		U		U	
460	3832	2	2	13	H		U	U	U	U		U		U	
461	3841	1	2	13	O		U	U	U	U		U		U	
462	3842	2	2	13	O		U	U	U	U		U		U	
463	3851	1	2	13	H		U	U	U	U		U		U	
464	3852	2	2	13	H		U	U	U	U		U		U	
465	3861	2	2	15	U		U	U	U	U		U		U	
466	3862	2	2	15	U		U	U	U	U		U		U	
467	3871	2	2	14	U		U	U	U	U		U		U	
468	3872	2	2	14	D		U	U	U	U		U		U	
469	3881	2	2	14	D		U	U	U	U		U		U	
470	3882	2	2	14	D		U	U	U	U		U		U	
471	3891	2	2	14	H		U	U	U	U		U		U	
472	3892	2	2	13	H		U	U	U	U		U		U	
473	3901	1	2	13	O		U	U	U	U		U	U	U	
474	3902	1	2	15	O		U	U	U	U		U	U	U	
475	3911	2	2	15	D		U	U	U	U		U	U	U	
476	3912	2	1	15	O		U	U	U	U		U	U	U	
477	5001	2	1	18	H		U	U	U	U	U	U	U	U	
478	5002	2	1	18	H		U	U	U	U	U	U	U	U	
479	5011	2	1	14	H		U	U	U	U	U	U	U	U	
480	5012	2	1	14	H		U	U	U	U	U	U	U	U	
481	5021	2	2	14	H		U	U	U	U	U	U	U	U	
482	5022	2	2	13	H		U	U	U	U	U	U	U	U	
483	5031	2	1	13	O		U	U	U	U	U	U	U	U	
484	5032	2	2	13	O		U	U	U	U	U	U	U	U	
485	5041	2	1	16	O		U	U	U	U		U		U	
486	5042	2	1	16	D		U	U	U	U		U		U	

259

OBS	ID	SEX	RACE	AGE	ZYG	_124	_125	_126	_127	_128	_129	_130	_131	_132	_133
487	5051	2	1	17	M					C	C		C		
488	5052	2	1	17	M					C	C		C		
489	5061	2	1	14	D					P	C		C		
490	5062	2	1	14	D					C	C		C		
491	5071	2	1	17	D					C	C		C		
492	5072	1	1	17	M					C	C		C		
493	5081	1	1	17	M					C	C		C		
494	5082	2	1	13	M					C	C		C		
495	5091	2	1	13	D					C	C		C		
496	5092	2	1	14	D					P	C		C		
497	5101	2	1	14	D					C	C		C		
498	5102	2	1	15	D					C	C		C		
499	5111	1	1	15	D					C	C		C		
500	5112	1	1	20	M					P	C		C		
501	5131	1	1	20	M					P	C		C		
502	5132	2	1	15	M					C	C		C		
503	5141	2	1	15	M					C	C		C		
504	5142	2	2	17	M					C	C		C		
505	5151	2	2	17	D					C	C		C		
506	5152	2	1	13	D					P	C		C		
507	5161	2	1	13	D					P	C		C		
508	5162	2	1	17	M					C	C		C		
509	5171	2	1	17	M					C	C		C		
510	5172	2	1	13	D					C	C		C		
511	5181	2	1	13	M					P	C		C		
512	5182	2	1	13	M					C	C		C		
513	5191	2	1	15	M					C	C		C		
514	5192	1	2	13	M					C	C		C		
515	5201	1	2	13	D					P	C		C		
516	5202	2	1	13	D					C	C		C		
517	5211	2	1	13	M					C	C		C		
518	5212	2	1	16	M					C	C		C		
519	5221	1	1	16	M					P	C		C		
520	5222	2	1	14	M					C	C		C		
521	5231	2	1	14	M					C	C		C		
522	5232	2	1	13	D					P	C		C		
523	5241	2	1	13	D					C	C		C		
524	5242	2	1	16	M					C	C		C		
525	5251	2	1	16	M					C	C		C		
526	5252	1	1	16	D					P	C		C		
527	5261	1	1	17	M					C	C		C		
528	5262	2	1	18	D					C	C		C		
529	5271	2	1	18	M					P	C		C		
530	5272	2	2	13	M					C	C		C		
531	5281	2	2	13	D					C	C		C		
532	5282	2	1	14	M					P	C		C		
533	5291	2	1	14	M					C	C		C		
534	5292	1	1	16	M					C	C		C		
535	5301	1	1	13	D					P	C		C		
536	5302	1	1	13	M					C	C		C		
537	5311	2	1	14	M					C	C		C		
538	5312	2	1	14	M					P	C		C		
539	5321	2	1	16	M					C	C		C		
540	5322	2	1	16	M					C	C		C		

OBS	ID	SEX	RACE	AGE	ZYG	_124	_125	_126	_127	_128	_129	_130	_131	_132	_133
541	5331	2	1	17	M					C	C		C		
542	5332	2	1	17	M					C	C		C		
543	5341	2	1	13	D					C	P				
544	5342	2	1	13	D					C	C				
545	5351	2	1	16	D					C	C		C		
546	5352	2	1	17	M					C	C		C		
547	5361	1	1	17	M					C	C		C		
548	5362	1	1	17	M					C	C		C		
549	5371	1	1	13	D					C	C		C		
550	5372	1	1	13	D					C	C				
551	5381	1	1	15	M					P	C				
552	5382	2	1	15	D					P	P				
553	5391	2	1	15	M					C	C		C		
554	5392	1	1	14	D					C	C		C		
555	5401	1	1	14	M					C	C		C		
556	5402	2	1	14	D					C	C		C		
557	5411	2	1	12	M					C	C				
558	5412	2	1	12	D					C	P				
559	5421	1	1	15	M					C	C		C		
560	5422	1	1	15	D					C	C		C		
561	5431	1	1	14	M					C	C		C		
562	5432	1	1	14	D					C	C		C		
563	5441	1	1	14	M					C	C		C		
564	5442	1	1	14	M					C	C		C		
565	5451	2	1	18	M					P	P		C		
566	5452	2	1	18	M					C	C		C		
567	5461	1	1	17	M					C	C		C		
568	5462	2	1	17	M					C	C		C		
569	5471	2	1	16	M					P	C		C		
570	5472	1	1	16	M					P	P		C		
571	5481	1	1	17	M					P	C		C		
572	5482	1	1	17	M					C	C		C		
573	5491	1	1	14	M					C	C		C		
574	5492	1	2	14	D					P	P		C		
575	5511	1	2	15	D					P	C		C		
576	5512	2	1	15	M					C	C		C		
577	5521	2	1	13	M					P	C		C		
578	5522	2	1	13	M					C	C		C		
579	5531	2	1	16	M					C	C		C		
580	5532	1	1	16	D					P	P		C		
581	5541	1	1	16	M					P	P		C		
582	5542	1	1	16	M					C	C		C		
583	5551	1	1	17	M					C	C		C		
584	5552	1	1	17	M					C	C		C		
585	5571	1	1	15	M					P	C		C		
586	5572	2	1	15	D					C	C		C		
587	5581	2	1	15	M					P	C		C		
588	5582	2	1	15	M					P	C		C		
589	5591	1	1	16	D					C	C		C		
590	5592	1	1	16	M					C	C		C		
591	5601	2	1	15	D					P	C		C		
592	5602	2	1	15	D					P	P		C		
593	5611	2	1	17	D					C	P		C		
594	5612	1	1	17	D					C	C		C		

OBS	ID	SEX	RACE	AGE	ZYG	_124	_125	_126	_127	_128	_129	_130	_131	_132	_133
595	5621	2	1	16	M					P	C		C		
596	5622	2	1	16	M					C	C		C		
597	5631	2	2	14	M					P	P		C		
598	5632	2	2	14	D					C	C		C		
599	5641	2	1	13	D					C	C		C		
600	5642	2	1	13	M					C	C		C		
601	5661	2	1	17	M					C	C		C		
602	5662	2	1	17	D					C	C		C		
603	5671	2	1	13	D					C	C		C		
604	5672	2	1	13	M					C	C		C		
605	5681	1	1	15	M					C	C		C		
606	5682	1	1	15	M					P	C		C		
607	5691	1	1	17	M					C	C		C		
608	5692	1	1	17	C					C	C		C		
609	5701	2	1	13	D					C	C		C		
610	5702	1	1	16	D					C	C		C		
611	5711	1	1	15	D					C	C		C		
612	5712	1	1	15	D					C	C		C		
613	5721	1	1	13	D					C	C		C		
614	5722	1	1	13	D					C	C		C		
615	5731	2	1	15	D					C	C		C		
616	5732	2	1	13	D					C	C		C		
617	5741	2	1	15	D					C	C		C		
618	5742	2	1	13	C					P	C		C		
619	5751	1	1	13	M					P	C		C		
620	5752	1	1	13	M					C	C		C		
621	5761	2	1	13	D					P	C		C		
622	5762	2	1	13	M					C	C		C		
623	5771	2	1	16	D					C	C		C		
624	5772	2	1	16	C					C	C		C		
625	5781	1	1	16	M					P	C		C		
626	5782	2	1	16	D					P	C		C		
627	5791	2	1	17	D					P	C		C		
628	5792	2	1	17	D					C	C		C		
629	5801	2	1	18	D					C	C		C		
630	5802	1	1	18	D					P	C		C		
631	5811	1	1	18	D					C	C		C		
632	5812	1	1	15	C					P	C		C		
633	5821	1	1	15	M					C	C		C		
634	5822	1	1	15	M					C	C		C		
635	5841	2	1	17	D					C	C		C		
636	5842	2	1	17	M					C	C		C		
637	5861	2	1	17	D					C	C		C		
638	5862	2	1	18	M					C	C		C		
639	5871	1	1	18	M					C	C		C		
640	5872	1	1	16	M					C	C		C		
641	5881	1	2	16	M					C	C		C		
642	5882	2	2	16	M					C	C		C		
643	5891	2	2	16	M					C	C		C		
644	5892	2	1	17	M					C	C		C		
645	5901	2	1	14	M					C	C		C		
646	5902	2	1	14	M					C	C		C		
647	5921	2	1		M					C	C		C		
648	5922	2	1		M					C	C		C		

APPENDIX H

OBS	ID	SEX	RACE	AGE	ZYG	_124	_125	_126	_127	_128	_129	_130	_131	_132	_133
649	5931	1	1	16	D					C	C		C		
650	5932	1	1	16	D					C	C		C		
651	5941	2	1	15	M					C	C		C		
652	5942	2	1	15	M					C	C		C		
653	5951	1	1	13	D					C	C		C		
654	5952	1	1	13	D					C	C		C		
655	5961	2	1	15	D					C	C		C		
656	5962	2	1	15	D					C	C		C		
657	5971	2	1	16	D					C	C		C		
658	5972	2	1	16	M					C	C		C		
659	5981	2	1	18	M					C	C		C		
660	5982	2	1	18	M					C	C		C		
661	5991	1	1	14	D					C	C		C		
662	5992	1	1	14	D					C	C		C		
663	6001	1	1	15	D					C	C		C		
664	6002	1	1	15	D					C	C		C		
665	6011	2	1	16	M					C	C		C		
666	6012	2	1	16	M					C	C		C		
667	6021	1	1	16	M					C	C		C		
668	6022	2	1	16	M					C	C		C		
669	6031	2	1	16	C					C	C		C		
670	6032	2	1	16	D					C	C		C		
671	6041	1	1	13	D					C	C		C		
672	6042	1	1	15	D					C	C		C		
673	6051	2	1	15	M					C	C		C		
674	6052	2	1	16	M					C	C		C		
675	6061	2	1	16	M					C	C		C		
676	6062	2	1	15	M					C	C		C		
677	6071	1	1	15	M					C	C		C		
678	6072	1	1	15	D					C	C		C		
679	6081	1	1	15	D					C	C		C		
680	6082	1	1	16	M					C	C		C		
681	6101	2	1	16	M					C	C		C		
682	6102	2	1	16	M					C	C		C		
683	6111	1	1	14	M					C	C		C		
684	6112	1	1	14	M					C	C		C		
685	6121	2	1	16	D					C	C		C		
686	6122	2	1	16	D					C	C		C		
687	6131	1	1	13	M					C	C		C		
688	6132	1	1	13	M					C	C		C		
689	6141	1	1	16	M					C	C		C		
690	6142	1	1	16	M					C	C		C		
691	6151	1	1	15	D					C	C		C		
692	6152	1	1	15	D					C	C		C		
693	6161	2	1	16	C					C	C		C		
694	6162	2	1	16	M					C	C		C		
695	6171	1	1	19	M					C	C		C		
696	6172	1	1	19	M					C	C		C		
697	6181	2	1	18	D					C	C		C		
698	6182	2	1	18	C					C	C		C		
699	6191	2	2	18	M					C	C		C		
700	6192	2	2	18	M					C	C		C		
701	6201	2	2	15	M					C	C		C		
702	6202	2	1	15	M					C	C		C		

OBS	ID	SEX	RACE	AGE	ZYG	_124	_125	_126	_127	_128	_129	_130	_131	_132	_133
703	6211	2	1	15	0					0	0		0		
704	6212	2	1	15	0					0	0		0		
705	6221	2	1	14	0					0	0		0		
706	6222	2	1	14	0					0	0		0		
707	6231	1	1	17	0					0	0		0		
708	6232	1	1	17	0					0	0		0		
709	6241	1	1	17	0					0	0		0		
710	6242	1	1	17	0					P	0		0		
711	6251	1	1	15	M					0	0		0		
712	6252	1	1	15	M					0	0		0		
713	6261	1	1	16	M					0	0		0		
714	6262	1	1	16	M					0	0		0		
715	6271	2	1	15	M					0	0		0		
716	6272	2	1	15	D					0	0		0		
717	6281	1	1	14	0					0	0		0		
718	6282	2	2	14	M					0	0		0		
719	6291	2	1	14	M					0	0		0		
720	6292	1	2	17	D					P	0		0		
721	6301	1	1	17	0					0	0		0		
722	6302	1	1	19	M					0	0		0		
723	6311	1	1	19	0					0	0		0		
724	6312	1	1	19	M					0	0		0		
725	6321	2	1	18	D					0	0		0		
726	6322	2	1	18	0					0	0		0		
727	6331	1	1	15	0					0	0		0		
728	6332	1	1	15	F					0	0		0		
729	6341	1	1	16	0					0	0		0		
730	6342	1	1	16	M					0	0		0		
731	6351	2	1	16	0					0	0		0		
732	6352	1	2	16	M					0	0		0		
733	6361	1	2	15	D					0	0		0		
734	6362	2	1	16	0					0	0		0		
735	6371	2	1	16	0					0	0		0		
736	6372	2	1	16	D					0	0		0		
737	6381	2	1	15	0					0	0		0		
738	6382	2	2	13	0					0	0		0		
739	6391	2	1	18	D					0	0		0		
740	6392	2	1	18	0					0	0		0		
741	6401	2	2	14	0					0	0		0		
742	6402	1	2	14	0					0	0		0		
743	6411	1	1	17	D					0	0		0		
744	6412	1	1	17	0					0	0		0		
745	6431	2	1	15	0					0	0		0		
746	6432	2	1	15	0					0	0		0		
747	6441	1	2	15	0					0	0		0		
748	6442	1	2	15	0					0	0		0		
749	6451	1	1	15	0					0	0		0		
750	6452	2	1	15	0					0	0		0		
751	6461	2	1	15	F					0	0		0		
752	6462	1	1	16	F					0	0		0		
753	6471	2	1	16	F					0	0		0		
754	6472	1	1	16	F					0	0		0		
755	6481	1	1	16	F					0	0		0		
756	6482	1	1	16	M					0	0		0		

APPENDIX H

OBS	ID	SEX	RACE	AGE	ZYG
757	6491	2	1	14	D
758	6492	2	1	14	D
759	6501	1	1	17	M
760	6502	1	1	17	M
761	6511	1	1	15	M
762	6512	1	1	15	M
763	6521	1	2	15	M
764	6522	1	2	15	D
765	6531	2	1	16	D
766	6532	2	1	16	D
767	6541	1	1	16	C
768	6542	1	1	16	M
769	6551	2	1	17	M
770	6552	2	1	17	M
771	6561	1	1	14	M
772	6562	1	1	14	M
773	6571	1	1	17	D
774	6572	1	1	17	D
775	6581	2	1	17	D
776	6582	2	1	16	D
777	6591	1	1	16	D
778	6592	1	1	13	D
779	6601	2	1	13	D
780	6602	2	1	18	D
781	6611	2	1	18	D
782	6612	2	1	18	M
783	6621	2	1	18	C
784	6622	2	1	14	M
785	6631	2	1	14	D
786	6632	1	1	19	C
787	6641	1	1	18	M
788	6651	1	1	18	F
789	6652	1	1	18	D
790	6661	1	1	18	D
791	6662	1	1	15	D
792	6671	2	1	15	C
793	6672	2	1	13	M
794	6681	1	1	13	M
795	6691	2	1	15	C
796	6692	2	1	15	M
797	6701	1	1	13	M
798	6702	1	1	13	M
799	6711	1	1	14	M
800	6712	2	1	14	M
801	6721	2	1	14	F
802	6722	2	1	16	M
803	6731	2	1	16	M
804	6732	1	1	17	F
805	6741	1	1	17	M
806	6742	2	1	15	M
807	6751	2	1	15	M
808	6752				

APPENDIX H

OBS	ID	SEX	RACE	AGE	ZYG	_124	_125	_126	_127	_128	_129	_130	_131	_132	_133
811	6771	1	1	17	D										
812	6772	1	1	17	D										
813	6781	1	1	14	D										
814	6782	1	1	14	D										
815	6791	2	1	16	M										
816	6792	2	1	16	M										
817	6801	2	1	15	M										
818	6802	2	1	15	M										
819	6811	2	1	16	M										
820	6812	2	1	16	D										
821	6841	1	1	13	D										
822	6842	1	1	13	M										
823	6851	2	1	15	M										
824	6852	2	1	15	M										
825	6861	1	2	16	M										
826	6862	2	2	16	M										
827	6871	2	1	19	M										
828	6872	2	1	19	F										
829	6881	1	1	14	M										
830	6882	1	1	14	M										
831	6891	1	1	13	M										
832	6892	1	1	13	M										
833	6901	2	1	13	M										
834	6902	2	1	14	M										
835	6911	2	1	14	D										
836	6912	2	1	17	O										
837	6921	2	1	17	D										
838	6922	2	1	15	D										
839	6931	2	1	15	M										
840	6932	2	1	16	M										
841	6941	1	1	16	D										
842	6942	1	1	15	D										
843	6951	1	2	15	M										
844	6952	1	2	13	M										
845	6961	2	2	15	D										
846	6962	2	2	15	D										
847	6971	2	2	15	M										
848	6972	1	1	17	M										
849	6981	1	1	17	D										
850	6982	1	1	15	M										
851	6991	2	1	15	M										
852	6992	2	1	15	M										
853	7001	2	1	16	M										
854	7002	2	1	16	M										
855	7011	2	2	15	M										
856	7012	2	2	15	M										
857	7021	1	1	17	M										
858	7022	2	1	17	M										
859	7031	2	1	17	D										
860	7032	2	1	17	D										
861	7041	2	1	17	M										
862	7042	2	1	17	M										
863	7061	2	1	15	D										
864	7062	2	1	15	D										

APPENDIX H

OBS	ID	SEX	RACE	AGE	ZYG
865	7071	1	1	18	M
866	7072	1	1	18	H
867	7081	2	1	14	D
868	7082	2	1	14	D
869	7091	1	1	15	H
870	7092	1	1	15	D
871	7101	1	1	17	H
872	7102	2	1	17	D
873	7111	2	1	17	H
874	7112	2	1	15	D
875	7121	2	1	15	D
876	7122	2	1	15	D
877	7131	1	1	15	D
878	7132	2	1	13	M
879	7141	1	1	13	H
880	7142	2	2	13	H
881	7151	2	2	13	H
882	7152	2	1	16	H
883	7161	2	1	16	H
884	7162	2	1	15	M
885	7171	2	1	15	H
886	7172	1	1	13	H
887	7191	1	1	13	H
888	7192	1	1	17	H
889	7201	1	1	17	M
890	7202	1	1	15	D
891	7221	1	1	15	D
892	7222	1	1	16	H
893	7231	1	1	16	H
894	7232	2	1	16	H
895	7241	2	1	16	D
896	7242	1	1	15	D
897	7251	1	1	15	D
898	7252	2	1	18	M
899	7271	2	1	18	H
900	7272	2	1	17	H
901	7281	2	1	17	H
902	7282	2	2	16	H
903	7291	1	1	16	H
904	7292	1	2	14	H
905	7301	1	1	14	H
906	7302	1	1	18	H
907	7311	1	1	18	H
908	7312	1	1	15	H
909	7321	1	1	15	H
910	7322	2	1	13	F
911	7331	1	1	13	H
912	7332	1	1	15	H
913	7341	1	1	15	H
914	7342	1	1	17	H
915	7351	1	1	17	H
916	7352	1	1	14	H
917	7361	1	1	14	H
918	7362	2	1	14	H

CBS	ID	SEX	RACE	AGE	ZYG	_124	_125	_126	_127	_128	_129	_130	_131	_132	_133
919	7371	1	1	16	M										
920	7372	1	1	16	M										
921	7381	2	1	13	D					U	U		U		
922	7382	2	1	13	D					U	U		U		
923	7391	1	2	16	D					U	U		U		
924	7392	1	2	16	D					P	U		U		
925	7411	2	1	14	D					U	U		U		
926	7412	2	1	16	D					U	U		U		
927	7421	2	1	16	M					U	U		U		
928	7422	2	1	16	M					U	U		U		
929	7431	2	1	14	M					U	U		U		
930	7432	2	1	14	M					U	U		U		
931	7441	1	1	16	M					U	U		U		
932	7442	1	1	16	M					U	U		U		
933	7451	1	1	14	M					U	U		U		
934	7452	1	1	14	M					U	U		U		
935	7461	2	1	16	M					U	U		U		
936	7462	2	1	16	M					U	U		U		
937	7471	2	1	17	M					U	U		U		
938	7472	2	1	17	M					U	P		U		
939	7481	2	2	14	M					P	U		U		
940	7482	2	2	14	D					U	U		U		
941	7491	2	1	18	D					U	U		U		
942	7492	2	1	18	D					U	U		U		
943	7501	1	1	14	M					U	U		U		
944	7502	1	1	14	D					U	U		U		
945	7521	1	1	17	D					U	U		U		
946	7522	1	1	17	M					U	U		U		U
947	7531	2	1	18	D					U	U		U		U
948	7532	2	1	18	M					U	U		U		U
949	7541	2	1	16	D					U	U		U		P
950	7542	2	1	16	D					U	U		U		U
951	7551	1	1	17	M					U	U		U		U
952	7552	1	1	17	M					U	U		U		U
953	8751	1	1	18	M					U	U		U		U
954	8752	1	1	18	M					U	U		U		U
955	9011	1	1	18	M					U	U		U		U
956	9012	1	1	18	M					U	U		U		U
957	9021	2	1	20	M					U	U		U		U
958	9022	2	1	20	M					U	U		U		U
959	9031	2	1	22	M					U	U		U		U
960	9032	2	1	22	M					U	U		U		U
961	9041	2	1	18	M					U	U		U		U
962	9042	2	1	18	M					U	U		U		U
963	9051	2	1	16	M					U	U		U		U
964	9052	2	1	16	M					U	U		U		U
965	9061	1	2	18	M					U	U		U		U
966	9062	1	2	18	M					U	U		U		U
967	9071	1	1	15	M					U	U		U		U
968	9072	1	1	15	M					U	U		U		U
969	9081	2	1	19	M					U	U		U		U
970	9082	2	1	11	M					U	U		U		U
971	9091	1	1	11	M					U	U		U		U
972	9092	1	1	11	M					U	U				U

APPENDIX H

18:06 TUESDAY, AUGUST 21, 1979

OBS	ID	SEX	RACE	AGE	ZYG	_124	_125	_126	_127	_128	_129	_130	_131	_132	_133	70
973	9101	1	1	18	M										C	
974	9102	1	1	18	M										C	
975	9111	2	1	11	M										C	
976	9112	2	1	11	M										C	
977	9121	1	1	21	M										P	
978	9122	1	1	21	M										P	
979	9131	1	1	19	M										C	
980	9132	1	1	19	M										C	
981	9141	1	1	11	D										C	
982	9142	2	1	11	D										C	
983	9151	2	1	15	D										C	
984	9152	2	1	15	D										C	
985	9161	2	1	12	D										C	
986	9162	2	1	12	D										C	
987	9171	1	1	18	D										C	
988	9172	1	1	18	D										C	
989	9181	1	1	19	D										C	
990	9182	2	1	19	D										C	
991	9191	2	1	19	D										C	
992	9192	2	1	19	D										C	

N=992

References

Allen, G. Within group and between group variation expected in human behavioral characters. *Behavior Genetics,* 1970, *1,* 175–194.

Allen, R. D., Bixler, H. H., Connor, W. L., & Graham, F. B. *Spelling achievement test; metropolitan achievement test.* Yonkers on Hudson, New York: World Book, 1946.

Barr, A. J., Goodnight, J. H., Sall, J. P., & Helwig, J. T. *A user's guide to SAS 76.* Raleigh, NC: SAS Institute Inc., 1976.

Bickford, R. G., Jacobson, J. L., & Cody, D. T. R. Nature of average evoked potentials to sound and other stimuli in man. *Annals of the New York Academy of Sciences,* 1964, *112* (1), 204–223.

Binet, A., & Henri, V. La psychologie individuelle. *Année Psychol.,* 1895, *2,* 411–465.

Blewett, D. B. An experimental study of the inheritance of intelligence. *Journal of Mental Science,* 1954, *100,* 922–933.

Bodmer, W. F. Race and IQ: The genetic background. In A. Montagu (Ed.), *Race and IQ.* New York: Oxford Univ. Press, 1975.

Bouchard, T. J. Genetic factors in intelligence, In A. Kaplan (Ed.), *Human Behavior Genetics.* Springfield, Ill.: Charles C. Thomas, 1976.

Breland, N. S. A new approach to estimates of heritability from twin data. Unpublished research qualifying paper, Department of Educational Psychology, State University of New York at Buffalo, 1972.

Burt, C., & Howard, M. The multifactorial theory of inheritance and its application to intelligence. *Brit. J. Stat. Psychol.,* 1956, *9,* 95–131.

Callaway, E., & Buchsbaum, M. Effects of cardiac and respiratory cycles on averaged visual evoked responses. *Electroencephalography and Clinical Neurophysiology,* 1965, *19,* 476–480.

Cattell, R. B. A universal index for psychological factors. *Psychologia,* 1957, *1,* 74–85.

Cattell, R. B. *Manual for the Cattell Culture Fair Intelligence Test.* Indianapolis, Indiana: Bobbs & Merrill Co., Inc., 1960.

Cattell, R. B. *Junior High Personality Questionnaire.* Champaign, Ill.: Institute for Personality and Ability Testing, 1969.

Cattell, R. B. *Abilities: Their structure, growth, and action.* Boston: Houghton Mifflin, 1971.

Cattell, R. B., Blewett, D. B., & Beloff, J. R. The inheritance of personality: A multiple variance analysis determination of approximate nature-nurture ratios for primary personality factors in Q-data. *American Journal of Human Genetics,* 1955, *7,* 122–146.

Cattell, R. B., & Cattell, A. K. S. *Manual for the Culture Fair Intelligence Test, Scale 2.* Champaign, Ill.: Institute for Personality and Ability Testing, 1965.

Cattell, R. B., Stice, G. F., & Kristy, N. F. A first approximation to nature-nurture ratios for eleven primary personality factors in objective tests. *Journal of Abnormal Social Psychology,* 1957, *54,* 143–258.

Cedarlof, R., Friberg, L., Jonsson, E., & Kaij, L. Studies on similarity diagnosis in twins with the aid of mailed questionnaires. *Acta Genetica et Statistica Medica* (Basel), 1961, *11,* 338–362.

Christensen, P. R., & Guilford, J. A. *Ship destination test.* Los Angeles, Calif.: Sheridan Supply Co., 1955.

Cleary, T. A. Test bias: Prediction of grades of Negro and white students in integrated colleges. *Journal of Educational Measurement,* 1968, *5* (2) 115–124.

Cronbach, L. J. A review of *How Well Do You Know Yourself?* In O. K. Buros (Ed.), *Sixth Mental Measurements Yearbook.* Highland Park, NJ: The Gryphon Press, 1965.

Darwin, C. *The descent of man, and selection in relation to sex.* New York: D. Appleton and Company, 1871.

Dixon, W. J. *Biomedical computer programs.* Los Angeles, Calif.: Univ. of California Press, 1973.

Droege, R. C. Sex differences in aptitude maturation during high school. *Journal of Counseling Psychology,* 1967, *14,* 407–411.

DuBois, P. H., & Gleser, G. Object-aperture test. *American Psychologist,* 1948, *3,* 363.

Dustman, R. E., & Beck, E. C. Long-term stability of visually evoked potentials in man. *Science,* 1963, *142,* 1480–1481.

Dustman, R. E., & Beck, E. C. The visually evoked potential in twins. *Electroencephalography and Clinical Neurophysiology,* 1965, *19,* 570–575.

Ehrlich, P. R. *The race bomb: Skin color, prejudice, and intelligence.* New York: Quadrangle/The New York Times Book Co., Inc., 1977.

Equality of Educational Opportunity. U.S. Dept. of Health, Education, and Welfare. Washington, D.C.: U.S. Government Printing Office, 1966.

Eysenck, H. J. Primary and second-order factors in a critical consideration of Cattell's 16 PF battery. *British Journal of Social Clinical Psychology,* 1972, *11,* 265–269.

Eysenck, H. J. *The inequality of man.* San Diego, Calif.: EdITS publishers, 1975.

Eysenck, H. J. Genetic factors in personality development. In A. R. Kaplan (Ed.), *Human behavior genetics.* Springfield, Ill.: Charles C. Thomas, 1976.

Fisher, R. A. The genesis of twins. *Genetics,* 1919, *4,* 489–499.

Flannagan, J. C., Dailey, J., Shaycoft, M. F., Gorham, W. A., Orr, D. B., Goldberg, I., Neyman, C. *Counselor's technical manual for interpreting test scores.* Project Talent Office, Washington, D.C., 1961.

Forrest, D. W. *Francis Galton: The life and work of a victorian genius.* New York: Taplinger Publishing Co., 1974.

Fowler, W. L. A. A comparative analysis of pupil performance on conventional and culture-controlled mental tests. Unpublished Ph.D. thesis, Univ. of Michigan, 1955.

French, J. W., Ekstrom, R. B., & Price, L. A. *Manual for a kit of reference tests for cognitive factors.* Princeton, NJ: Educational Testing Service, 1963.

Fuller, J. L., & Thompson, W. R. *Behavior genetics.* New York: Wiley, 1960.

Galton, F. Hereditary talent and character. *Macmillan's Magazine,* 1865, *12,* 157–327.

Galton, F. *Hereditary genius: An inquiry into its laws and consequences.* London: MacMillan, 1869.

Galton, F. The history of twins, as a criterion of the relative powers of nature and nurture. *Fraser's Magazine,* 1875, *92,* 566–576.

Galton, F. 'Typical laws of heredity.' *Proceedings of the Royal Institute,* 1877, *8,* 282–301.

Galton, F. Presidential address, section H, anthropology. *British Association Report,* 1885, *55,* 1206–1214. (a)

Galton, F. Regression toward mediocrity in hereditary stature. *Journal of the Anthropological Institute,* 1885, *15,* 246–263. (b)

Galton, F. *Natural inheritance.* London: MacMillan, 1889.

Goldberg, L. R., & Rorer, L. G. Test-retest item statistics for the California Psychological Inventory. *Oregon Research Institute Research Monographs,* 1964, *4* (1).

Gottesman, I. I. Heritability of personality: A demonstration. *Psychological Monographs,* 1963, *77* (9, Whole No. 572), 1–21.

Gottesman, I. I. Genetic variance in adaptive personality traits. *Journal of Child Psychology and Psychiatry,* 1966, *7,* 199–208.

Guilford, J. P. *The nature of human intelligence.* New York: McGraw-Hill, 1967.

Heim, A. W. Self-judging vocabulary test. *Journal of Genetic Psychology,* 1965, *72,* 285–294.

Hertzka, A. F., & Guilford, J. P. *Test of logical reasoning.* Orange, Calif.: Sheridan Psychological Services, Inc., 1955.

Holzinger, K. J. The relative effect of nature and nurture influences on twin differences. *Journal of Educational Psychology,* 1929, *20* (4), 241–248.

Huntley, R. M. C. Heritability of intelligence. In J. E. Meade & A. S. Parks (Eds.), *Environmental factors in human ability.* London: Oliver & Boyd, 1966.

Husen, T. Abilities of twins. *Scandinavian Journal of Psychology,* 1960, *I,* 125–135.

Jenkins, T. N. *How Well Do You Know Yourself?* New York: Executive Analysis Corporation, 1959.

Jensen, A. R. Estimation of the limits of heritability of traits by comparison of monozygotic and dizygotic twins. Reprinted from the *Proceedings of the National Academy of Sciences,* 1967, *58* (1), 149–156.

Jensen, A. R. Another look at culture-fair tests. In *Western Regional Conference on Testing Problems, Proceedings for 1968, Measurement for Educational Planning.* Berkeley, Calif.: Educational Testing Service, Western Office, pp. 50–104.

Jensen, A. R. How much can we boost IQ and scholastic achievement? *Harvard Educational Review,* 1969, *39* (2), 1–123.

Jensen, A. R. *Educability and group differences.* New York: Harper, 1973. (a)

Jensen, A. R. *Educational Differences.* London: Methuen & Co. Ltd., 1973. (b)

Jensen, A. R. Kinship correlations reported by Sir Cyril Burt. *Behavior Genetics,* 1974, *4* (1), 1–28.

Jinks, J. L., Fulker, D. W. Comparison of the biometrical genetical, MAVA, and classical approaches to the analysis of human behavior. *Psychological Bulletin,* 1970, *73,* 311–349.

Johnson, R. C. Similarity in IQ of separated identical twins as related to length of time spent in same environment. *Child Development,* 1963, *34,* 745–749.

Kamin, L. J. *The science and politics of IQ.* Potomac, MD: Lawrence Erlbaum Associates, Inc., 1974.

Kasriel, J., & Eaves, L. The zygosity of twins: Further evidence on the agreement between diagnosis by blood groups and written questionnaires. *Journal of Biosocial Science,* 1976, *8,* 263–266.

Keogh, B. K. Pattern copying under three conditions of an expanded spatial field. *Developmental Psychology,* 1971, *4,* 25–31.

Koch, H. L. *Twins and twin relations.* Chicago: Univ. of Chicago Press, 1966.

Kooi, K. A., & Bagchi, B. K. Visual evoked responses in man: Normative data. *Annals of the New York Academy of Sciences,* 1964, *112* (1), 254–269.

Last, K. A. Genetical aspects of human behavior. Unpublished master's thesis, Department of Genetics, Univ. of Birmingham, England, 1977.

Layzer, D. Heritability analyses of IQ scores: Science or numerology? In A. Montagu (Ed.), *Race and IQ.* New York: Oxford Univ. Press, 1975.

Levinsohn, J., Lewis, L., Riccobono, J. A., & Moore, R. P. *National longitudinal study of the high school class of 1972.* Research Triangle Park, NC: Center for Educational Research and Evaluation, Research Triangle Institute, 1976.

Lennox, W. G., & Lennox, M. A. *Epilepsy and related disorders.* Vol. 2. Boston: Little, Brown, & Co., 1960.

Loehlin, J. C., Lindzey, G., & Spuhler, J. N. *Race differences in intelligence.* San Francisco, Calif.: W. H. Freeman & Co., 1975.

Maccoby, E. E. Sex differences in intellectual functioning. In E. E. Maccoby (Ed.), *The development of sex differences.* Stanford, Calif.: Stanford Univ. Press, 1966.

Maccoby, E. E., & Jacklin, C. N. *The psychology of sex differences.* Stanford, Calif.: Stanford Univ. Press, 1974.

Merriman, C. The intellectual resemblance of twins. *Psychological Monographs,* 1924, *XXXIII* (5), 1–58.

Mooney, C. M. Age in the development of closure ability in children. *Canadian Journal of Psychology,* 1957, *11,* 219–226.

Mukherjee, B. N. Simple arithmetic test. Unpublished Ph.D. thesis, Univ. of North Carolina, 1963.

Newman, H. H., Freeman, F. N., & Holzinger, K. J. *Twins: A study of heredity and environment.* Chicago: Univ. of Chicago Press, 1937.

Nichols, P. L. The effects of heredity and environment on intelligence test performance in 4 and 7 year old white and negro sibling pairs. Unpublished Ph.D. thesis, Univ. of Minnesota, 1970.

Nichols, R. C. The national merit twin study. In S. G. Vandenberg (Ed.), *Methods and goals in human behavior genetics.* New York: Academic Press, 1965.

Nichols, R. C. The resemblance of twins in personality and interests. *National Merit Scholarship Corporation Research Reports,* 1969, *2* (8), (Reprinted in Manosevitz, M., Lindzey, G., and Thiessen, D. S. *Behavioral genetics: Method and research,* New York.)

Nichols, R. C. Heredity and environment: Major findings from twin studies of ability, personality, and interests. Invited address presented at the American Psychological Association meeting, Washington, D.C., September 4, 1976.

Nichols, R. C., & Bilbro, W. C., Jr. The diagnosis of twin zygosity. *Acta Genetica et Statistica Medica,* 1966, *16,* 265–275.

Osborne, R. T. Psychometric correlates of the visual evoked potential. *Acta Psychologica,* 1969, *29,* 303–308.

Osborne, R. T. Heritability estimates for the visual evoked response. *Life Sciences,* 1970, *9,* part II, 481–490.

Osborne, R. T. Race and sex differences in heritability of mental test performance: A study of Negroid and Caucasoid twins. In R. T. Osborne, C. E. Noble, & N. Weyl (Eds.), *Human Variation: The biopsychology of age, race, and sex.* New York: Academic Press, 1978.

Osborne, R. T., & Gregor, A. J. Racial differences in inheritance ratios for tests of spatial ability. Paper presented to the Instituto Internacional de Sociologia, XXII Congreso, Madrid, October 1967.

Osborne, R. T., Gregor, A. J., Miele, F. Heritability of factor V: Verbal comprehension. *Perceptual and Motor Skills,* 1968, *26,* 191–202.

Pampiglione, G. Some observations on the variability of evoked potentials. *Electroencephalography and Clinical Neurophysiology,* 1967, Suppl. 26, 97–99.

Paulson, E. An approximate normalization of the analysis of variance distribution. *Annals of Mathematical Statistics,* 1942, *13,* 233–235.

Race, R. R., & Sanger, R. *Blood groups in man.* Oxford: Blackwell Scientific Publications, 1954.

Remondino, C. Calendar test. *Revue de Psychologie Applique,* 1962, *12,* 62–81.

Revised Beta Examination. New York: The Psychological Corporation, 1962.

Rimland, B., & Munsinger, H. Burt's IQ data. *Science,* 1977, *195,* 246–248.

Scarr-Salapatek, S. Race, social class, and IQ. *Science,* 1971, *174* (4016), 1285–1295.

Schoenfeldt, L. F. The hereditary components of the Project Talent two-day test battery. *Measurement and Evaluation in Guidance,* 1968, *1* (2), 130–140.

Schwartz, M., & Shagass, C. Effect of different states of alertness on somatosensory and auditory recovery cycles. *Electroencephalography and Clinical Neurophysiology,* 1962, *14,* 11–20.

Shuey, A. M. *The testing of Negro intelligence.* (2nd ed.). New York, Social Science Press, 1966.

Smith, I. M., & Lawes, J. S. *Newcastle spatial test.* Bedford, England: Newnes Educational Publishing, 1959.

Smith, S. M., & Penrose, L. S. Monozygotic and dizygotic twin diagnosis. *Annals of Human Genetics,* 1955, *19,* 273–289.

Stinchcombe, A. L. Environment: The cumulation of events. *Harvard Educational Review,* 1969, *39* (3), 511–522.

Strong, S. J., & Corney, G. *The placenta in twin pregnancy.* New York: Pergamon Press, 1967.

Thoday, J. M. Educability and group differences. *Nature,* 1973, *245,* 418–420.

Thorndike, E. L. Measurements of twins. In J. M. Cattell & F. J. E. Woodbridge (Eds.), *Archives of Philosophy, Psychology and Scientific Methods.* New York: The Science Press, Sept. 1905–July 1906, Vol. I, 1–63.

Thorndike, R. L. Concepts of culture-fairness. *Journal of Educational Measurement,* 1971, *8* (2), 63–70.

Thurstone, L. L., & Thurstone, T. G. *Primary mental abilities.* Chicago: Chicago Univ. Press, 1938.

Thurstone, L. L., & Thurstone, T. G. *Multiple-factor analysis, a development and expansion of the vectors of mind.* Chicago: Chicago Univ. Press, 1947.

Thurstone, T. G. *Examiner's manual IBM 805 edition, primary mental abilities, for grades 9–12,* revised 1962. Chicago: Science Research Associates, Inc., 1963.

Thurstone, T. G., Thurstone, L. L., & Strandskov, H. H. *A psychological study of twins.* Chapel Hill, NC: Univ. of North Carolina, Psychometric Laboratory, 1955, Report #4.

Torrance, E. P. *Torrance tests of creative thinking:* Norms-technical manual, research edition. Princeton, NJ: Personnel Press, Inc., 1966.

Tyler, L. E. *The psychology of human differences.* New York: Appleton-Century-Crofts, Co., 1965.

Urbach, P. Progress and degeneration in the 'IQ Debate'. *British Journal of the Philosophy of Science,* 1974, *25,* Part I, 99–135 and Part II, 235–259.

Vandenberg, S. G. The hereditary abilities study: Hereditary components in a psychological test battery. *American Journal of Human Genetics,* 1962, *14,* 220–237.

Vandenberg, S. G. The developmental study of twins. Paper presented at the American Psychological Association meeting, Los Angeles, Calif., September 1964.

Vandenberg, S. G. Multivariate analysis of twin differences. In S. G. Vandenberg (Ed.), *Methods and goals in human behavior genetics.* New York: Academic Press, 1965.

Vandenberg, S. G. *A twin study of spatial ability.* Research Report from the

Louisville Twin Study, Child Development Unit, Department of Pediatrics, Univ. of Louisville School of Medicine, Report No. 26, April 1967. (a)

Vandenberg, S. G. Hereditary factors in normal personality traits (as measured by inventories). In J. Wortis (Ed.), *Recent advances in biological psychiatry.* New York: Plenum Press, 1967. (b)

Vandenberg, S. G. Hereditary factors in psychological variables in man, with a special emphasis on cognition. In J. N. Spuhler (Ed.), *Genetic diversity and human behavior.* Chicago, Ill.: Aldine Publishing Co., 1967. (c)

Vandenberg, S. G. A comparison of heritability estimates of U.S. Negro and white high school students. *Acta Geneticae Medicae et Gemellogia,* 1970, *19,* 280–284.

Vandenberg, S. G. Assortative mating, or who marries whom? *Behavior Genetics,* 1972, *2,* 127–157.

Wade, N. IQ and heredity: Suspicion of fraud beclouds classic experiment. *Science,* 1976, *194,* 916.

Warner, W. L., Meeker, M., Eells, K. *Social class in America: A manual of procedure for the measurement of social status.* Chicago: Science Research Associates, 1949.

We're all the same under the skin. *San Francisco Sunday Examiner & Chronicle,* Feb. 29, 1976, p. 16, Section A.

Whiteman, M. The performance of schizophrenics on social concepts. *Journal of Abnormal and Social Psychology,* 1954, *49,* 266–271.

Author Index

Subject Index